Contemporary History in Context Series

Published in association with the Institute of Contemporary British History

General Editor: **Peter Catterall**, Director, Institute of Contemporary British History

What do they know of the contemporary, who only the contemporary know? How, without some historical context, can you tell whether what you are observing is genuinely novel, and how can you understand how it has developed? It was, not least, to guard against the unconscious and ahistorical Whiggery of much contemporary comment that this series was conceived. The series takes important events or historical debates from the post-war years and, by bringing new archival evidence and historical insights to bear, seeks to re-examine and reinterpret these matters. Most of the books will have a significant international dimension, dealing with diplomatic, economic or cultural relations across borders. in the process the object will be to challenge orthodoxies and to cast new light upon major aspects of post-war history.

Titles include:

Oliver Bange
THE EEC CRISIS OF 1963
Kennedy, Macmillan, de Gaulle and Adenauer in Conflict

Christopher Brady
UNITED STATES FOREIGN POLICY TOWARDS CAMBODIA, 1977–92

Peter Catterall and Sean McDougall (*editors*)
THE NORTHERN IRELAND QUESTION IN BRITISH POLITICS

Peter Catterall, Colin Seymour-Ure and Adrian Smith (*editors*)
NORTHCLIFFE'S LEGACY
Aspects of the British Popular Press, 1896–1996

James Ellison
THREATENING EUROPE
Britain and the Creation of the European Community, 1955-58

Helen Fawcett and Rodney Lowe (*editors*)
WELFARE POLICY IN BRITAIN
The Road from 1945

Harriet Jones and Michael Kandiah (*editors*)
THE MYTH OF CONSENSUS
New Views on British History, 1945–64

Wolfram Kaiser
USING EUROPE, ABUSING THE EUROPEANS
Britain and European Integration, 1945–63

Keith Kyle
THE POLITICS OF THE INDEPENDENCE OF KENYA

Spencer Mawby
CONTAINING GERMANY
Britain and the Arming of the Federal Republic

Jeffrey Pickering
BRITAIN'S WITHDRAWAL FROM EAST OF SUEZ
The Politics of Retrenchment

L. V. Scott
MACMILLAN, KENNEDY AND THE CUBAN MISSILE CRISIS
Political, Military and Intelligence Aspects

Paul Sharp
THATCHER'S DIPLOMACY
The Revival of British Foreign Policy

Contemporary History in Context
Series Standing Order ISBN 0–333–71470–9
(*outside North America only*)

You can receive future titles in this series as they are published by placing a standing order. Please contact your bookseller or, in case of difficulty, write to us at the address below with your name and address, the title of the series and the ISBN quoted above.

Customer Services Department, Macmillan Distribution Ltd, Houndmills, Basingstoke, Hampshire RG21 6XS, England

Threatening Europe

Britain and the Creation of the European Community, 1955–58

James Ellison
Department of History
Queen Mary and Westfield College
University of London

ICBH

in association with
INSTITUTE OF CONTEMPORARY BRITISH HISTORY

First published in Great Britain 2000 by
MACMILLAN PRESS LTD
Houndmills, Basingstoke, Hampshire RG21 6XS and London
Companies and representatives throughout the world

A catalogue record for this book is available from the British Library.

ISBN 0–333–75363–1

First published in the United States of America 2000 by
ST. MARTIN'S PRESS, LLC,
Scholarly and Reference Division,
175 Fifth Avenue, New York, N.Y. 10010

ISBN 0–312–23609–3

Library of Congress Cataloging-in-Publication Data
Ellison, James, 1970–
    Threatening Europe : Britain and the creation of the European Community,
1955–58 / James Ellison.
      p. cm.
    Includes bibliographical references and index.
    ISBN 0–312–23609–3
    1. Great Britain—Politics and government—1945–1964. 2. Great Britain–
–Foreign relations—Europe. 3. Europe—Foreign relations—Great Britain. 4.
Great Britain—Foreign relations—1945– 5. European Community—History. I.
Title. II. Series.

    DA589.7 .E45 2000
    382'.9142'09045—dc21

                          00–033332

This book is printed on paper suitable for recycling and made from fully managed and sustained
forest sources.

10   9   8   7   6   5   4   3   2   1
09 08 07 06 05 04 03 02 01 00

Printed and bound in Great Britain by
Antony Rowe Ltd, Chippenham, Wiltshire

To my parents

Contents

List of Tables

General Editor's Preface

The story of Britain's first application for entry to Europe has so often been told it has almost become the subject of mythology. What has been much more obscure is the road trodden to reach that point. And a defining moment in that process is the subject of James Ellison's book.

During the 1950s successive British governments were confronted with a steadily shrinking range of options in terms of their European policy. They were pushed towards European integration by American administrations which saw this as a politically necessary step in a world viewed largely in Cold War terms. At the same time there was, it seemed, by 1956 a growing risk that this process of European integration would be to the economic detriment of Britain. Those who thought of themselves as Europeanists, such as Harold Macmillan, had not envisaged such an eventuality. As it became clearer that their vision of some kind of fairly loose European economic and military co-operation within broader international structures was not necessarily the one that would win out against the competing visions of continental neighbours, there were signs of mounting concern. Either as an island, or an imperial power, Macmillan mused in 1953, 'Are we really sure that we want to see a Six-Power Federal Europe, with a common army, a common iron and steel industry (Schuman Plan) ending with a common currency and monetary policy?'[1] The risk that the result would be dominated by the recent enemy, Germany, was often explicitly stated in such passages.

Solutions to this strategic dilemma were less readily perceived. At first the British seem to have hoped that it would simply go away, especially if they encouraged this to happen, as in the ill-starred attempt to sabotage the Messina negotiations in late 1955. The Free Trade Area negotiations represent instead an attempt to respond rather more creatively to the process of European integration. By trying to wrap the Customs Union of the Six within a Free Trade Area of the rest of Europe, Britain was arguably attempting

---

1 Public Record Office, London: CAB 129/60, C(53)108, Harold Macmillan, 'The EDC and European Unity', 19 March 1953.

to maximise the economic benefits for all, not least itself. In particular, Britain would have been able to maintain its Commonwealth
trading preferences while also preventing the closing of the markets of the Six against it. At the same time, the FTA accorded more
closely to the network of broad, ambiguous and loose Commonwealth ties with which the British were familiar through long
experience and felt to be compatible with Westminster systems,
rather than the more dirigiste structures the Six seemed to have in
mind.

British policy in the run-up to the first bid for entry in 1961 has
often been represented as being driven by delusions of grandeur
that were gradually stripped by a cold douche of post-Suez reality.
The Free Trade Area negotiations, instead, reflect a rational policy
choice as a means of maximising Britain's interests and advantages,
while also trying to offer enough to other countries to give the
policy at least a chance of success, even if, particularly as far as de
Gaulle was concerned, it looked too much like a British attempt to
have their cake and eat it to avoid eventual failure.

James Ellison's guidance through this process provides a model
reconstruction of European policymaking. He illuminates both the
bureaucratic politics of Whitehall and the broader process of European negotiations. In this particular round of negotiations Whitehall
was unsuccessful – though it should be apparent that the configu-
ration of British interests has not changed all that much subsequently,
even if the structures wherein these are pursued are different. It is,
of course, very difficult to speculate on the might-have-been if the
FTA negotiations had succeeded. What effect it might have had on
European growth rates, or on the outcome of the Cold War, is
impossible to tell. But it certainly would have resulted in a looser
and more open structure, more able to accommodate the Eastern
European applicants of recent years, not to mention the variable
geometry that their entry is likely to bring to the European Union.
That it failed in the 1950s does not mean it has no lessons to offer
for future international co-operation in the rapidly globalising world
of the twenty-first century.

PETER CATTERALL

Acknowledgements

There are a number of institutions which I must thank for their assistance in the production of this book. I owe a particular debt of gratitude to the British Academy for the studentship which facilitated the greater period of my research as a PhD student, and to Canterbury Christ Church University College and Queen Mary and Westfield College who provided funding which enabled me to complete additional research. Many thanks are due to the staff of various archives and libraries, mainly the Public Record Office at Kew and the National Archives and Record Administration at College Park, Maryland, but also the Bank of England Archives; Birmingham University Library; the Bodleian Library, Oxford; the Cabinet Office Historical Section, London; Churchill College Archive Centre, Cambridge; and Trinity College Library, Cambridge.

Kind permission to quote from private papers has been given by Lady Avon and the Avon Trustees; the Keeper of Western Manuscripts, the Bodleian Library, Oxford; the Macmillan Trustees; Mr Duncan Sandys; the executor of the estate of Selwyn Lloyd, and the Master and Fellows of Trinity College, Cambridge. I was lucky enough to correspond with, and interview, a number of retired diplomats and civil servants who provided informative and often amusing recollections for my research. Thanks go to the late Lord Gladwyn, John Moore Heath, Sir Guy Millard, Sir Michael Palliser – and, especially, to Sir Denis Wright for allowing me to quote from private correspondence with one of his former Foreign Office colleagues.

Many individuals have enabled me to write this book. My PhD supervisor, Sean Greenwood, deserves great thanks for his encouragement and guidance. I am especially indebted to Kevin Ruane whose help, as research companion and friend, has been invaluable, not least in his comments on drafts of this book. Two other friends, Piers Ludlow and Roland Maurhofer, also provided beneficial observations on the manuscript as well as many long and useful discussions and I am very grateful to them both. I am also thankful to Monika Dickhaus, Wolfram Kaiser, Gerold Krozewski, Frances Lynch, Alan Milward, Paul Pitman, David Welch, Hugo Young, John Young, Barbara Wells and my colleagues in the Department of History at Queen Mary and Westfield College. My appreciation also goes to Peter Catterall for his help as my General Editor and as Director of the Institute of Contemporary British History, an institution which has provided me with much support.

Finally, for their constant faith, encouragement and support, not just in the writing of this book, my warmest thanks are reserved for my parents, John and Linda, my family, and above all, Maggie.

J.R.V.E.

List of Abbreviations

BT	Board of Trade
CAB	Cabinet Office
CAP	Common Agricultural Policy
ECSC	European Coal and Steel Community
EDC	European Defence Community
ELEC	European League for Economic Co-operation
EEC	European Economic Community
EFTA	European Free Trade Association
EMA	European Monetary Agreement
EPC	Economic Policy Committee, Cabinet Office
EPU	European Payments Union
FBI	Federation of British Industry
FIG	French–Italian–German nuclear collaboration
FO	Foreign Office
FRUS	Foreign Relations of the United States
FTA	Free Trade Area
GATT	General Agreement on Tariffs and Trade
HOPS	Home and Overseas Planning Staff, Treasury
IGC	OEEC Intergovernmental Committee (also CIG)
IRBM	Intermediate Range Ballistic Missile
MAC	Mutual Aid Committee, Cabinet Office
MAD	Mutual Aid Department, Foreign Office
MAFF	Ministry of Agriculture, Fisheries and Food
MoD	Ministry of Defence
NATO	North Atlantic Treaty Organisation
NFU	National Farmers' Union
OEEC	Organisation for European Economic Co-operation
OFD	Overseas Finance Division, Treasury
PREM	Prime Minister's Office
T	Treasury
TUC	Trades Union Congress
WEU	Western European Union
WOD	Western Organisations Department, Foreign Office
WP17	OEEC Working Party No. 17
WP21	OEEC Working Party No. 21 (FTA/EEC association)
WP22	OEEC Working Party No. 22 (Agriculture)
WP23	OEEC Working Party No. 23 (Peripheral countries)

Introduction

The period 1955 to 1958 was a turning point in both British and European post-war history. It was at this stage that the Six powers (Belgium, France, Germany, Italy, Luxembourg and the Netherlands) resolved to create a European Common Market during a conference at Messina, Sicily, from 1 to 2 June 1955. Within two years, on 25 March 1957, the Six signed the Treaties of Rome principally establishing the European Economic Community (EEC). Britain was invited to join this movement from the outset but declined to do so. Instead, from 1955 to 1956, it developed its own proposal for economic co-operation which aimed to secure a European Free Trade Area (FTA) around the core of the EEC. It was the failure of this policy after Charles de Gaulle's intervention in late 1958 which began the process of re-evaluation eventually bringing Britain's first application to join the European Community in 1961.

These events have acquired historical notoriety due to the considerable and largely critical attention paid to them. The debate has its foundations in Miriam Camps' *Britain and the European Community 1955–1963*, a classic work which presented a thorough and mainly sympathetic interpretation of British policy.[1] With the release of British records in the 1980s, research concentrated on Britain's decision to reject EEC membership in 1955 and so built upon the developing interest in British policy towards European co-operation after 1945.[2] Encouraged by the contemporary importance of Britain's relationship with what has become known as 'Europe', scholars generated a proliferation of historical literature which soon made it a dominant historiographical subject in the study of post-war British history.[3] In 1996, the first archive-based studies were published, most notably Wolfram Kaiser's *Using Europe. Abusing the*

Europeans, and in 1998 two further publications extended the debate yet further.[4]

Given the extent of this scholarly enquiry, it is plausible to suggest that if historians can be said to plough furrows in their research, then perhaps Britain's initial reaction to the European Community is a furrow which would benefit from being set aside. Such a view would, however, be a misconception. Although research has recently concentrated on Britain's FTA proposal, it still remains true that it has received little attention.[5] Much of the debate so far has focused on whether Plan G, as Britain's FTA was known within Whitehall, was designed to sabotage the European Common Market, a negative view encapsulated in an enduring analogy which suggests that the FTA would have dissolved the European Common Market 'like a lump of sugar in an English cup of tea'.[6] Few studies have attempted to take a more complex view of the development of Britain's FTA proposal.[7] This is without question an important area of enquiry vital to understanding the development of Britain's reaction to the Six in 1955–56, but it is only a part of the story.

The present study sets out to provide an examination of not only the formulation of British policy towards European integration from 1955 to 1956 but also its implementation during the FTA negotiations from 1957 to 1958. In doing so it seeks to update the work of Camps which still remains the most detailed published account.[8] It also employs recent research on the attitudes of the Six towards Britain's FTA and considers their impact on British policy. This is in the knowledge that while historians have dealt with the response of the Six to Britain's first application and the Brussels negotiations from 1961–63 the same cannot be said of the period 1955–58.[9] Through analysing the parallel development of the Six's negotiations, the evolution of Britain's FTA proposal and the FTA negotiations, it becomes clear that the British and the Six feared the impact of each others' policy on their own chosen course. The idea that the EEC threatened Britain's political and economic position and that the FTA threatened the future development of the EEC is one which runs throughout 1955–58.

While it is written largely from the perspective of diplomatic history, the book attempts to present an interpretation which considers not only foreign policy but also economic and commercial interests. This has been influenced by necessity, in that the primary sources demanded such an approach, but also by intent. The history of Britain's policy towards European integration from the Schuman

Plan of 9 May 1950, which led to the creation of the European Coal and Steel Community (ECSC), to the Messina Conference of 1–2 June 1955 has been written separately by diplomatic and economic historians. What this historiography suggests is that reference has to be made to political and economic determinants in constructing an explanation of British decision making. At the risk of oversimplifying their complex arguments, a brief review of the diplomatic and economic schools will substantiate this view.

Ultimately, diplomatic and economic historians reach a very similar conclusion about British policy towards western European integration in the first half of the 1950s. Through its failures, Britain became 'in reality . . . only what Bevin had denied it to be, "just another European country"'.[10] However, these historians choose very different events and follow divergent analytical paths to reach their parallel judgement. Diplomatic historians focus their analysis on British attitudes towards the ECSC, the Six's proposals for a European army via the European Defence Community (EDC) and its British-inspired successor, the Western European Union (WEU). Their priority has been to explain, in foreign policy terms, why Britain remained detached from continental integration. Importance is placed on Britain's extra-European relations which acted as a barrier to more purposeful involvement in European co-operation. Conversely, economic historians concentrate on British external economic policy in relation to western Europe, highlighting attitudes towards the European Payments Union (EPU), the development of plans for convertibility and the goal of re-establishing the international role of sterling as an exchange currency. The work of Roger Bullen, Sean Greenwood and John Young on the one hand and Alan Milward on the other, are the most representative of the two approaches.[11]

It is accepted by diplomatic historians that British policy towards western European integration from mid-1950 to 1955 was remarkably consistent.[12] Young has described the nature of the policy as being one of benevolence towards, but non-involvement in supranational European schemes, seeking to associate with them where possible, while maintaining Britain's role in institutions such as the Organisation for European Economic Co-operation (OEEC). The motives for this attitude were extra-European. Successive British governments saw Atlantic and Commonwealth rather than European co-operation as the most effective form of international relations. British policy towards Europe was part of a greater global strategy of what Bullen describes as 'a declining power anxious to

shore up and protect both specific interests overseas, its own prestige and traditions of leadership in Europe and elsewhere'.[13] The
preservation and defence of Britain's status as a world power was
incompatible with membership of a supranational European Community. This did not, however, lead Britain into a hostile approach
to her western European partners' desire for integration in the first
half of the 1950s according to diplomatic historians who take a
relatively sympathetic view of British attitudes.[14]

Britain was forced into recognising her western European partners as a cohesive 'Six' for the first time in June 1950 during the
negotiations for the ECSC. British foreign policy foundations, diplomatic historians suggest, separated Britain from the Six from the
outset. Apart from the vital implication of forfeiting sovereignty
over two of the most politically sensitive sectors of the economy,
the British government maintained a preference for the intergovernmental co-operation of the OEEC as opposed to idealistic schemes
for a European federation. In a wider political sense, Britain's priorities were relations with the Commonwealth and the United States,
factors which would remain sacrosanct throughout the 1950s. Also,
Britain followed a different pattern of commercial relations than
her European neighbours.[15]

Another tenet of Britain's consistent policy towards western European integration developed from 1950/51: the desire to associate
with the Six rather than join their schemes. This was at the base of
the 'Eden Plan' in 1952 to reform the Council of Europe, and the
official policy London pursued towards the Six's plans for an EDC
from 1950 to 1954.[16] It emerged most significantly in the Council
of Association between Britain and the ECSC signed in December
1954. In response to this aspect of British policy, the Six also developed a continuum in their approach to London. Although
diplomatic historians argue that Britain was not 'anti-European' from
1950 to 1955, they qualify their view with the vital caveat that
some members of the Six were not always convinced of Britain's
sincerity. Association had always held the implication that Britain
would obtain certain advantages without significantly adding to her
obligations.[17] At best, therefore, British plans for association would
be received with cautious appraisal. At worst, as with Monnet's view
of the Eden Plan, there was suspicion of British motives mixed with
fear that London's ultimate goal was to sabotage the Six's efforts
towards federal integration.

The failure of the French National Assembly to ratify the EDC

Treaty in August 1954 and the consequent British proposal to transform the Brussels Treaty Organisation into the Western European Union is viewed by diplomatic historians as a triumph for Anthony Eden and British policy towards western European integration.[18] Bullen goes so far as to suggest that if it had not been for the WEU, the second phase of the integrationist movement, culminating in the Treaty of Rome, would not have been possible. Young and others, arguing from Whitehall's viewpoint, explain that the failure of the EDC had vindicated London's policy of the previous five years; supranationalism had succeeded in the economic field of the ECSC but not in the political/defence field.[19] Prior to the Messina Conference, therefore, diplomatic historians classify the origins of British policy towards western European integration as a desire to remain divorced from supranational schemes, to maintain traditional political and economic links with the Commonwealth and the United States, and to resolve European security problems in an Atlantic framework. Hence the benevolent yet non-involved policy towards the ECSC and plans for a European Army, and by extension, the desire to associate with these arrangements whenever possible.

For Alan Milward, the reason that Britain played 'so small and distant a role' in the historical evolution of European integration is that Britain's post-war tradition in external economic policy was crucially different to that of its western European partners.[20] Whereas the latter placed emphasis on the development of commercial economic policies, Britain pursued a reactionary financial economic goal of re-establishing the former glory of sterling as an international currency via sterling–dollar convertibility; 'The pound, once good as gold, would now be as good as dollars'.[21] Thus it was financial policy which was the true motor of Britain's attitudes towards western European integration. London had no desire to play a role equal to that of its European partners in new, possibly supranational European institutions because of its greater aim of creating a 'one-world economic system' in which sterling would be second to the dollar as an international currency.

This fundamental policy was revealed in Britain's attitudes towards the EPU and in the development of a secret economic plan in 1951, titled Operation ROBOT. The EPU was a central clearing mechanism for trade settlements between OEEC members in which they agreed within defined limits to make their currencies transferable for trade purposes. In the Europe of the Marshall Plan, the American government supported the EPU as a means of achieving multilateralism and promoting a further stage of European unity, two central aims in Washington's western European policies. Sustaining his argument that the convertibility of sterling was paramount for London, Milward explains Britain's reluctance to play a full role in the EPU and uses the example of Operation ROBOT as evidence of Britain's extra-European economic aims.[22] As the new Conservative government took office in London in 1951, officials from the Bank of England and some from the Treasury proposed a radical plan for the convertibility of all externally held sterling, and for the pound to float against other currencies. Milward sees ROBOT, which was ultimately still-born, as an example of Britain's reluctance to submerge itself in a European payments system and as an attempt to elevate British economic power via the strength of sterling. Moreover, it was reflective of Britain's disregard for relations with its western European partners. If ROBOT had been enacted, it would have had a detrimental effect on the EPU and would have been damaging to the economies of its members, but according to Milward, this was nothing more than a subsidiary consideration in London.[23]

The same disregard for her western European partners, developing into a misunderstanding of their aims, was at the basis of Britain's external economic policy from 1952 until the re-establishment of convertibility in 1958. The Collective Approach to freer trade and payments was no longer a plan for sterling–dollar convertibility alone, but also for the other major currencies to establish dollar convertibility at the same time as sterling.[24] Commonwealth, North American and European countries would steer a course towards the successful accomplishment of convertibility and multilateralism in trade. The limitations of this policy was its reliance on American financial support and the belief that western European countries would be willing to forfeit their preferred course of expanding intra-Western-European trade for an early move to convertibility. Milward argues that the negative reaction of western European countries to Britain's Collective Approach represents the gulf between their view of European economic co-operation and Britain's view. Furthermore, the Collective Approach was inimical to closer western European integration and as such fell foul of American policy aims. Milward suggests that by 1955 Britain was left isolated in a Europe of nation-states pursuing integration policies through the expansion of intra-Western-European trade under the protection of encouragement from Washington. Playing down what diplomatic historians see as a British triumph, Milward minimises the effect of the EDC's failure in 1954 by suggesting that it intensified efforts to guarantee intra-Western-European trade through the formalised institution of a customs union.[25] In summary, therefore, the thrust of Milward's argument identifies Britain's non-involvement in western European integration in the first half of the 1950s as being due to the contradiction between this process and London's sterling policy. The seam that ran through ROBOT, the Collective Approach and the quest for convertibility was the predominance of financial policy, a disregard for the trade and payments policies of Britain's European partners and a misreading of the intensity of American support for the Six powers. More recently, these economic explanations have been complemented by Andrew Moravcsik who has argued that British policy was motivated not by financial interests but 'the rational pursuit of commercial interest, in particular export promotion'.[26]

The purpose of these summaries has been to exemplify the complex motives for British policy towards European integration and to suggest that a balanced assessment should attempt to incorporate diplomatic and economic factors. Then, for instance, British policy from 1950 to 1955 might be described as being influenced by financial and commercial policy as well as Britain's extra-European political traditions and preference for intergovernmental co-operation over supranationalism. Surely a comprehensive analysis would integrate these varied arguments to reach the common conclusion that Britain was left, through its own policy choices, overpowered by the Six on the periphery of Europe by the end of the 1950s. The bias of the final analysis will depend very much on the inference the historian brings to the subject, and to be fair, diplomatic and economic historians do not completely rule out each others' case.[27] For instance, the policy staked out by the Foreign Office in the early 1950s can be read as a foreign policy or economic policy priority: 'Great Britain must be regarded as a world power of the second rank and not merely as a unit in a federated Europe'.[28] Maintaining 'power of the second rank' could have been achieved through the international prestige of dollar-sterling convertibility, or by fostering closer Anglo-American political/defence links while sustaining traditional ties with the Commonwealth or both. Anthony Eden offered retrospective advice to historians of British policy from 1951 to 1955: 'It will be remembered that the events which I now describe were never seen in isolation at the time. . . . None of them can be understood in isolation from the others'.[29] Perhaps this important suggestion should be borne in mind in reaching an understanding of British policy towards European integration.

This book attempts to adopt this approach in its analysis of British policy from June 1955 to December 1958. It concentrates on the roles of the Foreign Office, the Treasury and the Board of Trade in the formulation of Britain's FTA proposal from 1955 to 1956. It also analyses the implementation of this policy through reference to Britain's diplomatic relations with western Europe. Concurrently, it raises other issues such as the role of personalities, both ministerial and official, in policy development and diplomacy. It also seeks to explain British attitudes towards European integration with regard to wider foreign and economic policy. Hence, from the political viewpoint, for example, the Anglo-American relationship will be an important theme with specific reference to its effect on policy towards Europe. Similarly, from the economic viewpoint, sterling policy was not central to the FTA proposal, yet it is crucial in explaining many of the attitudes towards Europe, especially in the Treasury. The same can be said of Britain's commercial policy, particularly with regard to the Board of Trade's view of relations with the Commonwealth.

The book proceeds on a chronological basis and is divided into three parts. Part I deals with the development of British policy from the government's rejection of the European Common Market in autumn 1955 to its acceptance of the FTA proposal in autumn 1956. It was during this period that British policy underwent a three-stage evolution. Until now, the analysis of the FTA has taken 1956 as its starting point but, in fact, the idea was first raised in autumn 1955 during studies of a counter-initiative to lure the Six into the OEEC. After this was rendered impractical by failed British diplomacy, the FTA became a possible alternative to the Common Market as Whitehall continued to doubt the prospects of the Six. Only in autumn 1956 did the FTA proposal finally become an attempt to complement the Common Market after London had decided that any other course was unrealistic. Even then, the diversity of attitudes within the British government towards European integration suggests that not all had given up on overwhelming the Six's chosen course.

Part II examines policy development and Anglo-European relations from the aftermath of the Suez Crisis to the eve of the FTA negotiations in October 1957. It is already well established that the experience of Suez led Britain and France along diverse paths. Britain sought to restore Anglo-American relations and France embraced the European Common Market. These views are not disputed here although they are expanded somewhat. While the Macmillan government's priority was to rebuild relations with Washington, it nevertheless sought to give European policy a greater status by augmenting the FTA with proposals for political and defence collaboration via Selwyn Lloyd's Grand Design. Recently released Foreign Office documents offer new perspectives on this issue and reveal how Lloyd's post-Suez proposals for unprecedented Anglo-European nuclear collaboration were totally out of line with Whitehall opinion. Consequently, Britain's political dimension to its European policy was limited to proposals for a single European assembly which fell badly short of European, and particularly French, expectations. As a consequence, when Suez did not lead Britain towards Europe, the Mollet government seems to have adjusted the priority it placed on the FTA proposal. All efforts were angled towards securing the ratification of the Treaties of Rome. Thus, in May 1957, the British were forced to agree to French demands, supported by the Germans, for five months of delay in the FTA deliberations whilst the Rome Treaties were accepted by national parliaments. It was during this period that divergence between British and French positions became even more acute.

Part III considers the course of the Maudling Committee negotiations from October 1957 to December 1958. As little historical analysis has focused on the negotiations themselves, some of the most interesting interpretations are produced by this section of the book. Three factors are striking. First, it is clear that many in Whitehall, particularly at official level, had accepted that the negotiations were dead months before their final collapse in December 1958. Even British Ministers had concluded that the discussions would have to be suspended *before* the French actually broke off from the Maudling Committee in November. In light of this, it is difficult to sustain the view that the negotiations came close to success. Second, analysis of the negotiations reveals a more complex picture of Anglo-Six relations than has previously been depicted, with the British considering significant concessions on tariff policy and the French delaying the progress of the Maudling Committee. Third, despite the ill-feeling in Anglo-French relations at the end of the negotiations, Britain did not retaliate against General de Gaulle's termination of the FTA. This revealed that the government had no choice but to maintain a relationship with the EEC given that the alternative was isolation, something which it had been working to avoid since 1955.

A final point has to be made on the nomenclature used in this study. 'Europe' or 'European integration' refers to the countries of western Europe who were members of the OEEC.[30] Similarly, 'Germany' is an abbreviation for the Federal Republic of Germany or West Germany and should be read as such throughout. Finally, given this study's sensitivity to the complexity of opinion in the British government, whenever 'British policy', 'Whitehall' or 'London' are used generally in the text, this is in the knowledge that they are, as one historian has pointed out, 'convenient shorthand term[s] for numerous thought and action, not all of which may fit comfortably together'.[31]

Part I

From Counter-Initiative to Free Trade Area, June 1955–December 1956

1
Malicious Conception: the Counter-Initiative, June–December 1955

On 15 June 1955, in his inaugural speech to the House of Commons as Foreign Secretary, Harold Macmillan referred to 'important events' during the previous month which 'marked the opening of a new phase in post-war European history'.[1] Amongst these were the formal end of West Germany's occupation, its accession to NATO and the creation of the British-inspired WEU. Significantly, however, Macmillan made no reference to the conference of the Six powers which had taken place in Messina from 1–2 June. Yet the Foreign Secretary was fully aware of this most recent expression of the Six's determination to advance western European integration. On the day of his Commons speech, he had also officially informed the Luxembourg Minister of Foreign Affairs that the British government would 'consider most carefully' their response to an invitation from the Six to participate in studies for a European Common Market and a European Atomic Energy Community (Euratom).[2] Macmillan's exclusion of the Messina conference from his list of important European events was an early indication of British scepticism of the Six's plans which was to ensure that Britain was not amongst the founder members of the EEC. Instead, in autumn 1955, the Eden government mounted a failed attempt to prevent its creation.

This British reaction to the Six was the product of an agreed wisdom at official level in Whitehall, unchallenged by ministers, that the Common Market was contrary to British policy and should therefore be opposed. Such a view was fortified by the estimation of the Foreign Office that the Six would in any case fail in their endeavours, due mainly to the post-EDC condition of France, and that they could be diverted into the OEEC by British diplomatic intervention.[3] The motives for this policy are a matter of some debate. The threat posed to Britain's diplomatic and political policy in Europe and elsewhere by a German-dominated Common Market are prioritised by some whereas others emphasise the role played by Britain's financial interests in determining Britain's response.[4] Most recently, and in sharp contrast to the otherwise largely critical assessments of Whitehall decision-making, British policy has been described as 'rational, remarkably flexible, even far-sighted' and driven by the defense of commercial interests.[5]

Essentially, Britain's policy was a synthesis of these diplomatic, economic and commercial interests. This chapter will reconsider the narrative of Britain's response to the Messina Conference and the Spaak Committee to establish how the agendas of the dominant Whitehall departments combined and differed. The reaction of the Foreign Office can be seen to have reflected established attitudes towards European integration but also the impact of wider events, particularly in relation to the Cold War. Similarly, the Treasury's response was conditioned by earlier decisions taken during the late 1940s on a European customs union. In 1955, however, officials were also aware of the need to present the Six with opportunity for further economic integration via a British counter-initiative to the Common Market. For the Treasury this was to be little more than a tactic to divert the Six from their own plans but for the Board of Trade, the counter-initiative had greater potential. While the Board shared Whitehall's general opposition to the Common Market it did not share the opinion that the Six would necessarily fail. For this and other reasons, it played a leading part in the counter-initiative studies of autumn 1955 which, though preliminary in size and scope to those of 1956, nevertheless mark the genesis of the FTA, a fact underestimated by existing studies of British policy evolution.[6]

Whitehall and Messina

After Cabinet discussion on 30 June 1955, Russell Bretherton, Under-Secretary from the Board of Trade, was sent to play his now infamous part as Britain's 'representative' on the Spaak Committee in Brussels.[7] With the remit of 'cooperation without commitment', Bretherton and his colleagues made limited contributions to the Six's discussions on a Common Market and Euratom, and reported developments to London.[8] During the summer and early autumn of 1955, an interdepartmental Whitehall working party, chaired by the Treasury's Burke Trend, examined the implications for Britain of membership of, or isolation from, a European Common Market.[9] On 27 October, with little difficulty, officials reached the conclusion that 'the establishment of a European Common Market would be bad for the United Kingdom and if possible should be frustrated'.[10] In theory, once the Six had been redirected into the orbit of the OEEC, Britain was to produce 'a fresh proposal for an advance towards European integration' involving the lowering of tariff barriers and removal of general obstacles to trade in exchange for the Six abandoning their Common Market plans.[11] But not all in Whitehall were fully convinced of the necessity of such a new British initiative, and it is amongst the differing views of the three main departments involved in policy towards European integration – the Foreign Office, the Treasury and the Board of Trade – that the counter-initiative has its origins.

The Foreign Office has been widely condemned for its part in determining Britain's reaction to the Six in the summer and autumn of 1955.[12] The central question is why the Foreign Office broke so harmfully with its previous policy of benevolent neutrality towards Six power integration? Such a question is especially pertinent given the conclusions of a recent analysis which suggests that the Foreign Office dedicated itself to the success of the EDC and that 'The documentary record . . . provides minimal evidence that the British believed that federalism had died on 30 August 1954.'[13] One recent leading account argues that Foreign Office rejection of the Six's plans in autumn 1955 reflected innate opposition to European supranationalism and defence of the three circles doctrine of British foreign policy; the emphasis placed by the Office in Whitehall on maintaining the strength of the Commonwealth was a tactic 'to prevent a major debate about the future priorities of British foreign and trade policy'.[14] This response was driven by political decisions in a Foreign Office that 'simply ignored the economic aspects' of the Six's proposals and whose Foreign Secretary, Harold Macmillan, was dismissive of the Six and was personally responsible for disastrous diplomacy.[15] While having elements of accuracy, this explanation reveals little of the complexity of Foreign Office policy. The recently released files of the Western Organisations Department (WOD), the Foreign Office department responsible for the political aspects of the European policy, provide a fuller picture of decision-making than has previously been possible.[16]

Although in the immediate post-war period under Ernest Bevin's leadership the Foreign Office supported Anglo-European economic co-operation as a means of returning Britain to its 'former status of top dog', the onset of the Cold War and French plans for supranational European integration brought reassessments.[17] Believing that Britain was set apart from the Six by its defence policy, Commonwealth and Sterling Area commitments and a preference for intergovernmental institutions, the Office concluded that 'Great Britain must be regarded as a world power of the second rank and not merely as a unit in a federated Europe'.[18] The complement to this was the maintenance of NATO, as well as the OEEC, and Britain's position within these organisations, to justify British exclusion from the supranational institutions of the Six.[19] This did not mean that the Six were to be opposed or deflected as their integration served the fundamental foreign policy priorities of 'resolving the Franco-German conflict, and of successfully associating Germany in the Western democratic world for all purposes including that of common defence'.[20] The patronage given to the Six by the United States also conditioned attitudes in a Foreign Office acutely sensitive to the health of Anglo-American relations. Thus while Britain would not join the Six, it would, as Foreign Secretary Anthony Eden explained in 1951, wish to be 'closely associated' with their work.[21] This policy was pursued successfully in 1954 with the creation of the WEU after the EDC's failure and with Britain's Council of Association with the ECSC.[22]

Foreign Office policy was, however, essentially built on negative foundations, mainly the need to tie Germany to the western alliance and to prevent it from slipping into neutrality and the Soviet orbit. Alone, Six power integration did not offer the means to achieve this and, moreover, presented the threat of a resurgent Germany. In December 1951 the Permanent Under-Secretary's Committee warned that

> The main danger lies rather in the economic predominance which Germany's trained industrial man-power and her natural resources would certainly enable her eventually to assume in any continental union. We cannot be sure that she would not use this position to our disadvantage both in the commercial and political field.[23]

To avoid this eventuality the United Kingdom was to guide the Six's Communities into the wider Atlantic Alliance, the basis of British foreign policy. NATO was the preferred institution for future western co-operation, embodying the Anglo-American relationship and being central to western defence in the Cold War, and where West Germany could be best contained. By mid-1955, the Foreign Office believed that significant steps towards this goal had been achieved with the Federal Republic's membership of the WEU and accession to NATO. But just as events seemed to be following Britain's desired course, the Messina Conference presented a new threat and revived fears of West Germany and of the possibility that 'if a continental union emerged, and seemed to be prospering, those Europeans who fear Anglo-Saxon domination and resent American methods might try to resist its absorption into an Atlantic Community'.[24]

It is clear that in spring 1955, when early indications were received that plans for further European economic integration were 'rather more than "in the wind"', there was incredulity in the WOD whose head, Lord Hood, minuted on 19 April that 'I find this very ridiculous'.[25] Not all, however, were convinced that progress towards European integration had been stayed by the death of the EDC. More far-sighted analysis came from the Mutual Aid Department (MAD) which was charged with European economic questions. Its head, Alan Edden, warned on 14 May that 'We cannot dismiss the possibility ... that we are on the eve of developments of some importance'. Edden argued that if the Six insisted on further economic integration, Britain could not 'expect to hold them back'. He doubted the efficacy of delaying tactics or using the OEEC to placate the Six as its integrationary pace 'may not in practice be anything like fast enough for [them]'. The only feasible course was to await developments, and

> be ready, as and when any new bodies emerge, to make up our minds *quickly* about the merits of U.K. association with them and, where appropriate, to pursue the same 'bridge' technique that we have applied in the case of the ECSC itself. Only in this way can we hope to steer the Six in directions which are not too harmful to our own interests.[26]

In these early stages, Edden's suggestions received agreement throughout the Foreign Office.[27] Within a month, however, his tactical recommendations were surpassed by those of the dominant political and diplomatic side of the Office which, while aware of the economic aspects of the Six's plans, was motivated by doubt about their achievement post-EDC and fear of their implications for Britain's position in relation to West Germany.[28] Thus the political rationale which informed the Foreign Office response to Messina was more complex than opposition to European supranationalism and a restatement of the three circles doctrine. This view is further substantiated by analysis of the role played by Macmillan as Foreign Secretary and of Foreign Office reactions to developments in the Cold War during the second half of 1955.

At the beginning of June 1955, Harold Macmillan sent a directive on European unity to officials already aware of his interest in the subject: 'our purpose should definitely be, in my view, the strengthening of everything that leads to the unity of Europe on a basis which is acceptable to the British Government, that is what we used to call a confederation as opposed to the federal concept'.[29] Without doubt, Macmillan held a personal interest in the idea of European unity, and though his memoirs may portray an accurate enthusiasm for closer Anglo-European relations, this was always on British terms in search of sustained British power, particularly in relation to Germany. This chimed with Office opinion. At a high level meeting on 29 June 1955 to review European policy, Macmillan did not oppose the judgement of Sir Harold Caccia, Deputy Under-Secretary of State superintending the WOD, who cast a negative view of Messina, recommending that the Six be steered into the OEEC.[30] Instead, the foreign secretary added that 'the old plan for [a] federal Europe . . . was now losing out and we should not regret its defeat'. For Macmillan, resurgent German power was the main concern:

> We had always been inclined to say rather loosely that we did not mind other European Powers federating if they wished, but in fact if they did so and became really strong it might be very embarrassing for us. Europe would be handed over to the Germans, a state of affairs which we had fought two wars to prevent.[31]

With this statement, the foreign secretary dictated 'a complete thumbs down on Messina'.[32] Although Macmillan has been targeted as personally responsible for Foreign Office policy as it developed throughout 1955, in fact, once the foreign secretary's initial opinions were known, it seems that much of policy-making was delegated to Sir Harold

Caccia, with ministerial responsibility left to the Minister of State, Lord Reading.[33] If criticism has to be directed at Macmillan then it should be for his non-involvement in these events rather than his involvement. For most of his Foreign Secretaryship, Macmillan was greatly preoccupied by the Geneva four-power summit and the problem of Cyprus.[34] On the extremely rare occasion that the foreign secretary did comment on Foreign Office policy towards Europe, he evidently doubted current economic policy and saw an increased role for Britain in future Continental co-operation; in September 1955 he minuted Caccia, 'This is our second string – we may need it. The "one-world" approach isn't going with a swing at the moment. It may even bankrupt us'.[35] However, it remains true that these sentiments, which R.A. Butler suggested Macmillan had developed from 'his Strasbourg Goose days', were not deployed to modify the Foreign Office's negative view of Messina, thereby casting questions over Macmillan's self-defined Europeanism and the nature of his later enthusiasm for Plan G.[36]

Throughout the summer and early autumn of 1955, the Foreign Office line hardened towards the activities of the Six.[37] A combination of pro-OEEC, anti-Six rhetoric from Britain's Ambassador to the OEEC, Sir Hugh Ellis Rees, together with the estimation of Ambassador to Paris, Sir Gladwyn Jebb, that French conditions made the Common Market an impossibility, justified Office policy.[38] Developments in the Cold War had also fortified the need to ensure that the Six did not proceed along a course potentially harmful to British interests and were brought within the institutions of the Atlantic Alliance. The experience of Soviet attitudes towards European security during 1955, especially at the Geneva Summit of July and the Foreign Ministers' Conference of October/November, had confirmed Foreign Office fears that the Russians aimed to deny a united Germany, to destroy NATO and to engineer the withdrawal of American troops from Europe.[39] Hence, in December 1955, Macmillan was briefed by the WOD to stress to the North Atlantic Council meeting that despite the struggle for ideological spheres of influence in the Middle East and Asia, Europe was still the most important theatre of the Cold War and where the Soviet Union would continue to use every weapon in its armoury to undermine the cohesion and strength of the Western Alliance.[40] In this respect, enhanced NATO co-operation including the FRG and with sustained American involvement remained the basis for Foreign Office policy towards the Cold War in Europe and towards Six power developments.

It was for this reason that the Foreign Office welcomed the NATO Ministerial Council's decision in December 1955 to appoint Three Wise Men to investigate expanding NATO's competencies.[41] Invigoration of NATO in non-military areas such as political and economic co-operation via Article II of the treaty was thought necessary in light of East-West relations. If this could be achieved, and the Six diverted into the OEEC, Foreign Office policy towards Europe would be secure. Not all were assured of the likelihood of this; once more the head of the MAD, Edden, doubted whether enhanced NATO co-operation or the OEEC provided 'an answer to the European separatists'.[42] But by this stage, majority opinion was convinced of the chosen course. The aim was 'to cast out the devil in the German' and the proposed institutions of the Common Market and Euratom would create a 'straight-jacket [which] might bring out the worst in him'.[43] Reviewing NATO's development in 1955, one WOD official underlined the centrality of West Germany to British foreign policy:

> In 1955, the Germans have on the whole been modest and well behaved new boys. In 1956 (and still more in 1957) as they begin to feel their strength, we may not have such an easy time of it. One of the most important tasks of the Alliance for the coming year . . . is to ensure that the Germans continue to play the game and are not allowed to get above themselves.[44]

For the Foreign Office, the Six posed a challenge to British interests which could only be negated if they were subsumed within the wider Atlantic Alliance. It was this rationale which made it the leading Whitehall proponent of diverting the Six into the OEEC; it would also remain a factor in the Foreign Office response to Plan G throughout 1956, eventually producing Selwyn Lloyd's Grand Design. In autumn 1955, Sir Harold Caccia championed the Foreign Office argument. First, he was reluctant to produce an analysis of the potential impact of Britain's abstention from the European Common Market for interdepartmental Whitehall studies 'since, in his opinion, a proper tactical handling of the matter would ensure that the issue need never arise'.[45] Second, according to Eden's Private Secretary, Caccia informed the prime minister that he need not worry about the 'Messina business . . . because it [was] not going to happen'.[46] The most hawkish of the triumvirate of Whitehall departments dealing with Messina in autumn 1955, the Foreign Office, nevertheless did recognise the need for a future British counter-initiative in Europe as 'a genuine alternative to the Common Market' to be deployed once the Six had been side-tracked into the OEEC.[47] Yet there was only a half-hearted interest in an economic initiative. On 25 November, while noting that 'we feel that Messina is a doubtful, if not actually wrong, approach and that the OEEC is a better one', Sir Ivone Kirkpatrick, the Permanent Under-Secretary, informed Jebb of a possible future economic counter-initiative, but warned him not to 'bank on this'.[48]

It was on the feasibility of diverting the Six into the OEEC, and thus the importance of a new British initiative, that the Treasury differed most significantly from the Foreign Office. There was ultimately no fundamental conflict between the two departments over the basic question; in September 1955, the Permanent Secretary, Sir Edward Bridges, advised the Chancellor, R.A. Butler, that 'if the "little Six" form a zollverein without us, not only will the authority of the OEEC wither away, but in addition West Germany will gain an unhealthy position of power as the dominant partner in the new union'.[49] Despite counter arguments from the Economic Section which believed that the benefits of Common Market membership would outweigh the costs of exclusion, opposition towards the Six became the prevailing Treasury view.[50] This was mainly the result of Butler's own distaste for European federalism combined with similar attitudes in the Treasury's powerful Overseas Finance Division (OFD) and the Bank of England.[51] Hence, the Treasury's general attitude coincided with the judgements reached in the Foreign Office and also the Commonwealth Relations Office, which saw closer Anglo-European relations as a threat to Commonwealth ties.[52] The Treasury's policy in 1955 was in fact only an extension of its previous resistance to British membership of a European Common Market. In the late 1940s it had argued that the pre-eminence of sterling and the Sterling Area made extra-European trade more significant than intra-European trade. From the early 1950s, the Treasury persisted in its aim of re-establishing sterling as an international currency, second to the dollar, via global convertibility and multilateral trade under the 'one-world' system of the Collective Approach.[53] In London's view, uniquely European institutions were the antithesis of such a policy. This was revealed by the greater emphasis placed by Britain on convertibility, the dissolution of the EPU, and the move towards GATT trade rules during the OEEC Council meeting held in June 1955, days after the Messina conference.[54]

Accord with the Foreign Office's rejection of the Messina Common Market was thus easily achieved but Treasury officials doubted whether the Office tactics of attempting to divert the Six into the OEEC were viable. Burke Trend, the Treasury official who chaired interdepartmental studies on Messina, believed there were two possible outcomes from this course: first, the Six would fail to create a Common Market in the OEEC and blame Britain, or secondly, that the Six would succeed and the Common Market would swamp the OEEC.[55] As long as the Treasury supported the OEEC as a means of reconciling Britain's commitment to Europe with its world economic role, this institution had to be defended. Although Trend himself doubted the efficacy of an OEEC counter-initiative to the Messina plans, a high level Treasury meeting on 28 October sanctioned the proposals of Sir Leslie Rowan, head of the OFD, as a means of reconciling the harsh Foreign Office view with Treasury policy.[56] The government was to state that it could not join the European Common Market and that the OEEC should be fully consulted during the Six's further discussions, giving Whitehall 'time to formulate some alternative, but wider and non-discriminatory, scheme of economic co-operation intended to wean the Six Powers away from the Common Market'. Concurrently, the Treasury envisaged bargaining Anglo-European co-operation in the nuclear energy field as a sop for the Six's abandonment of the Common Market. Thus, although these proposals were more extensive than the tactics suggested by the Foreign Office, they were nevertheless equally negative; the counter-initiative was purely a more sophisticated method of undermining the Six's progress. Further support for Rowan's counter-initiative ideas was provided by the third Whitehall department with a significant interest in the Messina Common Market, the Board of Trade. While the Board shared the basic opposition to Common Market membership, of the three departments, it alone contemplated the Six's success and the consequent implications for Britain. In turn, this led to a more earnest view of a possible new initiative in Europe.

From the early 1950s, the Board of Trade placed importance on the expansion of British trade away from traditional patterns. Against the views of the Treasury's OFD and the Bank of England, the Board had argued that the Sterling Area and the system of imperial preferences would not alone provide the basis for the expansion of British trade necessary for the future strength of Britain's balance of payments.[57] Combined with his personal interest in trade liberalism, this had led the President of the Board of Trade, Peter Thorneycroft, to insist successfully on the relaxation of East-West trade controls in 1953–54 and gain Churchill's support in defeating Leo Amery's anti-GATT, pro-imperial preference motion at the 1954 Conservative Party Conference.[58] Thorneycroft's pursuit of redirecting British trade policy failed to extend to Europe, but not through lack of trying. In a far-sighted Cabinet memorandum of February 1953, Thorneycroft recognised the ambitions of the Six powers for European trade liberalisation and suggested that Britain take the initiative in Europe by bringing the Six, Switzerland and Scandinavia together in a 'wide common market' on an agreed list of goods.[59] This idea fell foul of a Cabinet riven by scepticism of an increased British role in European integration, but it goes some way to explain why Thorneycroft and his officials became so concerned about the European Common Market in 1955.

The Board shared the fundamental Foreign Office and Treasury opposition to the Messina Six. In July 1955 it had mounted a strong defence of British non-involvement suggesting that Britain's balance of payments position, especially in relation to the dollar area, and world-wide trade commitments with the United States, the Sterling Area, and the Commonwealth, via imperial preference, would be hindered by membership of a Common Market.[60] This was not based on a disregard for trade with Europe or the protectionist attitude it had taken to studies of a European Customs Union in the late 1940s.[61] Instead, it was a reflection of the fine and difficult balance of British tariff policy, committed on the one hand to negotiations for trade liberalisation in the GATT and OEEC, and on the other to the maintenance of the Ottawa system of trade with the Commonwealth which provided for over half of Britain's exports in 1955.[62] It was a precarious situation, as Sir Maurice Dean, Second Secretary in the Board, noted:

> Our difficulties really spring from the fact that we are trying to please everybody; to pacify the protectionists and to remain on terms with the free-traders; to sign up with the multilateralists but to raise our hat respectfully to the system of Commonwealth Preference and Commonwealth Free Entry. When we meet two of our ill-assorted friends simultaneously – as we sometimes do – we rely on our agility and speed of mind and foot to extricate us from embarrassment. It is not a restful policy.[63]

Joining a Common Market, which through its common external tariff would end Britain's imperial preference system, would have produced one of Dean's dangerous clashes and was thus anathema to the Board. Its policy, fashioned by Thorneycroft and Permanent Secretary Sir Frank Lee, aimed to manage Britain's changing traditional trade relations with the Dominions and the Sterling Area while at the same time developing trade elsewhere. In this calculation, European markets weighed heavily. British exports to the Six had, for example, risen from 10.4 per cent in 1951 to 13.0 per cent in 1955, and to Western Europe as a whole from 24.8 per cent to 27.2 per cent during the same period.[64] The prospect, therefore, of a successful Common Market from which Britain was excluded caused significant difficulties for trade policy. Whereas this failed to trouble the Foreign Office and the Treasury who doubted whether the Six would ever create a Common Market, it caused great anxiety in the Board of Trade which was less dismissive of the Messina powers. In July the Board too had doubted the Six, but by the autumn their progress created unease; in September, Sir Frank Lee first mooted his disquiet at a Whitehall policy which he described as an 'elaborate and embarrassing comedy of manners'.[65] Through his experience as British representative on the Spaak Committee, and with some irony considering the retrospective criticism of his role in Brussels, Russell Bretherton, Under-Secretary in the Board of Trade, was alone in warning that Whitehall underestimated 'the amount of steam, both political and economic . . . behind the Messina ideas, and also the dangers for the UK in a purely negative attitude'.[66] Opposed to the prevailing Whitehall policy in autumn 1955, but unable to influence it significantly, the Board in response took a far more serious view of a new trade initiative in Europe.

At a full Board of Trade meeting on 24 October, there was a general acceptance of the need to develop a more proactive policy towards Messina.[67] The potential of a European Common Market dominated by Germany which could develop into a discriminatory bloc led Thorneycroft and his officials to conclude that it would be unwise to take any decision which would shut Britain out of Europe. With the survival of trade within the 'walled garden' of the Commonwealth imperial preference system in doubt, the Board admitted that Britain might well wish closer association with Europe in the future.[68] Thorneycroft thus instructed Bretherton to consider British association with the Common Market as he planned to put a paper to Cabinet after the Spaak Committee had reported.

Prior to ministerial decisions on policy towards the Common Market, therefore, the Board of Trade was already looking past the negative Whitehall policy championed by the Foreign Office. A last attempt at demonstrating the Board's unhappiness was made by Sir Frank Lee at the Cabinet's Economic Steering Committee on 1 November 1955 when he actually argued in favour of joining the Messina Six on economic grounds. A lone voice, however, Lee conceded to the majority view of his colleagues. His foresight would soon be vindicated.[69]

Démarche and counter-initiative

During November and December 1955, the 'parting of the ways' between Britain and the Six was formalised with Russell Bretherton's final appearance as representative on the Spaak Committee and with a British ministerial decision which aimed to deflect the Six into the OEEC. From these events, two processes began which were crucial in the long-run for the development of Britain's FTA proposal. First, London made a series of diplomatic errors in the official démarche announcing its decision not to join a European Common Market which created an atmosphere of suspicion on the Continent from which the FTA would never escape. Second, ministers gave their approval to studies of a counter-initiative, setting officials on a course which would eventually lead to Plan G.

In his final statement to the Brussels Steering Committee on 7 November, Bretherton reaffirmed Britain's difficulties with the Six's plans and defended the OEEC's authority.[70] In what the Foreign Office described as a 'fighting speech', Spaak, in response, compared the Messina decisions to the creation of the OEEC and the ECSC; from this point on, the Six progressed alone in drafting the report which would form the basis of the Treaty of Rome.[71] Bretherton's statement was not well received in Brussels; its impact was described as 'that of the wettest of blankets' and British representatives were left unprepared for the dismay it caused amongst the Six at the ECSC's High Authority.[72] Its effect was, however, compounded by the result of disastrous decision-making in London.

On 11 November, officials' reports on the European Common Market and Euratom were finally considered by the Cabinet's Ministerial Economic Policy Committee (EPC).[73] With Butler chairing the meeting, and the Foreign Office represented by Reading in Macmillan's absence, there was unanimous agreement 'that it was against the interests of the United Kingdom to join a European Common Market'. As the Messina proposals threatened to 'infringe the wider interests of the OEEC', ministers decided that Britain should 'divert as far as possible the activities of the [Six] into the wider framework'. The tactics employed for this task were largely those advocated by the Foreign Office, as the Common Market plan was expected to 'collapse without [British] opposition being pressed too hard'. While ministers noted that officials had begun studies of a counter-initiative in Europe, expectation of the Common Market's failure made this a secondary consideration and 'it was important not to expect too much' from officials' efforts in this area. London aimed to avoid blatant hostility. Instead, Britain's views would be confidentially explained to the United States government, 'in order to secure their support', and also to the German government, 'in the hope that this would lead them to adopt a more realistic policy' of, in effect, opposing the Messina Common Market. The plan, therefore, was to inveigle the Six's projects under the aegis of the OEEC. Concurrently, accepting Ministry of Defence recommendations, the EPC rejected membership of Euratom but agreed that Britain might have to associate with it, in light of American interest in this project. It was hoped that association in the nuclear energy field would mitigate rejection of the Common Market.

The result of these decisions was by far the most conspicuous and enduring evidence of Britain's potential hostility towards Six power unity. On 17 November, Foreign Office telegrams were despatched to Washington and Bonn, inviting Ambassadors Makins and Hoyer Millar to explain British policy to their respective governments.[74] On 6 December, Ellis Rees officially pronounced the British démarche to his fellow OEEC Heads of Delegations in Paris.[75] These tactics were a complete failure, greatly damaging British reputations on the Continent, and ensuring that any future British policy towards European integration would be received with caution and scepticism. Without doubt, the Eden government made significant errors at this stage. Once Bretherton had left the Spaak Committee, there was no reason for Britain to make statements on its policy towards the Common Market until the details of the Spaak Report were known. If, as the EPC expected, the Common Market would 'collapse without [British] opposition being pressed too hard', and as the Foreign Office believed, the French would make the Common Market impossible, why court accusations of *perfidious Albion* by attempting to collude with Washington and Bonn? Instead, it seems that the ambiguous advice from an embassy official in Washington provided the extremely weak premise for informing the United States government of Britain's decisions. On 10 November, while admitting that some in Washington saw Britain as 'the anti-freeze in the [European] mixture', the embassy suggested that if the government decided against Common Market membership, from the American point of view, it would 'be far better for us to say so clearly at the earliest possible moment'.[76] A combination of this dubious logic and fear of leakage from Washington and Bonn led the Foreign Office to push for the Ellis Rees démarche, despite a warning from Bretherton that the government should make no final expression of policy on the Brussels developments.[77] But it seems there was no caution in British attitudes by this stage and, moreover, on 19 November, the EPC decision had received its final stamp of authority from Eden.[78]

The immediate response to the démarche, from British Ambassadors, the Six and the United States, was a condemnation of the strategy it represented. First, while British embassies in capitals of the Six would not go so far as to question Whitehall policy, there were high levels of consternation. Maintaining his scepticism of the Common Market, Gladwyn Jebb was nevertheless 'a little startled by the apparently extremely hostile view towards Euratom'.[79] From Bonn, Hoyer Millar counselled greater consideration of German political support for the Six, suggesting that Britain 'ought to try and be careful not to pour more cold water on these "Messina" ideas than is really necessary'.[80] In Brussels, Labouchere was frustrated by his instructions, and in The Hague, Mason was 'taken aback by the vigour and bitterness' of the Dutch reaction.[81]

Second, the démarche brought a furious reaction from Spaak and the Dutch Foreign Minister, Beyen. Both had recently discussed European questions with Butler in London and had received no indication of a possible British démarche. The minutes of Beyen's 2 November meeting justify his later shock as Butler had given assurances that if the Six accommodated British conditions, 'they would always find us sympathetic and "European"'.[82] It is no wonder that Beyen was left in a 'state of great perturbation and indignation' by the démarche, arguing that Ellis Rees had been 'very silly in [the] OEEC'.[83] Spaak also had cause for anger; he had been in London on 18 November for meetings with Eden, Salisbury and Butler and had received no hint of a changed British attitude.[84] On the contrary, after the London visit, Belgian officials informed the

American embassy in Brussels that Britain would try to be helpful and would 'certainly take no action which would increase difficulties or problems' for Spaak's Messina studies.[85] The climax of Spaak's and Beyen's reaction came at a WEU Council meeting on 14 December where they mounted a vengeful assault which left Macmillan clearly embarrassed but not contrite according to his diary entry.[86] The foreign secretary would not be drawn into a row at the meeting, pointing out that he had received no warning of the discussion. The Foreign Office had, of course, prepared a brief which warned of a potential Spaak/Beyen attack at the WEU and that 'in the coulisses' there would be 'the usual mutterings about the United Kingdom stabbing "Europe" in the back'.[87] Reflecting the still fluid views of the Common Market within their governments, the French, German and Italian reactions were less heated than the Belgian and Dutch. The French position was complicated by forthcoming elections, but there was surprise at British actions and support for Messina, mostly directed towards Euratom.[88] While accepting British reservations, but reminding London that the Six's aims were ultimately political, the Italians resolved to make Messina a success.[89] The Germans followed a similar line, but added that the OEEC no longer provided the impetus necessary for further European integration.[90] The effect of Britain's attempt to foster German opposition to the Common Market failed, however. In December, Foreign Minister, von Brentano, informed the US Secretary of State, John Foster Dulles, that Britain was causing problems for the Messina proposals which had the Adenauer government's full support. Although Brentano's request for a public statement indicating American preference for the Six above the OEEC was rejected, Dulles did promise to place pressure on Eden during his early 1956 visit to Washington.[91]

The third significant reaction to the démarche came from the United States. London believed the Americans were following a contradictory policy and found it difficult to reconcile their idealistic political support for the Six with their general advocacy of multilateral, non-discriminatory trade which, in British opinion, would not be upheld by the creation of a European Common Market with a high common external tariff. This was a paradox with which London battled throughout the FTA negotiations, yet it was not as if American support for Six power unity had been previously ambiguous; it was possible to see strong continuity in Washington's policy from the

Marshall Plan, through the ECSC to the EDC. Still, the terse response to Britain's démarche left one Foreign Office official complaining that the Americans were 'talking down [to Britain] in quite an objectionable manner'.[92] Makins was informed of Dulles' full support for the Six, and while the United States felt Euratom was the best means of progress, Dulles himself assured Macmillan that a protectionist European Common Market would be accepted, despite its effect on trade, for political reasons.[93] President Eisenhower's interest in European integration, which he himself admitted was 'one of his pets', was also made clear by Dulles in a meeting with Macmillan on 15 December.[94] From this point on, it is difficult to see why Britain could not accept that for the United States, commercial problems were subordinate to the ultimate political integration of Europe.[95] Nevertheless, London persisted in its anti-Common Market policy with the Americans during Eden's January 1956 Washington visit. The Prime Minister would gain no ground, however, as Dulles had already laid the foundations for this meeting in December 1955. After assuring Monnet, Spaak and von Brentano of American support for the Six, Dulles warned Eisenhower that 'the British are working hard to block the development of the European idea. . . . This is somewhat in the same pattern as their early opposition to [the] EDC'.[96]

In December 1955, the British démarche was aptly described by a Dutch Foreign Office official as a 'tragic blunder'.[97] The first tragedy was that any goodwill accrued by Eden's, albeit intergovernmental, WEU lifeline to the integration process after the EDC's collapse in 1954, had been frittered away. The second was that Anglo-Six relations had been damaged, and that any subsequent British policy would be tainted by the failed tactics of the démarche.[98] This would remain a problem throughout the course of the FTA negotiations. The third effect was on American views of Britain's attitude towards European integration. The Eden government's failure to look past its démarche tactics ensured that the doubt sown in Dulles' mind made US support for a future British approach to Messina harder to achieve. No one in London appeared to have considered with any seriousness the impact of the démarche if it fell flat. Perhaps the most significant outcome of British policy at this stage, and the reverse of its aim, was that the Six proceeded towards the Treaties of Rome possibly strengthened by their ability to resist British flak. Ultimately, it was an unfortunate indication of, at best, British misapprehension, and at worst, arrogance, that the Foreign Office felt Ellis Rees had 'batted very well, on [a] rather sticky wicket' when announcing the démarche, and that Eden later rejected as 'nonsense' criticism of it for which he maintained 'no guilt'.[99]

It was the failure of the démarche that intensified Whitehall interest in a new British initiative in Europe. On 11 November at the EPC meeting, Ministers had played down the counter-initiative studies, noting that options were limited by tariff policy and responsibilities to the OEEC and the International Monetary Fund. It was also noted, however, that 'in the much longer term, it was not impossible that the United Kingdom might be able to follow a policy of closer economic association with Europe'.[100] As the Six resisted Britain's diversion attempts and the Americans increased pressure on Britain not to interfere with their progress, the 'much longer term' shortened significantly. It was at this stage that the counter-initiative studies, which had been in process since mid-October, became more serious.

The origins of the counter-initiative idea were in the Treasury and the Board of Trade, both of which doubted the viability of the Foreign Office tactic of simply deflecting the Six into the OEEC. The significant difference between the Treasury and Board was in their differing views of the counter-initiative's goal. Sir Leslie Rowan, the main proponent within the Treasury of a counter-initiative, described it as a method 'to stifle the Common Market at birth'.[101] This intention, together with his later opposition to closer association with Europe via the FTA, suggests that Rowan simply wished to develop a more sophisticated version of the Foreign Office's diversionary tactics. With its greater awareness of the Six's potential, the Board of Trade took a more sincere view of the counter-initiative. On 22 October, Bretherton submitted a note to Thorneycroft on the possible alternative British courses to the proposals for a Common Market. There was, according to Bretherton, a 'strong case' for analysis of alternatives because British membership of, or exclusion from, the Common Market were impossible options. Membership would complicate Britain's commercial policy outside of Europe, while isolation would endanger Britain's export markets in the Six. There were two proactive courses, the first of which would loosely form the basis of the later Plan G: Britain could 'refuse to join the Common Market as a European Customs Union, but offer to join with it as a Free Trade Area'.[102] As representative on the Spaak Committee, Bretherton had promoted a FTA over a customs union in Brussels on a number of occasions.[103] But as the Six had decided on the latter, association via a FTA was a possible option. Tariffs and quantitative restrictions on mutual trade between Britain and the Six would be removed, but the government would retain its tariffs against imports from third countries and maintain autonomy in its general economic policy. Bretherton did note, however, that British industry and agriculture would probably object to a loss of tariff protection, and there would be difficulties over imperial preference. The second course was for Britain to make limited proposals on the tariff front, perhaps in a European 'Tariff Club', to satiate Continental desire for liberalisation of intra-European trade.[104]

The counter-initiative studies became an interdepartmental matter on instructions from the Cabinet's Economic Steering Committee on 1 November.[105] Once the EPC had taken its final decision on the Common Market, the Treasury's Otto Clarke circulated a paper to his Whitehall colleagues outlining the considerations which 'at first sight' would produce a 'fresh initiative' in British policy towards economic co-operation in Europe.[106] Clarke would later co-ordinate the studies which produced Plan G, remaining a key figure in FTA policy during the negotiations from 1957–58. In 1955, however, five options formed 'a single package' for Britain's initiative: tariff reductions; freer movement of labour; freedom of capital movement; harmonisation of social services; and abolition of passports and visas. While most of these alternatives would be surpassed by the considerations which produced Plan G in 1956, tariff reductions, which encompassed Bretherton's embryonic FTA and 'Tariff Club' ideas, would persist. On 16 November, under Clarke's chairmanship in the Cabinet's Mutual Aid Committee (MAC), officials began work on Britain's new initiative in Europe with the proviso that it would in no way damage Britain's interests in the Commonwealth and Colonies, and that it would be probably deployed in the middle of 1956.[107]

These studies mark the origins of British policy development which would produce Plan G in 1956. Clearly, it was the Board of Trade which took the most serious view of the Continental impetus for economic integration and the link between the counter-initiative and Plan G is strongest in Bretherton's suggestion of association with the Common Market via a FTA. But even then the Board's policy was based on negativity, a realisation that the Six might succeed in their efforts, and an interest in developing an *alternative* to their plans to protect Britain's trade policies and neutralise the threat of the Six. Similarly, the Treasury's support for a counter-initiative was grounded in a belief that the Six would only be successfully side-tracked by a British-inspired alternative in the OEEC. Unlike the Board, the Treasury, under the lead of the OFD, the most steadfast defender of established financial and economic policies, was inherently opposed to Britain developing a closer association with Europe. To the Foreign Office, ill-judged dismissiveness of the Six rendered the counter-initiative a tactical weapon only necessary if the Messina powers managed 'in spite of everything to go ahead'.[108] After the disaster of the December 1955 démarche, a combination of factors and re-evaluations within Whitehall significantly altered the emphasis placed on a British initiative in Europe.

A missed boat?

Before the analysis proceeds into early 1956 and the further development of Britain's FTA proposal, reference has to be made to one of the vital issues in the history of British policy towards European integration. Increasingly, the Eden government's response to the Messina conference and the consequent studies of a Common Market is depicted as one of the greatest failures in Britain's post-war foreign and economic policy.[109] Britain was condemned to a course of isolation from Europe until 1973 and deprived of the economic growth enjoyed by the Six powers in the first decade of the EEC's life. Macmillan himself admitted in hindsight that Britain 'should have been more alert to the dangers' in 1955, and there is a sense of lost opportunity amongst officials involved in policy at that time.[110] Historiographically, while there is general agreement that, in retrospect, Britain 'missed a boat' at Messina, there are those who take a more critical view, arguing that the trends were apparent, *not only* in retrospect, but in 1955.[111] A few, on the other hand, have suggested that there was some justification for Britain's hesitancy at this defining moment in post-war European development.[112] As one authority has said, debate about 'missing the boat' 'bristle[s] with methodological difficulties [being] both highly speculative and, in the end, rather unsatisfactory'.[113] However, given that this is an issue of historical interest, evinced by the attention paid to it by two recent accounts, it is necessary to consider it briefly.

According to one view, there was no boat to miss in 1955 as 'The success of the Messina initiative was not at all guaranteed' and, moreover, 'no minister seriously considered buying a ticket' anyway due mainly to 'strong traditions of political mentality' grounded in Britain's world power role.[114] British decisions are more extensively exonerated by another view which argues that 'British diplomacy was far-sighted, efficient, and well-informed' and that 'commercial interests in export promotion were predominant and sufficient motivations for initial British apathy and opposition to the E[uropean] C[ommunity]'.[115] Both of these argument have elements of reason in them; they suggest that the British government did not 'miss a boat' but rather decided, either for reasons of politics or economics depending on which account you read, to maintain a steady British course. But alone, they have shortcomings. To state that the success of the Six was not guaranteed does little more than stress the unpredictability of the Messina process, something which was as pertinent to the Six as it was to Britain; also, to describe British diplomacy as 'far-sighted' ignores the damage done to Anglo-Six relations by the close of 1955. More significantly, by accentuating political motives and economic motives for British policy separately, these accounts neglect the complexity of decision-making and the interplay between these factors.

When Whitehall's rejection of Common Market membership in autumn 1955 is analysed, it is clear that the Eden government was aware of the potential damage of exclusion but, given Britain's political position and its economic and commercial interests, together with doubt about the viability of the Six, it decided to pursue established policy. The United Kingdom had first rejected membership of a European customs union in November 1949 on terms explained by Sir Stafford Cripps, then Chancellor: 'We could not integrate our economy with that of Europe in any manner that would prejudice the full discharge of our responsibilities and interests as a leading member of the Commonwealth and sterling area'.[116] Wider commitments had been the main reason for opposition to a customs union, together with an aversion to European supranationalism. Six years later, these same reasons were the basis of Britain's dismissal of the Messina plans.

The final officials' report in November 1955 argued that Britain's world-wide interests, the federal aims of the Six, the necessity of maintaining economic and political links with the Commonwealth, and finally the continuation of protection for British industry, ruled

Table 1.1   UK balance of payments, 1946–55 (select items as percentage of GDP)

	(1) Manufactures	(2) Primary products	(3) Non-govt. services	(4) Commercial balance	(5) Basic balance
1946–50	+8.6	−11.4	+0.2	−2.6	−0.3
1951–55	+8.8	−12.4	+0.8	−2.8	−2.9

Source: Alford (1996), p. 225

out membership of a Common Market.[117] This analysis had been broken down into two separate studies, one economic, one political. The economic report had put two scenarios to ministers. First, if the comparison was between preservation of the status quo (no Common Market) and a Common Market including Britain, it was 'extremely difficult to strike any clear balance of economic advantage or disadvantage'. Conversely, if the Common Market was to succeed, despite British abstention, it was argued 'that the disadvantages of abstaining would, *in the long-run* (original italics), outweigh the advantages'.[118] Ministers, however, dismissed these considerations, finding an easier solution in the political report which argued that membership would not only be detrimental to Commonwealth political relations, but would offer 'no clear and definite' *quid pro quo* for the consequent weakening of Commonwealth links.[119] In 1948/49, despite dubious decision-making, the decision itself to reject a customs union had some defence, with the trends of sustained European growth of output and trade not yet proven.[120] In 1955, these trends, in parallel with the ECSC's success, were more evident. Moreover, the Board of Trade had come to recognise the weakness of imperial preferences and the Sterling Area for Britain's future balance of payments.[121] Also, the Treasury's Economic Section had concluded that on economic terms alone, Britain's interests were in Common Market membership.[122] The fact was that Britain's balance of payments were reliant, to a large extent, on the export of manufactures, and from 1950 to 1955, British exports in manufactures to the Six increased whereas exports to the Commonwealth remained relatively stagnant (Tables 1.1 and 1.2).

The long-term logic of such an evaluation was not fully considered by British ministers and the majority of officials who were largely sceptical of the Six and who almost unanimously believed that, in any event, Britain's future lay outside of a European politi-

Table 1.2 British exports of produce and manufactures to the Commonwealth, Western Europe and the Six, 1950–55 (percentage of total exports by value)

	Commonwealth	Western Europe	The Six
1950	48.7	21.5	11.1
1951	49.9	24.8	10.4
1952	47.9	26.0	11.3
1953	47.0	26.9	13.1
1954	48.5	27.6	13.1
1955	47.8	27.2	13.0

Source: Central Statistical Office, *Annual Abstract of Statistics*, Nos. 93 and 97, 1956 & 1960.

Table 1.3 The geographical distribution of British exports of produce and manufactures, 1955 (percentage of total exports by value)

	Commonwealth	Western Europe	The Six	North America	Rest of the world
1955	47.8	27.2	13.0	11.2	13.4

Source: CSO, *AAS*, No. 97, 1960.

cal federation. There was no widespread movement in Britain in 1955 for closer integration with the Six; membership of the Messina process would have been an unprecedented step for any government to take and the reaction of parliament and public was an unknown. Also, although trade with Britain's traditional markets was not increasing, manufactures to the Six in 1955 only accounted for 13 per cent of the total (Table 1.3).

Short-term political rationale therefore dominated the decision-making process; the possible advantages of membership advocated by the Economic Section, and of a more positive policy suggested by the Board of Trade, were dismissed. Ultimately, the decision to stay out in 1955 did not derive primarily from either political, economic or commercial interests but from the synthesis of these composite parts. The implementation of this policy decision, breaking from the established diplomacy of benevolent neutrality, was a damaging blunder born from underestimation of the Six's ambition and overestimation of Britain's ability to influence their course. This was a strategy championed by the Foreign Office which, influenced by its experience of the EDC's death and the WEU's birth, doubted the Six and saw danger in their potential development and safety in the Atlantic Alliance. It was also supported by the Treasury which held similar fears about the Six, especially in terms of growing German economic power. The Six's rebuff to Britain's intervention shocked the British and brought reassessments of their policy towards European integration. The solution was to invigorate the counter-initiative ideas, and it was Harold Macmillan who gave fresh impetus to Britain's new policy for Europe.

2
Fresh Impetus: Formulating Plan G, January–May 1956

In Anthony Eden's December 1955 Cabinet reshuffle, Harold Macmillan left the Foreign Office to become chancellor of the exchequer.[1] While this initially came as a 'shattering blow' to Macmillan, who was fond of the Office, it did free him from the prime minister's interference. It seems that Eden's own experience of a meddlesome superior had not prevented him from causing Macmillan frustration: 'It was quite clear that Eden wanted to get rid of me; he kept on sending me little notes, sometimes twenty a day, ringing up all the time. He really should have been both PM and Foreign Secretary.'[2] To prevent the continuation of this friction, Macmillan only accepted the Treasury post on a set of provisos which, according to his official biographer, 'verged on the insubordinate'.[3] The new chancellor demanded autonomy over his own department, that his predecessor not become deputy prime minister, and that the Treasury and the Board of Trade work as partners. Adept in political manipulation, Macmillan secured great power within the Cabinet and control over economic policy, as well as a degree of dominance over Eden who 'was probably just a little afraid' of him.[4] All of these factors were vital for the development of policy towards European integration, for which Macmillan, as chancellor, had primary responsibility.

The British government's search for a new initiative in Europe entered its second stage at the beginning of 1956, but the fresh impetus provided by Macmillan did not totally cleanse Whitehall of the previous autumn's negativity. Overt opposition towards the Six's plans was discarded rapidly after December 1955 with the Eden government returning (outwardly at least) to the wary benevolence which largely characterised British attitudes before Messina. This may account for early suggestions that Britain's ill will was short-lived.[5] Within Whitehall, however, majority opinion remained opposed to the Messina plans, and although the counter-initiative now became an initiative in its own right, no longer the tactical weapon of the démarche, it was designed to produce an alternative to the Messina process in expectation of its failure. It would remain as such until the success of the Six made an alternative to their plans less feasible and association with the Common Market vital. To talk of one Whitehall policy would, however, be to misrepresent the complexity of ministerial, departmental and intra-departmental agendas which conflicted and combined to produce Plan G. Thus, this chapter will analyse the development of policy from January to May 1956, concentrating on the internal divisions in London and also the British response to the progress of the Six powers in Brussels. To begin with, however, it will examine the circumstances which caused the re-evaluation in policy in January and February.

Birth of a new British initiative in Europe

Apart from the failed démarche and Macmillan's move to the Treasury, two other factors encouraged Whitehall's re-evaluation of its European policy in early 1956. The first was the formation of Guy Mollet's administration in Paris after the general elections of 2 January.[6] Doubts about ultimate French acceptance of the Common Market proposals had been widespread in London, and though they persisted, there was heightened awareness of new political momentum in France. Jebb reported that Mollet had shown interest in the Messina proposals as they were developing in the Spaak Committee and had appointed ministers who were sympathetic to European integration, particularly Christian Pineau at the Quai d'Orsay.[7] This suggested that blanket dismissal of the Six's efforts based on doubt about French enthusiasm was no longer a tenable position, particularly as the elections had seen the defeat of the Gaullists within the National Assembly.

The second and more powerful influence was that exerted by the Eisenhower Administration. The forceful reiteration of American preference for Six power integration in Europe and objection to British hostility towards Messina had great effect after the visit of the prime minister and foreign secretary to Washington at the end of January. 'Cross-currents of opinion' developed between Whitehall departments in the preparation of briefs for Eden's Washington trip which revealed the discord in attitudes towards European co-operation.[8] The final brief, which recommended that the prime minister take a firm line on Messina and urge the Americans to encourage the Six to discuss their plans within the OEEC frame-work, was a negative and bleak document, prepared mainly by the Treasury and the Board of Trade.[9] It seems that only the Foreign Office had learnt from the American response to the autumn démarche. Lord Hood, of WOD, believed the brief overlooked wider political implications and Edden, of the MAD, doubted whether the prime minister would be able to influence American support for the Six.[10] These views reflected a larger *volte-face* in Foreign Office policy towards European integration in early 1956 which discarded the hostility of the previous autumn. Recognising that London and Washington were 'more and more on the opposite side of the fence' over integration, and not wishing to be out of step with the Ameri-cans, the Office began to advocate American policy within Whitehall: the Messina process could be used to integrate West Germany into the Western Alliance. In January 1956, Sir Geoffrey Harrison, Assistant Under-Secretary, suggested that 'in the interests of our relations with Europe and with the Americans ... let us push inter-governmental co-ordination rather than attack Western integration'.[11] Such a view was also very much in accord with the pro-European tendencies of the Foreign Office Minister of State, Anthony Nutting, who later encouraged talks with Spaak to 'blow away some of the cobwebs of isolationism which clutter the corridors of H.M. Treasury – even H.M. Foreign Office'.[12] From early 1956, therefore, the Foreign Office supported Whitehall studies of a new European initiative, and worked to increase collaboration between Euratom and the OEEC as a means of smoothing Anglo-Six relations.[13] Nevertheless, the advice of his officials did not lead the new foreign secretary, Selwyn Lloyd, to urge the prime minister to moderate his negative view of the Six during meetings with Eisenhower and Dulles. This probably casts more light on Eden's personal attitudes than it does on Lloyd's views of European co-operation. One of the abiding legacies of the first half of the 1950s was Eden's reluctance to accept diminished status for Britain in Anglo-American relations.[14]

Eden's own prejudices were strengthened by the note of hysteria sounded by Thorneycroft prior to the Washington visit. The Presi-dent of the Board of Trade believed that the Americans were in a 'fool's paradise about Messina', having failed to recognise the risk of a European Common Market developing into a discriminatory *bloc*, endangering Anglo-American policies of non-discriminatory multilateral trade enshrined in the General Agreement on Tariffs and Trade (GATT) and threatening British trade.[15] Purposefully over-stated to catch Eden's attention and impress British fears on the Americans, the shortcomings of Thorneycroft's approach, in combination with the Washington brief, were recognised by some in Whitehall. In the Board, Bretherton warned that the Americans would not be moved by British arguments, and in the Foreign Office, Thorneycroft's recommendations only led to the conclusion that 'if a common market comes into being, we probably could not afford to stay out'.[16]

While it was true that the Americans placed greater importance on Euratom than on the Common Market in early 1956, believing it to be a more feasible proposition, the British were aware of the highest levels of support for the Six's general political goals in Washington. Dulles had clarified this in December 1955 and it was accepted in London that European integration was 'a hobby horse' of President Eisenhower.[17] Regardless of this, Eden and Lloyd revealed British opposition to the Common Market and expressed reservations about Euratom to Eisenhower and Dulles. The result was discord in Anglo-American attitudes with the American secretary of state stressing that 'the United States wished to encourage those who were anxious to co-operate in European affairs'.[18] Reporting to Cabinet on 9 February, Eden stated that 'on the main questions of policy in Europe there was complete identity of view between the two governments' but that there had been 'some difference' over the Messina proposals for which the Americans entertained 'an enthusiasm similar to that which they had shown towards the [EDC]'.[19] Integration was obviously not a 'main question of policy in Europe' and the prime minister did not mention this issue in any detail during his Commons report on the Washington talks.[20] His own opposition to Six power integration, encouraged by the negativity of the Economic Departments' advice, and perhaps a desire to resist American pressure, led Eden to attempt to convince the Eisenhower Administration of the dangers in the Six's plans. All this achieved, however, was enhanced American suspicion of British motives, with Dulles reporting Eden's anti-Common Market views to members of the Six thereby strengthening fears of *perfidious Albion* so soon after the démarche.[21]

It was against this background that Whitehall's Economic Departments began to re-consider policy towards the Common Market. Macmillan's move from foreign secretary to chancellor of the exchequer in December 1955 was the primary stimulus in enhancing Treasury interest in European integration. His actions reflect what was without doubt a personal interest in European co-operation, heavily influenced by fear of a united Europe dominated by Germany. This had been the basis of a March 1953 Cabinet memorandum which advocated action against a federal Europe controlled by Germany, otherwise Britain might have 'created the very situation in Europe ... which, in every century, since the Elizabethan age, [it had] fought long and bitter wars' to prevent.[22] On becoming chancellor, Macmillan was 'haunted by the fear' that Britain would 'fall between two stools' if it did not balance the declining importance of the Commonwealth preference system with new Anglo-European trade links.[23] This, together with the failed démarche and firm American pressure, encouraged Macmillan to invigorate Treasury analysis of European policy. On 23 January 1956, he complained to Rowan that Britain's policy was 'too negative', demanding fresh studies.[24] In his diary on 28 January, Macmillan spoke of finding a 'constructive alternative' to the 'merely negative attitude to European co-operation (as put forward by the Messina plan & the 6 powers)'.[25] Consequently, on 1 February, he increased the pressure with a minute to the Treasury's Permanent Secretary, Sir Edward Bridges:

> Our official view seems to be a confident hope that nothing will come out of Messina ... I think it is very probable that powerful forces in France and in Germany will prevent the Messina plan coming off ... [but] perhaps Messina will come off after all and that will mean Western Europe dominated in fact by Germany and used as an instrument for the revival of German power through economic means. It is really giving them on a plate what we fought two world wars to prevent. ... I do not like the prospect of a world divided into the Russian sphere, the American sphere and a united Europe of which we are not a member.[26]

Meeting this apparent threat of German power in Europe was thus a critical factor in Macmillan's search for a new British initiative, reflecting a long-held and widespread British attitude, exemplified in 1944 by Duff Cooper, then Ambassador to Paris: 'Throughout her history as a great power it has been the policy of Great Britain to prevent the domination of Europe by any one too powerful nation . . . that policy will be maintained in the future, for to abandon it would be to sign our own death warrant'.[27] Macmillan wanted his officials to develop a plan, 'however sketchy', which would reconcile Britain's position as head of the Sterling Area and Commonwealth with some degree of European co-operation.[28] Having seen the attempt to implement his 'thumbs down on Messina' fail in autumn 1955, Macmillan moved towards a more positive means of meeting the threat of the Six. Persisting with his characteristic military analogies, he felt that the real issue of a British initiative was whether it should be a rearguard action or an advance, and concluded on 6 February: 'I am anxious, if possible, for an advance which would be recognised as such'.[29]

Macmillan's directives created a split within the Treasury over Britain's relations with Europe which, in turn, reflected conflicts over external economic policy. Sir Leslie Rowan, head of the OFD, argued for the defence of the *status quo* in European policy, while his one-time 'evil genius', Otto Clarke, head of the Home and Overseas Planning Staff (HOPS), put the case 'in favour of a little bit of a tilt towards Europe'.[30] Ironically, HOPS had been born from the Treasury's decreased activity in the European field after 1952, but Clarke, in collaboration with the Treasury's Economic Section, worked for greater British involvement in European integration after 1955.[31] The clash between Rowan and Clarke centred on the viability of sustaining the accepted economic policy of the Collective Approach to global convertibility and multilateral trade with or without accommodation of the shifting sands in European economic relations. In Rowan's view, the primacy of sterling via the Collective Approach was the central plank of British external economic policy, especially after *de facto* sterling convertibility in February 1955, and closer economic relations with Europe would complicate this policy by unnecessary entanglement with continental economies.[32] The studies of a counter-initiative which the OFD instituted in November 1955 are cast in a dark light when considering Rowan's later insistence on 'some diversionary tactic in order to take peoples' minds a bit off Messina'.[33] His anti-European, pro-sterling views are further explained by later statements made in response to questions from the Radcliffe Committee on whether a pooling of UK and European reserves had ever been considered in the Treasury:

I think that the pooling of reserves is only another way of saying that you are going to have a common management of your currency, and if you have a common management of currency you are going to have a common management of economic policy; and if you have a common management of economic policy then you must have common legislatures, and so forth; therefore pooling our reserves is merely a way of saying a federation or confederation . . . The answer to your question is 'No'.[34]

Rowan's advocacy of undermining the Messina Common Market was, however, balked by Macmillan, who gave his full support to Clarke at the HOPS: 'I want this study to be made. But I don't want the study to be limited by any other doctrinaire assumptions. Let it be objective'.[35]

According to Clarke, Rowan's analysis of external economic policy was out of date.[36] The Collective Approach had been based on Britain's position at the centre of Churchill's 'three circles': the USA, the Commonwealth and Western Europe. Although Clarke admitted that the Collective Approach remained 'the only policy that aligns our political, military and economic interests', he added that the 'threat of Messina', as well as the importance of Western Europe for British defence policy, meant that the European circle had grown in stature since the Collective Approach was inaugurated in 1952.[37] Clarke's logic was clear: 'if Messina looks like succeeding, we shall have to move closer to Europe to avoid being excluded; if Messina looks like failing, we may want to move closer to Europe to keep it (and our defence) together'. Although on economic grounds the Treasury still hoped in February 1956 that Messina would fail, it was aware of the European resources committed to the Common Market idea and of the significant support from the United States with whom disagreement would tend 'to frustrate all policy'. Therefore, in order to reform the Collective Approach and meet European developments, Clarke advocated 'a genuine plan, representing a significant and real tilting of our policy towards Europe'.[38]

Clarke's general analysis coincided with the view of the Treasury's Economic Section under the lead of the Economic Advisor to the Government, Sir Robert Hall.[39] In autumn 1955, the Economic Section had been one of the minority in Whitehall arguing for membership of the Common Market, and in early 1956, Clarke's new approach provided the opportunity for Hall and his officials to influence policy development. Thus, whilst the role of the Economic Section in the formulation of Britain's initiative was officially confined to providing economic analysis for Clarke and his interdepartmental officials, there was in fact a greater degree of collaboration. Frank Figgures, a member of Clarke's staff at the HOPS, was also on secondment to the Economic Section from 1955–57, and this, together with cooperation between Clarke and Hall, ensured a great deal of unofficial communication between the two Treasury departments.[40] Hall himself had doubts about the Collective Approach and admitted that Plan G only formalised the accepted truth of Britain moving away from the Commonwealth and towards Europe.[41] Other members of Hall's staff argued that the Collective Approach in its 1952 form had 'exhausted its potentialities' and when analysing rates of growth abroad in August 1956 concluded that 'the faster [the Six] grow the greater our potential losses of exports if we are left with discriminatory barriers against us'.[42] Thus, there were those in the Treasury who recognised the necessity of altering Britain's economic policy in favour of closer links with the economies of western Europe prior to the inception of the European Common Market. Nevertheless, although Rowan's OFD had been unable to halt the impetus given to studies of a new British initiative in Europe, the established predominance of sterling policy in combination with other conservative aspects in the formulation of Britain's initiative, ensured that it failed to represent the revolution in British economic policy deemed by some contemporary commentators as vital to the country's future.[43] In the early months of 1956, the Treasury produced options for a British initiative in Europe, but it remained hostile to the Six, something that was exemplified by its approach to Eden's Washington brief in January. It is not too difficult to imagine that beneath the ideas of a genuine 'tilt' towards Europe there was expectation of Britain repeating in the economic field what it had succeeded in doing in the military field two years previously; the British initiative would replace the failed Common Market as the WEU had replaced the failed EDC.

Changes in Macmillan's and the Treasury's view of the European Common Market in early 1956 corresponded with the Board of Trade's interest in developing Britain's policy, and gave the president and his officials room for manoeuvre. Thorneycroft's February 1953 Cabinet paper suggesting a British-inspired European Common Market had been stark in its evaluation of Britain's trade relations with Europe. The government's choice, in the president's opinion, was not between taking risks in European commercial policy or avoiding them. Accepting the inevitability of Six power action on trade in the future, the real choice was between 'taking risks in . . . a constructive initiative under our own control and accepting whatever risks may be brought to us by leaving the initiative to the other Governments of Europe'.[44] Thorneycroft's frustration at seeing the latter course evolve in 1955/56 was intense and materialised in his negative recommendations to Eden prior to the Washington visit. The potential effects of the Messina developments on British commerce were, however, worsened by other difficulties in British trade policy in early 1956. To begin with, the Board came under pressure from British industry to adopt a more constructive European policy. In February 1956, the Federation of British Industry (FBI) actually advocated that Britain rejoin the Six's discussions, with the Director General, Sir Norman Kipping, warning Sir Frank Lee that the implications of Messina required a serious British response.[45] Based less on a positive interest in European collaboration, and more on a fear of being locked out of Europe as traditional markets stagnated and British competitiveness suffered, the FBI and other industrial organisations encouraged the Board of Trade to defend British markets in Europe.[46]

There were, however, wider trade concerns in early 1956 that heightened the necessity of protecting British interests on the Continent. In March, the Australian government informed London that it wished to renegotiate its 1932 Ottawa Agreements with Britain, reflecting the changing realities of Anglo-Commonwealth trade.[47] Under Thorneycroft, the Board had recognised the declining efficacy of the imperial preference system, but two factors prevented it from welcoming open season on the Ottawa Agreements. First, though the Board accepted the limitations of preferential Commonwealth trade, it had no desire to bring its benefits to a premature close. Apart from the unquantifiable political advantages Britain gained from relations with the Dominions and Colonies, a high proportion of Britain's trade was still with the Commonwealth, and the Board believed it was in British interests to sustain preferential trade agreements in the short term (Table 2.1).[48] Secondly, within the Conservative Party, and indeed within Eden's Cabinet, there were those 'Empire Men', led by Lord Salisbury as Lord President, who would have seen a proposal to demolish imperial preferences as

Table 2.1   UK exports of certain goods to the Commonwealth in 1956

	Percentage of UK exports to Commonwealth receiving preference	UK exports to Commonwealth as a percentage of total UK exports
Iron and steel	74	56
Electric machinery	65	55
Motor vehicles	71	54
Cotton textiles	57	63
Wool textiles	67	34
Synthetic textiles	72	67
Clothing	69	39
Paper and board	68	66
Chemicals	44	44
Machinery	44	48

Source: Economist Intelligence Unit (1960), p. 19.

sacrilege.[49] However short-sighted, this was certainly a conviction with which Thorneycroft had to grapple. A mixture of economic reality and *realpolitik*, therefore, pointed to a cautious approach in reforming Commonwealth trade. Furthermore, the Board was involved in a comprehensive review of tariff policy under Sir Frank Lee which had yet to be completed, and thus intermediate tactics were to resist any substantial alteration to Commonwealth preferences until this could be done on British terms.[50] Only then would a managed scaling down of preferences be countenanced; in the meantime, as the eventual agreement with the Australians in November 1956 reveals, the aim was to retain the margins of preference for British exports in Commonwealth markets.[51]

As British trade patterns began their revolutionary movement away from the Commonwealth and towards Europe in the mid-1950s, the Board of Trade attempted to balance tradition with innovation while at the same time meeting the ongoing impetus for trade liberalisation in the GATT. In April 1956, Thorneycroft noted, 'These related questions of Ottawa, GATT, [and] Messina are looming very close to us'.[52] The nexus of these factors, especially if Messina succeeded, pointed to a difficult future for British commerce. If Germany achieved, through the Common Market, a favoured position against British exporters in the Netherlands or Belgium, for example, the Board feared this would alter the whole attitude of the Commonwealth to world-wide freer trade and payments and put imperial preference into the melting pot. Britain would then be forced inexorably into a choice between Europe and the Commonwealth.[53] The balancing act of British trade policy was becoming ever more precarious and without successfully delaying Commonwealth inspired renegotiation of the Ottawa Agreements and protecting British export markets in Europe from a German-dominated Common Market, the Board faced unprecedented trade difficulties. This predicament explains its avid support for a new British initiative in Europe. Bretherton had lost no time after autumn 1955 in fostering studies of British association with the Common Market. On 27 January, he sent a memorandum to the Treasury:

> I think that a Common Market from which we were apart would be a mortal danger to us both economically and, in the end, politically. But if our present attempts to discourage it fail, as I think they probably will, we ought to be ready with a positive scheme for going in and moulding it on lines that are least dangerous to us.[54]

There was a definite negativity at the base of this argument, as there was beneath the majority of Whitehall thinking at this time. With the defence of British interests in mind, and building on his suggestions of October 1955, Bretherton personally concluded that a 'partial free trade area' associating Britain with the Six's 'Common Market Customs Union' was 'the most hopeful' choice.[55] There was a second option of all-OEEC tariff reductions via a 'European Commodities Plan', but this was very much the lesser of Bretherton's two alternatives having received no support in the Board when it was first mooted as an OEEC proposal in 1955.[56]

While British representative on the Spaak Committee, and without government instructions, Bretherton had promoted the concept of a free trade area over a customs union to the Six. He suggested that the absence of a common external tariff would reduce the modification of member states' tariff policies, especially in terms of preferential trade, and lessen the impact on industries. Indicative of his later approach to Plan G, Bretherton recognised that a free trade area would require origin controls to avoid trade deflection due to disparity in external tariff levels and even accepted the prospect of future tariff harmonisation. While these suggestions were rejected within the Spaak Committee as the Six accepted the customs union concept, a free trade area which would not impinge on imperial preference was thought to be a reasonable position for the British.[57]

This was probably in Bretherton's mind, as was knowledge of support amongst the Six, specifically in the Belgian government, for the idea of a European free trade area. In autumn 1954 and spring 1955 the Belgian Ministry of Economic Affairs had developed proposals for a western European free trade area as a future route for European economic integration.[58] Although they were surpassed by the Spaak Committee decisions, belief in some form of free trade area extension to the Six's customs union remained.[59] While such a course was known to raise difficult technical issues, it would nevertheless encourage Bretherton in his advocacy of the FTA within the Board of Trade and Whitehall as it moved towards full-scale interdepartmental consideration of a new British initiative.

Before studies of European policy were initiated in London at the beginning of March 1956, developments took place which further conditioned Britain's view of the Six's chances of success and added to Continental suspicion of British actions. The OEEC Council of Ministers' Meeting at the end of February provided the first opportunity since the December démarche for the British and the Six to face each other at the conference table. Although the Eden government had refrained from making any inflammatory statements in public, allowing 'the dust to settle', tempers were still high amongst the Messina powers.[60] At their meeting in mid-February to discuss Spaak's progress and plan further action, there was unanimous irritation over the alleged hostility of the British government.[61] Spaak himself was eager to ascertain the true nature of British attitudes towards the Messina goals. On 7 February, he personally invited Eden to clarify his government's views and also sent Baron Snoy et d'Oppuers, Secretary General of the Belgian Ministry of Economic Affairs, to gauge British opinion.[62] London's response did little to allay European scepticism. The Six were already aware of continued British opposition to the Common Market plans from Dulles's reports of Eden's Washington comments. Snoy's reports did not counter these negative evaluations; Macmillan warned him that the Six had 'commenced a very fine undertaking and we shall help it; but as for [the] Common Market ... it will kill our trade, and we will have to fight against it'.[63] Despite Foreign Office advice to the contrary, Macmillan implored the prime minister to respond vaguely to Spaak's letter, delaying a fuller statement of British policy until

Macmillan met Spaak after the OEEC meeting.[64] Spaak later claimed that these tactics 'left no room for illusion. Behind this show of good will, there were fundamental differences of view'.[65]

Spaak was accurate in his assumptions. Macmillan had stalled a reasoned reply to his letter to give London 'time to examine whether there [were] some counter-proposals' to the Common Market.[66] Little was being done to hide this fact from the Europeans and, in this sense, British diplomacy had a damaging effect. But this was the British plan. Overt and public explanation of British views had been suppressed only as a result of Foreign Office fears of American retribution. Otherwise, Britain maintained its sceptical attitude towards the Common Market. In doing so, encouragement was drawn from the troubles faced by the Spaak Committee negotiations in early 1956. First, it was Euratom that held the spotlight at this stage; after all, the French had shown little interest in the Common Market and even the Americans had admitted that it was of less immediate importance and that its prospects were not good.[67] The Six were also far from agreement on Euratom; the Belgians opposed French demands to use Euratom for military purposes and the Germans disagreed with French proposals to separate agreements on Euratom and the Common Market, and instead wanted parallel agreement, a *Junktim*, between the two negotiations.[68] At the same time, the German Defence Minister, Strauss, revealed his personal doubts about Euratom, stating that he would be reluctant to see Germany join that organisation without British participation.[69] The German Foreign Minister went so far as to inform Hoyer Millar, Ambassador to Bonn, that on the Common Market, 'the French were increasingly luke warm and very doubtful starters'.[70] Also, just prior to the OEEC Council meeting, the German Economics Minister, Ludwig Erhard, made his opposition to the Common Market plans very clear, arguing that 'there was the danger that the institutions proposed by the Six Countries would merely set up a facade behind which the old malpractices would continue'.[71]

Erhard's economic liberalism was in tune with the preferences of the British government and he would remain the FTA's greatest defender during the next two years, whether in Bonn or amongst the Six. Although his attitude would eventually prove to be out of step with the ultimate view of Adenauer, in February 1956, the British could be forgiven for doubting German support for the Common Market with three senior German ministers questioning the Messina proposals. This was, in fact, the aim of the Adenauer government according to recent research. While Erhard's line to the British was a genuine reflection of his policy, the doubt sown by the German Foreign Ministry may have been a ploy to appease the British. As defenders of the Common Market for the political benefits it would bring in binding Germany to the West – particularly to France – the German Foreign Ministry worked to defuse the threat posed to the Six by British intervention, especially after the démarche of autumn 1955. Consequently, in early 1956, efforts were made 'to reassure Britain and others that the Common Market posed no threat and that its membership should not be restricted to the Six alone'.[72] This evidence adds yet further complexity to the history of Anglo-European relations in early 1956 and conditions any criticism which might be directed at the British for doubting the Six's progress at this stage.

Uncertainty surrounding the Six's development added to the sceptical atmosphere in Whitehall, which was heightened further by the French chairman of the OEEC, René Sergent, urging Thorneycroft to 'be beastly to his compatriots' during the Council meeting.[73] The president of the Board of Trade needed little encouragement. While advocating close Anglo-Six co-operation on nuclear energy to maintain Britain's position in the OEEC and relations with the Six, he nevertheless wished to 'speak up in Paris' against the Common Market proposals, accusing the Six of planning a European discriminatory *bloc*.[74] While this found support from the Foreign Office Parliamentary Under-Secretary, Lord John Hope, who suggested to Lloyd that the government was 'too coy' in its desire not to criticise 'the Messina boys', it was firmly rejected by officials.[75] Assistant Under-Secretary Denis Wright cautioned Lloyd: 'With respect I urge that we strongly resist the President's wish to make a frontal attack on the Common Market. We made known our dislike of it last November and in doing so caused enough trouble for ourselves'. Edden, similarly, wanted to 'avoid a row in the OEEC'.[76] There is no record of Lloyd's opinion on this issue but his Minister of State, Lord Reading, seems to have achieved some moderation of the official line for the Council meeting, but the hostile Treasury/Board of Trade approach was dominant. Ministers agreed to pledge support for OEEC-Euratom co-operation, and not attack the Common Market proposals publicly, but conversely emphasise their opposition in private conversation.[77] While the Foreign Office may have avoided a public row at the OEEC, the net effect of backstage accusation would still damage British reputations.

The OEEC Council of Ministers' Meeting of 28–29 February was dominated by a common aim to reach agreement on collaboration between the Messina powers and the OEEC in nuclear energy. Britain, the Six and the United States were eager to prevent a clash of views and emphasise the compatibility of Euratom and the OEEC nuclear energy proposals. Controversy was avoided, but substantive decisions were postponed until the summer.[78] Macmillan had reached agreement with the Scandinavians before the Council that the priority was to secure a unanimous resolution on the OEEC Nuclear Energy Report; in the event, this left little opportunity to discuss the Common Market, reflecting the British aim 'to gain time'.[79] Despite evidence of a positive British attitude towards OEEC-Euratom collaboration, with Lloyd announcing to the Commons that the government would 'examine the plan sympathetically' and Jebb making an official démarche in Paris clarifying British interest in association, the Six were still suspicious of British motives.[80] They feared that the 'unaccustomed speed' with which the OEEC produced its nuclear energy plans was simply a move to prevent the establishment of Euratom.[81] Given the majority view in London at that time, these fears were probably justified, with the 1955 démarche strategy of a positive approach to Euratom compensating for the negative approach to the Common Market proposals still applicable. The State Department, keeping a close watching brief on the Six, certainly believed the British aimed to undermine Euratom.[82] Thus, British attitudes towards European nuclear co-operation, and by extension, European economic co-operation, both impaired by the 1955 démarche, were worsened by actions in February 1956.

Macmillan had meetings with Ramadier and Spaak during the OEEC Council. The record does not reveal discussion of Messina between Ramadier and Macmillan but the veil of the chancellor's protests at the French failure to meet their trade liberalisation obligations under the OEEC was very thin.[83] The meeting with Spaak was far more direct. Macmillan reported to Eden that Spaak took a very depressing view of Europe; the French were 'incapable of action . . . he had no belief at all that the French would do anything except back out when the moment for decision came . . . the French Government would never implement the Common Market'. Furthermore, Germany was becoming 'tougher' and Italy was 'like a man balanced on a wall – nobody knew at what moment he would topple, or to which side'. As Macmillan later noted, 'Spaak's most urgent plea was for Britain to seize the initiative . . .'.[84] These comments, in combination with the doubts already sown in British minds by German Ministers prior to the OEEC Council, encouraged British overestimation of Continental reception to any future British initiative in Europe. It also strengthened the prejudices of those sceptical of European co-operation, with Eden criticising French behaviour.[85] As Whitehall began its consideration of a new British initiative in Europe, therefore, the prevailing mood, both in London and amongst the Six, was one of suspicion: suspicion on the part of London that the Six would not succeed in their efforts, and suspicion on the part of the Six that British policy was designed to ensure they did not.

From Plan E to Plan G

Believing that Europe needed a British-inspired 'galvanic', Whitehall departments began their consideration of a new initiative in March 1956.[86] A small group of officials, dominated by the Treasury but including the Board of Trade, the Foreign Office, the Commonwealth Relations Office and the Colonial Office, met under the chairmanship of Otto Clarke to consider options for a new British economic initiative in Europe.[87] Informing senior Treasury colleagues of the first meeting, Clarke described the 'general feeling' amongst departments that the Working Group should 'not base [itself] upon the need to find a negative strategy to kill the "Messina" idea' but instead, seek to examine projects with the aim of binding Germany into the Western alliance.[88] While these sentiments seem to signify a change for the better in Whitehall attitudes, in fact, they reflected a greater confidence in the failure of the Messina powers due to their own difficulties. One day prior to the first meeting of his new Working Group, Clarke represented the Treasury on Sir Norman Brook's top level Cabinet Atlantic (Official) Committee, convened intermittently to develop government policy on NATO and related European affairs.[89] Although discussion points were not attributed to personalities in the minutes of the meeting, Clarke would have commented on the Common Market. Brook's Committee was informed that:

> Although it was unlikely that the common market proposed by the Messina Powers would ever come into effect, it must be recognised that it would either die as a result of internal opposition or, if it came into existence, would have to be lived with. A purely negative line was, therefore, unlikely to be helpful. The

Chancellor of the Exchequer was seeking to evolve a constructive counter-initiative which would demonstrate our willingness to associate ourselves with Europe while at the same time, it was hoped, administering a *coup de grâce* to the Messina proposals.

While it was also admitted that if a Common Market succeeded, it would be impossible for Britain to stand aloof, the expectation was of Messina's collapse. Yet Clarke's Working Group did not aim to produce a device that would directly sabotage the Common Market's development. Such blatant action would have been difficult to implement not least because of the post-démarche sensitivities of the Foreign Office within Whitehall. Instead, with reports of the Common Market proposals meeting difficulty in the Spaak Committee negotiations, British officials envisaged the new initiative providing an alternative route for European economic co-operation once the Six had foundered. Yet the hope that the initiative would administer 'a *coup de grâce* to the Messina proposals' also gives it a more offensive complexion.

During the Clarke Working Group's rapid consideration of possible initiatives in March and early April, the concept of an FTA linking Britain with the Common Market attracted increased support amongst key Treasury and Board of Trade officials. Of all the options, including revitalised OEEC co-operation, the European Commodities Tariff scheme and a more ambitious European–Commonwealth preferential trade area, the FTA quickly became the most popular plan. It also received wider approval. First, Macmillan commissioned memoranda from his friends in the European League for Economic Co-operation (ELEC), an organisation affiliated to the European Movement which included leading industrialists, economists and politicians. One member, Sir Roy Harrod, Nuffield Reader in International Economics at Oxford University, and often Macmillan's personal economic advisor outside of Whitehall, gave his support to an FTA in Europe and his arguments, together with those from ELEC, were circulated within Clarke's Group on the Chancellor's instructions.[90] Concurrently, James Meade, Professor of Commerce at the London School of Economics and former Director of Whitehall's Economic Section, wrote two articles in the *Manchester Guardian* explaining the advantages of an FTA with Europe.[91] As a neighbour of the Treasury's Figgures, and having first suggested the FTA option in January 1956, there can be little doubt that Meade received official encouragement to write the *Manchester Guardian* articles.[92]

It had been Meade's earlier involvement which had given birth to communication between Bretherton and Figgures on the FTA idea, leading to the first mention of extending its membership to include not only Britain and the Six, but also the Scandinavians.[93] It was on this basis that Bretherton circulated the FTA proposal within the Clarke Committee in mid-March.[94] Not all were enamoured with this policy option, however. In Rowan's OFD, Treasury officials mounted colourful attacks. Symons warned that 'there should be no illusion about the fact that pinning our faith on an association with a European common market is a counsel of despair and the beginning of the end of the U.K. as a first-class power'.[95] Arnold France reminded his colleagues that a price would have to be paid to Europe and as Britain already had too many economic commitments, a new initiative was not necessarily wise policy.[96] While the rationale beneath these narrow-minded attitudes was at fault – especially with the importance of developing Anglo-European trade links increasingly apparent – the idea that a price would have to be paid to Europe was a cogent one which was not too widely discussed amongst pro-FTA officials. Nevertheless, for the OFD, the idea of paying a price was more a tactical argument to defend the status quo than any positive encouragement to make the new initiative saleable on the Continent.

By 20 April 1956, Clarke's Working Group had prepared a report for Ministers which presented the case for an initiative in Europe.[97] This stemmed from 'the growing fear of a course of events in Europe which would disrupt [British] interests and undermine [Britain's] security and economy'. Thus the initiative was designed to meet the political priorities of the Foreign Office and the economic anxieties of the Economic Departments. Although the report stated that the predicament arose from the growing strength and independence of Germany, combined with the 'continuing deterioration' of France, the primary concern was the former: 'There are thus two threats – one that Germany will dissociate herself from the West, and the other that Germany, while remaining with the West, will establish a domination over Europe'. By extension, the Messina proposals presented Britain with a dilemma. If they succeeded, Britain would have to associate with them to protect its interests in Europe and elsewhere. If they failed, Britain would have to provide an alternative method of co-operation to avoid European disruption and difficulties within the Western Alliance. Six options were presented to Ministers beginning with Plan A, a vague policy of active co-operation in the

OEEC. Plan B suggested a Council of Europe/OEEC merger which would also keep open the possible development of Atlantic parliamentary institutions. Plan C was a 'European Commodities' tariff scheme for general tariff reductions on certain goods and Plan D envisaged an extension of the Council of Association with the ECSC through tariff reductions between Britain and the Six on steel. The two final plans were more ambitious. Under Plan E, there would be association with the Common Market via a FTA in 'a specified substantial list of commodities' excluding agriculture. Finally, Plan F, known as the 'Strasbourg Tariff Scheme', resurrected the 1949 Council of Europe idea for a grandiose European-Commonwealth preference arrangement that would ultimately replace the imperial preference system.[98] The report itself purely outlined the advantages and disadvantages of these schemes with the decision-making left to Ministers and their officials.

In the Board, Bretherton persisted with his interest in option 'E', the FTA. Options 'A' , 'B' and 'D' were thought to be insubstantial and unambitious. Bretherton felt 'C' could work, but that 'F' was not practical. As Whitehall was to agree, Bretherton felt 'F' wrongly assumed the support of the Commonwealth, involved alteration to Britain's agricultural policies and had formidable political implications for Britain's 'three circles' policy and the Collective Approach. Washington's reaction was also expected to be unenthusiastic; the Americans had been opposed to new preferential arrangements involving the Commonwealth since the end of the war.[99] 'E', the partial FTA, was the preferred option, but only if it was limited to manufactures, thus excluding agriculture or dealing with it separately. The Board of Trade moved to swift acceptance of option 'E' with the president claiming it was 'the inevitable solution'.[100] On 22 May, in a memorandum to ministerial colleagues, Thorneycroft warned that Britain's preferential arrangements with the Commonwealth and trade interests in Europe were in 'equal jeopardy'; a partial FTA provided the opportunity of 'taking the lead in Europe and securing the advantage of the fullest possible commercial opportunities [there], while holding the maximum we can of our preferential system'.[101] For Thorneycroft, the FTA represented a panacea for British trade policy as a whole, and meant far more than just a closer trading relationship with Europe.

The Board's support for option 'E' coincided with an identical conclusion in the Treasury. Referring to Thorneycroft's memorandum of 22 May, Macmillan minuted Clarke, 'I should be grateful for your comments on the B/T paper. But it is really E isn't it?'.[102] The chancellor's decision was taken despite continued opposition to this course from Sir Leslie Rowan.[103] There had been low-key Treasury interest in 'F', the European–Commonwealth preference scheme. Macmillan had been attracted by this option in the early 1950s when it had first been mooted, and both the HOPS and the Economic Section saw benefits in it to begin with.[104] By the end of interdepartmental studies on the six options in May, however, Clarke accepted the Board's dismissal of 'F', agreeing that there were over-powering arguments against it, not least that it was 'incompatible with the slimming of [Britain's] overseas commitments'.[105] Conversely, as long as compatibility with Commonwealth responsibilities was assured and British industry accepted the removal of protection, Clarke preferred the partial FTA. This plan also had two additional benefits. First, it would give the government 'an option to move more closely into Europe if the development and policies of U.S.A. and U.S.S.R. made this seem wise', and secondly, in the mood of cost-cutting within Whitehall during 1956, 'E' could also help Britain 'unload [its] commitments'. In this instance, Clarke was possibly alluding to sharing the burdens of decolonisation in the future, or engendering good creditor policies from the prosperous West German government once Britain's position in an integrated Europe had been secured. Ultimately, Clarke's recommendation to Macmillan was plain: 'If we cannot do E (the only possible form of association with the Messina common market) we must kill the Messina project stone-dead'.[106] This advice reveals the fine line between the advance in British policy represented by Whitehall consideration of a new initiative in Europe in spring 1956 and the opposition to the Six's plans which dominated the initial response to the Messina Conference. What lay beneath the search for an initiative throughout 1956 and would become established policy from November 1956 was that a Common Market could only be lived with if Britain could find a means to protect its interests.

For Whitehall's Economic Departments, Plan E, the FTA, met the necessary criteria for Britain's European initiative on three levels. First, apart from the discontinuation of protection for British industry, it was easily accommodated into existing external economic policy and offered a potential cure-all for trade policy. Secondly, it was also ambitious enough, in Whitehall's eyes, to carry weight with the Europeans, the Commonwealth and the Americans, although this had yet to be examined in full. Thirdly, with judicious presentation, the FTA was saleable to a Cabinet inherently sceptical of closer integration with Europe. It was due in great part to this latter consideration, as well as an overestimation of British power, that the FTA would fail to represent the startling conversion in British policy required for its eventual acceptance by the Six. Amongst officials, before the ministerial meeting of 31 May 1956, there was recognition of the need to meet European priorities in the FTA's design to make it negotiable.[107] In February 1956, Clarke had warned that 'neither the present UK tariff nor Imperial Preference must be regarded as sacrosanct' in the formulation of Britain's European initiative.[108] When introducing the FTA option in March, and drawing on his experiences of the Spaak Committee negotiations, Bretherton outlined a number of potential difficulties, including agriculture, tariff disparities and European opposition to Britain's preferential position, all of which would prove accurate during the eventual negotiations.[109] Finally, in May, the Board of Trade's Commercial Policy Advisor, Cyril Sanders, cautioned that the Six would not accept exclusion of agriculture from the FTA.[110]

While there were those in the Economic Departments who had misgivings about the Six's acceptance of a FTA excluding agriculture, it was the Foreign Office which held the strongest doubts, and this led to a parting of the ways within Whitehall in May 1956. Despite not being central to the economic deliberations in the Treasury and the Board of Trade, it was by no means 'indifferent' to them.[111] Since the turn of the year the Office had sought to improve Anglo-Six diplomatic relations and establish its policy towards European integration in light of the Messina powers' sustained efforts. During the preparation of Clarke's report to ministers, the Office had concentrated on analysis of a merger between the OEEC and the Council of Europe and argued for the general rationalisation of European institutions.[112] When presented with the Clarke Report, Foreign Office preference was for these measures in combination with the European Commodities Tariff Scheme.[113] Plans E and F were thought to be non-starters, causing difficulties externally with the United States who opposed discriminatory regional trade groupings, and internally with party political objections. These views were out of line with those of the Economic Departments and, as a result, Treasury representations were made in mid-1956 to Sir Harold Caccia, Deputy Under-Secretary, for the Foreign Office to leave the European initiative to the Economic Departments.[114] This intervention, together with a certain disillusionment with the FTA idea, accounts for Foreign Office marginalisation in the later formulation of Plan G. Caccia was realistic about the British initiative and caustic in his analysis of the Treasury and Board of Trade support for it:

> If we are to go European, let us do so for the right reasons with our eyes open, and not for speculative reasons of foreign affairs with a half belief that we can both move towards economic integration with Europe and at the same time keep up our impetus of the last centuries for trade over the Seven Seas. Of course, there are political benefits to be gained by a European economic initiative and, on the short run, the Foreign Office interest is clearly to support them. But again there are limits to what could be achieved and we should not pretend otherwise, or be put by economic Ministers in a false position of responsibility.[115]

Caccia nevertheless yielded to the pressure from the Economic Departments, even suppressing a Foreign Office memorandum which, in his view, went too far towards the Six for prevailing attitudes in Whitehall.[116]

Acceptance of Treasury and Board of Trade dominance in the development of Britain's European initiative did not mean, however, that the Foreign Office bowed out of policy-making altogether. Instead, it concentrated on the development of its preferred policy of tying Germany to the west within an Atlantic rather than a European Community. Although after the failed démarche of December 1955 it aligned itself with American insistence that the Messina process was the best means of achieving this goal, it privately criticised the Eisenhower government's rationale. The overt hostility to Six power integration may have been dropped, but the Foreign Office maintained its scepticism of Europe's future being on a Messina formula. In spring 1956, as the Economic Departments considered the idea of a new initiative in Europe, the WOD of the Foreign Office advocated a policy described by its head, Lord Hood, as a 'relance atlantique'.[117] Within Norman Brook's Atlantic (Official) Committee, the Foreign Office prepared plans for enhanced political and economic co-operation in NATO and increased Anglo-German co-operation.[118] These were designed to meet British anxieties over declining NATO viability as conventional weapons were surpassed by nuclear weapons and, at the same time, to prevent a 'neutralist Germany minded to barter its security for its unity'.[119] There was also the long-held fear that American support for European integration was part of a strategy to reduce its commitment on the Continent, thus increasing the burden on Britain. On 2 May 1956 the Office submitted a memorandum to Cabinet which explained these goals in relation to the future of NATO. Noting that the west faced a period of protracted 'competitive co-existence' during which the Russians would 'seek to undermine the strength and unity of the west and to lure the Germans into the eastern orbit', the Office presented plans for the development of western solidarity:

> [NATO] is the one western organisation which includes the USA as a full member and represents a real power grouping. It is our best counter to the feeling implicit in the Messina plans and never entirely absent from American thinking that if only Europe could be set on her feet the USA need concern themselves no longer with this continent.

To make NATO the focus of the western alliance, the Office recommended extending its Article II non-military competencies in areas such as countering the Soviet economic offensive, reviewing international trade and financial policies, and, in the long term, creating an Atlantic Assembly.[120] This political idea foreshadowed what would become Selwyn Lloyd's Grand Design in January 1957, a proposal to rationalise international institutions which had as one of its motives opposition to supranational integration. Foreign Office briefs for the visit of the Federal German Foreign Minister, Von Brentano, in May 1956 indicate the longevity of this view:

> While we wish to encourage closer bonds amongst European countries we do not like the Messina proposal which proceeds to political integration by economic means potentially harmful to the OEEC and the movement to freer trade and payments on a world scale.... We do not think the Messina approach is the best way to attract Germany into the political and military community of the West.... The advantage of the OEEC and NATO lies in the membership of the United Kingdom, the United States of America and Canada.[121]

From this point on, despite Treasury reservations, the Foreign Office developed its own policy towards Europe.[122] This dichotomy in British policy-making towards Europe reflected internal Whitehall power play on one level and the size of the challenge posed to British interests by the Six on another. At the beginning of 1957, however, it would do serious damage to Britain's new initiative in Europe.

Macmillan and Thorneycroft put the Clarke Working Group report to a small group of Ministers on 31 May 1956.[123] In an effort to achieve Cabinet agreement to further examination of Plan E, the FTA, Macmillan and Thorneycroft disregarded the warnings of officials about potential Six power reactions to agricultural exclusion and Britain's continued preferential trade relationship with the Commonwealth. Instead, concessions were made to sceptical ministers which drew what few teeth the FTA ever had. It was not an easy meeting. Macmillan introduced the discussion by making the case for action, criticising Plan F, the European–Commonwealth Tariff Scheme, for being 'out of date', and sponsoring the FTA. Reflecting Foreign Office attitudes, the Foreign Secretary, Selwyn Lloyd, had reservations about whether it was necessary to take policy action in the short-run. The political advantages that would flow from a British initiative in Europe were to him uncertain, and Whitehall was already preoccupied by the future role of NATO. Nevertheless, on balance, Lloyd favoured taking positive action, even though this might involve risks for Britain. Only Heathcoat Amory, Minister of Agriculture, Fisheries and Food, gave full support to the FTA, mainly as he shared Macmillan's and Thorneycroft's doubt of the Commonwealth which had 'too many disparate and incompatible interests' to remain a political force over a long period. Yet even Amory recognised that the FTA would face serious difficulties over agriculture. Conversely, fierce defence of the Commonwealth was put up by the Lord President of the Council, Salisbury, in combination with the Commonwealth Secretary, Home, and the Colonial Secretary, Lennox-Boyd. Reflecting the long-held pro-imperial preference sentiments of the Conservative old right, Salisbury criticised Thorneycroft's reasoning, opposed Plan E, and supported the 'magnificent' Plan F. Salisbury, Home and Lennox-Boyd only eventually agreed to further studies of the FTA after Thorneycroft had conceded that Commonwealth preferences in the British market would be preserved and agriculture excluded, thus ensuring the Tory shires would not lose the protection provided by guaranteed prices under the Agriculture Acts.[124] Plan E would thus be reshaped to combine 'its dynamic approach to Europe with something rather less static towards the Commonwealth'. To signify incorporation of the pro-clivities of its critics, Plan E was subsequently renamed Plan G within Whitehall.[125] However, by including the possibility of concessions to the Commonwealth, Plan G was compromised from the start. Still doubting whether the Six would succeed in their Common Market efforts, Macmillan and Thorneycroft placed greater import-ance on selling the FTA in London, rather than in Europe.

Macmillan and Thorneycroft had, at least, ensured that the FTA had passed the first hurdle within Eden's Cabinet. Salisbury and his supporters were a powerful group to circumvent, especially when matched with Eden and Butler's known apathy towards closer Anglo-Six collaboration. Apart from Macmillan and Thorneycroft, the FTA had few heavyweights in its defence; instead support came from more junior Conservative figures who had known interest in Euro-pean co-operation.[126] Yet securing the FTA's continued examination was not the only reason for Macmillan's and Thorneycroft's readi-ness to make concessions to the doubters, despite what the President of the Board of Trade claimed in retrospect.[127] Continued scepti-cism of the Six ever succeeding and belief in British strength on the Continent were also critical factors. When ministers took their decisions on 31 May, there was still a widespread tendency to dis-miss the Messina process, based mostly on German comments prior to the February OEEC Council and Spaak's anxieties of 28 Febru-ary. Moreover, there was a sense of superiority in London, fuelled by Spaak's appeal for Britain to take the lead in Europe and com-ments made by the German Foreign Minister, Von Brentano, during talks with British Ministers at the beginning of May. While Brentano said that the Spaak Committee had been making progress, he asked whether the Eden government could not join the Six powers in discussion of the Spaak Report: 'The Federal Government valued [Britain's] ideas so much that they would be prepared to modify their own if it would help make things easier'.[128] While this may have reflected the continued efforts of the German Foreign Minis-try to reassure the Eden government that the Six were not a threat to British interests, the result was to boost British self-importance.

There were also those amongst the Six who genuinely wished to see Britain play a part as the Messina negotiations entered a new phase after the completion of the Spaak Report on 21 April 1956. This particularly true of the Dutch.[129] It cannot be ruled out that for mainly political reasons, the French government may have been sympathetic to an enhanced level of co-operation with the British;

Mollet would develop concrete proposals on this later in 1956. More convincing evidence is provided by the comments of Hans von der Groeben, a German Economics Ministry official who, along with Pierre Uri and Albert Hupperts, had been responsible for the final preparation of the Spaak Report.[130] In March 1956, von der Groeben informed American officials in Bonn that 'Great Britain is [the] key of European integration' and suggested the

> desirability of having [the] Messina 6 countries 'join [the] British Commonwealth' on special status and added [that] Germany fully recognise[d] the particular ties that exist[ed] between [the] UK and [the] Commonwealth and would be willing to have [the] UK retain preferential arrangements with [the] Commonwealth and have a common market and general integration extend to [the] UK and 6 countries only.[131]

This comment is particularly interesting given that von der Groeben was not one of Erhard's supporters and, in contrast to the Economics Minister, had welcomed the Common Market proposals.[132] From this evidence, it is possible that despite suspicion of British motives, the situation amongst the Messina powers was fluid enough to have improved London's chances of preferential membership of a Common Market in spring 1956 had the British government decided on such a course. In retrospect, Thorneycroft made such a claim.[133] Similarly, it has been suggested that if Britain could have accepted the Common Market, it would have been able to secure 'sweeping exceptions' for agriculture and Commonwealth preference.[134] However, reminiscent of the 'missed boat' debate, such conjecture is always problematic.

What can be said with certainty is that there was no possibility of Britain deciding to join the Six at this stage. For the Eden government, the reasons which precluded membership of a European Common Market in autumn 1955 were equally applicable during the first half of 1956. Furthermore, enhanced doubts about the Six and indications that British involvement in European integration would be welcomed on the Continent further strengthened British rejection of Common Market membership. It also justified London's search for an alternative option to the Six's plans. Plan G was therefore designed to meet two contingencies. If the Six failed, the FTA would replace the Common Market as the WEU had replaced the EDC to prevent crisis in western Europe and the Atlantic Alliance. If they succeeded, the FTA would ensure association with the Common Market, protecting British interests.

During the first half of 1956, Whitehall was thus very much alive to the future of European co-operation. Amongst officials, there was widespread recognition of the need to direct Britain's economic policy more towards Europe. Amongst ministers, there was less enthusiasm for such a move, but through the leadership of Macmillan and Thorneycroft, agreement was reached to further studies of the FTA plan. Three factors predominate in the examination of British policy at this stage. First, the issue of European integration caused discord in London at many levels, between ministers, officials, and departments. The FTA was born from conflict between those in favour of meeting the changes in Britain's external relations, both with Europe and the Commonwealth, and those who believed that the *status quo* should be defended. There was also division between the Foreign Office and the Economic Departments on the means of achieving Britain's objectives. Secondly, whilst orienting trade towards Europe and abandoning protection for British industry were significant developments in British economic policy, the FTA was inherently conservative. It was a reactionary plan designed to protect traditional trade patterns while securing European export markets. At the same time, however, it was an innovation in British policy representing the first reassessment of external economic policy since the Collective Approach of 1952 and an attempt to address the issue of European tariffs and trade which was central to the plans of the Six. Thirdly, the focus of decision-making was introspective. Policy was designed to meet British requirements, mainly to bridge the Whitehall schisms, but also because of near universal disregard for the course chosen by the Messina powers. Policy-makers believed, not without reason, that in spring 1956 the ground was fertile for British intervention. As long as they did so, Plan G would remain an alternative to the Common Market rather than a means of association with it. At the end of May, as British ministers decided on the FTA, the Six foreign ministers met in Venice to review the Spaak Report. From this point on, and due in part to dramatic events in the Middle East, the Messina powers moved towards the realisation of their aims and Britain's initiative entered the third stage of its development.

3
Deliberation, Delay, Decision, June–December 1956

When announcing the European FTA proposal to the House of Commons on 26 November 1956, Harold Macmillan stated categorically that it was not the aim of the British government to upset the Messina plans or undermine the movement for European unity; this would be 'a very wrong decision' which could not be justified.[1] Macmillan in no way misled the House. By November 1956, British policy had matured into the third stage of its metamorphosis, becoming a serious attempt at securing an OEEC FTA around the kernel of the Messina Common Market. But this was not the result of enthusiasm for the Six's plans and a desire to complement them, despite what ministers would later argue during the FTA negotiations. Instead, it reflected Whitehall's acceptance of its inability to oppose the Six once they had overcome their differences, and a consequent desperation that British interests would be threatened unless a trade relationship with the Common Market was accomplished. However, it would be inaccurate to suggest that there was one universal Whitehall attitude towards European integration at this stage as ministerial and departmental differences worsened during the second half of 1956. Plan G was 'so politically explosive' that it provoked strong Cabinet splits.[2] These were only surmounted in the aftermath of the Suez Crisis, partly in the hope of providing a jaded Conservative Party with a European fillip, but also because of Macmillan's adept political manipulation. Before it is possible to analyse the connections between Suez and the Eden government's acceptance of Plan G, it is necessary to examine the six months of deliberations in London which ensured, ironically, that as the government decided that the Common Market would have to be accepted, the Six's suspicions of Britain's intentions grew, jeopardising Plan G's chances from the outset.

Inauspicious beginnings at the OEEC

Amateur diplomacy and underestimation of the Six's progress ensured that Whitehall did not give Plan G the most auspicious debut. While ministers had chosen the FTA as Britain's European initiative on 31 May, the foreign ministers of the Six had met in Venice to reach judgements on the Spaak Report. It is now clear that the Six took 'the utmost decisions' for Europe's future at the Venice Conference.[3] According to the communiqué, ministers agreed to use the Spaak Report as the basis for negotiations under a conference in Brussels, chaired by Spaak himself, whose task would be to draft the Common Market and Euratom treaties.[4] It has been suggested that the British government misread the Six's progress at Venice and on the basis of Foreign Office records, this appears to be an accurate criticism.[5] Despite positive reports from French, Dutch and Italian sources, the Foreign Office seemed determined to cast doubt on the Venice conference.[6] Edden advised Caccia that 'conflicting reports . . . are pretty clear proof that the results were meagre'.[7] Greater emphasis was placed on the difficult conditions the French had presented to their partners, demanding a solution to the Algerian problem and Common Market association for overseas territories, than on the general enthusiasm for future agreement.[8] This attitude persisted during mid-June meetings between Selwyn Lloyd and Maurice Faure, Minister of State at the Quai d'Orsay and head of the French delegation at the Brussels Conference.[9] Only Nutting provided an upbeat assessment; otherwise officials took Faure's conclusion that there was an 'unbridgeable gap' between Euratom and the OEEC nuclear energy scheme as an indication that the French would 'in their usual way . . . blame [Britain] for the eventual breakdown of Euratom'.[10] In London, therefore, there was a tendency to look on the negative side, rather than the positive, when considering the Six's future. Venice may not have provided final evidence of their success, but it did provide a further example of their intent. When combined with wider improvements in Franco-German relations, Foreign Office opinions seem even more dubious. On 5 June 1956, the French and Germans finally reached agreement over the Saar, a disputed territory on the western border of West Germany which the French had occupied since the end of the second world war.[11] Although Hoyer Millar reported from Bonn that this settlement removed one of the main sources of Franco-German dissension and furthered the 'European idea', there is no evidence that Whitehall made a connection between the Saar agreement and the Six's future.[12]

The Eden government's FTA proposal received a premature birth at the OEEC Council in July 1956 which undervalued the alterations in attitudes towards European tariff policy taking place within Whitehall. To understand fully how London compromised Plan G from the outset in Europe, it is necessary to explore briefly the complex issue of tariff negotiations within the OEEC during the first half of the 1950s. After 1952, Benelux, Denmark, Sweden and Switzerland, known collectively as the Low Tariff Club, worked within the OEEC to combat tariff disparities by securing general reductions in members' tariffs.[13] These small nations were dependent on intra-European trade, especially with West Germany and Britain, and thus the permanent removal of barriers to trade was vital to their economies. The Low Tariff Club's progress in achieving their aim was, however, often hindered by those OEEC members with high tariffs, especially Britain. A crucial condition for sterling convertibility, the central plank of British economic policy via the Collective Approach, was for Britain to retain autonomy in tariff policy. This was important for two reasons; first, technically, as a means of protecting British trade once quantitative import restrictions had been abandoned under OEEC liberalisation, and second, politically, to meet the demands of Conservative supporters of imperial preference and British agriculture, to whom tariff protection was vital.[14] Hence, the Churchill and Eden governments attempted to free Britain from the no-new-preference rule in the GATT and avoid commitments to OEEC tariff reduction negotiations. This revealed the paradox in British economic policy; on the one hand, London purported to be the main promoter of world-wide freer trade and payments, and on the other, it remained opposed to reducing tariffs as barriers to trade. Recognising this, the Low Tariff Club maintained their campaign against OEEC tariff disparities, supported by France, Germany and Italy who, for different reasons, feared that British policy would have a damaging effect on trade liberalisation.[15] It has been suggested that in 1954, the gulf between Britain, with its aims for a world economic order based on sterling convertibility, and these other members of the OEEC, who wished to preserve common positions in uniquely European institutions, was 'so wide that they were talking about different worlds'.[16] The Low Tariff Club's activities climaxed in July 1955 when, by threatening to block OEEC plans for 90 per cent liberalisation of quantitative import restrictions, they received general agreement to consider reduction of European tariffs in the GATT.

Such was the position in mid-1956 when Whitehall was informed by Bretherton that the Low Tariff Club 'had a scheme on the stocks'.[17] This was a plan for automatic and progressive tariff reductions on the basis of the OEEC European Commodities List, amounting to a 25 per cent cut which would be extended to all GATT members.[18] The timing of the Low Tariff Club's plan was all important for Britain. As Macmillan and Thorneycroft explained to their Cabinet colleagues, Britain could not simply oppose the Low Tariff Club plan when it was tabled at the July OEEC Council meeting.[19] To do so would weaken the OEEC at a vital moment 'when the initiative in the trade field may be felt to lie with the Messina powers'. However, Plan G, not yet having been submitted to full Cabinet, was in its infancy and therefore any announcement of Britain's intention to deal with the tariff issue and the Messina-OEEC relationship via a European FTA was impossible. Thus, while Britain rejected the Low Tariff Club plan, it could not do so in public without endangering the FTA's future by causing disagreement in the OEEC and therefore discrediting the institution in which the FTA would eventually operate. 'The tariff issue', Macmillan and Thorneycroft warned, was 'seen as a test of the OEEC's efficacy as an instrument of European co-operation; a patent failure at this point might leave the Messina group as the focus of further activity in Europe'. Two measures were proposed to neutralise this dilemma. First, Macmillan recommended Britain liberalise the final 5 per cent of its trade from quantitative import restrictions to meet the 90 per cent OEEC criteria, strengthening its position in the OEEC and emphasising the OEEC's progress in trade liberalisation. Second, to mollify the Low Tariff Club, Macmillan and Thorneycroft had 'arranged discreetly' for the OEEC Secretary-General to propose a study covering the whole relationship between the OEEC and the Messina Six with the aim of constructing an FTA. Britain would then be able to support such a study, having not publicly committed itself to a major review of external economic policy without prior agreement of Cabinet, country or Commonwealth. The tariff issue would therefore be delayed and the ground for the FTA prepared. The Cabinet agreed to these plans without debate.[20]

Britain's actions at this time have been depicted as an attempt to prevent the Six from creating a Common Market by providing a FTA diversion.[21] British collusion with the OEEC Secretary-General was not in itself a sabotage manoeuvre, more a guileless attempt to deter the Low Tariff Club from their plans and ensure the OEEC was not compromised before the FTA had been officially launched. However, as long as Whitehall doubted that the Six would succeed in their Common Market aims (as was the case in summer 1956), British policy was still based to some degree on constructing an FTA to meet that eventuality. Although the July OEEC Council tactic was not sabotage itself, the Eden government had not been converted to support the Six.

Unsurprisingly, Macmillan made no reference in his memoirs to the fact that Britain's amateurish collusion was exposed at the OEEC.[22] Where tactics failed was in the transparency of London's puppetry of the OEEC Secretary-General. According to Bretherton, 'everyone [knew] very well that the initiative came from the UK'.[23] The Low Tariff Club members were displeased at British actions, recognising that their cause had been diverted yet again. The Benelux countries were particularly angered on a more practical level as they had planned to use the European Commodities Tariff Scheme as a means of ensuring a low common external tariff in the Common Market negotiations. Britain's FTA intervention had prevented this and, in doing so, further discredited the OEEC.[24] More generally, the episode added to the legacy of European suspicion of British actions built up since the démarche of December 1955. In an attempt to secure support from other high tariff countries for Britain's OEEC intervention, the Foreign Office notified the French government of Britain's endorsement of the Secretary General's proposals prior to the Council meeting.[25] Robert Marjolin, senior official on the French delegation to the Brussels conference, noted that his government would not oppose the Secretary General's proposals, but were concerned that French opposition to the Messina Common Market would be strengthened by the prospect of a looser OEEC alternative.[26] One account suggests that Britain's July 1956 interest in the FTA partly forced the Mollet government to negotiate seriously for the Common Market as it included agriculture whereas the British plan did not.[27] Nevertheless, the concern that a FTA might cause those within the Six who were yet to be convinced of the Common Market to complicate the Brussels negotiations increased suspicion of British policy. The Messina powers were probably already cautious in their view of any British initiative because of Thorneycroft's hint at a change in policy in April, and also because of the Economic Secretary's vague Commons allusion to a possible advance in Britain's position in July.[28] Thus, even before it had received Cabinet authorisation, the FTA proposal faced a difficult reception in Europe. Bretherton had obviously recognised this: 'We shall be watched closely to see if we have constructive ideas to put forward; and any sign of holding back on our part will be taken as proof of duplicity or even ill-faith . . .'.[29]

Deliberation in London

When Macmillan and Thorneycroft presented their officials' studies of Plan G to Cabinet in July and August 1956 there must have been a sense of personal vindication for both ministers. For Macmillan, the FTA was reminiscent of the search for a 'middle way' in a January 1952 memorandum which advocated British membership of a European confederation. He may also have seen the FTA as a means of retribution for his Cabinet humiliation by Eden at that time.[30] For Thorneycroft, his 1953 Cabinet suggestion of a British-inspired, limited European Common Market could be seen as a loose blueprint for Plan G. Both ministers therefore fervently supported the FTA's passage through Cabinet in the second half of 1956, but while Thorneycroft constantly pressed for hasty decision-making, Macmillan urged caution upon his colleague. This may have reflected Treasury anxieties that progress on Plan G was too rapid for such a major re-orientation of external economic policy, but it also revealed Macmillan's own political skill. His desire not to alienate those opposed to Plan G, in order to ease Cabinet acceptance, would gain added importance when, amidst crisis in the Middle East, Eden's grip on the premiership weakened.

After ministers had authorised further study of the FTA at their 31 May meeting, Otto Clarke's Working Group was reconstructed to include officials from the Ministry of Agriculture, Fisheries and Food (MAFF), Customs and Excise and the Bank of England. However, due to the tendentious nature of Plan G, work was handled outside of the normal Whitehall channels 'within a restricted compass' and monitored by an *ad hoc* group chaired by Treasury Second Secretary and chairman of the Cabinet's Economic Steering Committee, Sir Bernard Gilbert.[31] Despite these attempts to limit Whitehall infighting, the formulation of Plan G was characterised by departmental friction. The Board of Trade was the most eager FTA advocate. Thorneycroft was quick to alert Eden to the necessity of an enhanced Anglo-European commercial relationship to offset the erosion of imperial preferences.[32] In a high level *ad hoc* Cabinet meeting, which included Eden and Butler, Thorneycroft intensified the pressure for speed in Plan G's preparation, suggesting that inaction would lead to the government forfeiting its leadership in commercial affairs in Europe and the Commonwealth.[33] On 25 June, he argued that officials' statistical and factual analyses need not preclude an early judgement on Plan G as 'the problem is mainly a political one and in so far as it is economic it is largely made up of imponderables'.[34] Thorneycroft and the Board's insistence on rapidity of decision-making is explained by two factors. First, the enduring fear of the Messina Common Market developing into a discriminatory *bloc* acted as a constant spur within the Board of Trade to ensure that an FTA removed that threat. Second, in July 1956, Thorneycroft's support for the new trade initiative in Europe was concurrent with his involvement in difficult trade negotiations with the Australians.

The Menzies government's intention to renegotiate the 1932 Ottawa agreements with Britain upheld the Board's doubt about the longevity of the imperial preference system. This in turn made Plan G's success even more crucial. Claiming balance of payments problems, the Australians required freedom to vary existing preference margins in order to expand and diversify export trade away from Britain.[35] Thorneycroft understood the Australian position; in a meeting between Eden and Menzies he admitted that 'it might well be true that the whole of the Ottawa policy was out of date and ought to be replaced'.[36] There was even suggestion within the Board that the negotiations with the Australians provided opportunity to un-freeze the UK tariff.[37] Nevertheless, with Plan G providing enough of a revolution in trade policy, and reflecting the Board's desire to maintain preferences for British exports in Commonwealth markets, Thorneycroft hammered out a compromise with his Australian counterpart, McEwan. The Australians would be given 'elbow room' in their bilateral trade relationship with Britain, which amounted to a retreat from their initial position, but they were assuaged with a preferential agreement on wheat exports.[38] In return, Menzies agreed to refrain from public reference to a revision of the Ottawa agreements. Thorneycroft had therefore prevented full renegotiation of the Ottawa system, but the Australian talks had provided further evidence of the changing nature of Anglo-Commonwealth commercial relations, making diversification of British trade vital. Moreover, Thorneycroft also used the Australian acceptance of the wheat concession to push Plan G even harder. Defending his argument for an early political decision, regardless of technical deliberations, to Heathcoat Amory at the MAFF, he noted that 'it does not look as if we shall need to contemplate doing as much for the Commonwealth as we had at one time thought'.[39]

The Board's enthusiasm was not equally matched throughout Whitehall. The Treasury was sceptical, reflecting its internal divisions over the FTA. This, together with Macmillan's belief that Cabinet would have to be persuaded diplomatically into supporting Plan G, led the chancellor to be less emphatic in his own note to Eden.[40] Furthermore, Macmillan toned down Thorneycroft's draft speech to the annual Commonwealth Prime Ministers' meeting at the end of June.[41] The guarded reaction to increased Anglo-European co-operation at this meeting underlined the arguments of those who suggested that the Commonwealth would have to be appeased over Plan G. The Commonwealth Relations Office entered the Plan G debate at this stage with a review of Commonwealth development into the 1960s which, according to the Treasury, gave the impression that the Commonwealth was a good thing in itself 'without enquiring why this should be so'.[42] At the MAFF, although Heathcoat Amory shared Treasury doubts of the Commonwealth's future, he warned that the government's room for manoeuvre on agriculture was 'pretty limited' and was critical of Thorneycroft's approach, arguing that detailed analyses could not be circumvented.[43] The political weight behind this MAFF position eventually led the Board of Trade to concede its suggestion for a limited definition of agricultural exclusion from the FTA for MAFF's more universal alternative.[44] This, in turn, created concern within the Foreign Office which reiterated its earlier warnings that positive European reactions to Plan G would be diminished by broad agricultural exclusion, and that as a result, the FTA would not be 'the exciting scheme it should be to appeal to Europe'.[45]

As Macmillan and Thorneycroft submitted a substantial Interim Report by officials to Cabinet explaining the details of Plan G on 27 July, Whitehall was riven by differences of opinion. On 26 July, Sir Bernard Gilbert reflected Treasury concern at the speed of events, suggesting that as Plan G involved such 'a drastic change of policy', it should be presented to Cabinet in an unbiased manner, not with the President of the Board of Trade urging ministerial acceptance.[46] Macmillan agreed to temper certain passages of his joint Cabinet submission with Thorneycroft, but ultimately, their support for Plan G was very clear.[47] The Interim Report explained that Britain would

enter an FTA with the Messina Six and the other main OEEC countries extending to all goods except agricultural produce.[48] Within
the area, tariffs would be progressively reduced over ten years with
a parallel reduction and elimination of quantitative restrictions, save
for the imposition of quotas in balance of payments emergencies.
Commonwealth free entry and preferences for Commonwealth agricultural products would be maintained in an attempt to ensure
Cabinet acceptance of Plan G, smooth Commonwealth reactions,
and preserve the Ottawa Agreements for the time being. There was
cautious confidence in favourable European and American reaction
to the FTA, but also admission of potential difficulties with the
French response and possible American scepticism of the discriminatory aspects of the Plan. As for the FTA's relationship to the
Collective Approach, the Report assumed future convertibility of
sterling but noted that further examination was required. Finally,
Plan G's implications for British industry were not thought to be
'disastrous for any principal sectors of the United Kingdom economy'.

The Cabinet had agreed to a general review of commercial policy
when discussing agricultural policy on 24 July and thus the Interim Report aimed to introduce Ministers to Plan G for consideration
over the summer recess.[49] As such, it was what its title suggested.
Frank Figgures, intimately involved in its preparation, was candid
in his view: 'our Report would provide the basis of rejection of the
scheme at this time'.[50] In order to avoid this eventuality, Macmillan
and Thorneycroft shadowed the report with a joint memorandum
explaining that they required no decision from their colleagues at
this stage.[51] The now familiar arguments were presented: Britain's
commercial policy was under pressure and to do nothing would
'be the most dangerous course'. Plan G was adroitly depicted as a
panacea both for British policy and the Conservative Party. It would
enable Britain to establish commercial leadership in Europe and
open the way for greater European unity, without German hegemony,
while at the same time making it possible to face inevitable adjust-
ments in Commonwealth trade. It would also be seen as a significant
initiative by the Opposition, and would provide the opportunity,
'which might not recur', of unifying 'the European and the Imperial wings of the Conservative Party', as well as gaining industry
support. There were, however, important questions left unanswered
by Macmillan's and Thorneycroft's memorandum. Exactly how Britain
would gain commercial leadership in Europe while maintaining
commitments to the Commonwealth was not spelled out, and there

was no mention of possible European resistance to aspects of the British plan. There was also underestimation of the rigidity of the Imperial wing towards any lessening of Commonwealth ties. These weak points, purposefully concealed by Macmillan and Thorneycroft to increase Plan G's chances, were rapidly exploited as the FTA began its difficult passage through Cabinet. Soon, another event far outside of the European arena would also hinder Plan G, in the short term at least. The day before Macmillan and Thorneycroft submitted the Interim Report to Cabinet, President Nasser nationalised the Suez Canal Company.

Plan G postponed

In light of the officials' Interim Report, the Cabinet's Economic Policy Committee agreed to further studies of Plan G with full Cabinet discussions deferred until these studies were complete. The Cabinet would not meet again until mid-September, and by then, high-level conflicts had developed.[52] The first recorded statement of discontent came from the Bank of England which, considering its traditionally close relationship with the Treasury's OFD and reluctance to see Britain entangled with European economies, was unsurprisingly cautious about Plan G. On 7 August, the Governor of the Bank, Cobbold, wrote to Macmillan, emphasising that sterling policy made 'it essential that before making new moves in Europe, we should take full account of our position with the Commonwealth and more particularly the sterling area Commonwealth'; he also questioned whether it was wise to link Britain with the Six when their financial policies were still uncertain.[53] From within the Cabinet, Lord Privy Seal, Butler, argued for delay, maintaining his scepticism of the Messina powers and questioning how far along the path towards European integration Plan G would lead Britain.[54] Heathcoat Amory, at the MAFF, reaffirmed that his agreement to Plan G was dependent on agricultural exclusion; for the MAFF, there was no room for manoeuvre without revising the Agriculture Acts or reducing Commonwealth imports.[55] On the last point, the Commonwealth Secretary, Home, warned that 'Plan G could lead to a permanent loosening of the Commonwealth bonds and through that to a weakening of the United Kingdom as a world Power' and he thus recommended to Cabinet that Plan G be dropped unless the Commonwealth could be compensated.[56] This reflected the reservations of the Commonwealth Relations Office, which argued, as much in defence of itself as anything else, that it was 'possible . . . to secure for the United Kingdom the advantages that flow from existence of the Commonwealth and our leadership of it' over the next ten to fifteen years.[57] At the Treasury, the Economic Secretary, Boyle, was anxious lest indications of continued balance of payments problems made the 'sound economic policy' necessary for Plan G an uncertainty.[58] Completing the attack, with probable encouragement from Home and Salisbury, Stuart, the Secretary of State for Scotland, appealed to the politician and nationalist in Eden. Britain's priorities were the Empire and the solidarity of the English-speaking peoples, 'Any idea that we are departing from these principles in favour of a mixed collection of Europeans, who have not all been our friends in the past, would have disastrous repercussions within and beyond our Party'.[59]

Plan G had thus triggered a debate about the heart of British and Conservative policy in the most colourful language. In defence, Treasury officials rejected Cobbold's and Home's criticisms. The Economic Section, much the most radical Whitehall group, argued in favour of harmonisation of European economic policies to avoid evasion from FTA commitments.[60] At the same time, it criticised the OFD's argument for an unreformed Collective Approach, estimating that 'the faster [the Six] grow the greater our potential losses of exports'.[61] Otto Clarke also dismissed Home's analysis: 'the triviality of the actual amount of trade on which the Commonwealth countries (excluding Canada) would be effectively losing Preference, should be the decisive consideration'.[62] The Bank and OFD anxieties were therefore overruled with the officials' Supplementary Report on Plan G concluding that the FTA could be integrated into the Collective Approach and should strengthen rather than weaken sterling.[63] Ultimately, therefore, the perceived divinity of sterling remained unaffected by Plan G, not that this was ever at contest. The reactionary nature of the FTA was that it did not represent a full revision of external economic policy, but even its tilt towards Europe was too great for those in the Bank and the OFD.

The Cabinet defence of Plan G came from younger ministers whom Macmillan commended in his memoirs.[64] But there is evidence that the chancellor himself was playing a delicate game from August onwards. He encouraged the Minister for Education, David Eccles, with whom he had previously urged a more European policy in the early 1950s, to write a Cabinet paper with political emphasis. He noted that the '[Suez] crisis may really help us. Europe must be united. But it must all be given a dramatic appeal. Economics are not enough'.[65] At the same time, within Cabinet, Macmillan allowed Thorneycroft to lead the charge, himself subduing his obvious personal support for Plan G with the comment, 'the arguments for and against proceeding with the plan were evenly balanced'.[66] Eccles responded to Macmillan's request with characteristic hyperbole which would, during the FTA negotiations, often harm British policy:

> For all living things the rhythm of their being is the same: birth, flowering, seed-time and then the challenge 'death or resurrection'? England has flowered and made much seed. Some has sprouted. Evidence of new growth is there in the Commonwealth. But it is not yet clear whether the mother-country can renew her position of leadership or must leave the high table to others . . . therefore we accept second class status or we share first class status by pooling our men and money with others who are to follow the same disadvantage in scale, and who are willing to follow our lead. This can only mean going in with Western Europe, not because it might not be safer to federate with North America, but because we cannot abandon Western Europe either to the Germans or to the Russians; and because the English want to join a show which they can run.[67]

At the Board, Thorneycroft was also aware of the need to underplay trade arguments and stress Plan G's political attractions, and he thus supported Plan G in the grandest terms:

> There was no prospect of our being able to pursue our traditional policies undisturbed and the proposals in Plan G had been devised to turn the developments in Europe to the advantage of the United Kingdom and of the Commonwealth as a whole. . . . this would place the United Kingdom for the first time in a combination equal in scale to the other two great trading units of the world, viz., the United States and the Soviet Union. . . . Moreover at the present time but no later we could enter such a combination on our own terms.[68]

The Cabinet divisions were most overt at the 18 September discussions on commercial policy.[69] Lennox-Boyd from the Colonial Office feared that the Six powers' decision to include overseas territories in the Common Market would place British colonies at an economic disadvantage and was not sure that the benefits of Plan G would outweigh the costs. Butler persisted with his earlier criticisms, joined by Lord Salisbury. Ultimately, however, the prime minister was swayed by the positive arguments from Thorneycroft and Macmillan, supported by Kilmuir, the Lord Chancellor, and Eccles.[70] Macmillan argued that 'the fact must be faced that the United Kingdom had declined in relative economic power' and a new base for the restoration and maintenance of that power was offered by Plan G. Eden, who would have preferred a Commonwealth foundation for Macmillan's economic argument, agreed that this was not feasible; thus, 'there seemed no alternative but to base [British] policy on the proposed plan for closer association with Europe'. Perhaps fatigued and influenced by the pressures of Suez, Eden admitted that 'although the Conservative Party had traditionally been a Commonwealth party, the younger generation were conscious of a need for new policies'. This seemed almost a reluctant conclusion which is not surprising given Eden's long-term view of European co-operation.[71] The prime minister played no significant part in the development of Plan G during 1956; as an indication of this, he made only one reference to it in his personal diary writing on 14 September: 'Cabinet on Plan G. Another very formidable issue that'.[72] However, Eden had recognised the importance of the FTA proposal and consequently gave it his support; on 2 October, Macmillan noted in his diary that the prime minister was 'himself very sympathetic' to the FTA but was concerned about 'some little troubles in the Cabinet and in the Party'.[73] Rab Butler was obviously one such trouble. Butler later maintained that his chance of succeeding Eden had been lost, in part, due to the FTA: 'I am convinced that what I affectionately call the "Young Turks Movement" had decided in their own minds to rally round the European Free Trade system, a military onslaught on Nasser, the retirement of Anthony Eden and the eventual succession of Macmillan'.[74] The Cabinet did not give its authority to Plan G at the September 18 meeting, however. All agreed, including Macmillan, that a final decision had to await the outcome of the Suez Crisis. Briefly, therefore, as the Middle East dispute worsened, Plan G was postponed. It was also complicated by another factor. The intimacy in Franco-British relations during the Suez Crisis led Guy Mollet to express interest in reviving Churchill's 1940 Anglo-French union proposal and Eden to instruct officials to consider this possibility.

Final decision: Suez and the Free Trade Area

At a meeting with Mollet in Paris on 27 September, Eden played down the French President's suggestion of France joining the Commonwealth on the terms of Churchill's 1940 offer, noting that 'in the world of to-day, we must work for co-operation on a broader basis'.[75] Nevertheless, *ad hoc* committees hastily explored the feasibility of Mollet's suggestion. French, Belgian, Dutch and Norwegian membership of the Commonwealth was briefly considered in London but the rapidity of the rejection of this course reflected its impracticality.[76] The Treasury saw nothing but economic costs in union with France and instead suggested that the 'most constructive course' would be to divert Mollet's interest in Anglo-French economic co-operation towards Plan G.[77] The Foreign Office concurred; Franco-British union would alter Britain's traditional three-fold link with the Commonwealth, America and Europe, and by its exclusivity, risk forcing other European countries, namely West Germany, 'into the arms of Russia'.[78] The Office also saw advantage for Plan G in Mollet's offer, suggesting that it should be the beneficiary of the French President's interest in Anglo-French co-operation. While the Anglo-French union idea evaporated due to rejection in London and events in the Middle East, it did give the Foreign Office opportunity to air its policies for Anglo-European political co-operation.[79]

During officials' meetings on Anglo-French union, the Permanent Under-Secretary, Sir Ivone Kirkpatrick, reminded his colleagues that if Plan G proceeded, there would be pressure for British association with the Six's supranational institutions.[80] Having been excluded from Plan G's formulation in May 1956, the Foreign Office used the Anglo-French union studies to re-enter policy-making on Europe. In August, it had pledged its support for Plan G to Macmillan as a positive contribution to western European solidarity which would 'counteract the likelihood of West German preponderance in a limited continental grouping'.[81] By October, the Foreign Office incorporated the FTA into what it saw as three possible elements of an initiative in Europe: Plan G, a merger of the Council of Europe and the OEEC, and finally, activation of the WEU.[82] Having accepted the Economic Departments' dominance in the FTA proposal, and also doubting aspects of Plan G's design, the Foreign Office directed its attentions towards non-economic European co-operation. First, the Council of Europe and the OEEC would be merged 'as the political complement to Plan G', with a longer-term aim of creating 'a single organisation responsible for broadly all forms of European co-operation'.[83] Thus, Britain's association with supranationalism would be limited and the profusion of European institutions rationalised. This proposal reflected a long-held Office view which had been the basis of the 1952 Eden Plan and had resurfaced during Macmillan's Foreign Secretaryship in 1955, as well as being option 'B' in the Clarke Committee's April 1956 report. Second, Anglo-European defence collaboration within the WEU would supposedly present more evidence of Britain's interest in Europe. More significantly, the Office also hoped to profit from developments in Adenauer's view of the western alliance. Suspicious of American policy, exemplified by the Radford Plan for US troop withdrawals from Europe and Washington's conduct during the Suez Crisis, Adenauer called for the creation of a European federation and expansion of the WEU's activities to include co-ordination of foreign policies.[84] While this ultimately proved to be a hiatus before the Six reached their final agreements, the Office saw an opportunity to align Anglo-German interests.[85]

What the Council of Europe/OEEC merger and WEU activation proposals represented was an attempt by the Foreign Office to give Britain's European policy, already spearheaded by Plan G, a politico-military dimension and to guide the Six into the wider Atlantic Alliance. In 1956, NATO, as an institution, gained in significance for British policy. In June, Eden initiated a comprehensive Whitehall review of national policy with the aim of highlighting areas for cost-cutting to off-set the constant danger of economic crisis. A full examination of this exercise is extraneous to the present analysis; nevertheless, its main conclusions are important in explaining Foreign Office policy towards Europe.

The government was to concentrate on developing its nuclear deterrent as a means of reducing defence expenditure and strengthening the Anglo-American relationship and British international prestige. Concurrently, in order to reduce the balance of payments burden of conventional forces stationed in Germany, Britain would attempt to negotiate a reduction in those forces. At the same time, requests for continued support payments for the British troops in Germany would be made to the Adenauer government.[86] However, European political reaction to these developments, especially in West Germany, was expected to be adverse and thus Britain planned to make proposals for greater allied co-operation in Continental defence within NATO to offset the impact of troop reductions. These proposals were combined with further British re-evaluation of NATO policy. Whitehall believed that the military side of NATO was becoming less important as nuclear weapons surpassed their conventional equivalent. As such, Norman Brook's Atlantic Official Committee concluded that greater emphasis should be placed on NATO politico-economic co-operation.[87] This met two criteria; first, it aimed to widen NATO's capabilities at a time when US and UK troop reduction proposals would cause suspicion in Europe. Secondly, it met what the Foreign Office saw as an important criteria for Plan G's success.

In August 1956, the Foreign Office was asked by the Treasury to provide views on the broad political implications of Plan G. With the greater emphasis given to Anglo-European relations by Plan G, Britain had to maintain its pivotal position in the Atlantic Alliance and the Commonwealth. Compensation for the Dominions and Colonies could be assured by economic concessions, but Britain's relations with the United States had to be boosted by enhanced political co-operation. Hence, the Office believed the launching of Plan G would 'make it all the more, rather than less, necessary for [Britain] to pursue [its] present policy of broadening the scope and strengthening the alliance in NATO'.[88] The Americans, it was felt, would not be persuaded to accept the discriminatory nature of Plan G by the promise of future sterling convertibility and freer dollar imports; for the Foreign Office, NATO was the key. It saw increased collaboration with the United States in NATO as a means of strengthening the Anglo-American special relationship, distinguishing Britain from the Six powers, and containing Germany's future growth.

The Foreign Office used the opportunity provided by the Three Wise Men's review of NATO non-military co-operation to present its case to the Americans for a general revision of NATO policy.[89] It aimed to develop Britain's nuclear deterrent and reduce conventional force costs by urging a new strategic concept within NATO. In turn, this would placate German opposition to troop reductions and enhance Plan G's chances by counter-balancing American opposition to the discriminatory nature of the FTA. Hence, the politico-military dimension to European policy suggested by the Foreign Office in autumn 1956 – namely merging the Council of Europe and the OEEC and activating defence collaboration within the WEU – have to be seen as component parts of this greater policy framework. These proposals would flank policy towards NATO and provide further evidence of Britain's new European profile. Ultimately, the Foreign Office contemplated a single assembly to oversee

European co-operation, with the WEU providing active defence collaboration on a seven-power basis, and with both institutions in line with NATO. These were ambitious plans by any standard. Ultimately, in 1957, when they were formalised in Selwyn Lloyd's 'Grand Design', they fell short of their intentions, as will be seen later. In late 1956, however, Foreign Office actions reveal that it recognised Plan G's limitations. More critically, it shows that the British design contained within itself an element of self-destruction. Despite what may have been believed in London, there was an irreconcilability about Plan G, the plans for a single European assembly, WEU and NATO policy. What they represented were policies tailor-made for British priorities. Unfortunately for Britain, they failed to meet the priorities of those involved in their success: the Americans and the Europeans.

While officials debated Anglo-French union under Eden's instructions, and a final decision on the FTA awaited the outcome of the Suez Crisis, Macmillan and Thorneycroft forced the pace of Plan G. At the end of September, they explained the FTA proposal to Commonwealth Finance Ministers at their annual meeting in Washington.[90] Returning to London, Macmillan and Thorneycroft rapidly sought Cabinet authority to clear up misconceptions about British policy after leakages to the press from the Washington meeting.[91] Thus, on 3 October, the two ministers held a press conference to explain Britain's FTA proposal in detail, noting that it had yet to receive final Cabinet assent.[92] From this point on, the Eden government's FTA policy was in the public domain; as Macmillan noted in his memoirs, 'we had now passed the point of no return'.[93] Despite Macmillan's innocent retrospective description of these events, it is possible that they were a deliberate diplomatic manoeuvre with a dual aim: first, to foil ministerial opposition to Plan G which had been so vociferous during August and September; and second, to influence developments on the Continent. It seems that Macmillan and Thorneycroft were responsible for the press leakages from Washington. According to the Bank of England's representative at the meetings, Sir George Bolton, there had been 'a great deal of inspired leakage, our ministers having spoken freely to the press'.[94] The result, perhaps as Macmillan and Thorneycroft had desired, was greater pressure for a definite government decision in London, and an ability to enter into early contact with the Six.

As the press statements were announced on 3 October, attempts were immediately made to influence the Six's development. Macmillan explained the British government position to Spaak, and pleading for time, asked that decisions taken at the vital meeting of the Six Foreign Ministers in mid-October be kept 'as fluid as possible' so as to permit FTA association with the Common Market.[95] In particular, the British were concerned that French demands for colonial membership of the Common Market would be accepted by the Six as a whole. The colonial question had the potential to disrupt the FTA before negotiations had begun. Common Market membership for the Six's colonies would give them a trade advantage over British colonies, yet British colonies could not be given FTA membership mainly because their exports were for the most part agricultural. Macmillan therefore appealed to Spaak for a postponement of the Six's decisions on colonies.[96] When Spaak's response was not as definite as hoped, Thorneycroft increased the pressure.[97] This attempt at delaying Six-power agreement on the colonial question, and therefore ultimate agreement on the Common Market, has been described as a British attempt to sabotage the Messina process.[98] As Plan G had been formulated as a possible alternative in the event of the Six's failure, and considering that the Six's success was, in British eyes, unconfirmed at this stage, it is not difficult to imagine that some in London hoped that the 3 October announcements of the FTA policy would give members of the Six pause for thought. This interpretation is given added weight when linked to Foreign Office plans to create a single European assembly and foster Anglo-European defence co-operation in the WEU, providing yet further potential alternatives to the Messina process. It was not surprising, therefore, that much of the initial reaction to Britain's FTA proposal was tainted by suspicion. Jebb warned that many believed Britain hoped to destroy the Six's plans.[99] At the same time, there were press reports of the FTA being seen, at best, as 'a clever move to induce France to stop short of the full integration process', and at worst 'as a mischievous move to torpedo the Continental efforts by raising false hopes of an even larger plan'.[100] French supporters of Messina certainly believed that Britain was attempting to attract those members of the Six who doubted the Common Market; Maurice Schumann, from the Quai d'Orsay, even blamed the failure of the Six Foreign Ministers' meeting in October on Britain for providing the German liberals with an alternative route for economic co-operation.[101]

It seems that Erhard had chosen the opportunity of Britain's announcement to step up his campaign to convince Adenauer of the
costs of the Common Market and benefits of Britain's FTA. Since
June, French demands within the Brussels negotiations for the
harmonisation of social costs had led Adenauer to comment in a
Cabinet meeting that the Six's Common Market was 'politically finished' and that the British FTA plan ought to be used as an indirect
route to its achievement.[102] By October, a battle was being waged
between the pro-Common Market Foreign Ministry and pro-FTA
Economics Ministry within the Federal government only to be won
by a combination of Von Brentano's political arguments and doubt
about the sincerity of Britain's new interest in Europe.[103] The result
was a breakthrough in the Brussels negotiations achieved by the
secret Adenauer–Mollet meeting at the climax of the Suez Crisis on
6 November 1956. The importance of this meeting to the completion of the negotiations leading to the Treaties of Rome has been a
matter of debate, the argument resting on whether Suez encouraged the French to embrace the Common Market or whether the
decision to sign a treaty had been taken earlier in 1956.[104] This has
been given further perspective by the recent judgement of one historian that Mollet's interest in reviving Anglo-French union and
joining the Commonwealth was a last attempt to keep France out
of the Common Market and reconcile French economic and financial problems with Britain's interest in European co-operation.[105]
With this in mind, perhaps the 6 November meeting was a success,
partly at least, because both the French and German leaders had
become disenchanted with the British. Suez most definitely led to
doubt about British motives for the FTA proposal in a wider sense.
The Swiss press, for example, saw a connection between the problems in the Middle East and Britain's change of attitude towards
Europe, with one source describing the FTA as nothing more than
an ingenious delaying operation.[106] Such were the anxieties caused
by these accusations in London that Otto Clarke urged Macmillan
'to let matters run' so as to avoid charges of 'perfide Albion'.[107]
Sensing the opportunity to force Plan G through Cabinet during
the Suez Crisis, Macmillan would reject such cautionary advice.

Events proceeded rapidly during October and November 1956 in
London, on the Continent and in the Middle East and were used
by Macmillan and Thorneycroft to their advantage within Cabinet.
On 6 November, as the Suez Crisis reached its climax with Eden
announcing a ceasefire to the Commons and Anglo-French troops

halting 23 miles south of Port Said, Macmillan and Thorneycroft put a memorandum to Cabinet recommending acceptance of Plan G.[108] This memorandum explained the general reaction to the Plan both domestically and externally. Thorneycroft had personally met with industry representatives from early October onwards. With the Board convinced of the need to expand trade with Europe, the president had adopted an uncompromising attitude. A firm belief that European competition would have to be faced with or without an FTA led Thorneycroft to discount certain industries' opposition to the FTA, warning that there would be no safeguards against the loss of tariff protection.[109] Concurrently, the Board's industry journal advocated both Plan G and the benefits of exploiting trade links with the Continent.[110] In the Cabinet report, therefore, Thorneycroft made much of an FBI survey which revealed majority support for the FTA proposal. Similarly, the Trades Union Congress's unqualified support was also used to strengthen Plan G's case. Externally, Macmillan and Thorneycroft described a positive reaction to Plan G. From Europe, there was supposedly 'considerable welcome'. This did not misrepresent Continental reaction which, though varying in degree, was generally enthusiastic, especially from the German and Dutch governments but less so from the French.[111] While reference was made to the problem of opposition to agricultural exclusion, Macmillan and Thorneycroft failed to explain fully that almost all responses had criticised this aspect of Britain's proposals or that many were suspicious of British motives.[112] The Commonwealth reaction was depicted as guarded though not unfavourable. The earlier trade agreements with the Australians had prepared the way for acceptance of Plan G in Canberra, and the New Zealand government, while concerned about losing preferences, did not object to the FTA.[113] The Canadian reaction was also cautious and support for Plan G was conditional on the continued reduction of discrimination against dollar imports.[114] To complete the picture, much was made of President Eisenhower's description of the FTA in a Miami election speech as 'a challenging idea'.[115] Having maximised the positive reactions to Plan G, and emphasised their support for the policy, Macmillan and Thorneycroft asked for Cabinet agreement to enter into negotiations in Europe. Rather similar to the 1961 decision to negotiate not for EEC membership itself, but to determine terms of membership, the Cabinet was reminded that a final decision on the FTA would only be necessary at the conclusion of negotiations, probably in 18 to 24 months' time.

Cabinet approval was only given to FTA negotiations on 20 November, after the postponement caused by the climax of the Suez crisis, and it is worth pondering whether Eden and the Cabinet doubters would have been swayed by Thorneycroft and Macmillan's arguments had it not been for the catastrophe in the Middle East.[116] Suez may not have turned Britain towards Europe in the long run but it gave weight to the arguments for closer economic ties in November 1956 and provided Conservative Party interest in new initiatives. Summing up the penultimate Plan G Cabinet meeting in Eden's absence, Butler stated that there was agreement in principle, though he added a caveat, reminding his colleagues that the 'disciplinary consequences' of the FTA on the economy should not be underestimated.[117] Perhaps, however, Suez had not alone convinced Butler, Salisbury and others to support Plan G. At that same penultimate meeting, Macmillan informed Cabinet:

> There was now some indication that, among the six Powers, both France and Germany might limit their aims to the establishment of a free trade area. If in negotiation, these countries were to pursue such an objective, this would create a new situation and it would be necessary to review our policy in the light of it.

In further discussion, the Cabinet Secretary noted 'It was not immediately apparent, however, that it would be contrary to our interests if the proposed Customs Union were in fact to be replaced by a wider free trade area in the creation of which we were to take a leading part'. This hint of Britain gaining precedence over the Messina Six, judiciously employed by Macmillan, may, in combination with the upheaval of Suez, have subdued Cabinet opposition to Plan G. What it represented, however, was an inaccurate description by Macmillan of the Six's progress. Although Whitehall had received mixed reports of the Six Foreign Ministers' meeting of 20–21 October, officials had concluded accurately that it would be wrong to exaggerate this apparent setback to the Messina plans.[118] Moreover, Whitehall was aware of the final breakthrough in the Brussels negotiations provided by the agreements reached by Adenauer and Mollet on 6 November.[119] Macmillan may himself have been unaware of these developments, especially amid the turmoil of November 1956 and the leadership struggle in the Conservative Party, or his previous doubts about the Messina process may have persisted. Conversely, the chancellor could have focused on a few reports of unattributed French and German interest in the FTA over the Common Market to clinch Cabinet agreement to Plan G. What is without question is that during this final Cabinet meeting, Macmillan prejudged incomplete studies by officials which concluded, within two days, that it actually *was* in Britain's interest for the Common Market to succeed.

From August 1956, officials had developed Plan G in Otto Clarke's Cabinet 'Sub Committee on Closer Economic Association with Europe', known as ES(EI), which was responsible to Permanent Secretaries on the Cabinet's Economic Steering Committee.[120] In November, Clarke's officials debated the possibility of the FTA replacing the Common Market in light of 'various indications' that Germany favoured the British scheme.[121] There were also similar indications from 'some official circles in the French government'.[122] Based on Foreign Office political arguments and warnings from Bretherton that the Messina delegations were now more optimistic of forming the Common Market, officials reached clear judgements. In terms of British economic interests there was 'no marked difference between a twelve country free trade area with a Customs Union of the six and without one'. From the point of view of the Commonwealth, however, the disappearance of the Common Market would ensure that their agricultural products were not discriminated against by a common external tariff. Thus, from the purely economic interests of Britain and the Commonwealth together, there was 'a slight balance of advantage' in favour of a FTA without a Common Market. Yet economic considerations were subordinate to political ones. The Clarke Committee concluded that it was 'Politically ... desirable to have a Customs Union as a nucleus [of the FTA], although the argument should not be put too strongly'.[123] This rationale was not based on a belief in the Common Market being the best means of achieving the FTA. On this point there were conflicting views; it was argued on the one hand that the Six provided impetus for European economic co-operation which would benefit the FTA, but it was equally argued that their agreements might delay its creation if they were unacceptable to Britain. What 'politically ... desirable' seems to have reflected was British officials' acknowledgement of the European and also American weight behind the Common Market. The lesson of the December 1955 démarche had been learnt, with the Clarke Committee admitting that 'It would be very damaging politically in the United Kingdom to incur the odium of appearing to have sabotaged the Messina proposals' and that 'the United States might regard such a suggestion as retro-gressive from the point of view of Western European solidarity'. What these decisions reveal is acceptance in London of the impos-sibility of opposition to the Six's Common Market and the paramount importance of complementing it with a FTA. For the Foreign Office, this policy was designed to help maintain Britain's strength both on the Continent and in the Atlantic Alliance when balanced by wider politico-military policies. For the Treasury, it represented an uneasy association between those who recognised the importance of Europe and those who placed sterling above all other policies. For the Board of Trade, it was an attempt to reconcile the changing nature of Britain's foreign economic relations. Yet at the same time, the FTA was only a positive proposal in the sense that Britain had accepted that an anti-Six policy was not feasible and that accom-modation and even containment was the best course. The final report to Macmillan and Thorneycroft stated:

> On wider political grounds... we should prefer there to be a Customs Union, but only provided a free trade area were also set up to include it. It would be politically as well as economi-cally to our disadvantage if a Customs Union were set up without a free trade area, but a combined organisation would be more stable when achieved.[124]

It is significant that while officials recommended that the FTA pro-posal continued to assume the existence of a Common Market, and that together these organisations would bring European stability, they also warned that a Common Market *without* an FTA would be to Britain's disadvantage. Thus, from early 1957, as the Six Messina powers moved towards the signature of their treaty, the Macmillan government struggled to create a European FTA around the Common Market.

The government's decision to enter into European FTA negotiations was announced to the Commons on 26 November 1956. The policy received bipartisan support, the ground having been prepared by earlier favourable meetings with Harold Wilson.[125] Roy Jenkins, the Labour member for Stechford, urged 'enthusiastic participation' in the FTA which, he argued, held political and economic benefits for

Britain and Europe.[126] Parliament was, of course, paralysed by external events in November, but nevertheless, the developments in Brussels had not received great attention in Britain, being presented mainly as a trade matter, and the uncontroversial Commons' reaction reflected this.[127] Closing the debate, Thorneycroft did not conceal the importance the government was placing on the FTA's success:

> We are taking the first step along a road which may lead to great opportunities in the future. . . . Let us not underestimate the prizes for the strong, the chances which a market of 250 million will give to our exporters and the fine opportunity which will lie ahead for our traders, our merchants, our financiers and our bankers. On the negative side, do not let us forget the dangers of staying out of a European *bloc* dominated by our principal competitor, Western Germany.[128]

This fear of West German economic and ultimately political power, and its potential effect on Britain's position in Europe, had been the primary motivation for the development of Plan G. The FTA had been seen as a possible alternative to the Common Market in expectation of its failure. By the close of 1956, however, with the Six finalising the treaties that would be signed in Rome, the FTA became a crucial means of association with the EEC, opposition to the Six having been ruled out by Whitehall. The caveat attached to this policy was that the formation of the EEC without the FTA would be to Britain's disadvantage. Such an eventuality would leave the Six dominant in Europe with British interests jeopardised. Great weight was duly placed upon the FTA and hence Bretherton's warning in December 1956 that 'Very firm action is necessary to keep the whole project on the rails' was disturbing news for Whitehall.[129]

It is clear that the FTA proposal faced significant difficulties at the close of 1956, months before the full OEEC negotiations commenced. The climate was complicated by two factors. First, the Six themselves were involved in the final stages of their negotiations and thus the British proposals were always subordinate. Second, the legacy of suspicion of Britain, grounded in enduring examples of questionable diplomacy such as the 1955 démarche, and heightened by more recent rumours of sabotage, impaired the FTA's chances from the beginning. The Six's determination to conclude their hard-fought negotiations was intensified by fears of retreat based on a possible FTA alternative. This would explain Six power insistence on their treaties remaining closed to future alteration, despite British demands for flexibility to ease EEC/FTA association, especially over the question of colonial membership.[130] That this came as a shock to the British government is evidence of their failure to grasp the level of Six power commitment to supranational integration. There was great Whitehall consternation at the Six presenting Britain with a *fait accompli* in their treaties. Bretherton made a 'strong protest' during an OEEC/Six meeting and Figgures noted that it was a 'very embarrassing' position.[131] In late December, despite the Six's decisions, Macmillan sent a memorandum to Spaak urging the Six 'to leave sufficient flexibility to facilitate the negotiations in O.E.E.C. and to make possible a very early agreement with other potential members of a Free Trade Area'.[132] The Foreign Office was particularly concerned about timing. Somewhat naively, the British hoped the Six would agree to the preparation of their treaties moving forward *pari passu* with the FTA negotiations.[133] London's frustration at the Six refusing to reopen their treaties and, moreover, possibly signing those treaties before the FTA negotiations began, can be explained by two interpretations. First, that there was still hope of the FTA superseding the Common Market. This view is contradicted by guidance sent to the UK Delegation in Paris on 9 December which stressed that 'there would be grave disadvantage in seeking to delay progress at Brussels'.[134] It is also contravened by the Clarke Committee's conclusion that on political grounds, it was in London's interest for the Common Market to succeed. However, although the majority seem to have accepted the impracticality of opposition to the Six, and with it, that the FTA could only be a complement to the Common Market, there may have been those who still hoped that Europe would be dominated by an FTA in the future. Realistically, the recurrent scepticism in Whitehall attitudes towards the Common Market has to point to this view.

Nevertheless, the second interpretation of British frustration in December 1956 offers a more plausible explanation. Bearing in mind that Whitehall had always expected Europe to welcome enthusiastically the announcement of the FTA as an expression of British interest in European integration, it is possible that British ministers and officials were genuinely surprised when this did not prove to be the case. Realisation that the Six might wish to conclude their agreements prior to negotiating a FTA, and that once those negotiations had started, the technical difficulties would *not* be suppressed by the greater political benefits of Britain's involvement, weakened the prospects of British policy at the outset. Yet if this was a surprise to Britain, and it seems it was, the catalogue of technical problems in the OEEC's early consideration of a FTA should already have disabused London of its misconceptions. Since September, based on the July OEEC Council meeting proposals, officials had prepared a report on a possible FTA within OEEC Working Party 17 (WP17).[135] These early deliberations, which included representatives from the Six and the rest of the OEEC, confirmed the fears of those who, during Plan G's formulation, warned that the exclusion of agriculture would be rejected in Europe. Britain was in a minority of one within WP17 when discussing agriculture, and in Anglo-German and Anglo-French Economic Committee meetings, appeals were made for British flexibility.[136] Although political priorities and the MAFF agenda ensured that London's position remained inflexible, both the Foreign Office and the Board of Trade sustained their earlier positions by concluding that Britain would have to make a possible future concession.[137] WP17 had revealed other technical problems which hinted at further difficulties in negotiation. The main difference between the Six's Common Market and the FTA was that the former would have a common external tariff on imports from third countries whereas the latter allowed members to set their own tariffs. There were those in the Six, especially the French, who argued that trade would be deflected in the FTA by the disparity in tariffs on imports of basic materials between high and low tariff members. Conversely, the British hoped to deal with this problem by defining the origin of goods entering the FTA so as to reduce any unfair competition caused by tariff disparities. Defining the origin of goods created great problems during WP17's studies and it would prove to be the most difficult technicality during the later FTA negotiations.[138] Further problems included the use of escape clauses from the FTA's commitments during balance of payments crises, the question of membership for the less developed members of the OEEC, such as Greece and Turkey, and also the lingering problem of colonial membership.[139] WP17 completed its report to the OEEC Council on Boxing Day 1956.[140] Its conclusions were hopeful; while there had not been time to study solutions to shared problems between the Common Market and the FTA, it had 'not discovered any fundamental differences' between the two. This was a superficial judgement that masked the technical difficulties which had plagued WP17 and was probably reflective of British and other OEEC countries' interest in getting the FTA negotiations moving at the February 1957 OEEC Council meeting. In the Foreign Office, however, there was anxiety about this strategy: 'one only hopes that the conclusion . . . on the workability of the fta (*sic*) as envisaged is not over optimistic when there are so many major problems which have barely been studied'.[141] Unfortunately for Britain and the FTA, it did prove over optimistic.

The significant question for the historian is how responsible the British government were for the difficulties the FTA proposal faced in late 1956? There can be little doubt that the second half of 1956 was a turbulent period in post-war history. The fortunes of the Six vacillated before finally meeting success in November. Britain was involved in a crisis which was devastating in its effect. This was not, therefore, a steady period in which to introduce new policy towards European integration. It is worth remembering that Plan G did represent a distinct development in British governmental attitudes towards Europe. Although it meant different things to different individuals or departments, the FTA proposal attached unprecedented significance to Anglo-European co-operation. Also, from the British point of view, the Six played a double hand after the FTA's announcement, welcoming the proposal on the one hand, and refusing to maintain flexibility to ease its passage on the other. However, these sympathetic arguments are outweighed by critical considerations. First, if the Six were obdurate in the defence of their treaties, it was as much to do with understandable anxiety generated by suspicious past British diplomacy as any European dogma. Ironically, British policy may have helped the Six here, by encouraging cohesion, despite what was feared at the time. Second, the FTA was blatantly designed for British interests. The difficulties over agriculture and the external tariff were genuine for those countries whose acceptance of British manufactured exports would not be matched by British import of their agricultural produce, or those who feared Britain enjoyed an unfair competitive advantage by maintaining imperial preference while gaining free entry into Europe. Considering that Britain's policy was not presented in the most effective manner, and that the FTA's design was dictated by commitments to the Commonwealth and the Agriculture Acts, the problems of late 1956 do seem to have been much of Britain's own making.

Where the British government's actions are even more questionable is in light of the Suez Crisis. Prior to the invasion's failure and the Mollet government's disappointment at Britain's decision to seek renewed Anglo-American relations post-Suez, Ministers might have used the political opportunity provided by close high-level Anglo-French relations to enhance Britain's position in Europe.[142] One year after the December 1955 démarche, and still suffering from the scepticism it caused, London would have been wise to exploit any opportunity to improve Anglo-European relations, especially once set on Plan G. Without question, with their fingers burnt by American actions during the Suez Crisis, the Mollet government looked with greater enthusiasm to a united Europe as a means of securing French power and independence.[143] There was hope on the Continent that feeling similarly aggrieved, the British would turn more than ever before to the benefits of European co-operation. On 26 November, Jebb reported that 'anxious to see some ray of hope', some in France comforted themselves with the thought that recent American policy would 'drive the United Kingdom further in the direction of Europe'.[144] Three days later, Hoyer Millar noted that in West Germany there was 'some optimism' that estrangement from America 'may at least lead to a greater willingness on the part of the United Kingdom to join in "European" projects'.[145] With Mollet's interest in revitalising Anglo-French union and Adenauer's vocal support for closer Anglo-European co-operation in mind, Britain might have had occasion to use the aftermath of Suez, with all Europeans stunned by American actions in the Middle East, and Soviet actions in Hungary, to the good of its new European policy. Even Anthony Eden, whose previous resistance towards European integration is well known, seems to have reached this conclusion. In a secret minute written in late December 1956 on the lessons of Suez, the prime minister suggested that a review of Britain's world position pointed to a closer relationship with Europe, but he also warned that:

> here too we must be under no illusion. Europe will not welcome us simply because at the moment it may appear to suit us to look to them. The timing and the conviction of our approach may be decisive in their in[f]luence on those with whom we plan to work.[146]

For a man who had shown little interest in Plan G's development this final comment held some foresight. That his successor did not capitalise on French, German, and perhaps other European enthusiasm for closer relations with Britain during and after autumn 1956 was a diplomatic loss. What the rapid restoration of post-Suez Anglo-American co-operation revealed was the real priority in British foreign policy, with Britain increasingly and willingly subordinate to American assistance both in the development of a nuclear deterrent and in providing support for the re-establishment of sterling convertibility.[147] European realisation of this, coupled with the humiliation of what Sir Ashley Clarke, Ambassador to Rome, described as the 'heavy blow' dealt to Britain's reputation for political wisdom, leading to diminished respect, was surely one of the factors which coloured the Six's reception of the FTA proposal in early 1957.[148] As such, perhaps Suez, rather than Messina, represented the real 'parting of the ways' between Britain and the Six.

Part II

Waiting Game, January–October 1957

4
Perfidious Albion? January–May 1957

The nature of Harold Macmillan's policies as prime minister from 10 January 1957 reflect the immense impact which the Suez Crisis had on Britain. Primarily, it had been American economic pressure which forced the withdrawal of British troops from the canal and this evidence of sterling's fragility and Washington's dominance moulded Macmillan's foreign, economic and defence policies. Securing the maintenance of the international value of sterling – the lifeblood for all British policies – was the first concern for the new government, as it had been for its predecessors since 1945. This produced three major policy aspirations. First was the re-establishment of strong Anglo-American relations which were vital for Britain's international standing and singularly important in ensuring that the United States would never repeat its Suez Crisis stranglehold on Britain's finances.[1] These relations were also necessary for the second policy initiative: the development of a British independent nuclear deterrent. This fulfilled the aim that had been constant since the 1952 Global Strategy Paper, and reaffirmed by the mid-1956 Eden Policy Review, that for reasons of international prestige and the reduction of defence expenditure, an independent nuclear deterrent was critical for Britain's future. Hence, from January 1957, Macmillan sought to foster unique Anglo-American nuclear relations as a prerequisite for the far-reaching defence policy review under his new Minister of Defence, Duncan Sandys.[2] Third, in a further attempt to strengthen sterling, there were significant developments in colonial policy. Immediately on becoming prime minister, Macmillan initiated a cost-benefit analysis of Britain's colonial commitments and, consequently, London pursued policies which aimed to reform financial relations within the Sterling Area and reduce claims of newly independent colonies on the Exchequer. As such, after Suez, the process of decolonisation continued with new British emphasis on decreasing the burdens for sterling.[3]

Ostensibly, policy towards western European integration played no major part in these reorientations.[4] Indeed, Europe was not one of the 'difficulties and dangers immediately ahead' which Macmillan listed on entering Downing Street.[5] Yet increased Anglo-European co-operation was part of the Macmillan government's overall strategy. Suez may not have led to acceptance of a European destiny for Britain, as it did in France, but the establishment of new Anglo-European links was an integral part of policy.[6] While the FTA proposal remained the centre of Britain's policy towards European co-operation, it was to be augmented by a Foreign Office political initiative, the Grand Design, to unify all European institutions under one General Assembly for Europe and to increase Anglo-Six non-nuclear defence collaboration in the WEU. This expansion in policy was partially the result of the Suez Crisis. At the beginning of 1957, there was some doubt about the future strength of the Anglo-American relationship and closer association with Europe was expected to add authority to Britain's international position. It was also a reaction to the general move towards European integration which Britain aimed to turn to its own advantage. Under Macmillan, therefore, European policy was to have greater status than that which it had enjoyed under Churchill and Eden.[7]

The irony of the post-Suez evolution in the Macmillan government's European policy is that it was short-lived and failed to improve Anglo-Six relations. In a crucial period, the Six finalised their negotiations, signed the Treaties of Rome on 25 March 1957 and proceeded to ratify them in national parliaments. Concurrently, Britain sought to avoid losing the initiative to the Six. However, the spearhead of policy, the FTA, was compromised by an atmosphere of suspicion; the Grand Design raised fears of *perfidious Albion*, and the prospect of WEU collaboration did not offset the impact of British troop reductions in Germany. By May, Britain had no choice but to accept five months' delay for the FTA as the Six ratified their treaties. Why the Macmillan government's post-Suez European policy suffered as the Six moved towards success can only be understood by explaining the development of the FTA negotiations from January to May 1957, and by examining how they were affected by wider British policies and accusations of sabotage. To begin with, it is necessary to turn to the Foreign Office's involvement in European policy after the Suez Crisis.

A Grand Design?

It was the Foreign Office which inspired the brief development in European policy under the Macmillan government. On 5 January 1957, resurrecting the name given to Ernest Bevin's August 1945 plans for Anglo-European co-operation, Selwyn Lloyd submitted a memorandum to Cabinet entitled 'The Grand Design: Co-operation with Western Europe'.[8] In it, the Foreign Secretary advocated unprecedented Anglo-European relations, arguing that 'We should take our place where we now most belong, i.e. in Europe with our immediate neighbours'. The first and most radical of the Grand Design's proposals was that Britain meet the costs of thermo-nuclear arms development through an association with the Six Messina powers in the non-supranational framework of the WEU. Such an association would not be a third force between the United States and the Soviet Union, but would develop as a powerful group within NATO 'almost as powerful as America and perhaps in friendly rivalry with her'. Second, the Grand Design supported the OEEC as the main instrument for European economic co-operation in which the FTA would eventually operate. Third, a single General Assembly for Europe was envisaged which would replace all existing assemblies, including future Six power institutions and already existing bodies such as those of the Council of Europe, the WEU and NATO.

Despite its timing, its revolutionary implications for British foreign policy and its importance in terms of Anglo-European relations, Lloyd's Grand Design has not received as much historical attention as it deserves.[9] One recent study suggests that the Foreign Office, which 'Throughout 1956 ... had been largely uninterested' in Plan G, was moved to advocate 'a substantial political supplement' to it by the 'shock of Suez'.[10] In fact, as this book has attempted to show, the Foreign Office was not 'largely uninterested' in Plan G but had acquiesced to the Economic Department's dominance in its evolution and pursued its own NATO-based strategy for European co-operation prior to Suez. The Grand Design was partly an expression of Foreign Office efforts throughout summer and autumn 1956 to give the FTA initiative a politico-military dimension, and partly a response, particularly for Selwyn Lloyd, to the Suez Crisis.[11] This view is supported by examination of the development of events in December 1956/January 1957.

The foreign secretary first attached the term 'grand design' to Foreign Office policy in a speech delivered to the North Atlantic

Council meeting on 12 December 1956. Responding to the report of the Three Wise Men on future NATO co-operation, Lloyd described three elements creating a greater strategy for the Atlantic Community: first, a high military and political directorate represented by NATO and the WEU; second, economic co-operation including the OEEC, ECSC, EPU, Common Market and Euratom; and third, a single parliamentary assembly.[12] In this form, the Grand Design was purely a codified version of the policies advocated by the Foreign Office throughout 1956. By widening Britain's European policy, the Office aimed to meet Six power interest in political co-operation, which it believed the FTA lacked, while ensuring that the format was intergovernmental rather than supranational. This was primarily a reaction to the proposals agreed at Messina but, more recently, to indications in autumn 1956 that the Federal German government was considering the expansion of WEU co-operation.[13] The Grand Design also aimed to soften the impact of British troop reductions on the Continent that would result from a nuclear-based defence policy. Finally, by including NATO, the single assembly would also work towards the affirmed government policy of broadening the scope and strengthening the alliance within that organisation.

Whilst it is possible to explain the foreign secretary's speech to the North Atlantic Council on 12 December, it is more difficult to account for the startling addendum which the Grand Design developed in Lloyd's Cabinet memorandum of 5 January 1957.[14] Using thermo-nuclear weapons capability as a symbol of Great Power status, the memorandum warned that Britain could bankrupt itself if it attempted to build a megaton bomb alone. This was based on the premise that the Suez Crisis had revealed the precarious nature of Britain's international power and the uncertainty of Anglo-American relations. Lloyd's solution was for Britain to base its future policy on western European co-operation through three initiatives in the arenas of defence, economics and politics. Proposals for enhanced OEEC co-operation and a single European parliamentary assembly remained consistent with those made in his North Atlantic Council speech, but Lloyd had far advanced his thinking on military collaboration.

He now advocated a nuclear association with Belgium, France, Italy, Luxembourg, the Netherlands and West Germany within WEU. Britain's superior nuclear know-how would enable it 'to dictate' to the Six powers, develop strong political links, correct tendencies towards neutralism and bind West Germany to the Western alliance, and perhaps even help Chancellor Adenauer to win the summer 1957 election in Germany. This new confederation would increase Europe's influence in Africa and the Middle East and while not being a rival to America, would offer insurance against an eventual American withdrawal from the continent. Furthermore, economic benefits would accrue; the financial contributions from the Six powers would, in Lloyd's view, help Britain considerably with its balance of payments while the British government would only have to meet 25 per cent of the costs of WEU nuclear weapons research and development.

The recently released papers of the WOD throw little light on the origins of these extraordinary proposals. What they do reveal is that they came as rather a shock to the Foreign Office and Whitehall. Within the Office there was immediate consternation. The head of the newly combined WOD and Western Department, Patrick Hancock, clearly objected, writing on 7 January that 'If we give up our own work on the bomb we are *cooked'*.[15] Hugh-Jones, another official in the Western Department, argued that the Grand Design would be launched when Britain was operating from a position of weakness, politically and economically, and when such a move might be seen as defiance by the United States and provocative by the Soviet Union.[16] From the economic side of the Office, Deputy Under-Secretary Sir Paul Gore-Booth expressed his doubts to the Permanent Under-Secretary, Sir Ivone Kirkpatrick, on 8 January: 'while I am not normally given to recommending hesitation', he wrote, 'I find myself compelled to do so now'.[17] There is no evidence of Kirkpatrick's view, either in favour or against Lloyd's proposals.

There is, however, strong evidence of resistance from elsewhere in Whitehall. In his new post as Permanent Secretary of the Treasury, after leaving the Embassy in Washington, Sir Roger Makins derided the foreign secretary's Grand Design, calling it 'rather half-baked' and 'premature':

I can only characterise a suggestion of such [a] light hearted approach to our future as a reckless plunge, and I can see no justification either politically, financially or economically for such precipitate action. If we were to embark on such a course in open contradiction in the nuclear field with the United States and Canada, I am certain that not only would our existing arrangements with the Americans in the whole field, particularly in the realm of intelligence, and collaboration in the research and development field, come to an end, but that any hope of our rebuilding relations of confidence with the United States would be extinguished.[18]

Makins also added that Britain was dependent on North America for the uranium supplies for its civil atomic programme and that consequently, Anglo-American relations had to be fostered; in Makins' words, this was 'A solid reason for not giving [the Americans] a smack in the eye'.[19] Otto Clarke, the official who had overseen the FTA's development within Whitehall and who was responsible for European policy in the Treasury, criticised Lloyd for the 'short notice' at which he demanded decisions on such fundamental issues.[20] Sir John Laithwaite, the Permanent Under-Secretary of the Commonwealth Relations Office, warned Home that he was 'frankly very disturbed' by Lloyd's proposals which asked Ministers to take decisions on 'issues of transcendent importance'.[21] Further rejection came from the Ministry of Defence (MoD). The MoD argued that 'the nuclear field is the one field in which we do not wish to share with the others on the Continent because they have nothing to offer us and we stand to lose all our co-operation with the U.S.'.[22]

From the reaction within the Foreign Office and elsewhere it is safe to assume that the WEU nuclear proposals were Lloyd's own. Their origins lay in personal conclusions drawn from the Suez Crisis, as Lloyd noted in a minute to Macmillan in February 1960:

> Towards the end of 1956 our minds were moving towards a closer relationship with Europe. That was the basis of the paper which I put to the Cabinet advocating a W.E.U. nuclear effort. Relations between Sir Anthony Eden and President Eisenhower had suffered a severe shock; Sir Anthony distrusted Mr. Dulles; it therefore seemed better to look towards the Continent. The fact that we had very close and friendly relations with Monsieur Mollet's Government reinforced this view.[23]

Disfavour with the Americans had thus led to the foreign secretary's initiative. Yet Anglo-European nuclear collaboration was a radical step and Lloyd's sponsorship of it requires further clarification, especially as it represented an isolated if poorly-timed example of originality in Lloyd's otherwise unremarkable career as foreign secretary.[24] It is possible to suggest why Lloyd was thinking in these terms. The idea had been discussed on 18 December by Eden's Cabinet Committee on the Long-Term Defence Programme when it was noted that 'Germany and France were known to be averse to relying entirely on the United States for the provision of atomic weapons and warheads and there might be advantage in our co-operating with such European allies in the nuclear field'.[25] It is also possible to imagine, but difficult to prove, that Lloyd had been encouraged by Conservative colleagues. Julian Amery, Conservative delegate to the Council of Europe in 1956, also a supporter of European unity and an overt critic of American actions during the Suez Crisis, was to propose Anglo-European nuclear collaboration to Macmillan on a number of future occasions.[26] Anthony Nutting, the Foreign Office Minister of State who resigned over Suez was actively pro-European and it is interesting that he advocated an Anglo-European nuclear alliance in his 1960 publication, *Europe Will Not Wait*.[27] Admittedly, there is great danger in creating such historical connections, but this evidence does offer a further perspective on Lloyd's initiative.

If there had been the political will in London, an Anglo-European nuclear association may have succeeded. It is now clear that the Suez Crisis inspired the Mollet and Adenauer governments to co-operate closely on European nuclear weapons development.[28] After discussion with the French Minister of Defence, Bourgès-Maunoury, about European military co-operation, Britain's Ambassador to NATO summed up the position as follows: 'We have either got to pull with Europe or continue to go cap in hand to the Americans. They [the French and German governments] believe that the last is becoming more difficult and more distasteful'.[29] This presaged Bourgès-Maunoury's request for British assistance with France's nuclear programme which was made during a visit to London in February 1957.[30] From this perspective, the defence aspect of Selwyn Lloyd's Grand Design was perhaps more than a simple reaction to the Suez Crisis; one study suggests that 'It was a persuasive argument, well-tuned to the thinking of people like Adenauer, Spaak, Monnet, Pinay and Mollet.'[31] Given the *volte face* that it implied for Britain's foreign policy, it had the potential to improve Anglo-Six relations significantly if it led to a synthesis in British, French and German nuclear policies. Ultimately, however, the Grand Design did just the opposite.

In light of Whitehall's reaction to the Grand Design and its timing –

coming just a few days before Anthony Eden resigned – it is not surprising that on 8 January 1957 Lloyd's nuclear plans were rejected by Cabinet.[32] It is possible to imagine that events would have been different had Eden remained as prime minister. Exasperated by American actions over Suez, perhaps Eden would have considered an Anglo-European defence agreement? This may have been something which Lloyd was banking on and it would certainly help explain the timing of his proposals. With Eden gone, however, Anglo-Six nuclear association conflicted with the post-Suez strategy of giving primacy to Anglo-American relations for foreign, economic and defence priorities. It also went too far for those who were ideologically opposed to closer links with the Continent, such as Lord Salisbury. The Cabinet nevertheless expressed 'strong support . . . for the general concept of a closer association between the United Kingdom and Western Europe' short of federation, commending advances in economic co-operation, including both the Common Market and the FTA. As a result, there was no opposition to Lloyd's General Assembly for Europe proposal, and even some consideration of future non-nuclear military association between Britain and the Six within the WEU. The rationale for these decisions was two-fold. First, it was noted that 'the Suez Crisis had made it plain that there must be some change in the basis of Anglo-American relations'; membership of a European association was expected to add authority to London's position in Washington after the damage done by Suez. Second, providing early evidence of the overestimation of British influence, the Cabinet was reminded that if Britain took the initiative with the Grand Design, it could seize the political leadership of Europe. Consequently, the public exposition of the Grand Design within WEU meetings from January onwards was limited to plans for increased WEU collaboration within NATO, OEEC primacy in European economic co-operation and the proposal for a single General Assembly for Europe.

Without its nuclear element, Lloyd's Grand Design was reduced to an enhanced version of the 1952 Eden Plan. The grandiose Foreign Office scheme aimed to construct a new European parliament. It would replace all existing assemblies, namely the Consultative Assembly of the Council of Europe, the Common Assembly of the ECSC, the WEU Assembly and the Conference of NATO Parliamentarians. The British were cautious about the degree of involvement of the proposed assembly of the EEC and Euratom, noting that this institution might continue to have special functions to fulfil but suggesting that it share the same geographical location and secretariat as the larger single assembly. The new organisation would meet annually and would be run by an international Steering Committee and Secretariat and be divided into five committees – Political, Economic, Social and Cultural, Legal and Administrative, and Defence – each with its own membership and rules of procedure.

Timed with total imperfection, the Grand Design's single assembly proposals were put to the WEU Council on 26 February as the Six worked to complete their hard-fought negotiations on the EEC and Euratom in advance of the Treaties of Rome in March.[33] It is true that other plans for rationalising European institutions were circulating; the Belgian President of the Consultative Assembly of the Council of Europe, Dehousse, had made suggestions which were discussed by the Foreign Ministers of the Six in early February.[34] But at best, Lloyd's Grand Design was seen as a reflection of British insensitivity to the Six's supranational aims, and at worst, as an attempt to frustrate them. The institutions outlined in the Treaties of Rome did include an Assembly, but the driving forces of the new Community were to be the Council of Ministers and the European Commission. Given the Foreign Office's emphasis on improving Anglo-Six relations after the 1955 démarche, particularly in relation to US attitudes, and the thrust of its policy development towards western co-operation, it is hard to imagine that sabotage of the Six motivated the Grand Design. It was, instead, a thoroughly undiplomatic attempt to realise Foreign Office ambitions for the pre-eminence of the Atlantic rather than the European Community. While in British eyes, this did not amount to hostility towards the Six's plans, it was a different story for those seeking a final conclusion to the Brussels negotiations. To them, and to the United States, it appeared that Britain was presenting a politico-economic alternative to their supranational course. This may have been the case for some ministers who sat around the Cabinet table on 8 January, but at official level the response to the Grand Design, and its non-discussion within Otto Clarke's ES(EI) FTA committee, reveals that there was no such co-ordination in Whitehall on Britain's European policy.[35] The lack of co-ordination, therefore, did the real damage and it was not to the Six, but to the British themselves as events drew on.

Complications for the FTA

While the Foreign Office was responsible for the Grand Design within Whitehall, independent of the Economic Departments, it did recognise that in terms of London's wider European policy, the FTA remained 'the spearhead of [Britain's] new approach to Europe'. Apart from its 'very considerable economic importance', the Office admitted that the FTA had also become 'a major political move'.[36] In January 1957, much was resting on the FTA for the Macmillan government; officials' recent warnings that 'it would be politically as well as economically to [Britain's] disadvantage if a Customs Union were set up without a free trade area' gained greater significance as the Common Market negotiations reached completion.[37] Consequently, to avoid losing the initiative to the Six, Britain's priorities were first, to start OEEC negotiations for a FTA excluding agriculture, and second, to secure flexibility in the Six's treaties to ease a future Common Market/FTA merger. During the first three months of 1957, however, the government failed in both these aims. To begin with, European rejection of the FTA's exclusion of agriculture frustrated the start of the OEEC negotiations and forced London into readjustment of its policy. Concurrently, the Six's agreement on colonial association with the Common Market presented London with a *fait accompli* which threatened the basis of the FTA policy. In a period complicated by the aftermath of the Suez Crisis, the British government witnessed the Six consolidate their lead in European economic co-operation and struggled to avoid the threat of a Europe with a Common Market but without a FTA.

Prior to the OEEC Council meeting on 12–13 February 1957, the Macmillan government aimed to ensure wide acceptance of the exclusion of agriculture from the FTA as 'an essential feature' of Britain's proposal.[38] Thus, in the publication of Britain's FTA memorandum to the OEEC as a White Paper on 7 February 1957, agriculture's exclusion was firmly restated.[39] There were two main reasons for this rigidity. Most importantly, as the MAFF reminded Whitehall prior to the OEEC Council, there was 'practically no possibility' of offering the Six a *quid pro quo* on agriculture: 'The only way we could import more from Europe would be by importing less from the Commonwealth, or reducing home production, and the impossibility of either of these courses is the reason for our decision to exclude agriculture from the free trade area'.[40] Political commitments to British farmers, and preferences given to Commonwealth agricultural exporters (on which reciprocal preferences for British industrial exports in Commonwealth markets relied), therefore conditioned the British position. As an indication of the importance of this trade relationship for Britain, in 1956, 50.98 per cent of all imports of food, beverages and tobacco came from the Commonwealth, and 49.13 per cent of all British exports of manufactured goods went to the Commonwealth.[41] The government's decision was, however, also determined to an extent by party politics. Those within the Conservative Party who opposed the FTA plan, encouraged by the hostile Beaverbrook press, were particularly sensitive on the agriculture question, and the unequivocal presentation of British policy was in part directed towards their proclivities.[42]

Britain's position was maintained despite significant evidence pointing to the impracticality of a blanket exclusion of agriculture. As officials had predicted during the formulation of Plan G, the British argument was not well received on the Continent. During a visit to London on 15 January 1957, Spaak told British ministers that their line on agriculture was unsustainable and suggested compensation advantages for those countries within the FTA who were dependent on agricultural exports.[43] In the weeks leading up to the meeting of 12–13 February, opposition to agricultural exclusion increased, both from the Six and the OEEC as a whole.[44] The importance of agriculture to the economies of France, the Netherlands, Italy and the Scandinavians (particularly Denmark) was so great that a purely industrial FTA was an unpalatable proposition. There was recognition of this within Whitehall. Given its resurgent interest in the FTA, the Foreign Office attempted to introduce flexibility into the government's position.[45] More significantly, the Board of Trade fielded suggestions for a modification of Britain's stance by going some way to meet the Six's proposals for a managed market in agriculture.[46] In the Treasury, Clarke noted: 'Bretherton thinks that unless we put forward positive further views, opinion will crystallise unfavourably. But is he right?'.[47] Bretherton was right, but the Treasury's reluctance to alter Britain's position on agriculture, at least until the Six's own plans were known, together with the MAFF view and ministerial predilections, ensured that Britain gave little ground at the OEEC Council.

Chairing the difficult two-day meeting in Paris, Thorneycroft, promoted to chancellor in Macmillan's government, reported that the 'formidable' strength of agricultural interests had forced him to concede discussions on agriculture parallel to the central discussions on the FTA Convention.[48] As such, the OEEC set up three official Working Parties (WP): WP21 on the FTA's association with the Common Market; WP22 on agriculture; and WP23 on the association of the five peripheral OEEC states with the FTA (Greece, Iceland, Ireland, Portugal and Turkey).[49] From London's viewpoint, parallel discussions on agriculture was a price paid to get the FTA negotiations moving.[50] Despite the evidence of the OEEC Council and the views of the Foreign Office and the Board of Trade, British Ministers nevertheless maintained their opposition to the inclusion of agriculture in the FTA. While it is true that not even the Six were envisaging free trade in agriculture, it is difficult to see how Thorneycroft, on his return to London, believed that in due course Britain's protectionist position would be accepted within the OEEC.[51] Apart from the overt Scandinavian interest in an agriculture agreement, the French had made it clear that they did not see where their country would gain by membership of a purely industrial FTA.[52] It was the strength and stamina of this argument which soon forced London into reconsidering its position.

On 13 February 1957 the OEEC Council resolved to 'enter into negotiations in order to determine ways and means on the basis of which there could be brought into being a European Free Trade Area which would, on a multilateral basis, associate the European Common Market with other members of the Organisation . . .'.[53] As such, officials were instructed to prepare reports within the three WPs for submission to the OEEC Ministerial Council by 31 July 1957. '[G]iven maximum goodwill', the British government hoped that the FTA Convention could be ratified by the close of 1957, therefore enabling synchronisation of the first round of tariff reductions between the FTA and the Common Market and thus averting trade discrimination between the two organisations.[54] In retrospect, these deadlines can be dismissed as impractical. Indeed, it has been suggested that with the 'lukewarm and ambiguous' OEEC Resolution, 'the Free Trade Area had started on its inexorable way to the scrap-heap'.[55] While this may be true, it begs the question why the British government believed in February 1957 that the FTA was achievable in under a year?

There was still doubt within Whitehall in early 1957 of France's ability to ratify the Common Market treaty. There was some justification for this as French ratification was not guaranteed. Even the Quai d'Orsay's Director of Economic and Financial Affairs, Olivier Wormser, considered that the treaties had only 'an even money chance', and the Luxembourg Prime Minister, Bech, also doubted whether they would survive the National Assembly.[56] How widespread scepticism of French ratification was at official level in London is difficult to assess, but it is revealing that Figgures, a prominent Treasury official working on the FTA, argued that 'we ought not to abandon our policy when so many difficulties in it flow from comparison with something which may never come into life'.[57] At ministerial level, Macmillan himself believed it possible that the French might 'back out of the plan', but by far the most cynical minister was Sir David Eccles, President of the Board of Trade.[58] Eccles converted his doubts about the Six's ratification into giving Britain an opportunity, once the Six had failed, to 'step in at once and take over the leadership of the Free Trade Area Movement' which he deemed to be 'one of the biggest political prizes of all time'.[59] Describing the Common Market arrangements to a Board of Trade meeting of industrialists as 'more sinister than had been expected', Eccles' hesitancy about the ratification of the Six's treaties was probably influenced by his interest in seeing them replaced by the FTA.[60] Out of step with many officials in the Board and throughout Whitehall, Eccles also distinguished himself from his political colleagues with such overt anti-Six views.

Linked to the doubt about the ratification process was an overestimation of London's power in Europe and a consequent belief that the FTA's progress was a prerequisite for the Six's success.[61] There was a pervasive view that the Common Market would not be able to succeed without British association. After the February OEEC Council meeting, Bretherton argued that in negotiating with the Six London had 'one ace – the realisation on their part that British participation in some form is essential if the Customs Union Treaty itself is to be ratified by their Parliaments'.[62] This attitude, though coloured with a degree of arrogance, had received some encouragement in early 1957. In January, Spaak admitted to British ministers that 'the six had a major interest in seeing the industrial Free Trade Area established'.[63] Similarly, Wormser, of the Quai d'Orsay, also agreed that the chances of the Common Market's ratification in France would be improved considerably if matters had progressed favourably in the FTA negotiations.[64] Final analysis on these estimations must rest with historians researching the policies of the Messina powers. However, there were those in the Six who wanted British participation in European integration as a counter-weight to prospective German strength and there were others who hoped the FTA would balance French protectionist economic policy in the Common Market. The Dutch were a particular example of this; they were described as 'smarting with resentment' as the Six finalised their agreements on the back of concessions to France.[65] For many in the Dutch government, the FTA was a necessary complement to the Common Market, as Ernst van der Beugel, Secretary of State at the Ministry of Foreign Affairs, put it in a Dutch Cabinet memorandum in April 1957:

> For the Netherlands the free trade area is of interest, both economically and politically. Politically because a stronger link between the United Kingdom and Europe (which would make other countries follow Britain's example) is one of the objectives of Dutch foreign policy; economically, because existing objections against some aspects of the Treaties among the Six could be mitigated or even taken away.[66]

While the Foreign Office understood that the Dutch would not oppose French safeguards in the Common Market Treaty for political reasons, it hoped that they would lend their support to the FTA.[67]

Britain adopted a similar approach to Ludwig Erhard, Minister of Economic Affairs in Adenauer's government. At the February OEEC Council, Erhard publicly announced his preference for the FTA and in a private meeting with Thorneycroft, instructed his interpreter to read from a memorandum sent to Spaak which stated that:

> the Federal [German] government is of the opinion that both the common market and free trade area should be realised and has adopted positive cabinet decisions to this effect. From this aspect the common market and the free trade area are a functional whole. . . . Within this comprehensive entity the common market and all the countries which form part of the free trade area will assume equal rank.[68]

It is clear that this independent action, coming soon after his autumn 1956 attempts to promote the FTA within the Federal government, led to a further curbing of Erhard's control with the pro-Six view of Adenauer and the German Foreign Office gaining greater precedence.[69] Nevertheless, the Economics Minister persisted with his support for the FTA; in March 1957 the Treasury was warned that he aimed to 'concert tactics with [Thorneycroft] with a view to seeing what could be done to substitute the Free Trade Area for the Common Market'.[70] This led the Permanent Secretary, Sir Roger Makins, to describe Erhard as a 'slippery customer' and added to Whitehall's growing impression that he was unrepresentative of German policy.[71] Yet London did hope that Erhard would use his influence in Bonn in the FTA's favour, the prospect of which seemed improved by reports suggesting that Adenauer saw British association with Europe as essential to the Six's success.[72]

Thus, it is possible to explain why Whitehall believed that an FTA was achievable by 1958. However, consideration of other complications in early 1957 disputes the feasibility of this aim. On the central question of reconciling the FTA with the Common Market, a fundamental difference of approach developed between Britain and members of the Six which would be sustained throughout the FTA negotiations. Within the British government, the majority saw the Common Market as the foundation or core of the FTA organisation but believed that the Six would have to be flexible to accommodate the wider periphery. Only Peter Thorneycroft seems to have taken a different view: 'his own feeling [was] that by and large the Free Trade Area would have to accept the arrangements relevant to it which had already been adopted by the Six even though this fact might not be apparent to the outside world'.[73]

Thorneycroft's judgement was an accurate estimate of the Six's attitude. Although Spaak welcomed the FTA proposal at the February OEEC Council meeting, he also clarified the position of the Six; it was not a question of their joining the FTA but rather how the greatest number of OEEC countries could cooperate with the Common Market.[74] While this may have been an ideological distinction for many in the Six, a similar argument was employed by the French National Assembly on a more technical basis. On 23 January 1957, an *Ordre du Jour* was passed which recommended that the FTA be 'pursued with determination and brought to a successful conclusion as soon as possible'.[75] The vital caveat, however, was that the

FTA include for France 'guarantees equivalent to those envisaged for the Common Market'. Taken literally, this suggested that the French would demand that compensation measures and safeguard clauses achieved in the Brussels negotiations be translated into the FTA Convention. Moreover, it raised questions as to whether the scope of the FTA could simply be limited to tariff reductions or whether it would have to include provisions for harmonisation of social charges and wages, something the French wanted but Whitehall rejected. Despite the attempt by Maurice Faure, Secretary of State at the Quai d'Orsay, to minimise the impact of the National Assembly's resolution, the Foreign Office was concerned that the French parliamentarians' demands would not be acceptable to Britain.[76] After all, it would be the National Assembly, not the French government, which would have to ratify the FTA Convention.

This vital issue of reconciliation was acutely exposed after the Six finalised their agreements on associating overseas territories with the Common Market. From late 1956, Britain had implored the Six to defer firm conclusions on this issue as it threatened to complicate the FTA proposal which made no provision for colonial association.[77] A Six-power colonial agreement would have jeopardised a simple Common Market/FTA merger and, with it, the Macmillan government's hopes of not losing the initiative in European economic co-operation. When the Six disregarded British pleas and reached agreement on 18–19 February 1957, London was faced with a *fait accompli* that threatened the basis of Britain's FTA policy.[78] Not only had the Messina powers agreed to associate their territories with the Common Market, but Maurice Faure also publicly raised the possibility of colonial association with the FTA, producing a terse Foreign Office response.[79] The French had negotiated Common Market association for their overseas territories to provide preferential markets for those territories, and to spread the financial burden of colonial development among the Six, thus assuaging domestic concerns that European unity would weaken France's imperial power.[80] Extending French overseas territories' association to the FTA seemed a logical evolution of these arguments. For the British, however, association raised serious questions.

The simplistic answer to the dilemma would have been for Britain to agree to associate its overseas territories with the FTA, thus meeting French demands and removing the unfair advantage the Six's overseas territories would have in the Common Market. Yet this was an impossibility for two reasons. First, it would contravene a vital principle of Britain's FTA proposal: the exclusion of agriculture. As the exports of the majority of British colonies were agricultural, an industrial FTA would no longer be sustainable.[81] Second, it would have caused major difficulties for Britain's decolonisation policy. Politically, the creation of 'Eurafrica' would have been opposed by newly independent colonies as an extension of the colonial system.[82]

Economically, the position was even more complicated. If the benefits of association were limited to dependent territories, then newly independent territories would be at a disadvantage. If, therefore, association was extended to newly independent or independent territories, this would raise the question of associating members of the Commonwealth. Consequently, as the Treasury noted, 'the FTA might imperil the conception of imperial preference. We had hitherto based our thinking on the assumption that, while we wished to join with Europe, we also wished to preserve intact our existing Commonwealth ties'.[83] Conversely, if imperial preference was protected by limiting FTA colonial association to dependent territories, this would act as a disincentive to colonies becoming independent. In turn, this would go against the spirit of Britain's decolonisation policy, especially after the Suez Crisis when emphasis was placed on encouraging independence to reduce burdens on sterling.

By removing the final obstacle to agreement on a Common Market treaty, the Six had, in the words of the Government's Economic Advisor, caused Britain 'frightful difficulties'.[84] On 5 March, Macmillan wrote to Thorneycroft: 'I understand that as the result of the decision of the six to include colonies in the Common Market a somewhat critical position has arisen'.[85] Thorneycroft's reply was reassuring; the Six's decision had 'undoubtedly complicated our position' but the problems were not insoluble.[86] Although Thorneycroft's prediction would prove accurate, in March and April 1957 Whitehall grappled with the overseas territories question while attempting to reach agreement with the Six and facilitate progress on the FTA. As a measure of the seriousness of the issue, officials concluded on 8 March that 'The fundamental problem . . . was whether the effects of the Messina arrangements [on overseas territories] would be so damaging both to our interests and also to those of the independent Commonwealth and the Colonies as to lead us to conclude that we should seek to destroy the Customs Union'.[87] Negative action was in fact ruled out at the highest levels. On 7 March, Macmillan convened an *ad hoc* Ministerial Cabinet Committee, GEN.580, to oversee policy on the Common Market and the FTA.[88] At its first meeting, ministers agreed that it would be 'politically damaging' for Britain to play a negative role. The rationale for this view, apart from the impact in Europe, was American influence. GEN.580 was told that Mollet had recently 'contrived to enlist' President Eisenhower's support for the Six in their political context.[89] To adopt a negative policy was thus impractical, as the Cabinet's Economic Policy Committee confirmed on 27 March.[90]

Having ruled out direct opposition to the Six on the overseas territories issue, the government moved rapidly to the only feasible policy option: the exclusion of colonies from the FTA. Whitehall did in fact briefly produce derivations of the original Plan G, described as schemes for 'building a colonial outhouse on to the main free trade area edifice'.[91] Plan H proposed full colonial association; Plan J confined association simply to African territories; and Plan K envisaged association of the whole Commonwealth.[92] Nevertheless, these were never serious options; the combination of the Colonial Office's opposition to such drastic alteration in its policy and the Treasury's interest in not complicating the FTA negotiations was readily accepted by Whitehall. The difficulty of the overseas territories issue was not economic; the Treasury admitted that the economic damage to Britain and her colonies from the Six's preferential colonial association was unlikely to be high. Ultimately, the real difficulty was political. British involvement in 'Eurafrica' would have destroyed the idea of an industrial FTA by including agriculture, involved the loss of imperial preference and caused significant complications for decolonisation as well as running the risk of accusations of new colonialism.[93] The pragmatic course, therefore, was for Britain to persist with the FTA negotiations as planned while seeking mitigation for the colonies from the effect of their exclusion from the Six's markets via the GATT. The Cabinet accepted this policy without debate, especially after an emergency conference of Colonial representatives in London had revealed a majority in favour of the government's proposals.[94] Subsequently, in early May 1957, British policy was squared with the Six, specifically the French.[95] French ministers seem to have been convinced by their officials' arguments that including British overseas territories in the FTA would lead to increased competition against their own colonies in the Common Market.[96] They were also swayed, as will be seen, by significant modifications in British tactics for the FTA negotiations. In the long-term, Britain sought mitigation for its colonies from the Six, but this issue became embroiled in the complications of the FTA negotiations during 1958. In the short-term, the overseas territories problem contributed to the growing difficulties between Britain and the Six over the FTA.

As the OEEC WPs began their discussions in March, it was clear that the French were increasingly reluctant to see rapid progress for the FTA.[97] The Foreign Office judged that while French officials had originally seen the FTA as a means of easing National Assembly acceptance of the Rome Treaties by providing British balance, it now threatened to give ammunition to those deputies opposed to the Common Market. The Office expected that at best, the FTA would 'take 2nd place' in French attentions, and at worst, that Paris would 'positively delay' the OEEC Working Parties until the Rome Treaties were ratified.[98] These conclusions had been reached after the British government had failed to move the French during talks between Macmillan and Mollet on 9 March.[99] Although an effort was made to urge flexibility in France's approach towards the FTA, Macmillan had rejected the aggressive brief prepared by Whitehall officials.[100] Much to the Treasury's later chagrin, Macmillan, according to Thorneycroft, 'deliberately pulled his punches' on the FTA while in Paris.[101] The prime minister's priority at this stage was not to force the French on the FTA but secure their acceptance of British troop cuts in Europe.[102] Reducing Britain's Army of the Rhine within the next year from 77 000 to 64 000 and cutting the Royal Air Force contingent in Germany by 50 per cent were major components of the 'fundamental revolution' in defence policy being overseen by Duncan Sandys.[103] Troop reductions in Germany were a component of the greater policy to decrease defence expenditure by moving towards a nuclear defence strategy, based on interdependence with the United States, and almost halving Britain's global forces by 1962.[104] London was aware, however, that withdrawing troops from Germany could be viewed as British dissociation from the Continent. To avoid this potentially damaging rift in Anglo-Six relations, Macmillan implemented the second post-Suez innovation in European policy: enhanced non-nuclear Anglo-Six collaboration within the WEU. He told Cabinet on 22 February that 'it was of the highest importance' to retain the goodwill of the Six on the issue of troop reductions and that Selwyn Lloyd's Grand Design and proposals for non-nuclear arms research and development within the WEU would help in this respect.[105] It seems that Macmillan also hoped the WEU offer would improve the general health of relations with the Six, thereby assisting the FTA negotiations.[106]

Although this was further evidence of Macmillan's interest in co-operation with western Europe, albeit with the parallel aim of facilitating British defence reforms, the strategy faced difficulties in practice. First, while the communiqué of the Macmillan–Mollet talks announced that the WEU proposals were noted 'with satisfaction', they did not give Anglo-Six relations the immediate fillip that Macmillan desired.[107] Three days after returning from Paris, Selwyn Lloyd told the Cabinet that the French Ministers had been unsym-pathetic to Britain's troop reductions and would probably try to frustrate them within the WEU.[108] Second, London's dependence on the United States in defence matters strictly limited the British proposals. Much of the military information Britain planned to share with its WEU partners was originally derived from its co-operation with the Americans. Thus, at the Bermuda Conference of March 1957, where Macmillan reaffirmed Anglo-American relations with Eisenhower and secured the defence collaboration necessary for the Sandys defence reforms, a request was made for liberalisation of previous Anglo-American agreements on the exchange of defence information with third parties.[109] The president welcomed this sug-gestion as a step towards greater European co-operation but only because of the non-nuclear nature of Britain's proposals. At Ber-muda, reflecting either American interest in avoiding nuclear proliferation or British interest in maintaining unique defence rela-tions with Washington, a secret agreement was signed between the two countries 'to adopt a very cautious policy... and to do very little by way of encouraging or assisting' French nuclear plans.[110] Britain was aware that France and Germany were eager to develop nuclear weapons, especially after the Suez Crisis. However, the agree-ments signed at Bermuda ruled out meeting the real interests of Britain's WEU partners. With this in mind, London's offer of non-nuclear collaboration was always going to fall short of Franco-German ambitions.

Thus, defence issues complicated Britain's European policy in March 1957 and Macmillan's diplomacy in Paris did not produce the im-provement in relations he had hoped for. In terms of the FTA, the French did agree to bilateral talks with Britain at official level after the Paris meetings, but these only contributed to Whitehall's growing unease. At a meeting of the Anglo-French Economic Committee on 16 April, Foreign Office suspicions that the French would delay the FTA negotiations until the Treaty of Rome had been ratified were given further credence.[111] First, French officials reaffirmed that the FTA would only be acceptable if it included guarantees equivalent to those gained in the Brussels negotiations and if agriculture was included. Second, they stated that there could not be progress in the FTA discussions until after July, fearing that anti-Common Market Deputies would use the FTA negotiations to delay National Assembly ratification. This only confirmed what Maurice Faure had hinted at one month earlier in a public speech, leading a Foreign Office official to describe French tactics as 'positively pathological', implying 'trouble ahead'.[112] This predicament led to reconsideration of tactics within Whitehall.

London accepts delay

France's position, supported by its partners within the Six, complicated London's planned timetable for the FTA. It precluded a review of the OEEC WPs' reports at the July Council meeting and consequently ruled out ratification of a FTA Convention by the end of 1957. This obstruction had serious implications for British policy, unveiling the impracticality of maintaining the strategy pursued by London since November 1956. First, the government had aimed to avoid being presented with a *fait accompli* in the Treaties of Rome; the Six's determination to conclude their negotiations without delay had ensured that this had failed. Second, Britain had nevertheless proceeded with the FTA on the basis that ratification of the Common Market treaty was not guaranteed in Paris and that the British plan was seen as a prerequisite for the Six's success. Increased chances of ratification in the National Assembly and the French government's insistence that the FTA would act as an impediment to the Common Market's safe passage overturned these hypotheses. One senior British official 'lamented' to the US Embassy in London that 'the cards Britain thought it would have in support of the FTA (e.g. [the] desire of the 6 and especially of France, to have Britain closely associated with the Common Market), [had] melted away'.[113] Thus, within five months of the FTA's public launch, British policy was in a precarious position. Progress could not be achieved without French acquiescence, and without progress, the FTA would lose the initiative to the Common Market.

Britain could not, however, demand that the French immediately participate in the OEEC WPs. Given France's determination to ratify the Treaties of Rome prior to entering into FTA negotiations, to force the French would have been to interfere with the Six's development. It was this dilemma which left the Macmillan government with no choice but to adjust its timetable and await ratification of the Rome Treaties before commencing full-scale FTA negotiations. To have pursued any other course would have inflamed already widespread suspicion in Europe that Britain's aim was to substitute the FTA for the Common Market. Although the resolve of the French, supported by their Messina partners, was the central reason for London's acceptance of delay for the FTA, the need to quash accusations of sabotage played an integral part in this decision.[114] Ironically, however, and despite recent historical judgement to the contrary, the British government was not intent on breaking the Common Market in spring 1957.[115]

It is true that at this stage, the Economic Departments concluded that the Six should be regarded with 'great hostility' if the Common Market was established without a FTA.[116] In this light, Eccles warned his colleagues on 18 April that if the FTA failed by October, 'the United Kingdom would have to consider trying to break the Common Market in [the] G.A.T.T.'.[117] It is also true that Figgures of the Treasury and Trend of the Cabinet Office both suggested soliciting Belgian or Dutch assistance in delaying their ratification of the Rome Treaties until the FTA 'had fair wind'.[118] Yet neither of these factors prove that London aimed to destroy the Common Market in April/May 1957. The first was only a harsh restatement of the long-held motivation for the FTA: to avoid domination of Europe by the Common Market. The second was a tactical option to ensure the FTA's creation, not the Common Market's failure; also, there is no evidence to suggest that it received serious consideration. The aggressive tone of the Economic Departments reflected their frustration at delay in the FTA negotiations and a fear of the Common Market gaining short-run precedence in Europe, perhaps to the FTA's detriment in the long-run. Yet complementing the Common Market was still the basis of policy. On 26 April, Sir Frank Lee reminded Eccles that 'the true position surely is that we do *not* want to sabotage the ratification of the Treaty of Rome.... What we want is for the Treaty to be ratified but to be supplemented by the association of ourselves and other countries in a Free Trade area'.[119] Similarly, the Treasury concurred with Sir Gladwyn Jebb's despatch of 27 April which advocated full British association with the Common Market via the FTA to avoid dependency on America as 'a sort of glorified 49th State'.[120] Jebb had also ruled out sabotage of the Common Market as a feasible British option, warning that the policy of:

> wrecking 'Europe' . . . is fraught with danger. . . . It is by no means certain that if we came to the conclusion that the Common Market was a menace we could now destroy it even if we wanted to. Uncle Sam may perhaps have his doubts about EURAFRICA, but I should be surprised if he did not vigorously protect his composite dreamchild in Western Europe from kidnapping or worse.

This view was fully supported by the Foreign Office which had surpassed the Economic Departments in its acceptance of the Six. While the Treasury and the Board still talked of hostility towards the Common Market if the FTA failed, as Jebb noted, the Office was 'unreservedly in favour of the constitution of the Common Market'.[121] From early 1957, the Office universally rejected the accusation that Britain aimed to break the Common Market.[122] In this vein, on 8 April, Assistant Under-Secretary Wright argued that 'Hostility to the Customs Union will serve no useful purpose as we shall have to live with it, whether we like it or not'.[123]

To Whitehall, the FTA was thus an essential complement to the Common Market. In November 1956 officials had advised ministers that 'It would be politically as well as economically to [Britain's] disadvantage if a Customs Union were set up without a free trade area, but a combined organisation would be more stable when achieved'.[124] These motives for Plan G's initial acceptance in London were even more critical given the Six's success in completing the Brussels negotiations. A FTA would provide, in Selwyn Lloyd's description, 'the best arrangement for coming as close to the Six, on a practical plane, as the shape of their own arrangements will allow'.[125] This would, of course, take place within the confines of Britain's external economic policy and in line with its political policy of maintaining intergovernmental rather than supranational links with the Continent. Attempting to sabotage the Six, while contravening this general approach, would also have brought the odium of many in Europe as well as the United States upon the Macmillan government. It was not a feasible diplomatic course. However, as London's FTA was not intended to destroy the Common Market, there seems to have been some misconception of British policy in Europe in mid-1957. On 26 April, Sir Frank Lee wrote an anxious minute to Eccles, President of the Board of Trade, in which he warned that 'A whispering campaign is going round Western Europe to the effect that we are trying to sabotage the ratification of the Treaty of Rome'.[126] A few days earlier, John Foster Dulles had invited US embassies in the Six capitals and London to comment on indications from 'non-British sources' that the Macmillan government's positive attitude towards the Six was weakening with the FTA seen not as a complement to the Common Market but as its substitute.[127]

Why this atmosphere of suspicion was prevalent in spring 1957 is explained by three factors. First, and most importantly, the FTA represented a threat to the Six whether it was perceived as a genuine or disingenuous British initiative. That Britain had attempted to steer the Common Market into the OEEC in autumn 1955 and was subsequently pursuing a large-scale policy in the same institution gave cause for suspicion. Spaak certainly voiced this concern during the February 1957 OEEC Council.[128] Erhard's intervention in support of the British plan at this stage, and statements from Thorneycroft and other British representatives that the FTA would go ahead even if the Common Market did not, caused further anxiety.[129] This was worsened by Britain's approach to the overseas territories issue. To ensure that a merger between the FTA and the Common Market was not complicated by colonial association, the British government had asked the Six to make their colonial provisions as 'little precise as possible'.[130] As the Mollet government had made it clear that assured clauses on overseas territories were a prerequisite of French agreement to the Common Market Treaty, the British request could have been viewed as an attempt to stall the Six's negotiations.[131] Apart from such fears of British tactics, there was the more fundamental consideration that if the Macmillan government was genuine in its European policy, then the FTA might endanger the EEC. The Common Market Treaty was a complex bargain between the Six amongst whom differences over economic policy had been overcome largely by political priorities. Those differences centred on the impact that a high common external tariff and harmonisation of social costs, both consequences of French economic policy, would have on the economic performance of France's EEC partners. This applied particularly to the Dutch, but also to the Belgians and the Germans, and it was known amongst the Six that they planned to use the FTA to 'battle behind the lines' against the less palatable aspects of the EEC.[132] To the most steadfast defenders of the EEC Treaty, therefore, the FTA had the potential to unravel its hard-won agreements.

Second, wider policy towards European co-operation had done little to improve Britain's reputation on the Continent during the first half of 1957. The European reception of the Sandys defence reforms and the concurrent proposals for troop reductions in West Germany had, in Macmillan's words, been 'pretty chilly'.[133] Selwyn Lloyd reported that the proposals were received 'without enthusiasm' by the Six and that the NATO discussion had not developed on 'wholly favourable lines'.[134] It was not so much the content of the defence reforms which had caused this reaction; British interest in altering the basis of its European troop commitment had been under discussion for some time, especially in terms of West German support costs. It was more the presentation of the defence reforms which damaged Britain's profile in Europe, along with little prior consultation within the WEU.[135] These developments, coming in quick succession after Macmillan's overt reaffirmation of close ties with the Eisenhower Administration at the Bermuda Conference of March 1957, generated doubts on the Continent about the British government's interest in European defence co-operation.

Alongside this suspicion of British defence policy was anxiety about Britain's attitude towards future political co-operation in Europe. Selwyn Lloyd's Grand Design proposal for an intergovernmental General European Assembly had been discussed within the WEU from January 1957. The offer of giving European institutions more coherent shape had not, contrary to Cabinet hopes, offset the impact of troop reductions in Germany.[136] Instead, the Grand Design had been received as a repudiation of the Six's supranational aims at the worst possible moment.[137] Closely watching this process, the American State Department circulated guidance to European embassies raising doubts about the Foreign Office plan: 'Flavor in [the Grand Design] paper of suspicion towards six-country institutions (CSC, EURATOM and Common Market) appears inconsistent with what we had understood to be Macmillan/Thorneycroft/Eccles position that Common Market necessary base for Free Trade area . . .'.[138] The combined negative effect of the doubts about the FTA, the Grand Design and the Sandys defence reforms was exemplified by German reactions in April 1957. The Foreign Office received reports that at an important *Bundesverband der Deutschen Industrie* Conference '. . . the wildest and most irresponsible views [were] being banded about on the British attitude towards Europe in general'.[139] The Free Trade Area was seen as 'a devilish trick to sabotage the Common Market itself'. The Germans had 'taken umbrage' at the Grand Design, interpreting it as an attempt to destroy all that was being done by the Six, and the troop reductions were seen as final proof of the British intention to disengage from Europe. Wright, of the Office, noted that these reports concurred with impressions gained from discussion with members of the German Embassy in London.[140] In a desperate attempt to smooth ruffled feathers, Lloyd instructed the British Ambassador to Bonn, Sir Kit Steel, to meet the German Foreign Office Minister and explain that the Grand Design was 'never intended to undermine the plans of the Six' or 'distract attention from ratification of the Rome Agreements'.[141] This followed up similar representations made to the Eisenhower Administration.[142] Nevertheless, the Grand Design was soon to be abandoned by Britain.

The third explanation for suspicion of British policy rests on rumours circulating in Europe in spring 1957. In late April, Sir Gladwyn Jebb dined with National Assembly Deputies known to be opposed to the Common Market. As the Mollet government was particularly sensitive that nothing should impede the Rome Treaties' passage through the National Assembly, Jebb's actions were viewed by some as an attempt to incite opposition; he was thus 'freely cast for the role of first murderer' in Paris.[143] Given the British Ambassador's recent conversion to European integration and his dismissal of wrecking tactics, described in the Treasury as 'a sea-change', it is hard to imagine that Jebb encouraged French dissent.[144] Although purely speculative, it is possible that French officials might have attempted to foster suspicion of British policy as a means of gaining support for a delay in the FTA negotiations. The FTA proposal had presented the French government with a troubling dilemma. There were powerful political arguments in favour of British involvement in European integration to balance West German power and to promote western solidarity; this had no doubt motivated Mollet's interest in Anglo-French union in autumn 1956. But there were also powerful economic arguments against British involvement; as one historian has put it, 'Essentially, the prospect of seeing the British participating in an FTA frightened the French'.[145] Britain's economic power, and that of the other members of the FTA, was a threat to France's economic position, especially given that a purely industrial FTA offered the French none of the safeguards secured in the EEC Treaty. At the same time, however, the FTA offered the potential benefit of diffusing the effect of France's real competitor, West Germany, within a wider trade organisation. In April 1957, therefore, government departments recommended that the Mollet government delay the FTA negotiations.[146] This not only aimed to gain time for reflection but also sought to prevent anti-EEC deputies using the FTA as an excuse to delay ratification of the Treaties of Rome. In light of this, the actions of Robert Marjolin are particularly interesting. It had been Marjolin, senior official on the French delegation to the Brussels Conference, who in July 1956 suggested that the FTA might encourage opposition to the Common Market in France.[147] Considering his personal support for a federal Europe, this was probably a genuine concern.[148] It would certainly go some way to explain why he privately accused London of attempting to wreck the Common Market in April/May 1957, informing the Americans that Britain's position reflected 'a basic desire to kill the common market and replace it by a free trade area'.[149] Within weeks, however, after a suspension of the FTA negotiations had been agreed, Marjolin admitted that Britain was 'not only serious about the Free Trade Area but that eventual agreement on a treaty was almost certain'.[150] Perhaps the rumours he had earlier inspired explain Foreign Office conjecture that the French would 'positively delay' the FTA until the Rome Treaties had been ratified?[151]

Given this widespread suspicion of British policy, the Macmillan government could not force the French to negotiate for a FTA as this would have exacerbated the already damaging rumours of *perfidious Albion*. Thus, Britain's FTA strategy was significantly adjusted. At this stage, the potential power of the Six finally dawned on London. Thorneycroft warned his colleagues that Britain was exposed 'to a most dangerous situation' to which there was 'no satisfactory or complete answer'.[152] The Six's desire to ratify their treaties before entering into OEEC negotiations meant that the Common Market would come into effect prior to the FTA, making its achievement less assured. Officials concluded that there was '[no] real confidence, as things now are, that a free trade area will be brought into being'.[153] In Cabinet on 2 May, Thorneycroft did not minimise the threat posed by the Six to British interests.[154] Without the FTA, the Common Market would discriminate against British exports and result in the loss of European markets and in intensified competition from the Six in overseas markets. Moreover, the Six's real objective was 'an integrated European Community capable of exerting a considerable political influence in its own right . . . a European "third force"'. Without association with this entity, ministers admitted that the consequences for Britain would 'be very grave. Our existing European policy would be undermined and our special relationship with the United States would be endangered if the United States believed that our influence was less than that of the European Community'. Macmillan had already reached this conclusion; on 18 April he wrote to the Chairman of the Conservative Party:

> What I chiefly fear, and what we must at all costs avoid, is the Common Market coming into being and the Free Trade Area never following. In that case, I believe the Germans would dominate the six countries and in a short time put us in a very bad position.[155]

With no choice but to submit to the Six's demands, the Cabinet considered suspension of the FTA negotiations until ratification of the Treaties of Rome was achieved, probably some time in summer 1957. In the meantime, Britain planned to obtain a gentleman's agreement from the French and the German governments: in return for the FTA moratorium, Paris and Bonn would agree to turn their attentions to the FTA once ratification was complete 'in order that they might not be able to subsequently break off the negotiations . . . or impose unacceptable terms as a condition of accepting [the FTA]'. Concurrently, British Ambassadors would be instructed to dispel 'the prevalent impression that our only purpose was to prevent the Customs Union from coming into being at all'. And revealing the Cabinet's disquiet, officials were instructed to begin work on positive inducements to entice the Six into the FTA negotiations and also to consider negative actions should those negotiations fail. In Cabinet, Macmillan concluded that a trade war might be one such option: 'if the members of the Customs Union felt unable to co-operate effectively with us . . . they must expect us to adopt measures of self-protection as we could devise in terms of our commercial policies'.

For Britain, all rested on high level diplomatic action to generate the political will in Europe in favour of the FTA. Thus, in early

May, a full-scale offensive was deployed. First, Foreign Office Minister David Ormsby-Gore attempted to quell anxieties over the Grand Design in a speech to the Council of Europe which met with some success.[156] Second, Selwyn Lloyd held separate meetings with Spaak, Pineau and Walter Hallstein, State Secretary in the German Foreign Office. Spaak welcomed the gentleman's agreement; Pineau assured Lloyd three times that the French wanted to make a success of the FTA; and Hallstein confirmed that once the Treaties of Rome had been ratified, the Federal government would tackle the FTA.[157] Third, Thorneycroft and Eccles held meetings with Maurice Faure in London on 6 May.[158] Rumours of sabotage were denied and the British agreed to accommodate French demands on the Rome Treaties' ratification. In reply, Faure likewise denied rumours that France planned to abandon the FTA, accepted the exclusion of overseas territories and agreed to a communiqué publicly stating the two governments' interest in seeing the FTA negotiations 'carried forward to a satisfactory conclusion'.[159] Fourth, to complete the diplomatic offensive and secure the gentleman's agreement that Cabinet desired, Macmillan visited Bonn 'to speak frankly to Adenauer' during meetings from 7–9 May.[160] The prime minister recognised that he would have 'a difficult passage' in Bonn; his private secretary had warned him that the German chancellor was not convinced of British sincerity in either European defence or economic co-operation.[161] This was an accurate assessment; the German Foreign Ministry had convinced Adenauer of the merits of the French case for delaying the FTA negotiations so as to avoid complications during the Rome Treaties' ratification.[162] Employing arguments which would become common place during the FTA negotiations, Macmillan stressed to Adenauer that failure to complement the Common Market with a FTA would lead to 'fresh division' in Europe with all of the far-reaching conclusions inherent in such a tragedy.[163] It seems that the prime minister's diplomacy had the desired effect. The Treasury later noted that prior to the meetings, Adenauer 'knew little or nothing about the Free Trade Area' but that afterwards, he appreciated its importance.[164] Macmillan's diary entry reveals that he had received the necessary assurances from Adenauer but still held some doubt about German intentions: 'the Germans were, or professed to be, entirely on our side. They would regard the union of the six Messina powers as a disaster if it were *not* followed by the Free Trade Area'.[165]

The gentleman's agreement achieved, London duly postponed the

FTA negotiations until autumn 1957 after the Rome Treaties' ratification.[166] It also agreed to abandon the troublesome Grand Design.
It seems that a deal had been struck between Adenauer and
Macmillan; soon after the Bonn meetings, the Foreign Office plan
was sent 'behind closed doors' at the WEU.[167] Combined with Britain's
acceptance of postponement of the GATT's April 1957 review of
the Rome Treaties, delay in the FTA negotiations and the demise of
the Grand Design met Six-power demands and quelled the spring
1957 rumours of British sabotage.[168] In separate representations, the
Belgians, the Germans and the French admitted to the United States
government that the British position had now changed significantly.
It was at this point that Marjolin admitted that the British were
serious about the FTA and that an eventual agreement was 'almost
certain'.[169]

Considering the lengths London had gone to improve relations
with the Six and rid the FTA of the aura of sabotage, it is difficult
to understand why, on 27 May 1957, Sir David Eccles made perhaps
the most damaging and inflammatory diplomatic blunder since the
autumn 1955 démarche. Addressing the Federation of Commonwealth and British Empire Chambers of Commerce, Eccles made a
fateful link between the Treaties of Rome and twentieth-century
German aggression:

> Twice in my lifetime the Commonwealth have come thousands
> of miles across the ocean to fight the war in Europe. These were
> the last two attempts of the Western European nations, or one
> of them, to dominate others and form a hostile bloc across
> the Channel which would threaten the very life of the United
> Kingdom.
>   All through our history we have had to take up arms against
> any such threat from the Continent of Europe.
>   Now, although it is not military or hostile in its intent, six
> countries in Europe have signed a treaty to do exactly what, for
> hundreds of years, we have always said we could not see with
> safety to our own country.[170]

The FTA, Eccles told his audience, would avert this risk by giving
Britain leadership of European unity: 'That, I think, would be a
great thing because it would mean, at any rate in Western Europe,
the germs of a Third World War would never live'. By threatening
to incite anti-German opposition to the Treaties of Rome in the

National Assembly when London had stalled the FTA negotiations to avoid just this eventuality, Eccles' remarks angered the French. To calm tempers, Sir Gladwyn Jebb made representations to Pineau on two occasions on 29 May, and Eccles himself extended an open apology to the French Ambassador to London on the same day.[171] Thorneycroft was also prompted to urge caution on Eccles in early June.[172] Why Eccles made his speech is unclear. The US Embassy in London reported that it had been made 'off the cuff' and there is no record in the British archives to dispute this.[173] What is sure is that Eccles was known for his tactlessness; his Permanent Secretary, Sir Frank Lee, asked the Foreign Office to prevent Eccles making further insensitive comments.[174] Perhaps, therefore, the speech had been made on Eccles' own volition; he had recently revealed a hawkish view of the Six in Whitehall correspondence.[175] Eccles excused the tone of his speech by noting that the Commonwealth trade representatives needed strong encouragement to surpass their opposition to the FTA. If this was the case, it was a high price to pay considering the collateral damage. It may be, however, that the tone was calculated not for Commonwealth but for European audiences. German officials in London suspected that Eccles' intention was to warn the Six that Britain would take a hostile view of the Common Market if, after ratification, the FTA negotiations did not commence.[176] Whatever the explanation for Eccles' actions, there is no question that they soured the recently improved Anglo-Six relations by making impolitic historical allusions, threatened to encourage opposition to the Rome Treaties in France, and hinted that Britain aimed to lead rather than join a European association.[177]

In his review of the 'gestation period' of the Messina process from June 1955 to March 1957, Anthony Nutting was struck by two things.[178] The first was the speed of the Six's success, and the second was that France had contrived arrangements 'which allowed her to have it both ways'. When a broad view of post-war European history is taken, one of the dominant facts to emerge is that in the mid-1950s France pursued a European destiny whereas Britain rejected such a course, following instead what had become traditional policies with greater enthusiasm. Thus, while Suez marked the nadir in the Anglo-American 'special relationship', the first period of Macmillan's prime ministership marked its apogee.[179] Furthermore, in executing revolutionary defence reforms and recasting its view of decolonisation, Britain also pursued its sterling policy for a one-world system with increased vigour. This is not to say, however, that London rejected the importance of Europe for its future. Indeed, by augmenting the FTA with the Grand Design and proposals for non-nuclear WEU defence collaboration, the Macmillan government did aim to make European co-operation a main pillar of its policy. In contrast with the French, the British planned a strategy which would maintain its established goals while simultaneously forging new relations with western Europe. As one historian has put it, 'European policy was only a function of wider British global policy; Europe did not have and did not get the status in London that it had in France'; France sought independence via Europe while Britain accepted dependence on the United States.[180] It was this difference, together with more specific problems in policy implementation, which ensured that the post-Suez evolution in Britain's European policy was short-lived and failed to improve Anglo-Six relations.

Established policies made Britain inflexible on the key issues in the FTA discussions, such as agriculture. They also ensured that the Grand Design was an intergovernmental as opposed to a supranational plan, and by prioritising Anglo-American relations, they rendered the offer of WEU collaboration toothless without nuclear content. In implementing European policy, London failed to gauge the mood of its Continental partners, especially the French. The Suez Crisis had left the Mollet government with a bitter view of not only the Eisenhower Administration.[181] Macmillan's pursuit of reaffirmed Anglo-American relations in the first months of 1957 disappointed those in France who had hoped that Britain would align itself with Europe after the shared experience of American hostility. This factor does not seem to have tempered Britain's view of its position in Europe as there was some overestimation of bargaining power with ministers expecting the offer of association with Europe to smooth over difficult technical issues and prepare the foundations for a FTA/Common Market merger. The Grand Design was also expected to be welcomed as evidence of Britain's interest in political co-operation; there was no recognition in London that the proposal might be viewed as rejection of the Six's plans. Ironically, the vehicle chosen by the Foreign Office to gain influence in Whitehall's European policy-making and enhance Anglo-Six relations after the Suez Crisis failed on both counts. Much of this is explained by the presentation of British policy. It is impossible to say whether the FTA's chances would have been improved by a more flexible British line on agriculture. What is sure, however, is that the way agriculture's exclusion was presented in the February 1957 FTA White Paper received the 'coldest possible reception in Europe'.[182] In general, the tone of British diplomacy, especially when in its worst form such as Eccles' May 1957 speech, was often patronising. The Germans believed the WEU's examination of the Grand Design revealed that it would 'be a long time before [the] Brit[ish] think as Europeans'.[183] It seems Britain failed to realise that from the Six's point of view it was still *in statu pupillari* despite the FTA proposal. As the *Economist* suggested in May 1957, Britain would have benefited by not behaving 'like a tourist walking into a café in a distinguished wine district and ordering a cup of tea'.[184]

The plain facts were that by May 1957, Britain was no longer in control of its European policy and that the FTA was in difficulties from these very early stages. It is true that by seeking gentleman's agreements Britain had colluded with the Six to delay the FTA negotiations over the summer of 1957 until the Rome Treaties were ratified.[185] Yet this was not something the British planned or desired. Given the need to dispel charges of *perfidious Albion* and France's temporary refusal to proceed with the FTA negotiations, Britain had no choice. This may have been much of its own making, although the intentions of the French were perhaps not without question at this stage. Regardless of this, it is clear that Britain was working from a position of weakness in spring 1957. London may have secured its gentleman's agreement from Paris and Bonn, but this was not agreement to the FTA *per se*, but to begin negotiations once the Treaties of Rome had been ratified. All of the early problems in the OEEC WPs, such as the agriculture question and the issue of the external tariff, remained to be resolved. Moreover, the Grand Design had been abandoned, the credit produced by the WEU proposals was unsure, and troop reductions had caused ill-feeling. On 26 May, Macmillan alerted Selwyn Lloyd to this dilemma: 'we are not making the progress we ought to be making about Europe'.[186] In response, the Foreign Secretary made one more attempt to breathe life into his original Grand Design proposal for an Anglo-Six nuclear agreement, arguing that there was little ground to be made on either the FTA or political co-operation, at least until the Treaties of Rome were ratified.[187] As Lloyd noted, however, Britain's commitments to the United States caused difficulties in this area. Thus, as Thorneycroft advised the prime minister, Britain had to suspend the FTA negotiations and use the summer months to square the agriculture problem, both in London and with the Commonwealth.[188] Ultimately, however, the British could only do so much. The future of their European policy now lay in the hands of the French and the Germans.

5
Philosophies Apart, June–October 1957

On 12 June 1957, Harold Macmillan affirmed Britain's support for the Six's progress in a letter to President Eisenhower: 'We have thought it wise not to press the negotiations for the European Free Trade Area too hard until the Rome agreements have been ratified. I do not want to see a repetition of what happened over [the] E.D.C.'.[1] In private, however, the fall of the Mollet government on 21 May had raised just this possibility in Macmillan's mind.[2] In a minute to Selwyn Lloyd in early June, the prime minister questioned the strategy of waiting for the Rome Treaties' ratification:

> The dangers of this plan are (a) that the French may not ratify; (b) that when the Six have ratified they may snap their fingers at the Free Trade Area and leave us in the lurch. In some ways I should be less worried about (a) because then we might be able to do an exercise as we did after [the] E.D.C. ... to pick up the pieces'.[3]

Macmillan's doubts about French ratification were soon to be proven groundless. The new government led by Maurice Bourgès-Maunoury from 12 June was as committed to the Treaties of Rome as its predecessor. Consequently, the Macmillan government had to keep its part of the May agreements and await ratification of the Rome Treaties before proceeding with the FTA negotiations. In return, when the Treaties were safe, the French and German governments were to direct their attentions to the British plan.

To lay the foundations for the autumn negotiations, and recover from the setbacks of the first half of 1957, the Macmillan government realised that the FTA would have to be augmented by some form of political content as well as a concession on the vexed issue of agriculture. The summer months, therefore, were dedicated to policy development in London leading to the appointment of a single minister responsible for the FTA, Reginald Maudling. Unfortunately for Maudling, by the time the Rome Treaties were ratified in Paris and Bonn, the fundamental difference in philosophy towards European integration between Britain and the Six caused serious problems for the FTA negotiations before they had even begun. To analyse this difference in philosophy, and measure its effect on British policy, it is necessary to examine the course of events from postponement in June to the eve of the negotiations in October. To start with, complications caused by Commonwealth relations must be explained.

Commonwealth complications

While in London for the Commonwealth Prime Ministers' Conference from 26 June to 5 July 1957, the newly elected Canadian Prime Minister, John Diefenbaker, announced two initiatives which had an indirect but important effect on the European FTA proposal. The first 'dramatic intervention' was the suggestion for a future full scale Commonwealth trade and economic conference which would aim to boost Commonwealth economic relations.[4] The second was to divert 15 per cent of Canada's imports from the United States to the United Kingdom.[5] Diefenbaker's motivation for these objectives rested on commitments made during his election campaign to increase Commonwealth trade and also a personal rejection of what he described to Macmillan as 'the tendency of America to treat Canada like Mexico or Brazil'.[6] Since the early 1950s, Canada's economic dependency on the United States had developed significantly. In 1956, for example, 73 per cent of Canada's imports came from America whereas the average amount for the other Dominions (Australia, New Zealand and South Africa) was approximately 13.6 per cent.[7] In the long run, Diefenbaker's Progressive Conservative government was unable to halt Canada's post-war integration into the North American market.[8] In the short run, however, as Britain's High Commissioner to Ottawa warned, the Canadian Prime Minister's proposals had the potential to land the United Kingdom in 'considerable embarrassments'.[9]

Although the Macmillan government was committed to strengthening Commonwealth economic links as other ties gradually loosened
in the second half of the 1950s, little advantage was seen in a
Commonwealth conference on Diefenbaker's lines.[10] Both Eccles and
Home concluded that the results 'would be disappointing'.[11] The
United Kingdom could not increase imports of foodstuffs from the
Commonwealth due to the protection given to British farmers and
the need to maintain agricultural imports from Europe for the benefit of the FTA negotiations. Conversely, the Commonwealth could
not increase imports of manufactures from Britain without contravening its policy of developing trade markets and protecting certain
domestic industries. The only method of increasing Commonwealth
trade would be by either erecting new preferences or cutting imports from the United States and Argentina, both of which might
cause problems in the GATT and complicate Britain's one-world
policy. Nevertheless, although Eccles and Home saw little advantage in a Commonwealth conference, they believed Diefenbaker could
not be rebuffed. If Britain failed to respond to his initiative, Anglo-
Canadian and Anglo-Commonwealth relations would be damaged
as would the Canadian Prime Minister's reputation with his electorate. Of wider concern, however, was the effect a rebuttal would
have on the European FTA proposal. Lloyd and Thorneycroft advised Macmillan that the 'danger' in Diefenbaker's conference proposal
was that it might provoke untimely doubts about Britain's interest
in European co-operation on the Continent.[12] Yet both Eccles and
Home believed that imperialists in the Conservative Party would
oppose the FTA if the Macmillan government failed to encourage
Diefenbaker's Commonwealth policy.[13] The prime minister's Private
Office received evidence of this on 11 July; an unauthored ministerial minute argued that 'it would be intolerable if we are not to
have a Conference on Empire Trade because it would embarrass
Free Trade Area plans'.[14] Moreover, while the government may have
needed no reminder of backbench support for the Commonwealth,
in July 1957 a group of Conservative MPs published a book calling
for its expansion.[15] In an attempt to juggle FTA and Commonwealth
policy, Macmillan therefore negotiated the compromise Home had
suggested to 'play [Diefenbaker] long': the Commonwealth Finance
Ministers would debate the idea of a conference at their annual
meeting in September with subsequent investigations by officials.[16]

The Macmillan government's more positive response to Diefenbaker's second proposal, to divert 15 per cent of imports from the

United States to the United Kingdom, was partly conditioned by the desire to maintain good relations with the new Canadian administration, the Commonwealth and Conservative Party imperialists. It was also influenced by the economic benefits such an agreement would bring: a potential gross increase of over one-third in British dollar export earnings or 6 per cent in total British exports.[17] However, just as the Commonwealth Conference threatened to raise doubts about Britain's interest in European co-operation, the securing of increased trade with Canada had to be similarly squared with European policy. Thus, in Cabinet on 9 July, Macmillan called for a 'fresh appraisal' of the FTA proposal.[18] This was not well received in Whitehall. In the Treasury, Clarke argued that there was nothing new to appraise and that without 'firmness and fortitude' the FTA would fail.[19] In the Board, Lee had similarly argued that 'We must not . . . be mesmerised into action by Diefenbaker's proposals'.[20] Less concerned with domestic politics, officials may have seen the only diversion created by Diefenbaker's 15 per cent idea as one affecting the FTA in Europe. There were doubts about the practicality of the offer and even indications that the Canadian Minister for Trade and Commerce did not agree with his prime minister's plan.[21] Regardless, ministers looked to exploit the opportunity provided by Diefenbaker. In a Cabinet minute, Eccles noted that although 'the wiseacres on both sides of the Atlantic' doubted whether a 15 per cent switch was feasible, the government had to respond positively to Diefenbaker to give him 'a partial success' with his electorate and to avoid entering the European FTA negotiations with 'our imperialists dissatisfied'.[22] Finally, Eccles suggested that it would 'be good [for European Ministers] to know that we have a line out to Canada' during the start of the FTA negotiations. Given the apparent weight of these arguments, Cabinet accepted Eccles' recommendations which went so far as to suggest that the best response to Diefenbaker's proposal would be an Anglo-Canadian FTA.[23] In time, however, the warnings of Lloyd and Thorneycroft that a new Commonwealth initiative could damage the European FTA and the scepticism of the 'wiseacres' that the 15 per cent switch was impractical proved to be correct.

While Commonwealth Prime Ministers had been in London for their conference, the British government used the opportunity to hold high level meetings with Commonwealth officials on agriculture and the European FTA proposal. In line with Cabinet decisions taken in May, Britain aimed to share the government's thoughts with the Commonwealth, without formally asking for its concurrence, on the need to offer Europeans a presentational concession on agriculture.[24] Commonwealth sensitivities on this issue were well known to Whitehall. The Commonwealth Chambers of Commerce in London had made it clear that their governments' reactions would be 'extremely hostile' if there was any discrimination against Commonwealth exports as a result of the FTA.[25] Thus, at the prime ministers' meeting, Macmillan and Thorneycroft gave assurances that the government would safeguard Commonwealth interests in the British market.[26] At the same time, however, in officials' meetings from 8–9 July 1957, Sir Roger Makins reminded his Commonwealth counterparts that his government's aim was not to 'buck the trend' of European integration but 'rather to try to guide it in directions which were helpful and not harmful to the interests of members of the Commonwealth, and, indeed, the rest of the world'.[27] Alluding to Commonwealth acceptance of Britain's changing position on agriculture, the Treasury Permanent Secretary added that it would be wise to remember this general aim when discussing the economic aspects of the FTA.

In July 1957, the Macmillan government sought to keep its consideration of an agriculture concession secret from the Europeans in the hope that it might be used as a strategically timed fillip for future FTA negotiations. The presentational nature of the concession made it so thin that all rested on its political impact rather than its substance. On substance, it became clear from the Commonwealth officials' meetings that anything more than a presentational concession would incite full scale opposition to the FTA.[28] This supported Britain's own interest in seeing agriculture excluded for domestic reasons and, moreover, Commonwealth determination was used as further justification for Britain's unequivocal stance on agriculture in Europe.[29] Similarly, Whitehall announced widespread concerns about the Common Market developing into a discriminatory trade bloc, noting that Commonwealth governments planned to apply the full rigours of the GATT during its autumn examination of the Rome Treaties.[30] The Commonwealth officials' meetings were thus used by the Macmillan government to secure agreement on an agriculture concession and to corroborate its long-held view that the Common Market was a potentially protectionist arrangement.

As an added complication, during the officials' meetings, the Australian and New Zealand governments announced their interest in long-term association with the FTA.[31] Concerned that Britain would be forced to concede more on agriculture than expected and eager to expand their own European markets, the Australians and New Zealanders persisted with their attempt to gain a foothold in the Paris developments.[32] However, based on decisions made earlier in 1957 concerning overseas territories, the British believed Commonwealth association would only complicate the FTA negotiations and possibly lead to revision of preferential arrangements which gave Britain lucrative markets for its exports of manufactures. Consequently, the government stalled the issue of Commonwealth involvement in European negotiations until it eventually died with the FTA negotiations' failure in 1958, only to be resuscitated again during the 1961–63 negotiations for British membership of the Community.

OEEC deadlock

On 26 July 1957, the Embassy in Brussels warned that Britain's inflexibility on agriculture was leading those Belgians concerned with the FTA discussions 'to predict ultimate deadlock'.[33] In response, the Foreign Office explained that 'the war of nerves' would have to continue as Whitehall had decided not to deploy its agriculture concession until the FTA negotiations were under way. Moreover, agriculture was no longer viewed as the most intractable of problems in London; Wright argued that 'The toughest nut of all to crack may in fact be something quite different, namely, the general scope and status of the industrial Free Trade Area vis-à-vis the European Economic Community'.[34] It was in July 1957 that studies on reconciling the FTA and the Common Market revealed the fundamental difference in approach to European economic co-operation between Britain and the Six powers. It is worth briefly comparing the two organisations to reveal their divergence in scope.

The Six's Common Market was an ambitious arrangement which would not only eliminate tariffs and quotas within the customs union, but also construct a common external tariff. It aimed to achieve free movement of persons, services and capital, to adopt common policies on agriculture and transport, as well as creating a European Social Fund and a European Investment Bank. It would achieve these objectives within the supranational framework of a

European Community administered by an Assembly, a Council, a Commission and a Court of Justice.[35] Conversely, Britain's conception was far more limited. An FTA would be established in manufactures which would aim to eliminate tariffs and quotas internally. Externally, however, member states would retain autonomy in setting tariffs against third countries. Agriculture would, of course, be excluded and the FTA would work within the OEEC via an intergovernmental Managing Board, avoiding the creation of a new institution. In simple terms, what the British envisaged was a concurrent reduction of tariffs and quotas between the FTA and the Common Market in manufactures; the FTA would include none of the more wide-ranging commitments of the Rome Treaties. It is when this basic distinction is drawn that the objections of those within the Six towards Britain securing FTA benefits without making wider commitments is fully understood.

The technical problems which were inherent in the difference between the two plans were highlighted by the report of the OEEC working party which had been charged with considering the FTA/Common Market association.[36] WP21 had taken the 'rules of the Rome Treaty as a basis for its discussions and sought for possible ways of transposing them into a Free Trade Area'. This had immediately revealed the dispute between members of the Six who had 'visualised the Free Trade Area Convention as a facsimile of the Rome Treaty', and the British and other OEEC states who viewed it as a limited trade arrangement. As the Chairman of WP21 noted, 'These differences of approach [went] to the root of the problems'. At that root was the issue of defining the origin of goods to qualify for FTA treatment. Within the Six, especially in France and Italy, the common external tariff and the protection it would bring to exposed industries was seen as a vital element of the EEC. That the FTA was not to have a common external tariff led the French and Italians to argue that trade would be deflected by the disparity in tariffs on imports of basic materials, semi-manufactures and components between high and low tariff members. What the French suggested, therefore, was harmonisation of external tariffs to eradicate disparities. Conversely, the British, supported by Norway, Sweden and Switzerland, hoped to deal with trade deflection by a less sweeping solution, namely a percentage criteria and certificates of origin.[37] The deadlock on this central issue had been previously encountered by WP21's 1956 predecessor, Working Group 17, and would remain the crucial technical problem throughout the FTA negotiations.

In July 1957, however, as the WP21 report concluded, the origin question, together with related technicalities, demonstrated that there was 'still no commonly held conception of the Free Trade Area'. This conclusion was further complicated by the reports of WP22 on agriculture and WP23 on the association of peripheral states. British officials had been forced to stall the report of WP22 because in draft, it had gone too far towards a compromise for London's taste; its final version thus reached the prophetic judgement that no progress could be made on agriculture 'unless substantially different instructions' were given to its members.[38] WP23, which had met infrequently, simply concluded that progress of peripheral associa- tion would only be achieved after some of the larger fundamental FTA questions were solved.[39]

The WPs having effectively stalled, and in line with the May agreements to postpone the FTA negotiations until ratification of the Rome Treaties, Thorneycroft, as Chairman of the Council, an- nounced that the OEEC would recommence its deliberations in the autumn.[40] To maintain the pressure for the British initiative, Thorneycroft's report also noted that it would 'be a very serious day for Europe if we are not able to create a Free Trade Area as a complement to the European Economic Community. . .'. This anxiety, worsened by the very real technical difficulties in the OEEC WPs' reports, created a two-fold reaction in London. First, the prime minister revealed frustration at the Six's growing strength. Second, Whitehall began to realise that it might have to depart from its original conception of a FTA if anything like success was to be achieved.

Macmillan directed much attention to the FTA proposal in mid- July 1957, possibly motivated by the increased chances of the Rome Treaties' ratification in Paris. It should be remembered that in his early June minute to Lloyd, Macmillan had aired the concern that 'when the Six have ratified they may snap their fingers at the Free Trade Area and leave us in the lurch'.[41] He wrote in his diary on 11 July that 'I feel more [and] more worried about the French, who are in one of their intransigent moods.'[42] It was this concern which contributed to the negativity in Macmillan's minute to Thorneycroft, Lloyd and Eccles on 15 July:

> We must not be bullied by the activities of the Six. We could, if we were driven to it, fight their movement if it were to take the form of anything that was prejudicial to our interests. Economi-

cally, with the Commonwealth and other friends, including the Scandinavians, we could stand aside from a narrow Common Market. We also have some politico-military weapons. . . . We must take positive action in this field, to ensure that the wider Free Trade Area is more attractive than the narrower Common Market of the Six. We must take the lead, either in widening their project, or, if they will not co-operate with us, in opposing it.[43]

From whatever angle these statements are viewed, they can only point to two conclusions: first, that Macmillan envisaged the FTA gaining some form of dominance over the Common Market, and second, that if this policy failed, the government would be forced to adopt an aggressive attitude. No doubt Macmillan's analysis was based on the November 1956 judgement that a Common Market without a FTA would be to Britain's disadvantage. However, in suggesting that the FTA be 'more attractive' than the Common Market, the prime minister had surpassed the official policy most recently reiterated by Otto Clarke. On 6 June, Clarke noted that in the long term Plan G implied 'permanent maintenance of [the] "3 Circles" . . . policy' with acceptance of the Six's consolidation, perhaps even federation including Denmark; Britain would 'unequivocally let them lead Europe' while itself remaining 'half-way between Europe and N. America, the linch-pin of N.A.T.O., G.A.T.T., etc.'.[44] Unless the official view had changed since Clarke's minute, there was a variance between the prime minister and the senior Treasury official co-ordinating FTA policy within Whitehall. That policy was not universal in London in 1957 should come as little surprise. In 1956, Plan G had been formulated from different agendas, both political and bureaucratic. Perhaps the explanation of this divergence between prime minister and civil servant rests on what was thought to be feasible. Whether Clarke and other officials shared Macmillan's belief in the FTA dominating the Common Market is unclear, though this was never a prospect recorded in Whitehall correspondence. Expectations were of the Six developing along their own lines as a component part of a wider FTA. It may be that, in private, officials imagined that the narrower, looser British-inspired proposal might gain precedence over the ambitious Common Market, especially if the French failed to meet their commitments or became too protectionist, say, for German industry. But these were improbables and there was mounting evidence that the Six would do all they could to ensure the Rome Treaties' success. Officials, therefore, may have ruled out FTA dominance. Macmillan, on the other hand, still seems to have been under the impression that Britain had the power and influence to dominate Europe's development. Consequently, he also believed that if forced, Britain could fight the Six. However, the prime minister's belligerence in response to potential FTA failure was not shared by officials when fighting talk reappeared in 1958.

Perhaps frustration at the achievements and potential of the Six accounts for the hot-headed tone of Macmillan's minute. Despite his negativity, the prime minister still wanted the FTA to succeed; Britain's position in Europe, both politically and economically, depended on it and the alternative of Anglo-Six hostility was not inviting. Thus, in two meetings of his *ad hoc* Cabinet Committee on the FTA in July 1957, and in his minute of 15 July, the prime minister made positive suggestions. Macmillan argued that the real pressure for European integration, though expressed in economic arrangements, derived from 'the strong desire' of many European countries for some form of closer political unity. He concluded that 'while we are in something of a strait jacket as regards economic integration, we may well be able to show Europe that we are prepared for a closer political association'.[45] The prime minister had been encouraged in this view by the intervention of Sir Gladwyn Jebb. On 28 April Jebb had urged the government to give greater priority to its European policy by, amongst other suggestions, making an institutional concession to the Six.[46] It was this which caught Macmillan's attention.[47] The FTA would still be run by a Managing Board of national officials within the OEEC which would be responsible to a Council of Ministers.[48] What Macmillan suggested was that this Managing Board might be called supranational and, through majority voting in certain areas, possibly involve some surrender of national sovereignty. Exactly what level of supranationality Macmillan had in mind is unclear. What is clear is that the European Commission was dismissed as dangerous because it involved a body of international officials having powers of initiative and recommendation over a Council of Ministers.[49]

These political proposals represented the limits of Britain's room for manoeuvre in the FTA negotiations as well as some misjudgement of Continental reaction. The OEEC WPs' reports had indicated that there was no fundamental agreement between Britain and the Six, particularly the French, as to what shape or scope the FTA should take. The real problems were the questions of agriculture and the external tariff, and although London was considering limited action on the former, it was opposed to French plans for the latter. At official level in Whitehall it was understood that political concessions would not deflect these issues. On 21 June, two key French Foreign Ministry officials, Wormser and Valéry, had made it clear to Figgures that the solution to the FTA's problems did not lie in the institutional field.[50] Within the Foreign Office, Hood also argued that majority voting in the FTA institutions would not be taken as an advance in Europe.[51]

The prime minister was either unaware of, or, more likely, disregarded such advice in the hope that any indication of British commitment to European co-operation would increase the FTA's chances. If this was the case, the recent actions of the President of the Board of Trade had already undermined such an aim. During a visit to London, the Dutch, who were recognised as Britain's closest allies within the Six, had been 'left breathless' by Eccles' references to Six power institutions. Describing them as 'irresponsible aggregates' of European civil servants, Eccles clarified his view by arguing that they were 'irresponsible' because 'they were not answerable to the House of Commons'.[52] Eccles may have given his characteristic inflexion to government policy, but the Dutch left London with an accurate view of Macmillan's proposals: Britain envisaged little more than some extension in the OEEC Council of Ministers' terms of reference, combined with majority vote instead of unanimity on certain issues. Although The Hague tried to see the positive side in British institutional ideas, it is probable that those dedicated to the supranational principle in the Six would have sensed further evidence of Britain's failure to comprehend the basic concepts of the European Community. This would only have enhanced the view that association between the Common Market and the FTA on British lines was impractical.

Macmillan's institutional proposal was not the limit of advances in FTA policy discussed at the July Cabinet Committee meetings. On agriculture, ministers reaffirmed the necessity of a concession which would be introduced later in the negotiations for greatest political effect. Furthermore, surpassing the brief provided by their officials, both Thorneycroft and Eccles raised the possibility of expanding the scope of the FTA to cover areas other than eliminating tariffs and quotas on manufactures.[53] Even Macmillan admitted that it would be difficult to adhere to a narrowly defined FTA if the negotiations were to have any success. He felt there might be presentational and political value in a FTA preamble which resolved ministers to undertake positive and constructive discussion on common economic problems in the broadest sense. Finally, to give weight to British policy on the Continent, Macmillan raised two options. First was the appointment of a single British minister responsible for the FTA.[54] Second, the Foreign Office was instructed to consider inducements to encourage the Six's acceptance of the FTA despite its economic imperfections. Considering that on 19 and 24 July 1957 the German and French parliaments had ratified the Treaties of Rome, success in the FTA negotiations was, more than ever, imperative for the Macmillan government.

Maudling's appointment

French Deputies' 'indifference or reserve' towards the FTA during the National Assembly's ratification debates on the Rome Treaties was described as 'rather frightening' by the Foreign Office.[55] Although the French leader, Bourgès-Maunoury, had assured Britain in June 1957 that his government would seek a successful solution to the FTA problems, there were indications in July that the French position had hardened, despite comments made by the prime minister to the Commons.[56] The Ambassador to London, Chauval, warned that the agriculture issue could bring deadlock; Pineau argued that there was no National Assembly majority for a FTA, and Faure reiterated French demands on agriculture and the external tariff.[57] Outside of the government, Jean Monnet told Jebb that OEEC negotiations could 'drag along to an ultimate failure'.[58] It may be that London hoped these views represented only initial negotiating positions; in mid-July, Britain's two representatives in Paris, Jebb and Ellis-Rees, told Ministers that a FTA agreement was likely after hard bargaining.[59] Clarke's deputy, Figgures, raised the hope that given ratification, other members of the Six might apply pressure to the French.[60] It was upon this strategy that London would base great weight during the FTA negotiations. In July, signals were already positive from Bonn; pro-FTA resolutions had been passed during the Bundestag ratification debates and Adenauer himself had reaffirmed his support for the FTA.[61] The Germans, however, were 'right in the "lame duck period" before the [Federal] elections' and could not be relied upon for action on the FTA until after September.[62] In the meantime, the Macmillan government hoped that the appointment of a single minister responsible for the FTA would give its European policy a boost.

Reginald Maudling, Paymaster-General since January 1957, was chosen for this post.[63] Described by *The Times* as 'one of the outstanding younger men in the Government', Maudling had entered the Commons in 1950 and had held a number of junior posts, including Economic Secretary to the Treasury.[64] It does not seem, however, that an interest in European integration and experience of international negotiation were the criteria for the job since Maudling possessed neither.[65] Instead, domestic considerations were paramount. According to Macmillan, Maudling was 'bienvu' in the Conservative Party (having not been a Suez rebel) and had a good reputation in his department; also, occasional projects, such as the FTA portfolio, were traditionally the responsibility of the paymaster-general in Whitehall.[66] It has even been suggested that the prime minister selected Maudling, a known protégé of Butler, to involve and neutralise the section of the party leadership who were sceptical of closer relations with western Europe.[67] On these lines, Maudling was not to be granted the title of Minister of State for Europe because this would have given the position more prominence than Macmillan wanted. Hence, the paymaster, who did not hold full ministerial rank, would be purely charged with 'special duties'.[68] This may have circumvented opposition to such concentration of efforts on Europe, but in the long run, Maudling's lack of authority did not ease what would be a difficult task in forcing FTA concessions through Cabinet.

Maudling's official responsibility was to co-ordinate the government's FTA preparations and represent Britain during the negotiations. He would work with the ministers interdepartmentally concerned and report directly to the prime minister.[69] Macmillan characterised the paymaster's role as being that of an 'Apostolic figure' who would have to 'hold firm the Eleven [non-Six OEEC states]' and 'break into the Six. He should therefore be something of a St. Paul: not merely the Jews but the Gentiles should be his care'.[70] Generally, Maudling would have to give British policy 'a positive and political character, to show that the wider Free Trade Area [was] a better conception than the narrower Common Market'.[71] In retrospect, Maudling described his appointment as a 'most interesting task . . . an excitement and a real challenge'.[72] But there were no false hopes. Macmillan warned that it was going to be 'difficult and exacting' and Maudling recounted that chances of agreement 'did not seem very good'.[73] Nevertheless, the paymaster was provided with a small staff and an office in Whitehall's Gwydyr House. On the prime minister's instruction, Sir John Coulson was recalled from his post as Minister (Economic) at the Washington Embassy to be Chief of Staff.[74] As Assistant Under-Secretary in 1955, Coulson had overseen Foreign Office policy on the Messina conference and was thus familiar with the issues at hand. Macmillan had been impressed with him as 'a very good economist' and his appointment, together with that of Guy Millard, a young Foreign Office counsellor and former Private Secretary to Anthony Eden, as his deputy, suggests that the prime minister wished to enhance the part played by the Foreign Office in European policy. Maudling's staff was completed by John Liverman, a senior Treasury principal who had been working on FTA policy, and would be Maudling's Private Secretary.[75]

British ministers also hoped to complement Maudling's appointment with inducements to encourage the Six to accept the FTA. This proved to be a fruitless exercise, however. It was first attempted by officials in early July and then reconsidered in August by the Foreign Office on the prime minister's instructions. On both occasions the options under consideration were defeated by the constraints of wider Whitehall policy. The first proposal was possible British membership of, or association with, Euratom. There was enthusiasm for this in Whitehall; both the Board of Trade and the Ministry of Power saw long-term commercial advantage in partial membership and Sir Frank Lee believed willingness to join could prove a 'significant political gesture' for the FTA negotiations. Conversely, the MoD believed Euratom membership would conflict both with Britain's nuclear policy and its bilateral relations with the United States. This idea, therefore, had serious objections.[76] The second option was for greater British association with the ECSC. This too held no hopes as it was thought that only membership would assist the FTA's chances and membership had been previously ruled out.[77] Third, officials debated British investment in North Africa to assist France's development of Saharan oil. With investment capital already limited and the potential for offending Arab, African-Asian and Commonwealth countries high, this was rapidly rejected.[78] Fourth, the Foreign Office considered two possible concessions on defence: enhancing co-operation with the Six within the WEU and maintaining British troops in Germany for longer than planned. In light of agreements with the Americans after the Bermuda conference of March 1957, Britain had constructed an Anglo-German Steering Committee on arms research and development to boost WEU co-operation. It was recognised, however, that this was already working to its full extent within the confines of Britain's bilateral agreements with the United States and relations with the Commonwealth.[79] Thus, little if anything could be done in this area and Britain's inability to be more forthcoming remained a problem in Anglo-German relations; in September, the British ambassador to Bonn warned that limited defence co-operation had 'not removed German suspicions that our only interest is to fob them off with out-of-date stuff'.[80] The ambassador also raised the possibility of Britain postponing the withdrawal of troops from Germany which, as a 'symbolic concession', might secure assurances on support costs and favourable action in the FTA negotiations. While there may have been something in this, Whitehall had already accepted that the timing of the forces negotiations made it impossible to assist the FTA in this respect.[81]

As a result, the Foreign Office paper on inducements, completed in late August, was accurately described by the Treasury as 'pretty thin'.[82] Although this exercise reveals that Britain was eager to make the FTA a success, it also shows that wider policies restricted British room for manoeuvre. Perhaps the only area where Britain might have scored diplomatic points in Paris and Bonn was nuclear defence co-operation. There were those, such as Jebb, who urged this as the only concession of any value, but Macmillan, committed by secret agreement with Eisenhower, could not envisage such drastic measures.[83] Consequently, as London moved into the final month before the start of full negotiations, it could not rely on inducements to compensate for the economic shortcomings of the FTA.

Preparing the ground

In May 1957, the French and German governments had agreed to direct their attention to the FTA once the Treaties of Rome had been ratified by their national parliaments. With this process complete by the end of July, the British government took immediate action to resuscitate the FTA negotiations. On 6 August, Thorneycroft, as Chairman of the OEEC Council, notified members that a ministerial meeting would be held in mid-October to consider the FTA and that Britain would be represented by Maudling.[84] On the same day, Selwyn Lloyd instructed British ambassadors in the capitals of the Six to 'stimulate a sense of urgency' in their respective governments and impress upon them the importance which the government placed on the forthcoming negotiations.[85] To give this diplomatic offensive yet more force, Maudling made visits to European capitals and Whitehall prepared its agriculture concession for the start of the negotiations.

Maudling's meetings with European ministers in late August and early October clarified the difficulties faced by Britain on the eve of the negotiations but also provided some hope. In Paris, Foreign Minister Faure and Finance Minister Gaillard both expressed their desire to see an agreement concluded and noted that since ratification, attention had been directed towards the OEEC negotiations.[86] Conversely, the French maintained their insistence on some form of external tariff harmonisation and a *quid pro quo* on agriculture. Maudling also noted that Gaillard was less enthusiastic about a possible agreement than Faure and believed that the OEEC would not produce successful negotiations. This did not augur well for Britain because within three months, Gaillard, a convinced European, a one-time collaborator of Jean Monnet, and a former French representative on the Spaak Committee, would form the next French government.[87] In Brussels and Rome there was little if any advance on a technical level as both governments revealed sympathy with the French position on agriculture and the external tariff.[88]

The meetings between Maudling and Federal German ministers and officials in Bonn on 4 October made these difficulties seem less threatening.[89] The Foreign Office had already received good indications of post-ratification German attitudes; on 25 September, Heath noted that the 'soft-pedalling policy [seemed] at last to be bearing fruit'.[90] Maudling managed to achieve a high level of agreement not only with Erhard and the Economics Ministry but also with the previously more sceptical Foreign Ministry. The paymaster was able to note, with support from the German Foreign Minister, Von Brentano, that there was sufficient unity between the British and German positions to get the negotiations started. Even State Secretary Hallstein, who was known to be the 'most stubborn contender for the Six, and the Six alone', was not dismissive of the FTA.[91] Hallstein spoke reassuringly of German interest in the FTA although he did see difficulties in the tariff problem and, more significantly, in reaching general agreement amongst the Six. What led the paymaster to report that he was 'very pleased', and the British Ambassador to write that meetings had been 'extremely friendly', was that the Germans claimed to have been exerting favourable pressure within the Six.[92]

This German intervention was the result of a compromise reached in the Federal government in June 1957. While the Foreign Ministry was still concerned to prevent any dilution of the EEC in a wider FTA, the Economics Ministry managed to secure agreement that the FRG would do everything towards realisation of the FTA, including mediating between extreme positions; it would also advise the British government that changes in its concept of a FTA would be necessary to achieve French and Italian agreement.[93] Consequently, the Germans led the work to co-ordinate the Six's positions on the FTA within the Brussels Interim Committee, the precursor of the European Commission, in summer 1957.[94] The result was a memorandum which presented four possible patterns for the FTA. These began with a complete copy of the EEC, a FTA very close to the British plan, and two less comprehensive proposals, one dealing with trade problems by escape clauses and the other achieving a FTA by piecemeal agreements with no timetable. It heartened the British considerably during Maudling's meetings in Bonn to hear of this memorandum and that the German government preferred the second proposal, in effect, the British FTA.[95] Moreover, there were promising words from Dr Müller-Armack, Head of the Economic Policy Department in the Economics Ministry and representative on the Brussels Interim Committee, about securing an agreement amongst the Six on the exclusion of agriculture and avoiding French suggestions of delay tariff reductions in the FTA. While he did not underestimate the difficulties faced in the FTA negotiations, Müller-Armack nevertheless had a positive outlook. This may have been an upbeat assessment of the Six's position, but it was not a wholly inaccurate one. There were rifts amongst the Six in the Interim Committee's study of the FTA and in summer 1957 agreement had not been reached on exactly which of the German options they should promote. At the same time, however, there was support, strongest from the Dutch and the Germans, less so from the Belgians, the French and the Italians, for some form of FTA agreement.[96]

In British Ministers' eyes this evidence of German support was encouraging as it complied with what Macmillan saw as the answer to the FTA negotiations' problems. In mid-August he had told Maudling that:

> The present position of France complicates, but perhaps in some ways facilitates your work. My feeling is that we must get the Germans on our side. When the election is over they will be

prepared to take a stronger line. The Germans really agree with us and are against the French ideas of a high productivity wall round the Common Market.[97]

France's position was one of political instability and Macmillan was suggesting that given this, others in the Six might be able to influence the French to depart from their growing hostility towards the FTA. Reliance on the Adenauer government was thus the main-stay of British strategy, as Maudling's reply shows: 'It certainly does seem, at first glance, that the Germans must hold the key to the solution of most of our problems'.[98] In this light, the Bonn meet-ings instilled confidence in the British position. With the Rome Treaties ratified and the Federal elections complete, the Adenauer government seemed to be turning its attention to creating the FTA. Certainly, Von Brentano's comment to Maudling that 'the Com-mon Market was not an end in itself, but a starting point for a new economic policy' pointed to this.[99] However, while there was some logic to British strategy, in the long-term, it presumed too much of the Adenauer government, which was committed to France in the Rome Treaties, and too little of the French, whose weakness did not prevent them from taking a strong line in the FTA negotiations.

During his talks with European Ministers, Maudling revealed that London was willing to accept agriculture discussions parallel to the FTA negotiations. This only confirmed growing rumours that the British government were to make a concession on 'the devil of a problem', agriculture.[100] Retrospectively, Macmillan claimed that it had become clear by the summer of 1957 that a negative attitude on foodstuffs would mean failure for the FTA.[101] This underesti-mated the longevity of the Europeans' opposition to British plans which had been a constant since the announcement of Plan G in late 1956. In a Cabinet report at the end of August 1957, officials clarified the two reasons that made a move on agriculture essen-tial.[102] First, 95 per cent of British exports to the OEEC were in industrial goods, whereas a varying but substantial percentage of exports from the OEEC countries to Britain were in agricultural products. The OEEC, and especially the Six, could not sell an in-dustrial FTA to their parliaments and public, without a *quid pro quo* on agriculture. Secondly, apart from their share in the British agri-cultural market, some OEEC countries had large interests in the markets of the Six which they were concerned to safeguard. This was

Table 5.1 OEEC exports of food, beverages and tobacco as a percentage of all exports, 1955 (figures in $ millions in brackets; metropolitan countries only)

Country	Exports to OEEC countries	Exports to the United Kingdom
Ireland	69.6 (195)	72.1 (191)
Iceland	81.8 (18)	90.7 (3.9)
United Kingdom	3.7 (85)	–
Fed. Rep. of Germany	2.5 (94)	3.3 (8)
Austria	2.0 (9)	0.7 (0.2)
Belgium–Luxembourg	4.0 (72)	7.3 (13)
Denmark	72.6 (567)	92.6 (323)
France	16.8 (348)	26.3 (93)
Greece	64.8 (83)	83.3 (15)
Italy	32.1 (309)	43.0 (58)
Norway	16.3 (66)	16.8 (23)
Netherlands	34.7 (600)	47.6 (158)
Portugal	41.1 (53)	31.8 (14)
Sweden	2.5 (31)	0.9 (3)
Switzerland	8.3 (58)	4.3 (3)
Turkey	59.8 (92)	52.2 (12)
All OEEC countries	15.9 (2680)	36.5 (918)

Source: CAB129/88, C(57)188, 24 Aug. 1957, p. 7.

especially true of Denmark which exported 72.6 per cent of its total produce to the OEEC and 32 per cent to the Six alone (Table 5.1).

For the government, the problem was simple: how far must it resign itself to, or participate in, agricultural arrangements to ensure the success of the Free Trade Area as a whole? Under the Treaties of Rome, the Six powers were committed to the reduction of tariffs and quotas on trade in foodstuffs with the future aim of a common agricultural policy.[103] They were not envisaging free trade in agricultural products but they did have the long-term goal of a single market which Britain, given its domestic and Commonwealth commitments, could not accept. From the very beginning, agricultural exclusion had been a prerequisite of the Free Trade Area. Assurances had been made to the Commonwealth that their stake in the British market would be protected, and domestically, under the 1947 and 1957 Agriculture Acts, the government could not make large-scale reductions in guaranteed prices. Horticulture was also protected by tariffs, and there were political and economic difficulties in adjusting the tariff on fish and fish products. As the Minister for Agriculture, Heathcoat Amory, had warned in February, there was no possible means of giving the Europeans compensation in the agricultural field for the industrial benefits that Britain would gain in the FTA without antagonising domestic or Commonwealth farmers.[104] In August, Butler reminded Macmillan that this subject was 'dynamite <u>for</u> and to the County constituencies' and indicated that he felt the officials' conclusions were dubious.[105]

The solution recommended by officials was for a presentational rather than a substantive concession. There would be a 'Statute' for agriculture, separate from the FTA Convention, but negotiated simultaneously with it. It would involve continuation of OEEC consultation on agriculture, rules for trade, the elimination of tariffs and quotas on foodstuffs over a definite period and, finally, strengthened institutional arrangements including possible association with the Six 'in differing degrees'. London, however, would demand a waiver on the reduction of tariffs to maintain its preferential trade with the Commonwealth, thus blocking increased access to the British market for European agriculture exports. Quite simply, as Macmillan summed up after a cautious Cabinet discussion, the 'Statute' was 'little more than an extension and strengthening of existing arrangements within [the] O.E.E.C.'.[106] This was essentially accurate and certainly how the British agriculture proposal was eventually received in Europe.

The agriculture concession was the primary advance in policy discussed by the Cabinet on 8 October.[107] In what Macmillan described as 'a remarkable combination of clarity and brevity', Maudling introduced detailed briefs in which he outlined the British approach towards the OEEC Ministerial meeting one week later.[108] The standoff between Britain and the Six was clearly drawn: 'it will not be easy to establish working arrangements between the two economic systems based on such different principles [EEC and FTA]. Yet we cannot subscribe to the European doctrines of integration; nor will they abandon the Treaty of Rome'. On the vital question of agriculture, Maudling supported the idea of a parallel 'Statute', adding that this had been canvassed with the Commonwealth during recent discussions during Finance Ministers' meetings.[109] In Cabinet there was general agreement that the proposals should be implemented, but conversely there was great reserve about making any more significant concessions in the future. This was a reaction to officials' warnings that the 'Statute' might be sufficient to start the negotiations, but not sustain them.[110] Implicitly, the Cabinet had ruled out large-scale concessions which might reduce British output or diminish control over agriculture policy. Domestic and Commonwealth considerations remained paramount, with the prime minister adding that the proposals not be called a 'Statute', but a charter or agreement. In summing up the Cabinet discussion, Macmillan was influenced by the advice of the Cabinet Office which suggested giving the FTA a 'specifically political colour' to 'blur the edges of the agricultural problem'.[111] He therefore concluded that the government should:

> seek to secure that [the FTA's] institutions were invested with at least as much dignity and authority as those of the European Economic Community. . . . discussion of our proposals should be elevated to the plane of [a] major political decision, and the Free Trade Area should be presented as a project which, so far from conflicting with our special relationship with the other members of the Commonwealth, was designed to strengthen and consolidate the political and economic resources which the free world as a whole could deploy against the Sino-Soviet *bloc*.[112]

Ostensibly, such language was intended to improve the chances of British policy, but the reality remained that Macmillan thought in such terms and saw the FTA as a component of greater British foreign and economic policy in the late 1950s.

On the eve of the negotiations that the Macmillan government had been waiting for since June, British policy in Europe faced an uncertain future. Maudling concluded that there was undoubtedly a genuine political desire throughout Europe for the FTA.[113] In the long run, however, success or failure would be determined by whether this would be sufficient 'to outweigh both the real technical difficulties and the many serious political drawbacks for the various countries involved'. Maudling did not overstate Britain's chances, warning that he had 'no exaggerated hopes' for the OEEC meeting. Yet he understated the mood of officials. From the Foreign Office, Gore-Booth noted that 'if there [was] to be a Free Trade Area at all' it would have to be put through by British initiative and leadership.[114] According to Bretherton, almost all diplomatic contacts, in London and in European capitals, reflected 'an air of gloom about the prospects of the Free Trade Area project'.[115] In what was a realistic assessment, Bretherton described political support for the FTA within the Six and the non-Six, but added that this did not always extend to facing the economic consequences. He argued that agriculture would no longer remain in the 'first rank' of problems, but would be surpassed by the basic question of reconciling the FTA with 'the institutions and spirit of the Six'. It was this philosophical division which caused so much difficulty; Bretherton noted that the Six's inability to see a solution to this problem was one of the main reasons for their pessimism.

Yet on this question, and its manifestation in the technical issues of the FTA's scope and the external tariff, the British were unable to make concessions to the Six. At the Cabinet meeting on 8 October, the only deviations from the February 1957 FTA White Paper were the agriculture agreement and the prospect of some limited majority voting. Although in July there had been talk in Macmillan's Cabinet Committee of extending the scope of the FTA, officials successfully reminded Ministers that it was axiomatic that the FTA operate within the OEEC, rather than replace it.[116] If not, the possibility of the FTA supplanting the OEEC would be raised and with it, the prospect of using the Treaties of Rome as a model for the FTA's scope. Consequently, London proceeded with an industrial FTA including a parallel agriculture agreement but which was otherwise limited in scope. On the question of the external tariff and the origin of goods, there was no flexibility. From the British viewpoint, the general acceptance of liberal rules of origin and the maintenance of national tariff autonomy on imports from third countries were essential to the design of the FTA. As Gore-Booth had said in July 1957, 'Commonwealth preference depends on a tariff. Therefore, if no tariff, no preference'.[117] However, if France decided to make external tariff harmonisation a breaking point, Britain's policy would face serious difficulties. As Maudling warned Cabinet, 'If France want[ed] to wreck the negotiations here [was] a simple way of doing it'.[118]

For Britain's FTA, then, all rested on the strategy of encouraging the Adenauer government, together with others in the Six and the non-Six, to influence the French and Italians.[119] This was a difficult task given the diplomatic situation in early October 1957; as Edden noted, there were 'some chill winds blowing up' against the FTA on the Continent.[120] It was also precarious in light of Bretherton's assessment of the Six's priorities which suggested that for the Six as a whole, the achievement of a FTA was officially regarded as secondary to the consolidation and unity of the Treaties of Rome.[121] Finally, on a wider scale, Britain's approach was further complicated by the impact of international events on Anglo-European relations.

Part III

The Maudling Committee Negotiations, October 1957– December 1958

6
The Negotiations Begin, October–December 1957

After five months of delay, the British government hoped that the OEEC ministerial meeting of 16 October 1957 would mark the beginning of serious negotiations on the FTA. There was no misconception about the formidable obstacles that lay ahead; the Cabinet was aware of the 'the real technical difficulties and the many serious political drawbacks for the various countries involved'.[1] Nevertheless, it was hoped that these problems could be surpassed if enough political will could be generated in favour of the FTA on the Continent. The following analysis of the first three months of the Maudling Committee negotiations, the name given to the OEEC's Intergovernmental Committee on the FTA, reveals the precarious nature of this strategy. The Macmillan government was right to believe that European political interest in Britain's proposals existed; where it miscalculated was in how effective this would be in solving the negotiating problems and influencing the French to soften their position on the FTA. This miscalculation also extended to the government's overestimation of its power in Europe. Hence, it wrongly believed that it could use Commonwealth initiatives to increase Britain's influence in the FTA negotiations. Furthermore, when Britain's international status was asserted in the form of strengthened Anglo-American relations after the launch of the Soviet satellite, Sputnik, the Macmillan government failed to see that this did not necessarily bring dividends in Anglo-European relations. Consequently, while October 1957 was supposed to hasten the progress of Britain's FTA, it actually began what Macmillan later described as 'long and dreary negotiations' which would eventually collapse in December 1958 amid much ill feeling.[2]

The OEEC Ministerial Meeting of October 1957

Returning from a short holiday in August 1957, Macmillan submitted a memorandum to Cabinet on Britain's economic situation.[3] Discussing action to deal with increasing pressure on sterling, the prime minister emphasised the necessity of boldness in economic policy. He added that restrictive measures in the economy would have to be balanced 'by the creative themes of closer union with Europe upon the one side and Canada upon the other. If we could hit all these marks, stability of prices and strength of sterling at home, and great openings of trade in Europe and Canada, we should have a fine and worthwhile programme'. Macmillan saw no incompatibility between the dual policy of increased trade with Europe and Canada. On 9 September he introduced a paper to Cabinet which suggested that in the context of the FTA negotiations, there was advantage in pursuing studies of a future, large-scale Commonwealth Conference to give the appearance of providing 'some alternative course' to Europe.[4] Prior to the all-important OEEC Ministerial Meeting of 16 October 1957, the Macmillan government attempted to increase its bargaining power in Europe by reminding its partners that Britain had a Commonwealth option should the FTA negotiations fail. Having the opposite effect, British tactics did little to improve the FTA's chances.

The ideas of a Commonwealth Economic Conference, and separately, an increase in Anglo-Canadian trade, had been suggested by John Diefenbaker, the Canadian Prime Minister, in July 1957. Doubting the potential of a Commonwealth Conference, the British government had decided to 'play it long' and use the September Commonwealth Finance Ministers' meeting at Mont Tremblant as an opportunity to debate the prospect. In response to Diefenbaker's second suggestion to switch 15 per cent of Canadian imports from the United States to the United Kingdom, the British had canvassed the idea of an Anglo-Canadian FTA confidentially with the Canadians over the summer.[5] As described in the previous chapter, this proposal planned to maintain good relations with the Diefenbaker Administration, the Commonwealth and Conservative Party imperialists, and aimed to secure the economic benefits of increased trade with Canada. However, there had always been doubts about the feasibility of Diefenbaker's switch, its support within the Canadian government and the potential impact on the European FTA negotiations. In fact, on 17 September, Thorneycroft had attempted to stall discussion of the Anglo-Canadian FTA proposal at the Mont Tremblant meeting.[6] The chancellor warned that the governor of the Bank of Canada had recently dismissed the Anglo-Canadian FTA as being unacceptable to Canadian industry and therefore a non-starter.[7] However, in Cabinet on 19 September, the president of the Board of Trade's contrary opinion was accepted.[8] Ministers did not wish to see the government criticised for failing to respond to Diefenbaker and thus his proposal was to receive 'sufficient publicity to illustrate [British] readiness, in principle, to engage in a continuous and long-term effort to foster Anglo-Canadian trade'. This message was directed at imperialists in the Party, the Canadians, and bearing in mind the prime minister's earlier reference to the appearance of an 'alternative course', the Europeans.

A few days prior to the October OEEC meeting on the FTA, Commonwealth Finance Ministers met at Mont Tremblant. A strong endorsement was given to the European FTA but it is unlikely that European Ministers were as comfortable with British policy towards Commonwealth trade. As London enthusiastically urged the launch of the FTA negotiations, the Europeans received reports of a Commonwealth Economic Conference planned for 1958, as well as private discussion of an Anglo-Canadian FTA. The effect on the Paris negotiations was to give those who doubted British exclamations of Europeanism more ammunition.[9] This was particularly true of the French. At the end of September, Wormser informed the Paris Embassy that French industries, and by inference the French government, were critical of Britain enjoying a preferential trade relationship with the Commonwealth while attempting to create another preferential position in Europe.[10] This criticism was firmly held by the French throughout the FTA negotiations and was based on the fear of the advantages that the British might secure if they gained access to two preferential worlds. Commenting specifically on Britain's proposal for an Anglo-Canadian FTA, the French Embassy in London claimed that it had created 'a bad impression in Europe. Nobody understood what [Britain] was after. It had long been thought that the British, after long hesitation as to where they stood, had decided that they stood in Europe and the question was asked whether [they] were now undecided once more?'.[11] Later in the year, Marjolin argued that common policies would have to be constructed in the European FTA to ensure, for example, that Britain would not be able to make proposals such as the Anglo-Canadian FTA without prior agreement from its European partners.[12] There is no doubt that the Anglo-Canadian FTA was a tactical manoeuvre to solve a difficult situation in Britain's relations with Diefenbaker, but it was also a tactical blunder in Britain's relations with Europe. Whitehall's claim that the Anglo-Canadian FTA in no way conflicted with the European FTA was a serious misjudgement.[13]

It is surprising that the British continued to use this precarious 'Commonwealth alternative' argument as a threat in Europe. Marjolin warned Maudling in October that British Ministers caused great difficulties in France when they stated that if forced they would chose the Commonwealth over Europe.[14] But the government seems to have overlooked this advice as the record of Eccles' conversation with the German Ambassador to London in early December 1957 reveals.[15] The president of the Board of Trade threatened 'that a main difference between [Britain] and the Six was that [Britain] had a Commonwealth alternative'. It is revealing that a key British minister believed such an exclamation would aid the government's cause. A more diplomatic course would surely have been to continue with Commonwealth discussions but also appeal to European sensibilities by disregarding the 'Commonwealth alternative' threat which did greater damage to British interests in Europe than good. Conversely, Commonwealth policy, designed to enhance Britain's bargaining position in the European FTA negotiations, in fact added to the government's problems. There was also no compensating profit in increased Anglo-Canadian trade as the FTA idea never came to fruition.[16]

Despite the complications caused by Commonwealth policy, from the British viewpoint, it was possible to see the OEEC Ministerial meeting of 16–18 October as a limited success. Sights had been set low. Maudling had told the Cabinet that he held no exaggerated hopes for the meeting. The simple objective was to secure the effective resumption of the negotiations after the postponements of the summer. There was no underestimation of the technical difficulties before the negotiating countries, but the government had set its strategy to overcome temporarily these problems by emphasising the danger of dividing Europe through the failure to complement the EEC with the FTA.[17] This was the basis of Thorneycroft's message to Erhard on 14 October, and the line followed by him with Spaak on 16 October. In both instances, under the recommendation of the Foreign

Office, the chancellor had stressed that division in the economic arena could lead to repercussions in all other fields, including defence.[18] This strategy, of embellishing the dangers of division in Europe to generate political will in favour of the FTA, was the basis of the chancellor's introductory speech to the ministerial delegates at the OEEC on 16 October.[19] Combined with Maudling's statements on the central problems and his indication that Britain would be willing to consider an agriculture agreement parallel to the FTA Convention, the strategy secured its objectives. It is true that the Council was 'resoundingly silent' on virtually all the central technical issues, but avoidance of such vexed matters as the basic relationship between the EEC and FTA, the scope of the OEEC arrangement, the question of the external tariff and the timetable for the reduction of tariffs, was part of British tactics.[20] The issues of substance were not supposed to be dealt with at the October meeting, and the Resolutions produced by it were simply announcements of procedure and intent.

The meetings themselves went in Britain's favour for two reasons. First, the French were unable to play a full role in the discussions. After the fall of the Bourgès-Maunoury government on 30 September, the Fourth Republic was once again in between administrations and thus French ministers had no political direction for the OEEC meeting. Consequently, comments made by the Six were relatively tepid. As a riposte to Thorneycroft's July report on the OEEC Working Parties' deliberations, the Six introduced a questionnaire produced by their Interim Committee (the forerunner of the European Commission).[21] This document, which made general commitments to creating a FTA under Article 238 of the EEC Treaty, raised the negotiating problems from the Six's point of view. Of these, the most basic was reconciling the divergent philosophies between the EEC and the FTA, overcoming the agriculture and external tariff problems, and working towards institutions governed by majority vote and common economic policy. Without French ministers to give political inflexion to the more extreme arguments, the Interim Commission questionnaire did not cause immediate problems for Britain. The second reason for the apparent success of the OEEC meeting was Britain's announcement of its agriculture concession. As Whitehall had hoped, the simple fact that Britain was willing to move from its previous position was enough to get the negotiations going. Moreover, the positive role played by Erhard assisted Britain's tactics. Pledging German support for the FTA, the Economics Minister argued that 'It was essential not to let things drag; people were looking for progress. Great political damage would be done if free Europe failed to achieve economic unity'.[22] With welcome words from the Scandinavian countries and qualified support from American and Canadian 'observer' delegates, the Resolutions were agreed. On 17 October, the OEEC Council declared its determination:

> to secure the establishment of a European Free Trade Area which would comprise all Member countries of the Organisation; which would associate on a multi-lateral basis, the European Economic Community with the other Member countries; and which, taking fully into consideration the objectives of the European Economic Community, would in practice take effect parallel with the Treaty of Rome.[23]

This Resolution held two important statements. The reference to the integrity of the EEC was a tactical reassurance directed towards the Six to convince them that the FTA presented no threat to their objectives. At the same time, however, reference to the FTA taking parallel effect with the EEC committed the OEEC to completion by 1 January 1959 when the first EEC tariff reductions were planned. Recognition of the impracticality of this deadline increased as the negotiations proceeded.

The Council also decided to 'reach agreement at the same time on methods of further co-operation between all member countries in agricultural matters with a view to assuring an expansion of trade in agricultural products' and there was a pledge to 'take full account of the interests of Member countries in process of economic development'. Describing the OEEC meetings, the permanent British representative at the OEEC, Ellis Rees, claimed that they had been 'remarkably successful and of political significance'.[24] Although Ellis Rees characteristically enhanced and even overestimated OEEC developments, his view of the October meetings reflected the fact that London's limited goals had been achieved. A start had been given to the FTA negotiations, and political will had temporarily overwhelmed technical difficulties. It is true that the October Resolutions only gave the illusion of progress, but this was what the Macmillan government desired, and in reality, was the only policy to pursue in autumn 1957.[25] However, the October meeting was affected by the French being unable to mount significant opposition to British plans. If a stable government had held office in

Paris, the OEEC meetings may not have passed so successfully. Regardless of this hypothetical point, it can be stated that the October meetings created the foundations for a precarious British policy. As the Maudling Committee began its work in November, there was a growing British optimism based on the premise that the negotiating problems, personified in the French, could be dissolved by political pressure, from within and without the Six.

The negotiations take shape

Anglo-Six relations were not wholly favourable at the start of the Maudling Committee negotiations. To begin with, members of Jean Monnet's Action Committee, together with some in the French government, such as Marjolin, argued that the FTA had the potential to jeopardise the integrity of the Six's achievement.[26] Max Kohnstamm, one of Monnet's assistants, told a British official prior to the OEEC meeting that 'it [was] quite vain to expect that it [would] be possible to break up the unity of the Six'.[27] Such sentiments characterised a break with the Action Committee's previously cautious welcome to the FTA.[28] Monnet himself warned London that the Paris negotiations would fail unless the Six spoke through a single voice via the European Commission.[29] He also suggested that the Six's inability to reach an agreed view might endanger the British plan and added ominously that 'the French would veto anything they did not like until such time as the French view was the Commission's view'. Macmillan was appropriately discouraged by Monnet's warning, the inference being that the French would control the policy of the Six towards the FTA, which was blatantly contrary to British strategy.[30]

There was also a resurgence in suspicion of British motives. Not all, for example, had welcomed Reginald Maudling's appointment in August 1957. Luxembourg's Ambassador to Brussels, who represented his country at the meetings of the Six, was another European official who felt the FTA was merely a device to wreck the EEC, and believed Maudling's appointment had been a convenient way for Britain to give the appearance of activity.[31] Although there is no evidence in the British record to suggest that this was a widely held opinion, it is not difficult to imagine that Maudling's tour of European capitals in August and October 1957 had been seen by some in the Six as an attempt to exploit their disagreements over the FTA to British ends.[32] Certainly, some members of the Council of Europe were sceptical of British sponsorship of the FTA. The Foreign Office realised that Strasbourg parliamentarians carried a good deal of influence on general European policy in their national parliaments and predicted that their positive votes would be needed in the future.[33] At the Council of Europe at the end of October, Maudling spoke in the highest terms, warning that unless the FTA was achieved, European politicians would 'be deemed in the eyes of history to have failed'.[34] Although the Council obviously responded to this message by passing a recommendation in support of the FTA, not all members were satisfied.[35] In particular, two parliamentarians from France and Belgium urged delay in the Paris negotiations on the grounds that simultaneous commencement of a FTA threatened the proper establishment of the EEC.[36] In general, other speakers in the debate believed that the sense of urgency and the fear of European division voiced by supporters of the FTA implied an unjustified criticism of the Six. As long as there were those willing to make such a defence and act as guardians of the Rome Treaties' integrity, both in Jean Monnet's Action Committee and elsewhere in Europe, the British faced an uphill battle that does not seem to have been fully realised in all quarters in London.

To compound an already difficult situation, diplomatic relations between Britain and the Six powers were further complicated by the Macmillan government's robust attitude in the GATT Contracting Parties' consideration of the Treaties of Rome from 28–30 October 1957.[37] Before the EEC Treaty could be implemented, the Six had to receive the approval of the GATT Contracting Parties and secure a waiver for the association of overseas territories which, by creating a new preferential area, was contrary to GATT principles. Britain's primary motive at the GATT meetings was to secure mitigation for its overseas territories from the preferential treatment that the Six's overseas territories would enjoy through Common Market association. In Cabinet on 8 October, Ministers agreed that:

Without provoking the Six Powers to retaliate by adopting a hostile attitude to the Free Trade Area negotiations, we should seek to prolong the GATT discussions, to ensure that the arrangements of the Six Powers would be effectively and continuously supervised by GATT and to secure adequate mitigation of the damage which would otherwise be caused to the trade of our overseas territories.[38]

This was a dubious tactic. Britain may have had to defend the interests of its overseas territories but this was an opportunity to improve Anglo-Six relations rather than worsen them. Prior to the GATT meetings, the French Ambassador to London, Chauval, had 'strongly pressed' the Foreign Office to ensure that Britain did not hold up the GATT review of the Rome Treaties.[39] Chauval referred to recent threats from unnamed British officials that 'if the French did not behave sensibly over the Free Trade Area negotiations, the United Kingdom might retaliate by making difficulties for the Common Market countries in the discussions in GATT'; this, the French Ambassador warned, had the 'worst possible effect on French opinion'. The Belgians even asked the British to use their influence to quell expected criticism of the Rome Treaties' overseas territories provisions.[40] There had been a hint that the *quid pro quo* for this assistance would have been reciprocation by the Six in the Paris negotiations. The Foreign Office was dismissive of such collusion: 'It is hard to see how the Belgians can really expect us to indulge in horse-trading of this kind when they know quite well that we are bound to represent the views of our overseas territories as well as our own'.[41]

The president of the Board of Trade's speech at the GATT ministerial meeting on 28 October did little to calm this situation.[42] Although Eccles welcomed the Treaties of Rome, he expressed great uneasiness about the provisions concerning overseas territories which he described as an extension of a preferential trading area. In response, the Six were 'hurt and surprised' at this criticism and wrote a letter of complaint to the chancellor of the exchequer.[43] All of the Six powers may not have been provoked into a hostile attitude to the FTA negotiations as a result of these tactics, but it is certain that Britain's actions affected the atmosphere of Anglo-Six relations. Ultimately, the interests of British overseas territories precluded tactical agreement to the Rome Treaties' swift passage through the GATT. However, although some in London may have seen the GATT as a potential lever over the Six, it was not in the British interest to delay the Rome Treaties. Difficulties with the Six in the GATT would have been too readily transposed to the FTA negotiations. There was also American policy to consider. Not wishing to see the Common Market held up in the GATT, but fearing that difficulties in the Maudling Committee negotiations might lead the British to cause the Six problems there, the Eisenhower Administration applied pressure on the British government.[44] On the recommendation of Dulles,

Macmillan's visit to Washington in October 1957 was used to 'extract from the British a firm commitment that they will not obstruct, through such devices as GATT consultations, progress towards [the] achievement of a common market'.[45] In return, the Americans would promise to reaffirm their support for the FTA. On 25 October, Selwyn Lloyd assured Douglas Dillon, Deputy Under-Secretary of State for Economic Affairs, that while Britain would seek mitigation in the GATT for overseas territories, it would not otherwise interfere with the Common Market.[46] Whether this was fully accepted amongst the Six is unclear, but even viewed in the best light, Britain's hard line on overseas territories was still further indication of the difference between the Common Market and the FTA.

Although the OEEC Ministerial meeting of October 1957 had got the negotiations underway, the atmosphere for progress was not, therefore, wholly propitious. To implement its Resolutions, the OEEC convened an Intergovernmental Committee at ministerial level which held its first procedural meeting on 18 October. As the Committee's permanent Chairman, Reginald Maudling's first task was to produce a single document, an Annotated Agenda, which would form the basis of future negotiation and would be discussed at the first substantive meeting of the Maudling Committee in November. With months of postponement and back-peddling behind them, officials were able to respond to Maudling's OEEC responsibility rapidly. Within days, the draft Annotated Agenda had been drawn up and debated by Otto Clarke's new interdepartmental *ad hoc* Cabinet Committee of officials, GEN.613 (designated 'The European Free Trade Area Steering Group', this committee became the primary official body during the FTA negotiations, surpassing Clarke's ES(EI) sub committee).[47] The Agenda represented a guiding structure for the forthcoming negotiations and included the major negotiating issues under five headings: problems of freeing trade; agriculture and fisheries; economic and financial questions; problems of particular sectors and constitutional questions.[48] During the first two meetings of the Maudling Committee in November 1957, Ministers addressed themselves to the Annotated Agenda although it soon became clear that the French position was little changed from the negative signals of the early autumn.

The first Maudling Committee meeting from 14 to 16 November was dominated by a policy statement given by Maurice Faure, the Foreign Minister in Félix Gaillard's newly convened French government.[49] The French exposition raised the fundamental problems of the FTA negotiations once more. Faure insisted that the FTA must include a common external tariff as a solution to trade deflection and be similar to the Treaty of Rome in scope; he also reiterated the French National Assembly's demand for identical guarantees in the FTA Convention as obtained in the Treaty of Rome. All of these demands, of course, were contrary to British policy and were re-stated more forcefully in private meetings between Maudling and Faure on 14 November.[50] First, when discussing the site of the Six's institutions, the British expressed interest in seeing joint location with the FTA's institutions. This brought a sharp reaction from Marjolin: 'You do not want us to be on our own for five minutes, do you?'. Second, on the central question of reconciling the FTA and the EEC, the French demanded consideration of a common commercial policy and external tariff harmonisation. They added that in their view, this should not be a problem for the British government and the only real block to such developments were the Scandinavians, with whom 'France was not in the least anxious to have a Free Trade Area'. Finally, the French intimated that unless there was some British movement on the external tariff and com-mercial policy, they would demand that the evolution of the FTA over its transitional stages be controlled by unanimity.[51] This was similar to the stance taken by the French in the Common Market negotiations. While they had agreed to the principle of irreversi-bility in the EEC treaty, the French had maintained that unanimity in the Council of Ministers would be required for the Common Market to progress from the first to the second transitional stage.[52] In effect, this amounted to the power of veto for the French which, when transposed to the FTA negotiations, conflicted with British policy. The Macmillan government's decision to pursue limited majority voting in the FTA institutions had been designed as a political concession but also as a means of ensuring that the French could not alone block the FTA's development.

Despite this negative evidence, British officials claimed there had been better progress than expected and that difficulties had been surmounted with comparative ease.[53] The outcome of the second Maudling Committee meeting, held on 28 and 29 November, did nothing to alter this perception. Maudling's deputy, Sir John Coulson, informed his Whitehall colleagues that the meeting had been 'eminently satisfactory'; Maudling himself told British industry rep-resentatives on a Board of Trade consultative committee that despite problems, the negotiation's atmosphere was 'universally a good one'.[54]

Reading British accounts, therefore, it seems that the negotiations were progressing successfully. An explanation of this rests on three main factors. First, the principal negotiating difficulties, agriculture and origin, had been effectively removed from the Maudling Committee's remit until January 1958. Only then would OEEC Ministers receive Britain's Agriculture Agreement and the Group of Trade Experts' report on defining the origin of goods and external tariff harmonisation. Second, Whitehall was placing great importance on the French attitude being only an initial bargaining position, and no doubt this was also the view held by other members of the Six and the OEEC who saw the current events as a repetition of French tactics during the Spaak Committee negotiations.[55] Third, and most significantly, there were positive signals of support from within the Six, and especially from the Adenauer government.

The vast majority of information received in London pointed to Bonn playing a role in the Maudling negotiations which was compatible with British strategy. Adenauer's policy seemed all the more coherent and satisfactory to the British when they considered its timing. Just as the chancellor had promised the prime minister in May, with the ratification of the Treaties of Rome complete, and also the Federal elections successfully over, the Germans had turned their attention to the Paris negotiations. At the end of August 1957, Sir Christopher Steel, Ambassador to Bonn, was anxious to impress on London the need for close Anglo-German relations, especially on a personal level between leaders, to prepare a safe passage through the difficult issues of the FTA and support costs which would loom later in the year.[56] Macmillan was impressed by the logic of this advice and wrote to Adenauer on a number of occasions throughout the autumn. After congratulating the chancellor on his election success, Macmillan took the opportunity to pursue beneficial diplomacy with Germany, minuting 'we must strike while the iron is hot'.[57] Linking the Paris negotiations with his desire to see Germany adopt good creditor policies, Macmillan wrote to Adenauer in early October:

> I feel that Europe is on the threshold of great advances if we can all work together which will add to our common strength and unity. Both in the political and the economic fields it would indeed be tragic if all this were frustrated by a failure to solve the initial financial problems on the solution of which, in a sense, all the rest depends.[58]

Selwyn Lloyd quickly followed up Macmillan's message in a meeting with Adenauer, and reported the chancellor's determination to co-operate fully with Britain.[59] Macmillan's strategy seemed to have achieved its objective. Prior to the OEEC meeting, the Foreign Office received indications that the paymaster's appointment had 'caused great pleasure in German circles', and Maudling's talks with German ministers in Bonn on 4 October had been very successful for the British.[60] Furthermore, there was evidence that the Germans were applying pressure favourably within the counsels of the Six. Due to the inability of the EEC powers to reach an agreed line on the FTA, demands were put to the British at the beginning of October to postpone the OEEC meeting, but the Germans ensured that the set date was guaranteed.[61]

As autumn progressed, further evidence pointed to a favourable German attitude towards the FTA negotiations. Any example of British interest in European co-operation was appreciated by Bonn, and the advance on agriculture was particularly welcome as a step towards ensuring that the Danes would not flood the German market with displaced agricultural exports.[62] The British received vocal support from the Germans within the Maudling Committee on many technical aspects, and on the vexed question of the external tariff in particular. There was also encouragement from leading German ministers. Erhard's advocacy of the FTA was a constant, and London must have been encouraged to hear that the German Finance Minister, Etzel, was 'convinced that there was now a new impetus in [Britain's] European policy and he would do all he could to see that the Free Trade Area came about'.[63]

German sympathy was the basis of Britain's strategy for the FTA negotiations and, from London's viewpoint, this seemed to be converging with Adenauer's policy in autumn 1957. There were also positive communications from the Dutch and the Belgians. It had been the Dutch who had typically responded most effectively to London's 'sense of urgency' campaign at the beginning of August and who were the strongest proponents of the political necessity of the FTA.[64] Their role was accurately summed up by one Foreign Office official as being a useful 'fifth column'.[65] It was also possible for London to view the Belgian position as offering no long-term obstacle to the FTA. The Belgian government emphasised its political support for the Paris negotiations on a number of occasions. After the October OEEC meeting the government communicated its interest in seeing Britain assume the leadership of Europe once more, and in November, the Foreign Minister, Larock, stressed that Belgian membership of the EEC did not mean severing traditional economic ties with Britain 'without whom the conception of Europe had no real meaning'.[66]

Thus, from Whitehall's vantage point, after two Maudling Committee meetings there seemed to be some tactical advance demonstrated by political will in favour of the FTA within the Six. There was also the constant support of the Scandinavians within the OEEC. The Foreign Office had been particularly interested to learn in November 1957 that the Scandinavian plans for a Nordic Customs Union had been postponed until October 1958 to await the outcome of the FTA negotiations.[67] Also, although early soundings from the Danish government on the draft Agriculture Agreement had not been wholly positive, in an early December speech, the Danish Prime Minister, Hansen, gave strong support for the FTA, leading one Foreign Office official to note that 'his final paragraph might have been lifted from any U.K. Minister'.[68] But while these were positive factors, the fact remained that the two main negotiating issues, agriculture and origin, and the position of France, were still unsolved. When Maudling held a meeting with officials on 2 December to review the situation after the two November Committee meetings, the importance of these points seemed to be underestimated.[69] Whitehall was rightly encouraged by the support for the FTA from within the Six and the non-Six, but it nevertheless overestimated the impact this would have on resolving the technical problems and influencing the French. Furthermore, with all resting on political influence, the wider impact on Anglo-European relations of the Macmillan government's search for ever closer Anglo-American co-operation relations does not seem to have been fully integrated into Whitehall's assessment of the FTA negotiations.

The side effects of Sputnik

On 4 October 1957, the Soviet Union launched the world's first man-made satellite, Sputnik. Although this event in itself did not directly effect Britain's FTA policy, it did heighten scepticism of British commitments to European integration. A by-product of the hysterical political and public American reaction to the Soviets' demonstration of their long-range missile capability was President Eisenhower's enthusiasm for enhanced nuclear collaboration with Britain.[70] The consequent agreements reached by Macmillan and

Eisenhower during meetings from 23 to 25 October amidst the immediate post-Sputnik atmosphere in Washington were beneficial for Britain's relations with the United States, but by causing concerns about Anglo-American hegemony, did little for Britain's profile in Europe.

Macmillan travelled to Washington with two clear objectives.[71] First, he hoped to achieve the repeal of the McMahon Act which had precluded significant Anglo-American nuclear collaboration since 1946. The second objective was more general. In his memoirs, Macmillan claimed that 'renewed impetus to Western co-operation against Soviet aggression or infiltration' was his goal, but his emphasis in Cabinet before the Washington visit was much more on 'unobtrusively' establishing joint Anglo-American machinery for implementation of wide-ranging agreed policies.[72] Ultimately, Macmillan's aim was to finalise the process begun in Bermuda and to stamp the seal on re-established Anglo-American relations. His private words after the Cabinet meeting revealed his intentions; Butler noted that Macmillan 'spoke of his ambition to merge US and UK policy.... He felt [the] US and [the] UK had [a] special relationship'.[73]

The prime minister's objectives were largely met by the Declaration of Common Purpose agreed with Eisenhower on 25 October 1957.[74] From American initiatives, the British delegation had obtained a general proclamation of Anglo-American unity and a presidential commitment to repeal the McMahon Act, which Macmillan deemed 'the great prize'.[75] Returning to London, the prime minister told the Cabinet that a declaration of 'inter-dependence' between the United States and Britain had been agreed, and Selwyn Lloyd added that 'we had now succeeded in regaining the special relationship with the United States which we had formerly enjoyed'.[76] The repeal of the McMahon Act (in July 1958) was indeed the 'great prize' as it secured unique nuclear collaboration with the United States, creating a solid basis for close and lasting relations, and provided a crucial ingredient for the Sandys defence reforms. For Macmillan and his government, however, the renewed intimacy in Anglo-American relations was perhaps the greatest achievement. Despite his contemporary and retrospective claims that the October agreements marked a desire to see the two countries work together not to rule or impose their will, but to serve the free world, Macmillan no doubt revelled in the special relations he enjoyed with the Eisenhower Administration.[77] But although the prime minister decried accusations of an Anglo-American directorate, a side effect of the post-Sputnik strengthening of relations with Washington was a certain souring of relations with Europe.[78] This adverse European reaction, particularly in France, was enhanced by further evidence of Britain's extra-European priorities, and did little to improve the chances of the FTA negotiations.

Prior to receiving reports of the Washington meetings, the French were already extremely sensitive to Anglo-American co-operation in autumn 1957. The escalation of French colonial difficulties in North Africa was of principal concern to France's new Prime Minister, Gaillard, and he and his country were incensed at recent British and American supplies of arms to Tunisia, sent to forestall similar supplies from the Soviets. The French claimed, with some justification, that these arms would be used to aid rebels fighting against their forces in Algeria, and the result was intense resentment towards London and Washington.[79] In retrospect, Macmillan admitted that the Tunisian Arms incident was 'a serious error' at a critical moment: 'It would have been wiser to take the risk of Soviet infiltration, in order to keep the French sweet'.[80]

The effect of the October 1957 Declaration of Common Purpose was to compound negative French attitudes. Distrust of Anglo-American relations was already in place. Bitterness at the repeal of the McMahon Act for Britain alone was a new factor. The French had applied to Washington for nuclear collaboration in July 1957 and it was not lost on them that the Americans had turned France down then, but signed agreements with Britain a few months later.[81] From the Embassy in Paris, Gladwyn Jebb clarified the level of French concerns in November 1957.[82] There was a fear that an Anglo-American directorate in world affairs would steamroller pre-arranged defence plans over European heads at the forthcoming high-level NATO meeting. There was also resentment over policies towards the French in North Africa and anxiety that Britain and the United States aimed to force Paris into playing a very minor role in defence matters. Finally, there was the opinion that Britain's attitude to the Common Market was 'anti-European'. All French attitudes and policies were coloured by these concerns and the FTA negotiations were no exception.[83] The combination of the joint action in North Africa and the Declaration of Common Purpose led to French anxiety that Britain and the United States were 'ganging up against them'.[84] Dulles attempted to cool French temperatures by stressing to Pineau in Washington that there was nothing exclusive about the US–UK relationship, especially in NATO, and Macmillan and Lloyd extended this process during a brief fence-mending visit to Paris on 25 November.[85] Macmillan was pleased with the outcome of these meetings and claimed the atmosphere had been greatly improved: 'Although we shall have to be careful of French suscep-tibilities for some time I now feel more sanguine about the NATO meeting in December'.[86] Evidence from Selwyn Lloyd's private papers suggests that the prime minister produced a biased view of the situation; he had failed to note that his remarks on the FTA to Gaillard, 'whom he lectured as though he was a small boy', had caused great offence to the French.[87]

The NATO meetings were held in Paris from 16 to 19 December under 'leaden skies', both in reality and metaphorically consider-ing the distrust of Anglo-American plans in Europe.[88] Nevertheless, both Eisenhower and Macmillan have described the meetings as a success. This was indeed true from their respective policy stances. For the United States, with the panic created by Sputnik still fresh, NATO agreement to the stationing of American intermediate-range ballistic missiles and stocks of nuclear warheads in Europe was a crucial Cold War stop-gap until Washington matched Moscow's inter-continental capabilities.[89] For Britain, and for the prime minister in particular, by obtaining European agreement to these defence plans and the concurrent price of American acquiescence to dis-armament discussions with the Soviets, the main objectives had been secured.[90] But what of European and mainly Franco-German distrust of Anglo-American relations? Macmillan claimed that one supremely important result of the NATO meeting was that these suspicions had been dispelled.[91] This may have been the case, but there is a sense that although suspicions had been allayed, the damage had already been done, especially to the Anglo-French and Ger-man relations.

There may not be a traceable link between British actions in Washington and the results for the FTA, but it is possible to sug-gest that they did little to improve the chances of the negotiations. The Washington meetings, the Declaration of Common Purpose and its unique repeal of the McMahon Act, together with British diplo-macy in the NATO Council, served as proof of Britain's extra-European priorities and Macmillan's desire to act as Washington's preferred ally and mediator in the Cold War. This policy was designed to set Britain apart from European states and, in late 1957, it succeeded in doing so. It is revealing that at the December NATO meetings, the French, Italians and Germans announced their tripartite co-operation in weapons development, an arrangement known as FIG.[92] This decision was influenced by the post-Sputnik UK–US special relations which encouraged the French and Germans into seeking defence co-operation within this European framework.[93] For Britain, however, being apart from the Europeans in defence collaboration was not wholly compatible with plans for closer economic co-operation. For those within the Six who were sceptical of British intentions, the close relations engendered with the Americans cast a damaging light on London's motives in the Maudling negotiations.

Despite the difficulties which external events caused the FTA, there was still a certain optimism in Whitehall at the close of the 1957. However, just as British ministers and officials neglected to place enough significance on the evidence of technical problems in the negotiations, it seems that there was a failure to recognise the diffi-culties generated on the Continent by Britain's earlier diplomacy with the Commonwealth and then, later, with the United States. Exactly why Whitehall did not take an all-inclusive view of these factors is explained by two possibilities. The first is that the Macmillan government failed to recognise the significant consequences of its wider foreign policies. A lack of appreciation of European sensi-bilities was a common denominator in much of British policy towards the Six. There is a sense that Whitehall failed to treat its proposed partners in Europe with the diplomatic gravity they deserved. The second possibility is that there was a general failure to place a high enough priority on European co-operation as a foreign policy goal, hence the disregard for the negative side effects of collaboration with the United States. It was almost as if soured relations with the French, Germans and other Europeans was a necessary price to pay for unique collaboration with the Americans. Perhaps the most balanced assessment would acknowledge these two factors and add that at the end of 1957, Britain had not recognised the incom-patibility between its foreign policy goals. Whitehall still expected to achieve preferred ally status with Washington, enhanced econ-omic and political relations with the Commonwealth, and new preferential links with Europe. What it did not fully grasp was that advances in the former two goals jeopardised the third, as the Six, and primarily France, were acutely sensitive to Britain's overt in-tentions to secure special status in all arenas. Yet if this was a failure in British diplomacy in late 1957, then it was one which had been encouraged by the United States. The Eisenhower Administration had, of course, lost no time in fortifying the British sense of superiority within the Atlantic Alliance when faced by Cold War crisis after the launch of Sputnik.

On 6 December 1957, Maudling submitted a progress report on the FTA negotiations to the prime minister.[94] The Paymaster noted that the discussions had been cordial and the majority of the Annotated Agenda points had been dealt with. The Germans, Dutch and Belgians had been particularly helpful, and even the Italians were searching for a solution.[95] Negotiations on agriculture had 'broken the apparent deadlock' and the problem was not thought to be insoluble. Although the French and Italians saw difficulties arising from the absence of a common external tariff, in practice Maudling believed that the problems would be far less difficult than they alleged. The passages which probably gave Macmillan most heart, and led him to thank the Paymaster for 'this excellent report', were those concerning France.[96] Maudling claimed that although the French posed the greatest problem, it was 'possible to detect some departure from their extreme position, presumably under the influence of their partners in the Six'. He then noted that there was a means of circumventing the French argument that the FTA would disrupt the Rome Treaties' 'careful balance of advantage and disadvantage'. What this amounted to was a special provision for France in the FTA, short of an empty chair, but designed to offer the French opportunity to escape if necessary. Although Maudling noted that the practicability and acceptability of these plans were uncertain, there can be no doubt that Macmillan was encouraged by this estimate of events.

The reason for Maudling's cautious optimism was recent evidence of German intervention against France on FTA matters. In a note to Eccles on 3 December, Maudling reported that the French were increasingly isolated in the Six and being 'driven quite a way in our direction'.[97] The evidence of Walter Hallstein's recent actions convinced Maudling that in Bonn, Erhard had persuaded Adenauer to support the FTA. In late November, the Permanent Under Secretary at the Foreign Office was warned by the German Ambassador that State Secretary Hallstein, confidant of Adenauer and known defender of the Rome Treaties, was 'going through one of his anti-British phases'; on other occasions, the Embassy advised that he

was susceptible to the large section of German opinion that believed Britain aimed to prevent the formation of the EEC.[98] It was
with some surprise, therefore, that Maudling reported Hallstein's
'extremely helpful speech' in Paris which had led to the complete
isolation of the French within the Six on the question of *décalage*,
or delaying the start of the Free Trade Area.[99] Even German officials
sensed a change in Hallstein's outlook. The German representative
to the OEEC, Werkmeister, advised London via Ellis Rees: 'You have
got hold of Hallstein now: don't let him go. Now is the time to
complete his conversion. He is fully seized of the importance of making the Free Trade Area succeed as a complementary force to the
Common Market'.[100] By the end of 1957, therefore, evidence pointed
to the beginnings of a beneficial German policy towards the FTA negotiations. Hallstein's apparent conversion was welcome news for
British plans, as was German influence within the Six. It was further
strengthened by assurances from Baron Snoy, Chairman of the Six's
Interim Committee, who told Maudling that 'as time went by the
other Five would necessarily exert great pressure on the French'.[101]

It had been this, together with some indications of a softening
of the French position that led to the hopeful tone of Maudling's
6 December report to Macmillan. There is no doubt that Maudling
recognised the size of the problems facing the FTA, but he hoped
the technical aspects of French opposition would be overwhelmed
by a political interest in British association with Europe and the
pressure evinced by Germany. There were problems with this analysis
however. First, as mentioned earlier, the two main negotiating difficulties of agriculture and origin remained. There had been evidence
in November that the French Farmers' Unions had decided not to
seek agriculture's inclusion in the FTA and the Danes, as mentioned
above, were sending positive signals.[102] Nevertheless, the Agriculture Agreement had yet to be presented to the Maudling Committee.
Similarly, there had been no ministerial discussion of the origin
question and the statements of France and Italy pointed to little if
any movement towards Britain's position. Maudling seems to have
rather underestimated this issue in his 6 December progress report.

Second, apart from the negotiating problems, there was also an
attempt by the senior Quai official, Wormser, to clarify Whitehall's
view of the French position on 5 December.[103] Concerned that London
had a false impression of French FTA policy, Wormser stressed that
unless there was a fundamental change in the political climate in
France towards the FTA, a Treaty would never be ratified in Paris.

Wormser was obviously referring to recent hostile resolutions of the French employers' association, the Patronat, against the FTA and to a hardening of ministerial attitudes after the Macmillan–Gaillard meetings in late November.[104] Whitehall's reaction to this is indicative of a general British misreading of the French position. The Permanent Secretary to the Treasury, Sir Roger Makins, argued that 'We should forge ahead without paying too much attention to the French or [being] deflected from our course by their diversionary tactics'.[105] In the Foreign Office, Rodgers minuted: 'In practice I think that France is going to have to drink its medicine in the next six months . . .'.[106] This Whitehall outlook was influenced by the confidence that the up-turn in German policy had imbued, and a belief that France would have to back down under pressure from within the Six and perhaps accept, as Maudling tentatively suggested to Macmillan on 6 December, a special position in the FTA. Such an option would not mature until early 1958, but even at this early stage, Whitehall was split on the issue. The Board and the Treasury saw advantage in the idea, but the Foreign Office accurately advised that the Five would not sign the FTA Treaty without France lest it threaten the integrity of the Six as a whole.[107]

Finally, it was misjudgement of the Six's determination to protect their recently won unity that was perhaps the greatest weakness in Britain's FTA strategy at the end of 1957. On 14 October, the American Embassy in London sent a report to the State Department on the views of an *Economist* journalist, Miriam Camps, who had recently completed a survey of the Six governments' views of the FTA.[108] Camps explained that the French and Italians, and to a lesser extent the Belgians, held little interest in the FTA on economic grounds but were unwilling to break off the negotiations. Conversely, both the Dutch and the Germans would be pleased if the FTA resulted in a low common external tariff and a liberal trade policy for the EEC. What united all parties was the priority given to starting the Common Market off satisfactorily; there was no compulsion, however, to see the FTA start concurrently. While the American Embassy generally agreed with Camps' views, it added that British officials believed they had received sufficient commitments from ministers in bilateral talks to doubt Camps' estimate of the cohesion of the Six and to argue that she had underestimated the political appeal of the FTA in Europe.

Although the Germans had agreed to turn their attentions to the FTA after ratification, they had never agreed to apply significant pressure to the French at the risk of serious division amongst the Six. Although German ministers and officials had fought Britain's corner by arguing, for instance, against postponement of the October OEEC meeting, and also by opposing French demands for *décalage*, wider support was not without confines. Bretherton's November 1957 conversation with Sonnenhol, the German delegate to the OEEC, epitomises this: 'Sonnenhol said that it was quite clear that somebody would have to talk turkey to the French at the highest possible level very soon. The German Government hoped . . . [Britain] would do this. I said that we rather hoped . . . they would'.[109] Adenauer's support for the FTA was far from absolute. In a Foreign Office brief for what became the chancellor's cancelled visit to London at the end of 1957, it was noted that although most senior German ministers and officials supported the FTA, 'Dr. Adenauer himself may be the weakest link, certainly not because of his dislike for the Free Trade Area but because he attaches prime importance to "bringing France along" in the European Economic Community'.[110] Eccles received corresponding evidence in conversation with the German ambassador in December.[111] The Ambassador stated that 'Adenauer was so set on the political side of European integration that he might be persuaded to support the French request for a delay in E.F.T.A.'. This would not actually occur until September 1958, although there can be little doubt that Adenauer's priority was always the security of the Treaties of Rome and the development of the Franco-German rapprochement.

The German chancellor may have been willing to agree to Erhard's pro-FTA position in the autumn of 1957; there was in fact significant support for the FTA in Germany, especially amongst industrialists.[112] This may have led to some German pressure on the French during that period and would account for the more malleable and co-operative attitude exhibited by Hallstein.[113] However, the major constant in German communications with Britain was an insistence on the integrity and the cohesion of the Treaties of Rome being unaffected by the FTA negotiations. This had been particularly evident in Maudling's meetings in Bonn at the beginning of October. Any German support for the FTA in the Six's Interim Commission, and any pressure on the French, was thus limited by this important condition. As van Scherpenberg, Chief of the Foreign Trade Division of the German Foreign Office, told the Eisenhower Administration in November 1957, Germany 'welcomed the wider membership of the FTA as a counterpoise to the protectionist sentiments of France and Italy'.[114] However, because the French position was 'exceptionally delicate', it was necessary to treat Paris with caution and tact. The German government did wish to see Britain involved in the development of the European Community. However, as one ex-Foreign Office official commented in retrospect, although this did 'often result in them saying "no" to the French, [it] didn't result in making the French say "yes"'.[115] It seems that the Macmillan government failed to grasp the gravity of this factor in its reliance on German advocacy. Yet as a study of Germany's role has suggested, the Germans had fostered British confidence. Erhard's interventions in defence of the FTA and the belief that the German Economics Ministry would fight its cause within the counsels of the Six, 'hardened, rather than softened' Britain's negotiating position. It also masked the fact that the German Foreign Ministry still held doubts about the FTA and that the failure of the Germans to bring their influence to bear on the French within the Six's Interim Committee was an ominous development.[116]

German co-operation was, of course, dependent on favourable relations between London and Bonn. For Germany to be the key to the success of the FTA negotiations, links between the Adenauer and Macmillan governments had to be harmonious, both in the Paris negotiations and also wider afield. But not enough significance was placed on damaged German sensitivities as a result of Macmillan's actions in Washington in October and in the NATO Council in December. From Bonn, the form did not look good. For some time, the Germans had been very suspicious of reductions in British and American troop levels in Germany and were especially anxious about the implications of the Sandys defence reforms. The Adenauer government also doubted the rationale of 'trip-wire' defence and reliance on the nuclear deterrent.[117] Thus, the announcement of increased unique nuclear collaboration between Britain and America in the Declaration of Common Purpose, followed by the NATO decisions to station IRBMs in Europe, and the resultant accusations of an Anglo-American directorate, all had a negative effect on the German outlook. These factors, combined with anxieties about the crucial issues of reunification and disarmament, as well as lingering suspicion of Britain's motives in the FTA, did little to breed German confidence in the Macmillan government. It is very likely that at this juncture, Adenauer's disillusion with the Western alliance and with Britain contributed to the developing Paris–Bonn axis, especially in terms of defence co-operation.[118]

For Germany to have fought for the FTA, Britain would have had to have treated her with more diplomatic sensitivity and revealed a new enthusiasm for closer political ties. Sir Kit Steel had given exactly that advice in September 1957 and on other occasions.[119] As a signal of his dedication to European co-operation and close relations with Germany, Macmillan could have increased the profile of collaboration with Adenauer before and during the NATO meeting in December 1957. If the prime minister had truly been working for the Western Alliance, and not the Anglo-American dominance he rejected in hindsight, collaboration with the Germans as well as the Americans should have been a priority. Ultimately, it could not have been lost on Adenauer, whose relations with the British prime minister were already difficult, that Macmillan was searching for a greater role for his country than an equal partner in a united Europe.[120] This must partly explain Adenauer's often lacklustre approach to the FTA negotiations.

Just over a year on from the British government's official announcement of its FTA proposal, Whitehall believed that its strategies were working. With the Treaties of Rome successfully ratified, the Germans, supported by the Dutch, and to a lesser extent the Belgians, seemed to be fulfilling their May 1957 commitments by directing their attentions to the FTA's creation.[121] With the 'key in the lock' – German co-operation and pressure on France within the Six – there appeared to be positive prospects of success. There was some accuracy in this evaluation as the Germans and the Dutch did want the FTA to succeed. Yet there was British miscalculation of first, the limits of this support, and second, the effect it had on the position of France. The reality of this situation would dawn on London as the FTA negotiations took another frustrating turn in January 1958. When considering the French position in early December 1957, Figgures of the Treasury minuted: 'We must obviously be ready for some new French line'.[122] Within weeks, the announcement of French counter-proposals to Britain's FTA proved him right.

7
Impending Crisis, January–May 1958

On 1 January 1958 the Treaties of Rome formally came into force marking a turning-point in Europe's history.[1] To maintain parity with the Six, the British hoped to finalise the FTA Convention in time for the first EEC tariff and quota reductions exactly one year from this date. There was, however, an immediate complication for British plans. On 9 January, the Ambassador to Paris, Gladwyn Jebb, informed the Foreign Office of the French government's intention to submit a counter-plan to the FTA.[2] This produced an anxious response in Whitehall with fears that the French were 'simply finding the best way of stalling or, worse, of artificially putting [Britain] in the wrong instead of themselves'.[3] From January to May 1958, the government struggled through a period of impending crisis in the FTA negotiations months before their final collapse. The proposals of the French counter-plan not only complicated the OEEC negotiations but also exposed an incongruity in Britain's external economic policy. The price of French agreement to the FTA was access to the preferential markets of the Commonwealth and tariff harmonisation to deal with the problem of defining the origin of goods entering the FTA. Britain's response to this predicament confirms that the FTA was founded in traditional policies but also that Whitehall was prepared to make an unprecedented concession on external tariff harmonisation to secure a relationship with the EEC. As ministers were about to implement this advance in policy, however, a *crise de régime* threatened the Fourth Republic and momentarily threw the whole situation out of kilter. To establish a background to these arguments, it is necessary to look first at how Whitehall perceived Britain's external economic and foreign policies in 1958.

'The position of the United Kingdom in world affairs'

In December 1957, Harold Macmillan initiated a comprehensive review entitled 'The Position of the United Kingdom in World Affairs' which, like its predecessor under Anthony Eden in 1956, aimed to analyse government expenditure against Britain's essential interests.[4] As the review involved each of the main Whitehall departments stating exactly what those interests were, it provides an important source for the historian of general British policy in the late 1950s. Economic policy was the primary focus for departmental studies although wider questions were raised by officials, including Britain's policy towards Europe. As such, the review process reveals the importance of European co-operation for Britain, but confirms that despite the FTA, the Macmillan government departed little from traditional British attitudes pursued in the post-war period. It was these attitudes which would be called into question by the French counter-plan in the Maudling Committee negotiations.

There were two common denominators in departmental submissions on Britain's external policies: first, the necessity of maintaining the value of sterling as an international currency, and second, Britain's dependence on trade for the health of its economy, its living standards and its international position. In its review, the Foreign Office re-stated the main policy goal pursued in common with the United States and other allies, namely 'the prevention of global war and the spread of Communism'. However, revealing the relationship between foreign and economic policy, the Office added that the United Kingdom also pursued the individual goal of gaining through trade 'the strength to play [its] part in these international objectives'.[5] According to the Commonwealth Relations Office, Britain's global status was dependent on its leadership of the Commonwealth, which set it aside from Continental European powers.[6] This leadership was preserved by political ties but more significantly by economic links, mainly the volume of intra-Commonwealth trade and the status of sterling as the currency of the Sterling Area. For Britain, as the Treasury noted, the international value of sterling was 'a matter of life or death'.[7]

Since the early 1950s, British governments had sought the international convertibility of sterling not as an end in itself but as a means of freeing multilateral trade. In its review of external economic aims, the Treasury explained that Britain survived by buying, processing and selling: 'Thus we must import; and therefore must

earn the means of paying for our imports by exporting. Freedom
from restrictions for our exports must always be more important
for us than liberty to keep out imports from others'.[8] Consequently,
Britain would seek to increase access to markets and play a full
part in international institutions designed to promote the expansion of world trade (IMF, GATT and OEEC). It would also seek,
through the European FTA, 'to ensure that the E.E.C. [was] an instrument of freedom not restriction'. The British government had
sponsored the FTA for a number of reasons, but one of the priorities
had been to protect access to European markets. In the first half of
1958, the world economic situation made this vital. Officials predicted
a decline in world trade and economic conditions due mainly to
the recession in the United States, a lull in European industrial
production, and a weakening of commodity prices. In such an economic climate, export prices would be critical in maintaining overseas
trade and ministers recognised that all steps should be taken to
stimulate exports. At the same time, it was suggested that 'the only
major component of world trade likely to continue expanding [was]
intra-European trade'.[9] Thus, European markets would be essential
for British exports.

Britain's European policy had been designed to maintain the *status
quo* in wider foreign and economic policy while meeting the development of the Common Market. It was framed to gain access to
Continental markets for manufactured goods while sustaining protection for British agriculture and the system of preferential trade
with the Commonwealth. There would be no concessions on
Commonwealth trade or on tariff policy as a whole. However, the
prospect of surpassing this position was raised in the working party
of permanent secretaries which prepared the review of Britain's world
situation for ministers. On 18 February 1958, officials debated the
possibility of going 'in with Europe' and abandoning 'the attempt
to synthesize co-operation with Europe on the one hand, and the
Commonwealth and the United States on the other'.[10] The response
was reminiscent of arguments rehearsed since 1945:

Our economic prosperity was dependent on world trading, and
the maintenance of sterling as an international trading currency.
We were a part of each of the three important international groupings: the Commonwealth, the Anglo-American nexus, and Europe.
We could not cut ourselves off from the Commonwealth, nor
abandon our relationship of 'inter-dependence' with the United

States, and still hope to maintain our world-wide trading position and the international status of sterling. . . . Our present policies, which were designed to maintain our position in each of these three groupings, were broadly acceptable.

This analysis was eventually accepted by ministers even though officials concluded that additional resources to continue these aims could not be found from reductions in Britain's overseas commitments.[11] From Whitehall's viewpoint, the three circles policy was ingeniously devised to maximise external relations. The FTA was an extension of this traditional policy aiming to secure the best of all worlds for Britain. From the very beginning, however, this had been inimical to many on the Continent, especially the French, who argued with justification that the British would achieve disproportionate benefits to those enjoyed by their FTA partners. In early 1958, the formulation of these objections in a French counter-plan revealed an incompatibility within the three circles policy which held serious consequences for Britain's position in world affairs.

The French counter-plan

Harold Macmillan returned to Downing Street after a six-week tour of the Commonwealth on 14 February noting that he faced 'All the same problems – all important, and all insoluble'.[12] Certainly, the complications of the FTA negotiations had worsened. On 20 February, the Cabinet Secretary, Sir Norman Brook, informed the prime minister that some members of the Cabinet 'were evidently anxious about the scale and nature of any concessions which [the government] might need to make, particularly in the politically sensitive areas such as agriculture, if the negotiations were to succeed'.[13] The following day, Macmillan noted in his diary that the French were being 'very difficult'.[14] These concerns were quickly worsened by the French counter-plan's proposals.

The FTA negotiations had not got off to a good start in 1958 with all effectively in limbo until the details of the French plan were known. The two Maudling Committee meetings, of 15–16 January and 17–18 February, had only confirmed the difficulties faced by the OEEC negotiators. Despite Maudling's positive public portrayal of the meetings, Bretherton described the first as 'profoundly depressing' and noted after the second that it had been 'ten months since the same body tackled [the] same problems in more or less the same form'.[15] Postponed from the autumn, agriculture was the main subject for the Maudling Committee. Discussion centred on Britain's 'Draft Outline of an Agreement on Agriculture and Fisheries' which had been submitted to the OEEC on 6 January.[16] The draft agreement made a number of proposals including annual reviews of prices and trade; confrontation of members' domestic policies; elimination of quantitative restrictions; commodity arrangements; controls on subsidies and a complaints procedure. It did not, however, commit Britain to the abolition of tariffs on agricultural trade and thus effectively blocked increased access to British markets.[17] While these suggestions represented an advance on the original FTA White Paper position, they adhered to Cabinet decisions taken in October 1957 to maintain Britain's domestic policy and preferential trade with the Commonwealth and to avoid the political ramifications of a substantive agricultural concession (Macmillan had only recently been reminded of Commonwealth sensitivities on this issue during his tour).[18]

The mid-January Maudling Committee referred the agriculture question to discussions between the Six, Denmark and Britain with the aim of reviewing the results in March. At that stage, the Swiss delegation submitted a memorandum to strike a compromise solution.[19] Still, the fundamental divergence between British policy and the plans of the Six precluded agreement even though neither Britain nor the Six wanted to see free trade in agriculture. What the EEC envisaged was a short-term preference system to meet French proclivities and a long-term Common Agriculture Policy (CAP).[20] While the German government sought to engineer a settlement on this issue, it could not secure British flexibility.[21] As long as Britain was committed to trade with the Commonwealth and protection for domestic agriculture, it could not co-operate in a European agriculture policy which precluded preferential trade with third countries. Consequently, agriculture remained a divisive issue until the FTA negotiations' failure in December 1958. It was also complicated by the fact that the Six had not finalised their own agriculture arrangements (the CAP was agreed in January 1962).[22]

On 30 January 1958, Maudling submitted a progress report to Cabinet.[23] Although he noted that the three main problems (agriculture, the external tariff and the attitude of France) were not 'in the long run insoluble', Maudling failed to present any concrete solutions. Instead, he reminded his colleagues of the threat posed by the Six to British interests:

I have become more than ever impressed by the dangers of failing to reach an agreement. The European Economic Community
has now been launched; the Six countries are committed to forming
one single economy based on 160 million hard-working people,
including some of the ablest scientific and technological nations
in the world. If no Free Trade Area agreement is achieved, this new
industrial giant will increasingly overshadow our trading future
throughout the world. The centre of gravity in European economic affairs will shift inexorably to Bonn (or Paris). The smaller
Continental countries will have willy-nilly to come to terms with
the Six. The attractions of the Continental market will grow in
the eyes of the Commonwealth, and the power of the Six to
compete with us in Commonwealth markets will steadily increase.

Maudling's extreme prediction of the EEC having the potential to
dominate almost three-quarters of Britain's trade was deliberate. His
memorandum closed with a warning: ' . . . the negotiations will be
hard, and we shall be pressed more and more on many points. I
am not at this moment asking my colleagues to give me any more
elbow room in the negotiations. But I should warn them that the
time may come when I shall have to do so'. During the first few
months of the FTA negotiations it had become clear to Maudling
that success would only be achieved through significant British
concessions. To obtain Cabinet consideration of such concessions,
it seems that Maudling was not totally candid about the FTA's chances
with his colleagues. While he told them that the problems were
not insoluble, he also told Frank Lee that he was pessimistic about
the negotiations' future and, despite Treasury reluctance, authorised Board of Trade studies of alternative projects in case of the
FTA's failure.[24]

Prior to Britain receiving the details of the French counter-plan,
there were indications that France's position towards the FTA had
hardened. Gaillard made a particularly negative speech in Lille on
27 January in which he stated that his government did 'not intend
to embark on an adventure that might threaten either the economy
of the country or the building of Europe that [was] going on within
the Common Market'.[25] Although Gaillard's speech probably catered
for its sceptical audience of commercial and trades union
representatives, Jebb found it 'unfortunate and rather disquieting'.[26]
Similarly, Lloyd had received the impression from Pineau that the
French wished to delay the FTA negotiations.[27] Wider policy also

led Whitehall to question French interest in co-operation with Britain. It was during the first half of 1958 that French–Italian–German (FIG) collaboration on arms production and development fully got under way.[28] This initiative would be abandoned after General de Gaulle's return to power in June 1958, but it was initially seen by Makins at least as another sign 'of French inclination to disengage from [a] close Anglo-French relationship' and led to the conclusion that Whitehall 'ought now to reckon seriously with the prospect that the French will block an agreement on the Free Trade Area'.[29] This was a fair assessment of the French position. On 9 January 1958, French Ministers had been unable to agree a policy except that Britain's plan was impossible; only a minority of Ministers wished to see some form of FTA whereas a majority rejected it but could not see how this could be politically implemented.[30] While one historian doubts whether the French developed their counter-plan to end the FTA negotiations, it is clear that their conception of it was completely at odds with that of the British.[31]

Whitehall was determined not to kow-tow to further French-initiated delay in the FTA negotiations; at the Foreign Office Wright was typical in rejecting the French 'go-slow' arguing that 'the longer the negotiations drag on the more likely they are to founder'.[32] Nevertheless, as further confirmation of its inability to control the Maudling negotiations, the Macmillan government had no choice but to accommodate the complications caused by France. The French counter-plan was revealed during discussions between Lloyd and Faure on 6 March 1958 when a member of the British staff in Paris managed to glance at a copy of the French document.[33] Apart from the relatively minor point that the French wished to see the FTA renamed as the 'Union for European Economic Co-operation', there were essentially four proposals. First, the French suggested that there be three years *décalage* (or delay) between the commencement of the Common Market and that of the Union. This was a reversion to suggestions made by the French during the previous autumn. Second, the scope of the new Union would be determined on a sector basis, industry-by-industry, with variable trade arrangements according to different industries settled via negotiation. Third, the French reiterated their demands that external tariff rates on imports into the Union be harmonised. This would settle the problem of Union members paying different prices for imports of basic materials. Wormser had previously said that the French would never accept a FTA in which some countries (namely Britain) imported basic materials at a low tariff rate, and exported semi-manufactured and manufactured goods produced from those materials duty free.[34] This, Wormser argued, would put those French industries which paid substantial tariffs on basic materials imported from the United States out of business. Finally, the French addressed their long-term criticism that via the FTA and the system of imperial preference, Britain would enjoy a uniquely privileged position in both Europe and the Commonwealth. Consequently, France proposed that members of the new Union share the preferential markets of the Commonwealth, so enabling European exporters to sell a negotiated quota of their products to the Commonwealth at the imperial tariff rate rather than the most-favoured-nation rate agreed by the GATT. The justification for this demand was that by excluding agriculture from the Union, the British would deprive France and other members of compensation in the agricultural field for the opening of their markets, duty free, to British industrial exports. This was more important to the French since they had given up on pursuing an agriculture concession from Britain. On 11 March, Faure had told Maudling that there was little between the French and British positions on agriculture.[35]

The French had always argued that the FTA had the potential to destroy the very favourable terms they had secured in the Common Market negotiations. In a FTA, the French economy would be exposed to competition not just with its EEC partners, but also the other eleven OEEC members. Such a prospect had produced the National Assembly's January 1957 *Ordre du Jour* which demanded that the FTA include for France 'guarantees equivalent to those envisaged for the Common Market'.[36] This had always raised the possibility of French insistence on the translation of its EEC safeguards into the FTA Convention. Considering the contents of the counter-plan, French policy can therefore be seen as constant. *Décalage* would give French industries protection from seventeen-nation competition in the short-term, leaving those outside the Six at a disadvantage until the FTA was inaugurated three years after the EEC's 1 January 1959 tariff and quota reductions. It would also ensure EEC pre-eminence in Europe for the same period. Via the sectoral approach, France would have the potential to protect those industries it believed would suffer from European competition, eliminating free trade where it wished to do so. Harmonisation of external tariffs would have wiped away the advantages that low tariff countries would enjoy on imports of basic materials by creating a common external tariff on certain products. Finally, securing access to Britain's preferential Commonwealth markets would, on the one hand, weaken Britain's privileges, and on the other, provide possibly lucrative markets for French exports. The *Economist* predicted that Australia would be an ideal export market to meet booming motor car production in France which in January 1958 had come near to British and German levels of output.[37]

Singly and collectively these propositions were inimical to Britain's concept of the FTA. *Décalage* would have denied parallel introduction of the FTA with the EEC, upon which London placed great importance to avoid losing the initiative in European co-operation. The sector approach, apart from holding no guarantee of ultimate agreement on an industry-by-industry basis, would potentially have restricted access to French export markets for British manufactures and jeopardised the concept of industrial free trade. Figgures believed that this would fundamentally alter the FTA and involve Britain in '*de facto* membership of a Customs Union'.[38] Harmonisation of external tariffs, albeit on basic materials imports, endangered Britain's aim of maintaining liberal rules of origin for goods and a low tariff regime, and would also limit Britain's national autonomy in imposing tariffs on imports from third countries. Finally, France's proposal for sharing Britain's preferences in Commonwealth markets amounted to a threat, from London's perspective, to the FTA negotiations and to Britain's wider commercial policy. It had always been Whitehall's aim to maintain its trade within the 'walled garden' of the Commonwealth, unaffected by trade relations with Europe via the FTA.[39] Hence the original British decision to pursue a purely industrial FTA rather than a customs union, which would have included a common external tariff and deprived Britain of protection for its agriculture industry. In sum, the four proposals of the French counter-plan would transform the FTA and with it, Britain's trading patterns. By setting the price for their agreement to a FTA on limited external tariff harmonisation and sharing Commonwealth preferences, the French had exposed the Achilles heel of Britain's external economic policy and, in the process, the incompatibility of British policy in two of its three circles. Consequently, the Macmillan government faced the difficult dilemma of making concessions in Commonwealth policy to secure the European FTA, or rejecting French demands and risking the collapse of its European policy. Either course would mean reassessment of Britain's position in world affairs.

Whitehall's response

Britain could not immediately reject the French counter-plan. Such a move would have been premature as the Gaillard government had made no official submission to the Maudling Committee; it would also have risked Britain incurring responsibility for a breach in the negotiations. Moreover, France's EEC partners had made their doubts about the counter-plan clear to Whitehall. According to the German Foreign Ministry, it had not found favour in Bonn and a representative of the Belgian government 'expressed the fervent hope that [Britain] should never see the [counter-plan] because he feared a violent reaction'.[40] There were similar views from the Dutch, the Italians and the European Commission which had joined the Maudling Committee negotiations after its formation in January 1958.[41] However, London also received less encouraging reports. Although Hallstein, President of the European Commission, had told Maudling that the French counter-plan would have to be altered, he also noted how disturbed he was by the amount of technical work still necessary in the FTA negotiations.[42] Worse, senior Dutch officials warned Britain that the Belgians, Luxembourgers, Italians and Germans would feel EEC-bound to back the French.[43] On returning from meetings at the Bank of International Settlements in Basle, Bank of England officials also had the impression that the Five would 'support the French even if this meant no Free Trade Area'.[44]

The Maudling Committee meeting of 11–14 March 1958 exposed the disparity in British and French views which had characterised the FTA negotiations until that point, and would do so until the end of the negotiations in December 1958. With tempers raised on both sides, Maudling pulled no punches during what was described as 'a vigorous discussion' and 'a frank encounter' with Faure over dinner on 11 March.[45] In official session, Maudling threatened a crisis in the negotiations because of France's position and caused Faure 'great discomfort' by demanding indication, within a month or so, of whether the negotiations would succeed or fail. Faure protested that he could not meet this deadline, being unsure of Cabinet support.[46] To break this stalemate, and to try to modify the French position, the Six announced that the European Commission would revise the French counter-plan with the aim of submitting it to the Maudling Committee at the end of April. The work would be undertaken by a committee chaired by Roger Ockrent, the Belgian permanent delegate to the OEEC.[47] For the Macmillan government, this was a mixed blessing. It avoided immediate collapse caused by the French plan but gave the European Commission effective control of the FTA negotiations' timetable. Bretherton was right to see great danger in this; the European Commission would not present a revised counter-plan to the Maudling Committee until October 1958.[48] In the meantime, the FTA negotiations were on hold. This was exemplified by the Maudling Committee meeting of 31 March. Lasting only five hours, ministers used the excuse of a threatened French railway strike to leave Paris rapidly, but the reality was that while the European Commission revised the French plan, the Maudling Committee could make no significant progress.[49] As Hugh Jones of the Foreign Office lamented, 'things [were] grinding to a halt'.[50]

Macmillan's reaction to this situation after a discussion with Maudling on 17 March was to suggest that France be offered special treatment in the FTA.[51] This would have amounted to delaying French membership while the other FTA members proceeded. In Eccles's words: 'The solution seemed to be to form the club and let the French pay their subscription when they felt able'.[52] However, this idea was rapidly dismissed as officials predicted – accurately, as it turned out – that a special position would be rejected by France and the Six.[53] The Dutch opposed the idea in the strongest terms and in a speech on 20 March in Strasbourg, Hallstein stressed that 'the Six-Power Community [could] only accept measures which [left] the community itself inviolate'.[54] Although Maudling recommended to Cabinet on 21 March that a special position for France be examined, after further European objections, the idea was dropped.[55] British ministers had still not grasped that cohesion and unity were the priorities of the EEC powers.

With no alternative, therefore, the Macmillan government had to deal with the demands of the French counter-plan. Consequently, in spring 1958, Whitehall considered an unprecedented concession to the Six which aimed to either secure the FTA or ensure that Britain would not shoulder the responsibility for the failure of the negotiations. The concession did not come from sharing Commonwealth preferences. There was unanimous agreement, both at ministerial and official level, that Britain had to kill this aspect of the French proposals.[56] Officials explained the issue succinctly:

For the United Kingdom, much is at stake. We receive preferences on about 25 per cent of our total [Commonwealth] exports

– the same proportion as our exports to Europe. Whether in the last resort we should sacrifice one in order to hold the other is a nice economic judgement. But it is contrary to the basis on which we have considered the Free Trade Area so far; to inject the preferences and to bring the 'Southern Dominions' into the bargaining would create a new negotiation.[57]

There was also the concern that members of the Commonwealth, particularly Australia and New Zealand, might wish to negotiate with the Six to gain access to European markets, possibly bargaining away British preferences in their own markets. Clarke's analysis was typical: 'we should be buying agreement with Europe at an altogether excessive price if we prejudiced the 75 per cent [of our exports] outside Europe for the benefit of the 25 per cent within'.[58] Given the support for the three circles policy described above, this conclusion is not surprising. Constrained by its own policies, the Macmillan government could not offer the Six a concession on Commonwealth preferences. Thus, it turned its attention to the most divisive issue in the FTA negotiations.

Defining the origin of goods to qualify for FTA treatment had always been much more than a technical issue. It represented the basic distinction between the Six's Common Market, which would be surrounded by a common external tariff on imports from third countries, and the FTA, which would allow its members to retain external tariff autonomy. As instructed by the Maudling Committee during the previous autumn, the OEEC's Group of Trade Experts completed their report on the origin question at the end of January 1958.[59] This clearly exposed the deadlock between the French view and the contrary British view. The French, supported by the Italians and Belgians, argued that without a common external tariff, free trade would be deflected by the disparity in imports of basic materials, semi-manufactures and components between high and low tariff members. Low tariff countries would import basic materials at a cheaper price than high tariff countries. This would enable them to sell manufactured goods, produced with low cost materials, within the FTA, putting high tariff members at a trade disadvantage. Their manufactures would be produced using more expensive materials thus raising their market price and reducing their competitiveness. Consequently, the French, Italians and Belgians believed this problem ought to be eradicated by external tariff harmonisation agreed before the inauguration of the FTA. Hence the proposal incorporated in the French counter-plan for limited harmonisation. Conversely, Britain, supported by others in the OEEC, preferred a wait and see policy and suggested that problems would be eliminated by defining the origin of FTA goods with customs certificates including rules of percentage content and processing criterion.[60] In simple terms, what this divergence represented was France's desire to construct a protectionist Europe in which to modernise its economy and Britain's interest in perpetuating the system of preferential trade with the Commonwealth. The issue of origin, therefore, went to the heart of the Anglo-French dispute.

In mid-March 1958, the Italian Minister of Foreign Trade, Guido Carli, submitted a compromise plan to the Maudling Committee on the origin question.[61] This was proof of the anxiety of France's EEC partners to achieve progress in the FTA negotiations. The Carli Plan entailed the creation of a tariff band, with maximum and minimum limits, within which FTA members could fix their own tariffs on imports from third countries. Any commodity which was imported by a member country within this tariff band would qualify for FTA treatment. However, member countries could maintain tariffs outside of the tariff band, but where they did so, goods produced using materials imported at such tariff rates would be liable to compensatory taxes, thus raising their market price.[62] This proposal was, in effect, tariff harmonisation 'by a round-about route'.[63] The threat of compensating taxes on goods made from materials imported at tariffs outside of the agreed band would tend to force tariff rates closer together, or harmonise them. The initial British reaction to Carli's proposals was one of scepticism; harmonisation of external tariffs was inimical to Britain's commercial policy. Bretherton felt that the Plan was 'nonsense, and probably dangerous nonsense' but ruled out immediate rejection, seeing negotiating advantage in keeping it alive.[64] This became Britain's position in the short-term and was the governing factor in remitting the Carli Plan to the OEEC's Steering Board for Trade.[65]

At this stage Whitehall began to consider softening its position on the origin issue even though it was increasingly admitted that the FTA's prospects were bleak. For example, in a diary entry of 17 March, Macmillan wrote that 'It looks as if the French are determined to wreck [the FTA]', and on 1 April Maudling warned the Cabinet that the Five seemed to be unwilling to apply pressure to France.[66] Despite these predictions, the Macmillan government considered a concession to the Six for two reasons. First, origin was the key issue in the negotiations. As Clarke suggested, failure to find a solution would mean failure of the FTA negotiations; on the other hand, if the wrong solution was found on French lines, British trade would suffer.[67] As Britain had to do something to regain the initiative in the FTA negotiations, either to achieve their success or their failure, and in case of the latter, to avoid blame, addressing the origin issue was imperative.

Second, Britain received external encouragement from the United States and Germany. In late March, Douglas Dillon, Deputy Under-Secretary of State for Economic Affairs in the Eisenhower Administration, assured the British Ambassador to Washington, Sir Harold Caccia, that 'we in the United States Government are alert to the unhappy consequences for Europe, and for the Atlantic Area as a whole, which might result from the ultimate failure to work out a suitable form of association between the Six and the other OEEC member countries'.[68] This was appreciated by the Foreign Office; Edden minuted that 'The move away from American "passivity" on the Free Trade Area is indeed welcome, if a little late in the day', and Gore-Booth believed the Americans had 'seen the light' over the FTA.[69] Whitehall did not seem to grasp, however, that the change in American policy was based on national interests and did not represent a significant shift from long-term American preference for the Treaties of Rome. For political reasons, Washington wished to see stability in the western alliance, but more significantly, for economic reasons, it was seriously concerned that a FTA agreement would include French proposals for sharing preferences and an industry-by-industry approach.[70] As the American economy entered sharp decline in 1958, the prospect of being walled out of a Europe controlled by a preferential bloc built around the EEC and the FTA forced American intervention. US diplomatic missions in Europe were to assist the FTA negotiations and promote common action amongst the Six to mitigate extreme French positions.[71] By this approach Washington hoped to reinforce liberal elements, sustain European-wide trade liberalisation and multilateralism, encourage economic growth and facilitate currency convertibility.[72] But the State Department always stressed to its diplomatic missions that at no point should the cohesion of the EEC be jeopardised by divisions over the FTA.[73] Whitehall's misjudgement of these motives would cause it to despair at the lack of American assistance in the second half of 1958 when the FTA negotiations reached crisis point.

The British government was also encouraged to move in the FTA negotiations by meetings between Macmillan and Adenauer in London from 16–18 April 1958. Whitehall placed great weight on the German chancellor's visit as perhaps the last hope of advancing the FTA negotiations.[74] Macmillan employed a mixture of European rhetoric and Cold War threats to implore Adenauer to intervene on Britain's behalf with the French. He depicted the failure of the FTA as a Cold War catastrophe with political, economic and strategic repercussions: 'The Russians would score their biggest triumph since the war, if we had to set up a counter-organisation to compete with the Six.'[75] In response, Adenauer's emphasis on securing agreement between Britain and the Six and his assurance of impressing this on Hallstein led the British to see the meeting as a success.[76] Forceful diplomacy had seemingly overcome the Bonn Embassy's recent warnings of 'misunderstandings' and 'friction' in Anglo-German relations based on uncertainty about British policy in Europe; writing in his diary after the meetings with Adenauer, Macmillan was confident, noting that they had 'certainly helped to counteract the poison which the French have been pouring into his ears'.[77]

In fact, wider events, not Macmillan's diplomacy, had led to the more positive German tone at the April meetings. As Adenauer arrived in London, the Gaillard government resigned amid further crisis in France.[78] Thus western European stability was all important; there can be no doubt that the German chancellor hoped to avoid division over the FTA at this stage.[79] Adenauer had also received briefs from the otherwise cautious German Foreign Office casting the FTA in a better light. This derived from awareness of new American interest in a FTA agreement, German industry's pro-FTA position, and a concern to safeguard the EEC from British retaliatory action in the trade field.[80] The temporary result was the strengthening of those sections of the German government more favourable to British policy, namely Erhard and his State Secretary Müller-Armack who were developing compromise proposals.[81] Consequently, Whitehall's tactical approach towards the FTA negotiations continued: reliance on German influence within the EEC and joint effort with the Scandinavians in the OEEC.[82] There was no alternative to this strategy but believing that its diplomacy had generated German support for a FTA agreement, the Macmillan government proceeded under some misapprehension about the German position.[83] The British were soon to discover that they expected too much of the Federal government.

Against this background, Whitehall developed policy on the origin question. Finding a solution had become essential as OEEC studies of the Carli Plan had produced no progress.[84] Furthermore, it did not bode well that the European Commission was floating suggestions to stall the FTA negotiations and reach an interim agreement to avoid trade discrimination caused by the EEC's 1 January 1959 tariff and quota reductions.[85] The modification in British policy came from an intense period of Whitehall deliberation from 1 to 20 May 1958. Britain was to propose simple origin rules for the first four-year stage of the FTA with negotiations to achieve low tariff rates on basic materials. It would concede external tariff harmonisation on machinery, textiles and chemicals, the latter having been demanded by the French, Italians and Belgians in the OEEC Group of Trade Experts' report.[86] Otherwise, normal origin rules (percentage content and processing criterion) would apply to manufactured goods but there would be provision for compensation taxes in certain cases.[87] For the Macmillan government, this represented a distinct advance from the original FTA position which had envisaged the universal application of simple origin rules for all goods and categorically rejected any external tariff harmonisation.[88]

It was a measure of the changing attitudes towards Britain's external economic policy that officials 'generally agreed' that 'a breakdown in the Free Trade Area negotiations . . . would be so serious that on balance it would be justifiable to take the calculated risks inherent in trying to negotiate a settlement' on the origin question.[89] Not all were convinced of this. There is no record of which personalities or departments in the crucial Economic Steering Committee meetings took opposing sides. Nevertheless, when the long-term support for the FTA from the Board of Trade, Treasury and Foreign Office is considered, it is safe to say that these departments supported the origin concession. Conversely, given their reluctance to see economic links with the Commonwealth weakened in favour of Europe, it is probable that the Commonwealth Relations Office and the Colonial Office argued against the concession on tariff autonomy fearing it would lead to disintegration in British–Commonwealth trade links.[90]

Underlining the significance of these issues, on 15 May 1958 Macmillan reconvened his *ad hoc* FTA Cabinet committee which had been in abeyance for ten months.[91] Acting upon his warning earlier in January, Maudling asked his colleagues for latitude in the FTA negotiations.[92] Although concerns about the effect on

Commonwealth trade were raised, ministers agreed that Britain had no alternative option in the FTA negotiations other than the origin concession. It is not surprising that this found support from the prime minister. Throughout Plan G's formulation Macmillan had argued that the Commonwealth preference system could not remain unaltered in the future. In September 1956, for example, he had said that 'the Commonwealth countries will wish to bargain if we retain preferences. But we are in for this anyway. . . . In the long run it may be easier to make bargains of this kind on the basis of a big policy . . .'.[93] Only the president of the Board of Trade disputed the origin concession in May 1958.[94] Eccles predicted a gradual erosion of Britain's Commonwealth preferences if the government conceded any tariff harmonisation in the FTA. Given the French governmental crisis and the forthcoming Commonwealth Trade and Economic Conference, Eccles also suggested that now was not the time to enter into negotiations with the Europeans. The president had not been prompted by his officials to take this stance; Sir Frank Lee fully supported Maudling's proposals.[95] Instead, this episode was symptomatic of Eccles' personal hostility towards yielding to the Europeans, a fact which caused friction with the views of Lee on many occasions.[96]

Ministers did accept Eccles' arguments on timing, agreeing that the origin concession be subject to Commonwealth agreement and conditioned by any major constitutional developments in France.[97] Nevertheless, on substance, the Economic Policy Committee recommended that Maudling implement the origin concession. The necessity of securing access to European markets had won the day. Still, the concession was not unconditional. Its limits were to be firm sticking points even if this entailed a breakdown in the negotiations. Furthermore, the policy would also have to be endorsed by the Commonwealth, the FBI, the NFU and the TUC. Nevertheless, there is no doubt that from the British viewpoint, the acceptance of limited tariff harmonisation on basic materials and for certain industrial sectors represented a far-reaching concession to French demands. Whether the French, together with the Italians and Belgians, would have received it as such is questionable. Britain's proposals were carefully and cleverly designed to circumvent the immediate problem by promising negotiation on basic materials tariffs and by offering the inducement of tariff harmonisation on machinery, textiles and chemicals. It was hoped that this would bring enough satisfaction to ensure early agreement on the FTA, leaving the detailed negotiations until after signature of the Convention. Yet because of Britain's scarcely concealed intention to retain low or nil tariffs on basic materials imports as well as maintain Commonwealth free entry, it is likely that the French, Italians and Belgians would have found the proposals unacceptable and stalled or ended the negotiations. There may also have been others in the Six who might have seen the British proposals as a complication for their own unfinished negotiations on basic materials tariffs under List G of the Treaties of Rome.[98] Conversely, British movement on the origin issue may have been enough to force the FTA negotiations forward by generating support amongst the Six, particularly amongst the Dutch and Germans.

Ultimately, this debate is hypothetical as events precluded Britain from implementing its origin concession. In May 1958 France moved closer to constitutional crisis as the Algerian problem threatened to destroy the Fourth Republic.[99] There was also further delay for the Maudling Committee as the European Commission agreed with the French request to postpone the Ockrent Committee's report on the FTA for a month; in fact, as Sir John Coulson estimated, the delay would be closer to four months given the upcoming holiday season.[100] Thus in Cabinet on 22 May, when ministers were to give their final approval to the FTA concession, Maudling himself had to admit that the political situation in France made it difficult to foresee the future attitude of the French government towards both the Treaties of Rome and the FTA.[101] In these circumstances, it was thought best to defer further consideration of the origin problem until the French position became clearer. Britain, it could be argued, had given up a chance to take the high ground in the FTA negotiations at this stage when the French were without firm political direction. After rejecting the Carli Plan in early May, Britain could have regained some initiative by announcing its advance on the origin question.[102] This was certainly seen by one official as a missed opportunity.[103] Instead, given de Gaulle's outspoken criticism of supranational integration, British ministers probably wondered whether their previous doubts about France ever implementing a European Common Market would be finally justified. In this scenario, the need for a concession to the Six on origin was questionable.

The crisis in France also altered the perspective of those Whitehall officials closely involved in FTA policy. As they were recommending that ministers accept the concession on origin, key officials seemed to be turning away from full-scale, seventeen-nation FTA negotiations and looking towards a breakdown followed by negotiations of a much smaller kind. This supports the view that the origin concession was expected to either secure the FTA or otherwise ensure that the negotiations broke amicably, allowing Britain to move swiftly to a post-FTA policy. On 5 May, Bretherton suggested that the chances of achieving the FTA were very slight and recommended 'systematic consideration' of alternative options.[104] In 1955 it had been the Board of Trade that had pioneered the FTA within Whitehall. Three years later, it was the same department which led policy on its replacement. From as early as January 1958, Board officials had been developing alternative courses and, by March, had decided on a Uniscan FTA, comprising Britain, Scandinavia and Switzerland, as the best choice.[105] Bretherton played a significant role in this; his support for the Uniscan FTA and his belief that the French proposals for sharing Commonwealth preferences should have represented a breaking point in the negotiations indicates that he had given up on the FTA in March 1958.[106] The Board also received encouragement outside of Whitehall from Scandinavian governments and from the FBI. During the first half of 1958, Scandinavian governments were increasingly pessimistic about the FTA's chances and encouraged Britain to consider a non-Six arrangement.[107] Scandinavian industrialists were of a similar view and began a process of co-ordination with the FBI which would eventually lead to the creation of the European Free Trade Association (EFTA) once the FTA negotiations had collapsed.[108]

Outside of the Board of Trade, there had been little support for alternative courses. For the Foreign Office, great political weight was attached to securing agreement with the Six; in early 1958 there had even been brief flirtation with abandoning the FTA for an Anglo-Six bilateral deal.[109] A non-Six arrangement thus held few attractions and the Office instead pursued co-operation with the Eisenhower Administration to influence the OEEC negotiations.[110] The Treasury had also initially rejected the Board's initiative.[111] Regional groupings were inimical to the Treasury's primary policy of world-wide multilateralism and apart from the fact that a non-Six arrangement was thought to be a 'second-best' policy, Clarke believed it would be premature to consider alternatives until the FTA had reached crisis point.[112] Nevertheless, with French governmental crisis in May, the Treasury altered its view. Figgures discounted the FTA's chances and warned that 'the breakdown of the Free Trade Area negotiations creates the possibility of the division of Europe;

we must be careful that it does not lead to the effective isolation of the UK'.[113] Figgures believed that it would be desirable if the FTA negotiations broke down causing minimum loss of temper and leaving open the possibility of returning to them in the future. Clarke, though more cautious, was developing similar thoughts; on 13 May he advised Makins that the concession on origin would probably not meet the French position.[114] In the event of the FTA's failure, therefore, Clarke recommended that Britain should consider interim arrangements, continue OEEC trade liberalisation and the EPU, and seek rapid negotiation of a Uniscan FTA. During the second half of 1958, these ideas would become dominant. Once more in British policy towards European integration, the decision-making process in Whitehall would be instigated by officials rather than ministers. At ministerial level, acceptance of the FTA's failure would have to await Macmillan's forlorn attempt to benefit from the relations he had established with de Gaulle in Algiers in 1943.[115]

It is true that the FTA negotiations were in trouble before the collapse of the Fourth Republic in May 1958.[116] This much is clear from the examination of events from January onwards. It has even been suggested that given French hostility towards the whole FTA concept, there was little hope from the beginning of the negotiations in autumn 1957.[117] This may also be true, but what is sure is that from the moment the French counter-plan's proposals became known, the differences between the negotiators seemed insoluble. For Britain, the fact that the French remained unmoved in this period revealed that its tactical approach was ineffective. The Five may have criticised France's diplomacy but there was sympathy for the French position, born of the unity produced by the Rome Treaties.[118] In retrospect, even Maudling admitted that the French had many good arguments against the FTA but added that 'for every solution they could find a new problem'.[119] The French counter-plan was ingenious in that it offered the prospect of success if the British wanted to pay a high price, but potentially avoided responsibility for the breakdown of the Maudling Committee being shouldered by France. The widespread speculation in Whitehall from January to May 1958 that the French aimed to wreck the FTA negotiations was probably warranted. It is not too difficult to imagine that the French had chosen the vexed issue of origin and sharing Commonwealth preferences as their line of attack.

The Macmillan government's response to these proposals reveals the progression and also the limitations of British attitudes towards

European co-operation. The origin concession represented a significant advance in British policy going further towards external tariff harmonisation than had previously been envisaged. In this, the striking factor was the majority in favour of the concession amongst both ministers and officials. Just as striking, however, was the unanimity against sharing Commonwealth preferences with the Europeans. Whitehall was right to rule this out in March/April 1958. It would have meant suspending the Maudling Committee negotiations, opening negotiations with the Commonwealth, ensuring that the result was acceptable to all seventeen OEEC states and Commonwealth countries, and then applying to the GATT for a waiver which was unlikely under the no-new-preferences rule. It would also have probably fallen foul of the Eisenhower Administration's defence of multilateralism and, apart from this, it is debatable whether such a concession would have secured the FTA, especially given French political instability. It now appears that only through a final caesura in the FTA negotiations could Britain embark upon a re-evaluation of its European policy and its place in a changing world. In the event, it would be General de Gaulle who would act as the catalyst for this fundamental reassessment.

8
The Demise of the Free Trade Area, June–December 1958

General de Gaulle's return to power in June 1958 created a period of short-lived uncertainty about the prospects for European integration. British ministers were not alone in wondering whether the General's personal opposition to supranational schemes would jeopardise the implementation of the Treaties of Rome.[1] In Washington, the State Department considered that de Gaulle might favour the FTA over the Common Market as a looser arrangement.[2] There was also anxiety within the Adenauer government that the new French leader would frustrate its European policy. In what can only have been a brief knee-jerk reaction, the Foreign Minister, von Brentano, informed Macmillan that the Germans were considering slowing the Common Market down until it could proceed in parallel with the FTA.[3]

It soon became clear, however, that such measures would be unnecessary as de Gaulle's government affirmed continued French support for the Rome Treaties. Amid the pressing problems of Algeria, the constitution and the weak financial situation, the General embraced his predecessors' policy of securing France's future stability within a united Europe.[4] Moreover, he had done so with characteristic nationalism; according to Antoine Pinay, the Minister of Finance and Economic Affairs, de Gaulle favoured a European Community, 'but one built around France rather than France acting only as a partner therein'.[5] It was de Gaulle's pursuit of this policy and his skilful diplomacy, especially with the Adenauer government, which put an end to Britain's FTA. After a brief period in July 1958 when Whitehall believed de Gaulle might have accepted the FTA, the Macmillan government could do little as the French continued to block the Maudling negotiations. What ensued was a period of diplomatic manoeuvres with neither the French nor the British wanting to accept responsibility for the FTA's demise. When de Gaulle did eventually hasten the break in November, however, Britain did not retaliate despite Macmillan's belligerence within Whitehall in the preceding months. Even when its FTA policy had been rejected by the French, the Macmillan government could not afford to turn its back on Europe and consequently sought ways to maintain a relationship with the EEC.

False remission for the Free Trade Area

It was not until Macmillan's visit to Paris from 29–30 June 1958 that de Gaulle's endorsement of the Rome Treaties was fully grasped by the British. In the meantime, unsure of the French attitude, Whitehall prepared itself for failure rather than progress in the FTA negotiations. Maintaining their spring 1958 scepticism, officials worked rapidly towards a post-FTA policy by considering contingency plans.[6] To deal with trade discrimination after the EEC's 1 January 1959 tariff and quota reductions, Whitehall began preliminary consideration of the European Commission's proposal for a provisional agreement. Concurrently, the Economic Departments extended their studies of a possible Uniscan FTA.[7] Two factors had encouraged officials to contemplate the Maudling Committee's collapse. There had been early indications that the European Commission's revised version of the French counter-plan presented no basis for negotiation and also reports that de Gaulle's Foreign Minister, Maurice Couve de Murville, had ruled out completion of the FTA by 1 January 1959.[8]

These developments led the Prime Minister's *ad hoc* committee to conclude on 23 June that it was impossible to achieve a FTA by the end of the year.[9] Macmillan had told Butler privately that he feared the FTA would suffer as a result of the new French government.[10] Despite this concern, Ministers recommended further studies of a future agriculture concession and planned to apply diplomatic pressure to Germany and France via Maudling's meeting with Erhard and Macmillan's visit to Paris.[11] There are two explanations for the less fatalistic approach of ministers in comparison with their officials. First, there was little to be gained from aborting the negotiations when de Gaulle's policy was unknown and, furthermore, the Macmillan government did not wish to incur responsibility for the FTA's breakdown. Second, the prime minister still hoped to influence de Gaulle to follow a positive policy towards the FTA. Macmillan had first encountered the General while Minister Resident at Allied Headquarters in Algiers during the early 1940s.[12] According to his memoirs, he hoped to use this familiarity in favour of Britain's FTA policy when he met de Gaulle in Paris at the end of June.[13] However, Macmillan's statements prior to the Paris trip reveal that he may not have been too confident about dealing with the General.

At the close of his *ad hoc* FTA committee meeting on 23 June, Macmillan had warned ministers that if the FTA negotiations failed, 'our whole policy towards Europe would need to be reconsidered'.[14] In 1956, when the British government had formulated Plan G, and when doubts about the Common Market were prevalent, Britain had sought to avoid a fundamental re-evaluation in its relationship with Europe. As such, the FTA was a reactive policy designed to accommodate either the failure or the success of the Six. In the latter case, Whitehall had always affirmed that a Common Market without a FTA would be to Britain's disadvantage. It is only Macmillan's fear of this prospect which can explain his loss of composure in mid-summer. On 23 June he wrote in his diary that if efforts to engage German support failed, it would mean 'the end of much more than trade cooperation in Europe. I don't see how NATO could survive'.[15] He formalised these views the next day in a startling minute to the foreign secretary and the chancellor:

I think sometimes our difficulties with our friends abroad result from our natural good manners and reticence. We are apt not to press our points too strongly in the early stages of a negotiation, and then when a crisis arises and we have to take a definite position we are accused of perfidy. I feel we ought to make it quite clear to our European friends that if Little Europe is formed without a parallel development of a Free Trade Area we shall have to reconsider the whole of our political and economic attitude towards Europe. I doubt if we could remain in NATO. We should certainly put on highly protective tariffs and quotas to counteract what Little Europe was doing to us. In other words, we should not allow ourselves to be destroyed little by little. We would fight back with every weapon in our armoury. We would take our troops out of Europe. We would withdraw from NATO. We would adopt a policy of isolationism. We would surround ourselves with rockets and we would say to the Germans, the French and all the rest of them: 'Look after yourselves with your own forces. Look after yourselves when the Russians overrun your countries'. I would be inclined to make this position quite clear to both de Gaulle and Adenauer, so they that they may be under no illusion. What do you say?[16]

It is telling that neither Lloyd nor Amory had anything to say. Briefing the chancellor, Makins explained Macmillan's minute as 'an emotional reaction ... to the present state of negotiations on the Free Trade Area and their probable failure'.[17] The chancellor did not reply to the prime minister, doubting 'whether this isolationist policy is practicable'.[18] The fact that the Foreign Office also failed to respond to Macmillan indicates that it too rejected his analysis. This was the first of a number of occasions during the second half of 1958 when the prime minister's frustration at the FTA's demise resulted in aggressive and impractical outbursts. As the Maudling Committee negotiations reached crisis point, however, Macmillan found himself out of step with the majority of opinion in Whitehall which advocated calm rather than retaliation.

Macmillan travelled to Paris in the knowledge that Britain's European policy rested on his discussions with de Gaulle. Although Maudling's talks with Erhard in Bonn from 25–26 June had produced commitments to the FTA, the Germans had made less promising comments on the origin issue which revealed similarities with the French position.[19] But Macmillan did not go to discuss technicalities with the General who, Whitehall considered, did not understand economics.[20] Instead, the prime minister was to concentrate on the importance of retaining political cohesion in Europe which would be undermined should a split occur between the Six and the OEEC. The Macmillan–de Gaulle discussions from 29–30 June are significant in what they reveal of British and French priorities. By his own admission, Macmillan spoke 'very strongly' on the FTA and begged the General to turn his attention to the matter, warning that failure might spell the end of NATO.[21] In response, de Gaulle gave little indication of enthusiasm for the FTA; his government 'would be glad to listen to [Britain's] proposals, but they could not enter lightly into any agreement on the subject'. France had obligations under the Treaties of Rome and 'it was impossible for the French government to go fast'. The success of Macmillan's efforts was, therefore, dubious; he himself later noted that de Gaulle was 'clearly ... neither interested nor impressed'.[22] A review of the minutes of the meetings confirms that the French leader was preoccupied with other issues, such as the future of NATO, nuclear weapons development and Algeria.[23] Before departing from Paris, Macmillan once again pressed de Gaulle on the FTA and went so far as to leave a written exposition of his fears: 'Europe is already tragically divided from Stettin to Trieste and I am very anxious to avoid further division'.[24]

At the beginning of July 1958, Macmillan remained doubtful about the FTA's chances; 'I fear it looks as if the whole of this great effort will break down, foiled by the selfishness [and] insularity of the French.'[25] It was at this stage, however, that Whitehall received a good deal of evidence pointing towards a more positive French approach to the FTA negotiations. On 1 July, the Cabinet had been told that although de Gaulle was 'not well-informed' about the FTA, 'there was some hope that he might exert his personal authority to secure a resumption of practical negotiations in the near future'.[26] There was, therefore, a certain symmetry between Macmillan's Paris visit and reports that the French government had decided in principle to co-operate in the FTA negotiations.[27] This seemed to be confirmed by a letter from de Gaulle to Macmillan on 5 July.[28] The General stressed that France was 'not at all unfavourable, quite the contrary, to an enlargement of economic co-operation in Europe, in which Great Britain [was] naturally included'. He added, however, that some way had to be found of preserving both the equilibrium of France's economy and finances and the agreements reached by the Six. This in itself represented a strictly conditional advance on the previous French position but was augmented by reports of de Gaulle's comments to Dulles on 5 July. The American secretary of state informed Lloyd that 'On the free trade area, de Gaulle seemed to appreciate your preoccupations and [the] consequences of not reaching agreement with you on this matter. He indicated [that] he thought [a] compromise arrangement might be found'.[29] This was more promising, especially when matched with further reports of a new French interdepartmental committee on the FTA, in which the Quai d'Orsay had rejected the Ministry of Industry's opposition to any further participation by France in the FTA negotiations.[30] In response, and on the eve of the Maudling Committee meeting from 24–25 July, Macmillan replied to de Gaulle. He welcomed the General's interest in the FTA and assured him that his national preoccupations could be met in the negotiations.[31]

In spite of this apparent development in the French attitude towards the FTA, Whitehall remained sceptical of de Gaulle's policy.[32]

Although there were reports of a new French approach, the French had not moved significantly from their previous negotiating positions. Just before the Maudling Committee meeting, Whitehall was warned that the French wished to agree a common position amongst the Six before proceeding with the FTA negotiations.[33] Moreover, although they had dropped demands for *décalage* (delay between EEC and FTA development), the de Gaulle government retained key aspects of the original French counter-plan including escape clauses, eradication of trade distortion and sector analysis. To this list they had added unanimity for transition from phase to phase in the FTA.[34] This did not bode well and thus, on 22 July, Cabinet agreed that if the forthcoming Maudling Committee meeting failed to provide some advance, Britain would seek a temporary pause in the negotiations.[35] Preparing the ground for this possibility, Maudling proceeded to brief Scandinavian ministers of Britain's intentions.[36]

It was with surprise then, and some hope, that Maudling reported 'a change in the French attitude' to Macmillan after his Committee meeting of 24–25 July 1958.[37] Erhard had gone so far as to describe it as a '"break through", a view which was confirmed by the Dutch'. Maudling attributed this development to 'an important political decision' recently taken by the French Cabinet which saw the Quai's support for continued French involvement in the FTA negotiations overpower the arguments for withdrawal from the Ministry of Finance and the Ministry of Industry. According to Couve, Macmillan's letter to de Gaulle had been 'the decisive factor'. Although Maudling welcomed this development, he did warn the prime minister that the OEEC still faced significant problems and that the French Ministries of Finance and Industry might seek to obstruct the negotiations. Officials also admitted that even though the French seemed anxious to settle the FTA, if the de Gaulle government adhered to its present position, then there would be no chance for the Maudling negotiations.[38] Sir Frank Lee felt that 'the *general* outlook [was] pretty gloomy' and his concerns were justified as the events of July proved to be nothing more than an 'ephemeral burst of optimism'.[39]

Impasse

On 3 August 1958, Macmillan wrote a brief minute to Maudling: 'What is your *real* feeling about [the] F.T.A.? Is there a good chance of success?'.[40] The prime minister had been encouraged in this enquiry by the apparent advance of the recent Maudling Committee, but also by a submission from the president of the Board of Trade. Implying that the FTA negotiations were lost, Eccles dismissed the alternative promoted by his own officials; a Uniscan FTA 'would be a climb down – the engineer's daughter when the general-manager's had said no'.[41] The answer was something much grander: a United States–Canada–United Kingdom-Six free trade arrangement in manufactures with possible association of the Commonwealth in agriculture. Once again, Eccles had shown himself to be a maverick within Whitehall. His proposal, remarkable both for its overestimation of British influence and its misunderstanding of the global political economy, was rightly dismissed as unrealistic.[42] Maudling had some sympathy with Eccles' view of the Uniscan FTA in his reply to Macmillan on 5 August, but otherwise saw the president's ideas as impractical.[43] Obviously temporarily boosted by the July Committee meeting, Maudling was resolute:

> I believe the Free Trade Area is a fundamental British interest. There is no satisfactory alternative – indeed there may be no alternative at all. . . . I think there is little doubt that we shall have to face some awkward decisions but it is still my hope that they will be no more than awkward. But I do believe that so much work has now been done and so much impetus been given in Europe, and that so many of our friends, including the Germans, are now deeply attached to the whole concept of a Free Trade Area that the negotiations cannot, and will not be allowed to fail. . . . I conclude therefore that we must press on with the negotiations which, owing to the political impetus you have personally given at the highest level, can now continue on a genuine basis.

Macmillan agreed 'sincerely with this'.[44] However, the key FTA official, Otto Clarke, did not. Indicating that the Treasury was increasingly disillusioned with the FTA, Clarke had suggested prior to the July Maudling Committee that a forward movement by France would raise great difficulties for Britain, making it more difficult to break off the negotiations.[45] He was less pessimistic than Maudling about Britain's ability to live with the Common Market economically as long as a 'really vigorous' one world policy was pursued with the Commonwealth and the USA.[46] The real difficulty, according to Clarke, was political: 'if the Common Market does work itself up into a European Federation we shall become a poor No. 3 politically in the West instead of No. 2'. Clarke's answer, therefore, was to take further decisive steps towards sterling convertibility which, when achieved, might make Britain's priorities in Europe altogether different. In this respect, it is interesting that within a month, the chancellor of the exchequer recommended to the prime minister an early move on convertibility.[47]

Any optimism that British ministers had about the FTA negotiations was dashed by developments in French policy and by France's leadership of the Six during September 1958. It is now clear that when Adenauer visited de Gaulle at Colombey-les-deux Eglises on 17 September, the sceptical German chancellor was won over by the General's masterful diplomacy.[48] De Gaulle succeeded in assuring Adenauer of his interest in Franco-German relations and in the implementation of the Rome Treaties; *Die Welt* observed that 'more than one remark Konrad Adenauer made in the presence of journalists gave an inkling of the great weight that had been lifted from his heart'.[49] To contemporaries, the immediate product of Colombey was German agreement to French demands for the FTA negotiations during meetings of the Six in Venice from 18–20 September.[50] Confirmation of the deal struck by de Gaulle at this stage is provided by a copy of his brief for the Colombey meetings that was leaked to a member of the British delegation in Paris.[51] The brief's contents correspond with the development of EEC policy after 17 September. It recommended that the price for de Gaulle's support for the EEC and France's commitment to tariff and quota reductions on 1 January should be German acceptance of the French approach to the FTA negotiations. The French government would be prepared to consider a FTA but only if it preserved the basic interests of the French economy, allowed fair competition and did not compromise the development of the Rome Treaties. While the Germans, Italians, Belgians, and more reluctantly the Dutch, agreed to these French terms, the French were nevertheless isolated within the Six.[52] Recent research has suggested that while the Colombey meetings had gone generally well, Adenauer had defended Britain's FTA motives.[53] Furthermore, the Germans' acquiescence to French demands at Venice has been depicted not as acceptance of their position but as a means of avoiding further postponement of the Maudling Committee negotiations.[54]

To Whitehall, however, the French appeared to be gaining dominance within the EEC in autumn 1958. Ellis Rees reported that 'The Venice conference shows that our hopes were vain and there is a danger that if any agreed view emerges from these conferences it will be a French view'.[55] The implication of this was troubling for British policy as it sterilised the long-term strategy of applying pressure on the French via the Germans. In the technical discussions of the FTA negotiations themselves, this was particularly worrying given recent French tactics. The July 1958 Maudling Committee had agreed to Couve de Murville's insistence that the problem of defining the origin of goods should be analysed on a sector basis, industry-by-industry.[56] Consequently, the whole issue was remitted to the OEEC's Steering Board for Trade where Russell Bretherton represented the British government. This was a substantial concession on Britain's part meeting one of the demands of the March 1958 French counter-plan.[57] Whitehall could be forgiven for hoping that this would bring corresponding goodwill from Paris, but in the event it ran into 'unashamed French dilatory practice'.[58] The French had promised to submit a sector report in time for the Steering Board's meeting of 11 September but failed to do so.[59] Their excuse was an inability to identify industries requiring special treatment until they knew what the general treatment on origin would be. According to the Board of Trade's tariff division, 'The origin negotiations had now entered their lunatic phase, the French, in particular, having given up all pretence of co-operation'.[60] The French representative, Bernard Clappier, caused consternation on the Steering Board with the suggestion that it concentrate on universally applying the Carli Plan. This, of course, had been rejected by the British government in May 1958.

On 30 September, Maudling produced an explanation of these events for Macmillan.[61] Although there had been a political commitment by the de Gaulle government to the FTA negotiations in July, this had been at the expense of the reluctant Ministries of Finance and Industry. The vacillations of officials in the Steering Board for Trade thus represented these Ministries fighting 'a vigorous rearguard action'. The Ministry of Industry's hostility to the whole FTA concept, buoyed up by the Patronat, had been made clear to Whitehall even when the French had announced its change of tack in early July 1958.[62] It was also confirmed in more detail in early October.[63] While this offered some explanation of French actions, Maudling also raised the possibility that de Gaulle had not been 'wholly sincere' in his approval of continued involvement in the Maudling Committee negotiations.[64] This was probably an accurate estimation of French policy. Recent research suggests that de Gaulle had not only adopted his predecessors' support for the EEC but also their reservations about the FTA. Seeing the issue as 'a power struggle between France and Britain over who should control the economic development of Europe', de Gaulle had decided against the FTA from June 1958. Recognising that France's EEC partners did not share this view, however, he had to resist blame for breaking the negotiations and foster their opposition to the British position.[65] This would account for early conciliation in June/July 1958 and the tougher stance thereafter. What is sure is that French stonewalling in the origin negotiations ended Maudling's effort to meet the Six on this issue. In May, the Cabinet had postponed Maudling's proposals for limited tariff harmonisation amid the uncertainties of the French constitutional crisis. The paymaster had subsequently made a failed attempt to resuscitate the idea in July and, in preparation for the Commonwealth Trade and Economic Conference from 15–26 September, he once again raised the possibility of movement towards the Six.[66] Commonwealth insistence on liberal origin rules for goods produced from their basic material exports together with French tactics in the Steering Board for Trade discouraged Maudling from pressing Cabinet on the origin concession after September.[67] If there was to be any progress, it was to come from diplomatic pressure applied at the highest level. Thus, Maudling urged the prime minister to foster Adenauer's support for the FTA when in Bonn on 8 October.[68]

Macmillan's response to the problems faced by the FTA negotiations suggests that he was ill at ease with developments in Europe. Exceeding his Whitehall brief, the prime minister threatened Adenauer: 'it would be very bad if the United Kingdom found herself economically isolated as the result of French difficulties. No British government could continue to take part in the military defence of a continent which had declared economic war upon her'.[69] In his memoirs, Macmillan notes that his task in Bonn was assisted by de Gaulle's recent mishandling of Adenauer.[70] The German chancellor was supposedly 'very hurt and angry' by the General's proposals for a tripartite directorate of the western alliance including Britain, France and the United States.[71] Although de Gaulle had circulated a memorandum outlining these aims to Washington and London on 17 September, he had revealed nothing of them during the Colombey meetings with Adenauer on the same day. On learning of this, the German chancellor assured Macmillan that his government would use its influence in support of the FTA. For a brief period, therefore, as the French became more isolated in the Ockrent Committee and the Maudling Committee, Franco-German relations were strained.[72] They were not, however, broken. Macmillan's aggressive diplomacy ultimately failed to move the German chancellor.[73] As Cold War struggles over Berlin heightened in autumn 1958, Adenauer looked for stability and support, not threats of division in Europe. It did not help, therefore, that after the Bonn talks Macmillan warned Adenauer that failure in the FTA negotiations could have ramifications for Britain's defence commitments in Europe and the cohesion of NATO.[74] On two occasions in October 1958 the prime minister repeated his frustrated outburst of the previous June. On 15 October he outlined retaliation measures in case of the FTA's failure that amounted to a trade war and the withdrawal of British troops from Germany; in Macmillan's view, 'Fortress Britain might be our reply'.[75] On 26 October, he went further and suggested that the most practical course would be to denounce the WEU Treaty.[76] These were unrealistic proposals which would have done more harm to Britain's international standing than good. They were certainly received as such by Whitehall. In the Treasury, Clarke argued that if the FTA negotiations failed, Britain ought to turn to a Uniscan FTA and otherwise 'reduce the temperature rather than . . . increase it by slashing out wildly in all directions'.[77] Rowan supported this view and suggested that the government should now move towards sterling convertibility as the only effective alternative course.[78]

The Foreign Office was similarly dismissive of the prime minister's ideas. Anthony Rumbold, Assistant Under-Secretary, argued that 'Fortress Britain would mean neutralist Europe, Communist dominated Germany, and eventually the end of us. "Air-strip 1" is another way of expressing it'.[79] Gore-Booth, Deputy Under-Secretary, took a pragmatic view: 'A nation of shop-keepers living on international trade and finance and importing 50% of its food-stuffs cannot turn itself into a self-supporting fortress'.[80] Obviously concerned by the prime minister's intervention, the Treasury and Foreign Office combined their efforts in a submission on 31 October.[81] This rejected Macmillan's proposals and advised that until the FTA negotiations had collapsed, there should be no precipitate action. Moreover, even when they had collapsed, warnings of the effect on North Atlantic co-operation should not take the form of threats. Whether this was in response to, or in ignorance of, Macmillan's recent comments to the American under-secretary of state for economic affairs is unknown. But either way, officials would not have been pleased to hear that on 23 October, the prime minister told Douglas Dillon that if the FTA negotiations failed, 'the British would not go down without a fight . . . [the] UK would organize a counter-movement of their own and would have to reevaluate her position in NATO'.[82] Macmillan was clearly troubled by European developments, confiding in his diary on 26 October that 'De Gaulle is bidding high for the hegemony of Europe'.[83]

This divergence between the prime minister and Whitehall reflected officials' acceptance that the FTA negotiations were dead but could not be broken off by belligerence. Public opinion in Britain and elsewhere was expected to have sympathy for the de Gaulle government's refusal to negotiate against a background of fundamental constitutional changes in France.[84] As long as this was the case, Britain had to continue a futile game of manoeuvring to avoid blame for the negotiations' demise and accusations of anti-Europeanism. If there was no progress in the OEEC at the end of October, officials would recommend that Maudling suspend the FTA negotiations.[85] 'The most profitable line' in this situation would be to ensure that 'the onus of causing delay lay firmly on the Six . . . implying that their attitude was largely dictated by French intransigence'. Two events confirmed the impasse in the FTA negotiations prior to the Maudling Committee of 23–30 October. First, on 14 October, Wormser, the Quai official who had as much power as most of de Gaulle's ministers, visited London.[86] While clashing with British officials on every point, Wormser explained frankly that France only remained in the FTA negotiations because it could see no way to end them without causing political problems with Britain and its EEC partners.[87] Second, on 20 October, the European Commission's Ockrent Committee submitted its revised version of the French counter-plan to the Maudling Committee.[88] The Ockrent Report, while restating the interest of the Six in a multilateral arrangement with the OEEC, recommended the strengthening of institutional checks on members of the European Economic Association (as the FTA would be renamed) in their trade with third countries. It also promoted the Carli Plan solution to the origin question with tariff harmonisation, around the EEC's common external tariff, and compensating charges either side of it; specific settlements were to be agreed in the sector studies underway in the OEEC. Although Coulson, Maudling's deputy, believed that there 'was nothing fundamentally abhorrent' in the Ockrent Report, he nevertheless argued that there was little chance of progress due to French obstruction.[89] Over six months in preparation, the Ockrent Report was rendered bankrupt by France's position in the Steering Board for Trade's examination of the origin question where it continued to obstruct progress on sector analysis.

Confirmation of this predicament was provided by the penultimate Maudling Committee meeting of 23–30 October 1958. In Bretherton's view, the French position, and its acceptance by France's EEC partners, brought 'two years' work into question'; there was absolutely no chance of securing a FTA on terms acceptable to Britain in the near future.[90] Consequently, in Cabinet on 30 October, Macmillan admitted that the time was approaching 'when a political settlement of this problem should be sought'.[91] In his diary, he noted that the French had just 'wasted time' and that 'even the 5 . . . are shocked [and] angry at French insincerity [and] trickery'; he therefore agreed with Maudling's suggestion that if there was no progress by the end of November, Britain should break off from the negotiations.[92] On 31 October, the prime minister also turned his attention to the Treasury's proposals for sterling convertibility known as Operation Unicorn.[93] It was during the final months of 1958 that Whitehall was forced to confront the conjunction of these two major events: the end of the FTA negotiations and Britain's move to currency convertibility along with France, Germany and other OEEC member states.

'Crowning folly'

On 3 November 1958, Adenauer informed Macmillan that the President of the European Commission, Walter Hallstein, did not believe the FTA negotiations to be 'seriously endangered'.[94] This had little effect on Whitehall which had concluded that there was no hope for the FTA and whose regard for German opinion had now reached a low point. Gore-Booth was representative of widespread disillusion with the Adenauer government in November 1958: 'At every stage in this argument, the Germans have arrayed themselves in a great panoply of doctrine and defiance, only to run away when the first shot is fired by the Grande Armée of M. WORMSER'.[95] Thus, all efforts were directed towards bringing the FTA negotiations to a satisfactory close and developing policy in that event. Clarke's interdepartmental committee urged a suspension of the negotiations for at least six months and no 'rock-slinging (verbal or commercial) against France or the Six' to keep the FTA alive for the future.[96] Whitehall's plea for calm does not seem to have had the desired effect on the prime minister, however. In a memorandum submitted to Cabinet on 4 November outlining possible policy, Macmillan still talked of threatening reappraisals of Britain's role in European institutions and of denouncing the WEU Treaty if the FTA failed.[97] Concurrently, he made more considered suggestions including measures to avoid trade discrimination caused by the EEC's 1 January 1958 tariff and quota reductions and the possibility of a Uniscan FTA.

The crisis in the negotiations was precipitated by early French action. On 6 November, the French foreign minister visited London for talks on the FTA. Couve surpassed the Ockrent Report and explained that what France envisaged for the FTA was an exchange of preferential positions, not merely free access to markets.[98] Maudling was incensed by this: 'the object of the Free Trade Area had been to preserve the integrity of the O.E.E.C. and to avoid discrimination. M. Couve now said that there never could have been a Free Trade Area on this basis, that there was bound to be discrimination and that the Free Trade Area could not involve wider competition'. Introducing a further meeting between Couve and Macmillan, Selwyn Lloyd informed the prime minister that 'he and Couve had just finished a bad meeting at which they had finally torpedoed the Free Trade Area'.[99] In what he described as 'a painful discussion' in which he talked to Couve 'roughly', Macmillan said that he 'was very sorry to hear this':

It depressed him to feel that the French Government had decided that Sparta and Athens must quarrel. The Russians were getting stronger all the time and here was the free world voluntarily weakening and dividing itself. History would regard this as a tragic decision and the crowning folly of the twentieth century in Europe.[100]

Events now proceeded rapidly. At the final Maudling Committee meeting of 13–14 November, there was a reasonably good atmosphere even though no substantial progress was achieved.[101] However, all was overshadowed by the now famous statement made by de Gaulle's Minister for Information, Jacques Soustelle. As the Maudling Committee was in session on 14 November, Soustelle announced to the press that:

it was not possible to form a free trade area as had been wished by the British, that is to say by having free trade between the six countries of the Common Market and the eleven other countries of the OEEC, without a common external tariff and without harmonization in the economic and social spheres.[102]

The General immediately followed this up with a letter to Macmillan on 15 November.[103] The message was the same although the tone more diplomatic. Having begged de Gaulle not to regard the FTA as a technical issue one week previously, the prime minister was curt in his response: 'I cannot conceal from you my concern over the situation which developed from the breakdown of these prolonged negotiations, and especially the effect upon Western Europe'; he also ignored de Gaulle's offer of bilateral talks to solve the immediate problems of 1 January 1959.[104] Subsequently, Maudling postponed his Committee's studies.[105]

French diplomacy may have been 'brutal', as Macmillan later described it, but the content of the Soustelle announcement and the de Gaulle letter was only what Wormser had conveyed to London on 14 October and what Couve had told Macmillan, Lloyd and Maudling on 6 November.[106] As Makins put it: 'The French attitude is no surprise to me, indeed, the outcome has been pretty clear for some months. We have been "fishing in a rain barrel" since last July'.[107] The reason Britain took the opportunity provided by the French to suspend the FTA negotiations was that it had planned to do this by the end of November anyway; Soustelle had just given the British government the chance to lay the blame at France's door.

Although the FTA's suspension was in line with Whitehall's tactics, it still left the serious problem of establishing a relationship with the EEC in the FTA's absence. De Gaulle's diplomacy had created the situation that Britain had been working to avoid since Plan G's formulation: the establishment of a Common Market without a FTA. As Maudling explained to his colleagues on 25 November, the strategy of tackling the French via her EEC partners had failed; 'As a result the French [had] taken trick after trick without playing a single card of their own'.[108] In Macmillan's view, the 'European Trade picture [was] darkening' and Britain's impending exclusion from Europe was due to Washington's lack of interest in the FTA and the Franco-German 'unholy alliance' against Britain.[109] This alliance had been confirmed by reports of the General's discussions with Adenauer at Bad Kreuznach on 26 November. Steel, Britain's Ambassador to Bonn, was 'filled . . . with the most unrelieved gloom' by reports of the meeting: 'the Chancellor really understood nothing about the Free Trade Area and the French had buried everything in a cloud of bonhomie and produced a quite specious atmosphere of euphoria'.[110] Similarly, Maudling informed Macmillan that 'the Germans gave in to [the French] all along the line'.[111] It is now clear that de Gaulle obtained Adenauer's agreement to terminate the FTA negotiations at Bad Kreuznach.[112] Their joint recommendation that the Maudling Committee be suspended with the task of negotiating a long-term multilateral agreement placed in Hallstein's hands was perhaps the best indication of this at the time.[113] Britain initially rejected this idea and demanded that a further OEEC meeting be held.[114] Cold War tensions had played a part in determining Adenauer's actions at Bad Kreuznach. On 27 November, the Soviet leader, Nikita Khrushchev, sent an ultimatum to the Western allies demanding that West Berlin become a demilitarised 'independent unit – a free city'.[115] Adenauer held doubts about British reliability on the Berlin question bred from the Macmillan government's failure to take a firm stand in favour of German interests.[116] Thus it is probable that the price for Adenauer's agreement to the General's plan to end the FTA was French opposition to Khrushchev's ultimatum.[117] Adenauer remained anxious that Macmillan would use the Berlin Crisis as a means of retribution for German policy towards the FTA.[118] However, these fears proved unfounded.

Given Macmillan's proposals for retaliatory action in his baleful minutes of June, October and November, it would be supposed that he might have reacted with some hostility to continued Franco-German opposition to the FTA. Yet as events developed, the prime minister implemented none of his more aggressive ideas. He did make links between the FTA negotiations and the Berlin Crisis in Whitehall communications, but they came to nothing possibly because of Foreign Office insistence that these volatile issues be kept apart to avoid further tension in Europe.[119] This was due to the government having no choice but to maintain relations with France and the Six. Macmillan was forcefully reminded of this imperative by Whitehall which ruled out economic or political reprisals.[120] Britain could not cut itself off from Europe; this had become increasingly apparent after 1955 and had been the main motivation for Plan G. Apart from the political importance of retaining influence in Europe, Britain's trade with the Continent was too significant to be jeopardised by a clash with the EEC. There were already 'disquiet-ing' signs of pro-German and anti-British attitudes evinced by industrialists in the Six; Eccles warned that 'shortening order books were the rule'.[121] But the Macmillan government could not deal with this by joining the Common Market. Such a move would have entailed fundamental alteration of the three circles policy and was probably impractical given de Gaulle's political opposition to British association via the FTA. Consequently, the prime minister's only feasible policy was to suppress any anger he might have felt towards the Six and search for a relationship with the EEC. Hence, on the one hand, the British government prepared proposals to avoid trade discrimination on 1 January 1959 and considered a Uniscan FTA as a bridge to a long-term European multilateral association. On the other, Macmillan stalled Britain's move to sterling convertibility to avoid giving France reason to accuse Britain of being anti-European and thereby end any hope of a future agreement.

Whitehall had been urging ministers to consider a short-term *modus vivendi* to deal with discrimination on 1 January 1959 and a medium-term Uniscan FTA since June 1958. After the Soustelle announcement, officials stepped up their preparations of these plans. For a brief period, however, ministers clung to the possibility of circumvent-ing the problems caused by France by offering the French a special position in the FTA. This had previously been ruled out by officials as impractical earlier in 1958, and now, in November, they again warned that it would probably be received by the Six as an attack on the integrity of the Rome Treaties.[122] Clarke urged the chancel-lor 'to throw his weight on the side of disengagement and [a] "modus vivendi"' because a special position was 'very foreign to General de Gaulle's basic concepts of the position of France in the world'.[123] Nevertheless, for a brief period a special position remained a possi-bility and had some support from the Foreign Office which believed that the French were thinking in these terms themselves.[124] When it became clear that this was an inaccurate assumption, the idea was dropped in London.

Consequently, Whitehall concentrated first on avoiding discrimi-nation against British exports to Europe, and second on developing an alternative trade association with the non-Six powers. The dis-crimination issue was imperative because of the impending 1 January

1959 EEC tariff and quota reductions. At the Bad Kreuznach meeting, the French and the Germans had agreed proposals for a *modus vivendi* to avoid discrimination between the EEC and other OEEC states. These amounted to extending the 10 per cent EEC tariff cut to all GATT countries and possibly extending the 20 per cent quota increase to OEEC members.[125] The problem for Britain came with France's insistence that the increase in nil or negligible quotas be reserved for EEC members only.[126] Britain reacted to this on two levels. First, it opposed the threat of discrimination especially when France had not yet fulfilled her obligations on OEEC trade liberalisation.[127] Some British exports would suffer as a result of the French plan; according to the *Economist*, 'The quota for German and Italian cars, for instance, [would] be increased by more than 10,000, the British by a few hundred'.[128] Second, Britain opposed the ethos of discrimination between the EEC and the OEEC which had been at the root of the Anglo-French dispute throughout the FTA negotiations.[129] Consequently, the Board of Trade developed counter-proposals to eradicate discrimination by the extension of the EEC's increase in nil or negligible quotas to all OEEC members on a reciprocal basis.[130] This was discussed at the OEEC Council meeting of 15 December 1958 that marked the end of the FTA.[131] The Council meeting was notorious for the public split between Eccles and Couve on the issue of the *modus vivendi*; for Sir Paul Gore-Booth, it was 'unquestionably the worst conference' he had ever attended.[132] With French dismissal of the British proposals, Eccles threatened a trade war after 1 January 1959. In response, Couve 'jumped in to say that the French Government could not negotiate under a threat' and effectively abandoned the FTA negotiations.[133] Lord Gladwyn recalled that Couve and Wormser were left 'literally quivering with emotion' by Eccles' speech: 'They looked for all the world like cats which had just survived the charge of a powerful mastiff'.[134] Although France was isolated in its opposition to the British proposals at the Council, in the long-run, Britain's effort to defend trade liberalism throughout the OEEC fell victim to the support France had secured within the Six.[135] The prospect of facing EEC discrimination, albeit on nil and negligible quotas, made Britain's defence of its trade relations outside of the EEC all the more important and was one of the reasons for the Macmillan government's interest in a Uniscan FTA.

The Macmillan government had been carefully fostering non-Six relations during the final months of the FTA negotiations.[136] Most recently, meetings of the eleven non-Six powers had taken place on 1 December at Geneva where it was confirmed that the FTA negotiations had created a sense of common interest.[137] Bretherton also reported that in a private meeting at Geneva, the Swiss and Norwegian representatives had raised the issue of a non-Six FTA agreement.[138] These suggestions augmented the collaboration which was already taking place between British and Scandinavian industrial organisations.[139] The Board of Trade had, of course, been considering a Uniscan FTA since the beginning of the year, while the Treasury had dropped its previous hostility to the idea in May. After the French had finally ended the FTA in November, the Economic Departments mounted a campaign in favour of a Uniscan FTA within Whitehall.

On 18 November, Clarke's Committee concluded that a non-Six trade agreement 'appeared to be the best, if not indeed the only alternative, policy' and proceeded to make this recommendation to ministers.[140] There were three main arguments in support of a Uniscan FTA. First, it was thought to be a 'viable project in its own right' and acceptable to British industry by offering exporters an opportunity to expand their sales to Scandinavia. Second, it would be a valuable insurance policy against the danger that Scandinavian countries might otherwise be drawn into the orbit of the EEC. Third, officials believed that a Uniscan FTA 'might become a bridge to an association with the Six equivalent to a European Free Trade Area' or at least some form of multilateral European economic co-operation. These arguments no doubt made the Uniscan FTA more saleable at ministerial level, but with the FTA negotiations over and Britain still committed to some form of association with the Six in the long-term, the truth was that Britain had no choice but to pursue the Uniscan course.[141] It was this stark reality which converted previous doubters. The Foreign Office, which had opposed the plan for causing division in Europe, now supported it.[142] Even Sir David Eccles, who had criticised the proposal for being 'a climb down – the engineer's daughter when the general-manager's had said no', now suggested to Macmillan that although it remained second best, 'half a loaf is better than none'.[143] Thus, at critical meetings in December, ministers approved the Uniscan FTA studies but suggested that they remain low key; Britain did not wish to attract accusations of dividing Europe when it had been a vocal defender of OEEC unity over the past three years.[144] With their eyes still on achieving a FTA agreement with the EEC in the long-run, British ministers eventually entered into negotiations with the Scandinavians in early 1958, leading to the creation of the European Free Trade Association (EFTA, including Austria, Denmark, Norway, Portugal, Sweden, Switzerland and the United Kingdom) in November 1959.[145] This, however, was a defensive policy from the beginning and when EFTA failed to provide the stepping-stone to the original FTA concept, the Macmillan government soon lost interest in it and moved towards making an application for membership of the EEC in 1961.

The Macmillan government's search for a *modus vivendi* and its examination of a Uniscan FTA in December 1958 reflected its aim of maintaining Britain's position in Europe after the failure of the Maudling negotiations. Hence the importance placed on not being blamed for the FTA's breakdown and avoiding accusations of anti-Europeanism that would have jeopardised a future agreement with the EEC. These same priorities also governed ministers' considera-tion of Britain's move to currency convertibility along with France, Germany and other OEEC member states on 29 December 1958. Britain had been committed to making sterling held by non-residents freely convertible into dollars since the collective approach to freer trade and payments in 1952.[146] The re-establishment of sterling as an international currency had, of course, been the aim of success-ive governments as confirmed most recently by Whitehall's review of Britain's position in world affairs.[147] From early 1958, there was pressure from the Bank of England for the government to unify the official and transferable rates thus making sterling convertible on the international markets. It was felt that the process started in 1955 with *de facto* convertibility had to be completed by seizing the earliest and most favourable opportunity to establish *de jure* convertibility.[148]

At the end of July 1958, the Treasury believed that the time was ripe to re-establish convertibility and therefore recommended an early move to the prime minister on 8 September.[149] Treasury officials had been urging convertibility as a possible option during the stale-mate in the FTA negotiations as European monetary co-operation offered Britain the chance to maintain links with Continental econo-mies outside of the conflicts over trade policy.[150] However, smooth establishment of currency co-operation was complicated at this stage by the need to maintain good relations with the French in order to avoid breakdown in the FTA negotiations. In his memorandum of

8 September, the Chancellor, Heathcoat Amory, noted that a move to convertibility would bring the EPU to an end and bring its successor, the European Monetary Agreement (EMA), into force.[151] Amory warned that this could be viewed by the de Gaulle government as an unfriendly act which would impel France to repay its size-able EPU debts on transition to the EMA when the country already faced significant economic problems.[152] At a meeting on 5 November at Downing Street, therefore, Macmillan stalled the Treasury's plan for convertibility, known as Operation Unicorn, for fear of causing the French to end the FTA negotiations.[153]

Ironically, the Macmillan government only eventually made ster-ling convertible when France itself had decided to proceed with convertibility. After the suspension of the FTA negotiations in mid-November, Britain still postponed a move on sterling to avoid further conflict with de Gaulle.[154] It was only when Whitehall heard that the French were considering a change in their own exchange rate policy that Macmillan agreed to convertibility lest Britain lose the initiative and sterling suffer as a result.[155] In contrast to the tensions of the OEEC Council on 15 December, Heathcoat Amory eventu-ally secured agreement from the French and German Finance Ministers, Pinay and Etzel, to synchronise the convertibility of sterling, the franc and the mark in a friendly meeting on 17 December.[156] There was some contemporary conjecture which suggested that Britain pressed for convertibility to force France into a difficult position vis-à-vis the EPU in retaliation for French actions in the FTA nego-tiations.[157] Macmillan's hesitancy to precipitate French rancour would seem to discount this, yet British ministers did believe that con-vertibility might lead, through the manipulation of EMA loans, to some degree of control over France and encourage a more outward-looking economic policy from Paris.[158] Despite the differences over trade relations, it seems that the French and Germans were eager to co-operate with Britain over monetary policy. This was probably due to the support France received from Germany for its compre-hensive financial reforms and also German interest in seeing convertibility finally established.[159] One recent study argues that de Gaulle's decision to liberalise trade and accept devaluation and convertibility was, in part, a *quid pro quo* for German agreement to the demise of the FTA negotiations.[160] Ultimately, what the conjunction between the end of the FTA negotiations and currency convertibility represents is proof of Britain's impotence in the face of de Gaulle's France in 1958. De Gaulle may have had to pay a

financial price 'to secure the future of the EEC a[n]d French leadership of it' but in the longer-term the greatest costs were those
shouldered by the British.[161]

In his memoirs, de Gaulle states that he decided to put an end to
the Maudling negotiations because they 'were calculated to submerge the Community of the Six at the outset in a vast free trade
area together with England and eventually the whole of the West'.[162]
This view is also held by one of the most comprehensive studies of
de Gaulle.[163] Recent research has added clarity to this explanation
by showing more clearly how the General saw the FTA as a political threat to the EEC and to the policy of French national greatness
that he wished to develop through it.[164] Wider foreign policy no
doubt influenced de Gaulle's decision. The rejection of his tripartite directorate proposals in September 1958 by Eisenhower and
Macmillan confirmed the General's long-term hostility towards Anglo-
Saxon hegemony. There is even conjecture that he submitted the
tripartite memorandum knowing it would be rejected thus enabling
French withdrawal from NATO in the long-term.[165] In late 1958,
however, de Gaulle played his hand with diplomatic finesse. In
killing the FTA, the General had to be sure that he would not bring
international retribution upon France. The French Ambassador to
Washington's discussion with the American under-secretary of state
for economic affairs on 30 October is very interesting in this light.
Alphand received assurances from Dillon that the United States had
no plans to intervene in the FTA negotiations and would always
put the Six first.[166] Having squared the Americans, de Gaulle had
only to ensure Adenauer's agreement. This, of course, came from
the Bad Kreuznach meeting, accurately described by one Foreign
Office official as a *'tour de force'*.[167] De Gaulle had thus prevented
Britain associating with the EEC and possibly endangering the position
France had secured in the Rome Treaties. He had done so within
the boundaries of American interests and the Franco-German
rapprochement.

The consequences of de Gaulle's skilful diplomacy were momentous for Britain. First, the long-term strategy of applying pressure
on France through Germany was exposed as a failure. Even Britain's
champion amongst the Six, Ludwig Erhard, had shown signs of
giving up on the FTA negotiations in autumn 1958.[168] This was

probably a tactical retreat under pressure from Adenauer but the Foreign Office had received reports that Erhard was charmed by de Gaulle during the Bad Kreuznach meeting.[169] Second, the end of the FTA negotiations confirmed that the Anglo-American relationship amounted to very little in terms of European integration. After the final OEEC Council meeting of 15 December, Sir Roger Makins, former Ambassador to Washington, described the State Department's instructions to their representative as 'deplorable'.[170] This was characteristic of widespread Whitehall frustration at the Eisenhower Administration's reluctance to support Britain's FTA policy, a reluctance exemplified during a meeting on 16 December when Dulles appeared to be anxious to help but 'was uncertain [about] what to do'.[171]

It was perhaps an early realisation of the forces ranged against his European policy and an overestimation of Britain's ability to resist them which led Macmillan to advocate retaliation in June, October and November 1958. Only due to Whitehall's caution did the prime minister refrain from implementing his ideas. Caution, given the confines of British policy, was the right approach, despite the undiplomatic actions of de Gaulle. The re-evaluation in British governmental attitudes towards European integration which would produce the first application for EEC membership in 1961 was still perhaps a year off in December 1958.[172] In the interim, London remained paralysed by French actions and committed to some form of multilateral association with the EEC, perhaps via a Uniscan FTA. As an indication of this intent, and of Macmillan's personal view, when presented by his private secretary on 30 December with a choice of either 'try[ing] to break up the Common Market, or . . . concentrat[ing] on watering it down', the prime minister favoured the latter course.[173] The former was an impossibility although it is revealing that someone so close to Macmillan still felt able to raise the idea. While this strategy may have persisted into 1959/60, the means of achieving it altered with recognition that a multilateral association was not acceptable to de Gaulle. The General wasted no time in making this clear. When asked about the FTA at an Elysée reception in January 1959, he 'drew himself up and, with great solemnity, made the following pronouncement *ex cathedra*: "Be sure of this – France will never agree to join a Free Trade Area" and with a decisive sweep of the arm thus closed the conversation'. In response, Otto Clarke wrote one word: 'FINIS'.[174]

Conclusion: Threatening Europe

The failure of the FTA negotiations in December 1958 marked a crisis in post-war British history. In rejecting membership of the Common Market and instead promoting a wider organisation, the Eden and Macmillan governments had committed Britain to 15 years of exclusion from the EEC and contributed to decades of uneasy Anglo-European relations thereafter. These events have been the focus of particular attention in the troubled history of Britain's relationship with the European Community. In the first and now classic treatment, Miriam Camps presented a largely sympathetic account of British decision making, arguing that while the FTA was 'ineptly presented and badly negotiated ... it was not maliciously conceived' and represented a 'real and substantial shift in the British Government's attitude towards Europe'. Such sympathy was, however, conditioned by Camps' wider criticism of the 'essentially negative character of so much of Britain's post-war policy towards Europe, the lack of imagination, the timidity, and the half-heartedness of the few British initiatives'.[1] Leading diplomatic and economic historians have also portrayed Britain's rejection of EEC membership as a great error, although they have been cautious in their criticisms admitting the hindsight involved in them. John Young has argued that if there was a 'lost opportunity' for Britain's relations with the Community then it came with the Conservatives between 1955 and 1957.[2] Similarly, Alan Milward has suggested that Britain's 'failure to sign the Treaties of Rome was a serious mistake'.[3]

This book has rejected such a perspective. It has not done so because it believes that there was no boat for the British to catch at Messina in 1955, as Wolfram Kaiser has suggested.[4] While there is something in this view, it is fraught with methodological difficulties and in itself proves nothing more than the unpredictability of events for Britain *and* the Six.[5] Neither does the book share Kaiser's largely dismissive assessment of Plan G.[6] At the same time, it does not go so far as Andrew Moravcsik who has described British policy as 'a rational, remarkably flexible, even far-sighted defense of enduring British economic interests'.[7] Instead, while sharing some of the conclusions of Kaiser and Moravcsik on the motives for British policy, it offers an interpretation which emphasises that Britain's response to the creation of the European Community is an historical question too complex to lend itself to condemnation or vindication. This conclusion results partly from the nature of the subject matter and partly from the book's research methodology. Distinguishing itself from previous studies, it analyses not only the evolution of policy that produced the FTA proposal from 1955 to 1956, but also the consequent FTA negotiations from 1957 to 1958. It also draws on the recent research of historians writing about the attitudes of the Six powers towards the FTA, particularly the French and German governments. While it has its foundations in diplomatic history, it recognises that a full explanation of Britain's FTA policy has to deal not only with diplomacy, but with economic and commercial interests as well. In doing so, the book offers a more detailed picture of the early years in Britain's relationship with the European Community and produces a number of new interpretations.

There are five major findings. First, British policy can be seen as far more sophisticated than previously depicted, developing from negative origins before eventually becoming an attempt to complement the Common Market. This said, the diversity of attitudes in London indicates that for some, the FTA was still a means of supplanting the Common Market. Second, although it is fair to say that the FTA represented an advance in policy towards European co-operation, and one which was not as uninspired as is often thought, it was nevertheless securely founded in traditional British attitudes. Third, British diplomacy, both in the European arena and outside of it, did little to improve the FTA's chances and confirmed that Britain's priorities remained very much extra-European. While the difficulties this posed for the FTA were largely of Britain's own making, it is also possible to suggest that the British were misled into thinking that their policy was in better shape than it actually was by members of the Six. Fourth, it was during the FTA negotiations that the incompatibility of attempting to tilt towards Europe while maintaining otherwise traditional policies was revealed. It was not that Britain had dismissed the EEC out of hand in 1955/56, rather it had taken a calculated decision to pursue another course. The FTA negotiations proved that this course was unobtainable. Fifth, it is clear that the FTA negotiations were in difficulties months before their final termination by de Gaulle in December 1958. Whitehall was quick to move to a post-FTA policy and recommended conciliation rather than retaliation to ministers, advice that was symptomatic of Britain's inability to turn its back on Europe. Each of these points will now be discussed more fully.

It is now accepted that the FTA was the result of an evolution in British attitudes towards Messina during 1956.[8] What needs to be stated clearly, however, is that the evolution had its roots in the negativity of British policy in autumn 1955 and that while the FTA was ultimately designed to complement the Common Market, it cannot be assumed that all in London had given up on dominating the Six in future. Analysis of the FTA proposal has to begin with the autumn 1955 Whitehall studies of Britain's reaction to the Messina developments. As a result of the disastrous attempt to steer the Spaak Committee into the orbit of the OEEC, both the Board of Trade and the Treasury concentrated on developing a counter-initiative to the European Common Market. It was these counter-initiative ideas and the attitudes surrounding them which suggest that the FTA was, in fact, maliciously conceived.[9] The option of a FTA association with the Six's customs union was first mooted by Russell Bretherton in October 1955 and it was at this point that British policy entered the first of its three stage transformation.[10] From the beginning, however, there were different motives for different individuals and departments. The Board of Trade, heavily influenced by Peter Thorneycroft, Sir Frank Lee and Bretherton, was interested in developing an alternative trade plan to protect access to the markets of the Six and to maintain the forum of the OEEC for trade liberalisation. The Treasury, dominated by R.A. Butler's scepticism of European integration, wished to use the counter-initiative, in Sir Leslie Rowan's words, 'to stifle the Common Market at birth'.[11] Under Harold Macmillan, the Foreign Office was the main source of opposition towards the Six's plans in autumn 1955 and saw no reason for a counter-initiative, expecting the Messina powers to fail after they had been diverted into the OEEC. When events did not follow this pattern, the counter-initiative matured into the second stage of policy evolution.

The fresh impetus given to the development of a British initiative in Europe by Harold Macmillan, Chancellor from December 1955, did not cleanse policy of the previous autumn's negativity. It was in March 1956 that Otto Clarke, the Treasury official who chaired interdepartmental formulation of Plan G, told the Cabinet Secretary's Committee that 'the Chancellor of the Exchequer was seeking to evolve a constructive counter-initiative which would demonstrate [Britain's] willingness to associate [itself] with Europe while at the same time, it was hoped, administering a *coup de grâce* to the Messina proposals'.[12] This rather contradicts the view that a desire to 'undermine' the Common Market was not what prompted Britain to propose a FTA.[13] During the first half of 1956, while London still held doubts about the Six's potential, Britain's initiative in Europe developed as a possible alternative to the Common Market in expectation of its failure. It was after the Six had bridged their differences, from the Venice Conference of May to the meetings between Adenauer and Mollet in November 1956, that Plan G evolved into its third and final stage.

In November 1956, postponed by the Suez Crisis, but also assisted by it in encouraging the Cabinet to accept a new dynamic policy for Europe, the FTA became a fully fledged proposal to complement the European Common Market. In finally recommending the policy to ministers, officials determined that it was 'Politically . . . desirable to have a Customs Union as a nucleus' of the FTA.[14] What this judgement implied was not that Whitehall had embraced the Six's goals but that it had accepted the impossibility of obstructing the Messina developments given the strength of support for them in Europe and the United States. This remained a policy foundation throughout the FTA negotiations, as did the second of Whitehall's major conclusions. Officials stated that they 'would prefer there to be a Customs Union, but only provided a free trade area were also set up to include it. It would be politically as well as economically to [Britain's] disadvantage if a Customs Union were set up without a free trade area . . .'.[15] Thus, from early 1957, the newly formed Macmillan government worked to construct an OEEC FTA around the kernel of the Six's Common Market. Ultimately, however, it cannot be ruled out that some in London, including Macmillan himself as revealed in July 1957, still hoped that the FTA might, in the long-term, gain some form of dominance over the Common Market. Conversely, the prevailing mood amongst officials was that this was not Britain's goal. Instead, the FTA was designed to sustain the established three circles policy, with Britain remaining

'half-way between Europe and N. America' while accepting the consolidation of the Six.[16] Anxiety that this would not be achieved
accounted for a great deal of the frustration displayed in Whitehall,
especially at ministerial level, during the latter half of the Maudling
Committee negotiations in 1958. The reason for this anxiety is explained by the second conclusion of this study.

In 1959/60, a number of the principal officials involved in Britain's
FTA proposal commented on a post-mortem of the negotiations
produced by Frank Figgures of the Treasury.[17] Officials mainly considered negotiating procedure, which will be discussed below. There
was little analysis of the FTA policy itself, although Clarke stressed
that the 'United Kingdom proposal for a European Free Trade Area
in autumn 1956 was a historical departure' and that it was difficult to
appreciate 'what a tremendous leap in the dark it was for Ministers'.[18]
Camps supported this view with her description of the FTA as 'a
real and substantial shift in the British Government's attitude towards
Europe' which marked 'the beginning of a questioning of the priorities
that had hitherto conditioned all official, and most unofficial, thinking
about the United Kingdom's external relations'.[19] The result, so this
argument suggests, was that 'Europe began to move up the scale,
the Commonwealth to move down, and the nature of the British
relationship with the United States began to come into better perspective'. One recent study has sustained Camps' view by claiming
that the FTA represented 'a truly momentous decision and was more
than an incremental step in a gradually evolving policy'.[20] While it
is accurate to say that the FTA attached unprecedented importance
to Anglo-European relations in Whitehall, it is not true that the
policy 'represented a real and substantial shift' or 'a truly momentous decision'. In fact, the FTA was conservatively designed to meet
the threat of the Six and to maintain the *status quo* in Britain's
extra-European relations, both political and economic. It did represent changes in Britain's trade policy but these were set firmly in
traditional British policy foundations which only began to alter as
a result of the failure of Plan G and the success of the Six in combination with wider historical movements at the end of the 1950s.
  An explanation of how the FTA proposal was rooted in established policies is achieved by a summary of the varying motives of
Ministers and Whitehall departments during its preparation. This

analysis also supports one of the contentions of the present study, namely that the FTA proposal was more sophisticated than has previously been thought. For Macmillan, political concerns had a primary, not secondary, role in decision making.[21] The threat of German domination of Europe was a critical rationale from the outset and was combined with the need to avoid French political leadership at the end of the negotiations. Such considerations were important for three reasons. First, Macmillan had a personal interest in Britain playing a part in European co-operation, an interest he had exhibited earlier in the 1950s as a member of Churchill's Cabinet. Second, as an *'aficionado* of the Cold War', Macmillan believed that Europe should be united rather than divided in the face of the Soviet Union.[22] This argument may have been used tactically in the FTA negotiations but it did fit into Macmillan's view of East-West struggle. His unrealistic and ultimately still-born threats of withdrawing from Europe in 1958 were a frustrated response to the possible failure of this policy. Third, Macmillan was aware, as were many of his colleagues, that Britain's relationship with the United States might be undermined if Washington believed that the Six held greater influence than Britain itself. When Anglo-American relations represented the core of Macmillan's policy as prime minister, this concern became more acute. Yet despite the weight of these political criteria, they did not mean that the 'economic perspective was completely alien to Macmillan'.[23] He was conscious of the limited future benefits of the imperial preference system and hoped to see Britain balance this changing trade pattern with access to European markets. As chancellor he directed the development of Treasury policy and supported Otto Clarke over Sir Leslie Rowan in 1956. Clarke argued in favour of modifying the one-world approach to incorporate the rising importance of Europe. That Plan G would address this and do so without drastic alteration of existing external economic policy was one of the main factors that led Macmillan and the Treasury to support the proposal.

Commercial considerations motivated Peter Thorneycroft to direct the Board of Trade's attention to a new European initiative from late 1955 onwards. Thorneycroft's trade liberalism, his reservations about the imperial preference system and his long-term desire to see European commercial relations organised in a manner acceptable to Britain, led him to champion Plan G alongside Macmillan. In a wider sense, however, the FTA represented a potential cure-all for British trade policy. It was created to prevent the formation of a discriminatory *bloc* in Europe and protect trade liberalisation. The Board received some encouragement for this policy from British industrial organisations and, at the same time, it understood that members of the Commonwealth were planning to expand their export markets in Europe which might involve bargaining away preferences for British goods in Commonwealth markets. Consequently, for the Board of Trade, the FTA was, as Thorneycroft stated in May 1956, the most efficient method of 'taking the lead in Europe and securing the advantage of the fullest possible commercial opportunities [there], while holding the maximum we can of our preferential system'.[24] Both Lee and Bretherton advocated this view and continued to defend a diplomatic approach to Europe even when Thorneycroft had been replaced as president by the sometimes bellicose Sir David Eccles.

Of the three main Whitehall departments involved in European policy it was the Foreign Office whose attitudes underwent the most overt shift. Having instigated the negative British response to the Spaak Committee in the démarche of December 1955, the Foreign Office was then criticised by the Treasury for moving too close to the Messina position, an attitude that led to its exclusion from the formulation of Plan G in mid-1956. The reason for this altered Foreign Office outlook was recognition that an obstructive policy was not feasible given the unfortunate effect of the démarche, especially in light of American reactions. This does not indicate that the Foreign Office had accepted the Six's ambitions as the best course for Europe's future; in May 1956 an internal brief stated that 'We do not think the Messina approach is the best way to attract Germany into the political and military community of the West. . . . The advantage of the OEEC and NATO lies in the membership of the United Kingdom, the United States and Canada'.[25] What the change in Office attitudes represented was a return to its position of the early 1950s when it had been argued that Britain could not be seen as a saboteur of Six power unity. At the same time, the policy of the Atlantic Alliance was paramount and, in this context, the German question was a primary consideration. The reason that the Office promoted an extension of European policy in autumn 1956 to include the FTA proposal, a rationalisation of European institutions and activation of the WEU, was to widen European integration away from the economic forum. This was because officials had doubts about Plan G's potential given its lack of political content and the exclusion of agriculture, but also because politico-defence co-operation would be in an Atlantic rather than a European framework. The Foreign Office had been encouraged in this by reports that Adenauer was thinking in such terms in autumn 1956.

Selwyn Lloyd's Anglo-Six nuclear proposals in the January 1957 Grand Design were influenced by knowledge of French and German interest in defence collaboration but were primarily motivated by the experience of American policy during the Suez Crisis. While the Grand Design was rejected by a Cabinet determined to rebuild Anglo-American relations and which included ministers such as Lord Salisbury who were still sceptical of links with the Continent, it nevertheless reveals the level of importance attached to European co-operation by the Foreign Office. This view is supported by the conciliatory tone taken by the Office during the final breakdown of the Maudling negotiations and in response to Macmillan's 1958 suggestions for a 'Fortress Britain'. But even though the Office may have recognised the importance of Europe for British foreign, economic and defence policy, it had not lost the arrogance of its approach to the Six exhibited during autumn 1955. In a telling paradox, the Foreign Office accurately assumed that the Six had political ambitions but inaccurately believed that the intergovernmental Single Assembly for Europe proposal of the Grand Design would be marketable on the Continent. The widespread rejection of this idea, leading to a final deal between Macmillan and Adenauer in May 1957 to send the Grand Design behind closed doors at the WEU, had two effects. First, it dashed Foreign Office hopes of making a significant return to Whitehall decision-making on European policy after its exclusion by the Treasury in mid-1956. Second, it worsened rather than enhanced Anglo-Six relations after Suez, contrary to what had been planned. Consequently, the Foreign Office directed its attentions to the FTA as 'the spearhead of [Britain's] new approach to Europe'.[26]

Throughout the remainder of the FTA negotiations, Foreign Office officials made few efforts to shape Britain's European policy but maintained instead a watching brief via Maudling's Chief of Staff, Sir John Coulson, and took opportunities to remind Whitehall of the political importance of strong Anglo-European relations. Having misread Britain's ability to influence the Six in autumn 1955 and spring 1957 with such damaging consequences, and having recognised the implications of their development thereafter, the Foreign Office was the first of Whitehall departments to move towards a new policy after the demise of the FTA. In October 1959, it concluded that the

European Community was fast 'gathering momentum' and had the potential to 'completely out-class the U.K. in terms of military and economic importance'.[27] From 1959 onwards, the Foreign Office played a leading role in seeking British entry in to the EEC due mainly to changing attitudes towards foreign policy that were born, in part, from the experience of 1955–58.[28]

Plan G, therefore, was a culmination of different ministerial and departmental agendas and addressed different aims. Ultimately it did represent an advance in British policy towards European co-operation in that it proposed free trade in manufactured goods between Britain and its European partners. Otherwise, however, it was a conservative plan to preserve Britain's wider interests within the confines of the three circles. In terms of external economic policy, the FTA would not entail any major alteration to the one-world approach. The Six's plans would be accommodated within the preferred institution of the OEEC where Britain hoped to gain support from those countries outside of the Six. At the same time, the design of the FTA would enable Britain to maintain its preferential trade with the Commonwealth while it adjusted to new Commonwealth trade patterns. By excluding agriculture, it also continued protection for British farmers. This sensitivity to the Commonwealth and British agriculture, while having an economic rationale, was also a response to Conservative Party political interests. On a grander political scale, the FTA would not call in to question Britain's fundamental relations with America, the Commonwealth or Europe. The FTA would prevent Britain's relationship with the United States from being eclipsed by a successfully united European Community. As long as Commonwealth interests were protected, there was no reason to believe that the FTA would lead to disintegration of Commonwealth relations and with it the loss of Britain's claim to world-wide influence. Finally, the FTA would prevent a German-dominated European *bloc* weakening Britain's position in Europe and leading to its isolation as smaller states were attracted to the Common Market. As such, while the FTA was inspired by the Economic Departments, and particularly the commercial motives of the Board of Trade, it reflected a synthesis of interests which included foreign policy and domestic politics.[29]

Kaiser's judgement on the FTA is that as a 'modernization strategy' it may have 'provided the right answer, but it was to a question with which only Britain was faced'.[30] The implication of this argument is that the FTA was not designed to meet the demands of the Six and, as such, was misconceived. It is clear that the Six had chosen another route in the Treaties of Rome. Some might argue that this was political in conception. A 'sense of common cause', according to one commentator, 'helps to explain how the Treaties of Rome were possible so soon after the traumatic rejection of the EDC and why the British Free Trade Area proposals a little later made so little impression on the founding states of the European Community'.[31] British records also suggest that the Community spirit that would present Britain's first application for membership of the EEC with difficulties in the early 1960s was also in existence in embryonic form during the FTA negotiations.[32] In April 1957 Sir Gladwyn Jebb warned that 'Most of [the Six] (though not, of course, all) are concerned to "make Europe" in a physical sense. To that extent, when they meet with us, they are often really talking a different language.'[33] In July 1957, a Foreign Office official criticised Sir Christopher Steel's scepticism of Franco-German relations arguing that 'He misses the growing *mystique* of Europe.'[34] That this political sentiment existed cannot be questioned but that the FTA had none of it did not necessarily make it an uninspired British response to the Six.

What the British were trying to do via the FTA was rally the support of those elements of the Six who, for political and economic reasons, were favourable to British involvement in European integration. Politically, the desire to see Britain play a central role in Europe either as a counterweight to German power or as a link to the Atlantic Alliance existed amongst the Six. There was also economic support for Britain's chosen FTA, most vociferously expressed by Erhard, but also having been discussed as a concept in Belgium during 1954–55. The Dutch too hoped to see the FTA act as a counterbalance to French economic policy. While it was recognised in London that the FTA created technical difficulties, it was hoped that they would be overcome by a reservoir of support within the Six, as well as in the wider OEEC amongst those countries who shared Britain's opposition to their chosen course but were interested in European trade liberalisation. The flaw in this reasoning was that during the Common Market negotiations, for many different reasons, the reservoir of support upon which the British were depending drained away. This was largely due to the Six having chosen to pursue commercial relations based on 'a guaranteed, protected European market'.[35] It was also due to the detrimental effect that British diplomacy had upon its own European policy, which is the focus of the third conclusion of this book.

It was the insensitivity of British attitudes towards the Six, and the fact that the advance represented by the FTA proposal was not matched by a similar advance in diplomatic attitudes, which accounts for many of the problems faced in the Maudling Committee negotiations. As British strategy was based primarily on generating enough political will on the Continent to overcome the self interest of Plan G's design, paradoxically there was very little effort to foster favourable Anglo-Six relations. There were many examples when the effect of diplomacy in Europe was to increase suspicion of Britain's aims rather than encourage interest in the FTA. Of these, Macmillan's request for the Six to delay their agreements in late 1956 and Eccles' ill-considered speech to Commonwealth industrialists in May 1957 were perhaps the most damaging for the FTA's prospects. Otherwise, the general spirit of British diplomacy was that the FTA represented a move towards Europe which in itself, regardless of substance, should have been rewarded by flexibility from the Six.

The reason diplomacy failed, as officials admitted in their postmortem, was that Britain assumed it was wanted in Europe.[36] This supposition was not based on an entirely objective reading of recent events. First, it is true that Whitehall failed to grasp the damage done to its reputation on the Continent by the démarche of December 1955.[37] Second, and as an extension of this, during 1956 there was a tendency amongst officials and ministers to work on the premise of the Six's failure rather than their success. This attitude, of course, is why Plan G was formulated as an alternative to the Common Market in 1956 and it is also why Britain misread the ambitions and progress of the Messina powers. Yet if the aim was to achieve a FTA association with the Common Market by gaining the support of those within the Six who were sympathetic to Britain, such as the Dutch and members of the German and Belgian governments, a more diplomatic approach was necessary. For example, London might have adopted a positive stance rather than just warning of splits in Europe, as it continued to do throughout the negotiations. The strategy on which Britain relied (the application of pressure on France via Germany) was only going to be profitable if Britain remained on the side of the Germans and gave the Treaties of Rome the credit they deserved, recognising that the unity of the Six was their first priority. While a growing number of officials seem to have accepted this reality as the Maudling Committee negotiations commenced, ministers failed to realise fully the implications until the end of the negotiations. Ministerial myopia was exemplified by

Macmillan's aggressive tactics in Bonn in October 1958 and also by the debate about whether France would accept a special position in the FTA. Ministers contemplated such an idea in November 1958 even though officials had accurately warned earlier in the year that it would be received by the Six as an attack on the integrity of the Rome Treaties. When, ultimately, the Germans did not influence the French to support the FTA negotiations, many in Whitehall were left frustrated and angry. Yet the weakness was not in the Adenauer government but in British expectations of what it could achieve. In the long-term, the Macmillan government presumed too much of the Germans, who were committed to France in the Rome Treaties, and too little of the French, who though weakened by constitutional crisis managed to maintain a strong presence in the Maudling Committee negotiations.

Such criticism of British diplomacy and of a general British over-estimation of the FTA's chances has to be balanced by consideration of the diplomacy of the Six, particularly the Germans and the French. At key moments in the FTA negotiations, Adenauer promised to intervene on Britain's behalf but ultimately this had little effect. One historian has suggested that 'Alienating the British was ... far from Adenauer's mind, though he unintentionally raised expectations of German support, which his government could not fulfil.'[38] Erhard and the German Economics Ministry also led the British to imagine that circumstances were more hopeful than they actually were. It is worth noting that until the Venice Conference of September 1958, the Dutch believed that the Germans were seriously working towards the creation of a FTA.[39] It is also important to consider the diplomatic tactics of the French throughout the Maudling Committee negotiations, but particularly during 1958. With a majority in successive governments arguing that the FTA was contrary to the interests of France, the French sought to play the negotiations long. It now seems that the brief period of high hopes for the FTA negotiations in early summer 1958 (due to de Gaulle's supposed intervention) were in fact based on deception. To engineer the collapse of the FTA, but to avoid blame themselves, the French set the price of agreement high and became the defenders of the Treaties of Rome within the Six. In 1958, this strategy succeeded much as it would do during the Brussels negotiations from 1961 to 1963.[40]

Wider British diplomacy outside of the European arena did little to improve this situation. Under both Eden and Macmillan there was no significant attempt to present Britain as a power with European priorities on the international stage. Whether such a judgement of Eden would be accurate had he remained prime minister after the Suez Crisis is an interesting point on which to speculate. It is not impossible to imagine that Eden would have been far less willing to accept junior status in the Anglo-American relationship than his successor. Welcomed by the Eisenhower Administration, however, Macmillan did accept such status. Given the new prime minister's personal interest in Britain playing a role in European integration, it might have been expected that his government would have pursued a more European diplomacy. Instead, while Macmillan gave greater significance to European policy and more readily questioned the long-term importance of the Commonwealth and colonies, his foreign policy was otherwise conventional.

In this respect, the Suez Crisis has to be seen as a crucial turning point in Anglo-European, and specifically Anglo-French, relations. Given the weight placed on the European initiative by Britain in late 1956, together with the fact that Whitehall had rejected obstruction of the Common Market, more might have been made of the intimacy of Suez-inspired Anglo-French relations. Certainly, immediately after the Crisis there were indications that the French and Germans hoped that the hostility of United States' policy would encourage Britain to look more towards Europe. That the Macmillan government pursued Anglo-American relations with increased vigour after the breach at Suez must have had a negative impact, particularly on the French, but also more generally on Continental views of Britain's enthusiasm for European co-operation. In fact, the Macmillan government did aim to give European policy a boost after January 1957 with the Grand Design and WEU non-nuclear arms research and development. However, the insensitivity of the former and the limitations of the latter did not compensate for Macmillan's otherwise Atlanticist foreign policy. While it is now generally accepted that Suez gave the French the final impetus to join the European Common Market, less has been made of the effect of the Crisis in relation to the FTA proposal. It seems that as hopes of Britain embracing a European future diminished after November 1956, the Mollet government changed its attitude towards the British proposal. It is interesting that to begin with, the French argued that the FTA might assist the Common Market's passage through the National Assembly in so far as it offered a British counterweight to the partnership with Germany in the Rome Treaties. By spring

1957, however, the Mollet government reversed this view, suggest-ing that the FTA would hinder ratification by offering a looser alternative to the Common Market. As a result, Britain was forced to accept five months' delay in the FTA negotiations which was crucial in giving the French time to secure the Rome Treaties and develop a common identity amongst the Six.

Post-Suez diplomacy with the Commonwealth and the United States also had a negative effect on the FTA proposal. In general, the use of the argument that Britain had a Commonwealth alternative which set it apart from the Six did nothing to strengthen the government's negotiating position. Instead, it gave those sceptical of the FTA further ammunition with which to prove that Britain's priorities had not changed despite the apparent movement towards Europe. A particular example of this was Whitehall's consideration of an Anglo-Canadian FTA in the summer and autumn of 1957. The view of the French Embassy in London was probably representative of the general re-action to this development: 'Nobody understood what [Britain] was after. It had long been thought that the British, after long hesita-tion as to where they stood, had decided that they stood in Europe and the question was asked whether [they] were now undecided once more'.[41] It is clear that the Anglo-Canadian FTA was pursued for Commonwealth and Conservative Party political reasons. This is just another indication that British ministers looked first to calming domestic and Commonwealth, rather than European, opinion and that they overestimated their influence on the Continent. It is also an example of what Bretherton saw as the 'deliberate obstruction' of the Commonwealth Relations Office and the Colonial Office.[42] These two departments constantly fought to ensure that Anglo-Commonwealth relations would not suffer as a result of the development in Anglo-European economic ties. This often had a negative effect in Whitehall and in the presentation of policy, not least because effort was expended on achieving consensus in London rather than in the OEEC.

British diplomacy towards the United States also made Britain's priorities look very much anti-European. This did not occur solely in the aftermath of the Suez Crisis but on a number of other occa-sions. For example, in autumn 1957 the joint supply of British and American arms to Tunisian rebels caused significant friction with the Gaillard government which argued, with justification, that these arms would be used against French forces fighting in Algeria. Anglo-European relations also suffered as a result of the October 1957

Anglo-American Declaration of Common Purpose with its unique repeal of the McMahon Act for British nuclear development. Having themselves been turned down by the Americans on the nuclear question, this left the French dissatisfied, especially as the British had refused to co-operate in the production of a European nuclear weapon in February 1957. Moreover, the Adenauer government doubted the rationale of the Eisenhower Administration's decision to develop a 'trip-wire' defence policy and station IRBMs in Europe in December 1957. The result of French and German discontent were accusations of Anglo-American dominance, something which preoccupied de Gaulle in the latter half of 1958. In fact, perhaps the most serious diplomatic by-product in Europe of Anglo-American relations was caused by the rejection by Eisenhower and Macmillan of the General's proposals for a tripartite directorate in September 1958. This was ultimately one of the factors which contributed to de Gaulle's decision to seek the end of the FTA negotiations. It should be remembered, however, that the British alone were not responsible for this. On this occasion, and more significantly in fostering unique nuclear relations with the British, the United States administration was quick to confer preferred ally status on Britain, encouraging the perpetuation of traditional foreign policy assumptions.

There are a number of explanations for Ministers' failure to recognise the negative impact of their international diplomacy on European relations. Not attaching political weight to the views of the Six has to be one, as does a possible failure to place a high enough priority on Anglo-European political co-operation as a foreign policy goal. A balanced assessment might include these factors and add that Whitehall may not have fully recognised the incompatibility of attempting to maintain a unique position in the United States, the Commonwealth and Europe. The Six, and particularly France under de Gaulle, were acutely sensitive to Britain's strategies for securing special status in all arenas and it is this point which is the subject of the fourth conclusion.

It was during the course of the FTA negotiations that the French exposed the incongruity in the British attempt to tilt towards Europe while otherwise maintaining traditional policies and attitudes. The specific focus of the French criticism was that through the FTA and sustained Commonwealth preferences, the British government would obtain benefits disproportionate to those enjoyed by its FTA partners. The technical dispute on which this larger question rested was defining the origin of goods qualifying for FTA treatment. The basic distinction between the aims of the Common Market and the FTA were most vividly displayed by this issue with the French arguing that the balance they had secured in the Treaties of Rome would be upset by the FTA's lack of a common external tariff. Hence, in their counter-plan to the FTA of spring 1958, the French demanded external tariff harmonisation and sharing of Commonwealth preferences. By setting these conditions as the price for their agreement to a FTA, the French had revealed the incompatibility of Britain's trade policies in Europe and the Commonwealth. Britain could either make concessions in Commonwealth policy to secure the FTA and Britain's place in Europe, or reject French demands and risk the collapse of its European policy. It was a difficult dilemma, especially given the obduracy of the French. Yet it was one that always threatened to develop if the Six proved successful in the formation of a European Common Market and if Britain had correspondingly failed to generate political will in favour of the FTA. At the outset, doubting the Six's potential, Whitehall was not thoroughly alive to this prospect. It was only when the Six signed the Treaties of Rome in March 1957, and when the EEC looked like succeeding, that the problem of reconciling trade policies towards Europe and the Commonwealth became a reality.

As a measure of the importance the Macmillan government and Whitehall placed on securing a FTA in Europe, Britain did attempt to meet French demands on the origin question in 1958. First, Reginald Maudling put proposals to Cabinet for a concession on limited tariff harmonisation in May. Second, after the Maudling Committee meeting of July, the British agreed to the French request for sector studies on an industry-by-industry basis to solve problems caused by variable external tariffs. Although the Macmillan government rightly refused to share Commonwealth preferences given the state of the negotiations in mid-1958, it was nevertheless ready to contemplate some limited loss of tariff autonomy. To be fair, these were significant advances in British policy, going further towards the French position than had previously been envisaged. Reacting to events rather than directing them, however, the British only considered dealing with the origin question when it had become clear that the negotiations would otherwise fail. The French, effectively in control of the negotiations since they had obtained the delay for ratification of the Rome Treaties in May 1957, rendered Britain's concessions ineffective. In May 1958 the French constitutional crisis delayed Maudling's proposals for limited tariff harmonisation which subsequently were never implemented. In September 1958, after de Gaulle had taken charge of policy and probably decided to terminate the FTA negotiations, the French failed to play any constructive part in the FTA sector studies. The British movement on the origin problem, though confounded by the French, was too little too late. The same can be said of the less substantive agriculture concession in autumn 1957. It is possible to imagine that the FTA negotiations would have taken a different course if Britain had been more flexible on this crucial issue from the beginning.

The fifth conclusion of this book deals with the end of the FTA negotiations. Contrary to the view that the Maudling Committee came close to success, many in Whitehall had given up on the negotiations months before their eventual collapse.[43] For example, it was in January 1958 that Bretherton and other members of the Board of Trade began to consider alternative projects in expectation of the FTA's failure. Once more, as with Plan G in 1956, it was the Board which instigated development of British policy towards European co-operation by raising the possibility of a future Uniscan FTA. The Permanent Secretary of the Treasury, Sir Roger Makins, had also concluded by January that Whitehall 'ought now to reckon seriously with the prospect that the French will block an agreement on the Free Trade Area'.[44] It took the May 1958 crisis in the Fourth Republic to bring other key Treasury officials around to this point of view. In the post-mortem discussions, officials argued that the coming to power of General de Gaulle was the point at which the FTA negotiations reached a terminal stage.[45] Although officials had recognised in May 1958 that any hopes were forlorn, it took much longer for ministers to accept this fact. In Macmillan's case, this may have been because he still believed that his personal intervention could have an effect on French and German policies. For other ministers, including Maudling, there was the unpalatable prospect of a failure in government policy. As a result, it was only at the end of October that ministers decided to break the negotiations if there was no movement in the French position. From the Whitehall viewpoint, the negotiations did not come close to success and after the false remission for the FTA in July 1958, the latter months of the negotiations were characterised by diplomatic manoeuvrings to avoid attracting responsibility for the breakdown in the negotiations.

The dénouement of the Maudling Committee negotiations in November/December 1958 represents the culmination of the Anglo-French dispute about the European order which had first been exposed over the Schuman Plan in 1950–51. Then, the French had pursued their European political ambitions for a supranational arrangement through two key sectors of the economy. In January 1958, the inauguration of the EEC was the logical evolution of these aims. Britain's response to the Schuman Plan had been dictated by its aversion to European federation, its world-wide commitments and a belief in being 'with but not of' Europe. At the end of the FTA negotiations, Britain faced unprecedented crisis in this policy. Since November 1956, the government had worked to ensure that a European Common Market was complemented by a FTA to defend Britain's political, economic and commercial interests. Yet although de Gaulle's hostile diplomacy had ensured the failure of this policy, Whitehall's reaction was to recommend conciliation rather than retaliation to ministers. The reason for this was that Britain had no option other than to maintain a relationship with the EEC. The FTA negotiations had exposed the weakness of the strategy of influencing France via Germany, and also that in terms of Britain's European policy, the Anglo-American 'special relationship' counted for little. In Macmillan's view, Britain faced impending exclusion from Europe because of Washington's lack of interest and a hostile Franco-German 'unholy alliance'.[46] It was probably frustration at the prospect of this situation, together with a certain overestimation of Britain's international influence, which had led the prime minister to advocate an aggressive response to the EEC in the final months of the FTA negotiations. But ultimately even Macmillan recognised the need to maintain relations with the Six, as exemplified by his cautious policy towards sterling convertibility in the final months of the FTA negotiations. It was the continued development of the Six after the failure of the FTA negotiations which forced the Macmillan government and Whitehall to re-assess the foundations of policies pursued since the late 1940s and begin the process which would eventually culminate in Britain's first application for EEC membership in 1961.

A number of themes run through this study of Britain's reaction to the creation of the European Community from 1955 to 1958 which may inform the larger debate on the question of Britain and Europe. The first concerns the degree to which Britain's historical experience accounts for why it sought to remain 'with but not of' European integration until 1961 and has, since then, often resisted its further advancement. For John Young, 'Britain's historical experience and attitudes towards external affairs do not fit in well with European integration'.[47] Yet conversely, Wolfram Kaiser describes British exceptionalism as a myth, 'created by the British political elite'.[48] A sense of difference informed the decisions taken in the 1950s which set Britain apart from the Six. There was an unquantifiable psychological factor strongly linked to Britain's unique history and strengthened by inter-war and wartime experiences. Britain saw the outcome of the war as a triumph for which it could expect to be rewarded, and this attitude extended into institutions where old powers and practices survived conflict unchanged and less malleable to unprecedented development, such as the pooling of sovereignty. British uniqueness and defence of parliamentary sovereignty have been common denominators in debates since 1961 and may have been used by leaders and parties for political reasons but their importance to the history of Britain's relationship with the European Community cannot be doubted. To understand the part played by such issues over the long-term will mean adopting a methodological approach which analyses the relationship between governments' policies and public attitudes.[49]

The second theme is that for the British government, European integration created conflicts at many different levels. It was and has been essentially divisive. In the 1950s, the success of the Six presented Britain with a choice. It could either hope that they failed in their efforts, seek to contain them within a British-inspired organisation or abandon an independent policy and join them. Set against wider changes affecting Britain's political and economic interests, the issue of Europe came to represent the doorway between two worlds. In the old world, Britain acted as a global power whose pre-war independence had been replaced by post-war dependence on the United States; in the new world it would be a European power with unknown ramifications for its wider international status. From 1955 to 1958 there was no consensus on how to deal with this issue. Conflicts arose throughout the British government, from the Cabinet through Whitehall in general down into the departments.

That Europe had such an effect in these early stages, even at the purely élite level, helps explain why it has remained a divisive issue for the British ever since.

The third and final theme deals with Britain's reputation in Europe. During the FTA negotiations and the Brussels negotiations thereafter, there always existed a good deal of positive opinion amongst the Six for British involvement in European co-operation. This had much to do with political affinities, some born from the war, and expectations of Britain improving the form and future of the European Community. At the same time, converse opinion saw Britain as a threat to this same form and future. Such concerns existed in a triumvirate of interests. First, the French, who wished to protect the preferential status they had and, under de Gaulle, realise *la grandeur* through Europe. Then the Germans, who under Adenauer, sought to cement the foundations of the Community in an alliance with the French and who feared that the promise of European integration could be dashed by British involvement. Finally, the 'Europeanists', who were most significantly found in the European Commission. To them, the defence of the new Community was paramount and no matter how much of a transformation British ministers appeared to have undergone in their attachment to a European future, there was always anxiety that Britain might complicate rather than facilitate the further integration of Europe.

The FTA was designed to meet the threat posed to British interests by the creation of the EEC but in itself it was seen as threat to this new institution. Given the objectives of the FTA policy, namely to protect access to European export markets and maintain Britain's position in Europe, the British government can be said to have made mistakes in its response to the formation of the European Common Market after June 1955. Those mistakes were in the design of the FTA, which concentrated less on achieving acceptance by its prospective partners and more on attaining domestic approval. Mistakes were also made in the implementation of the policy, not least when diplomacy did not match the supposed new British initiative in Europe. Yet if the British government is to be criticised on its record from 1955 to 1958, then these criticisms have to be directed at the failure in approach, in dealing with the Six and in the general diplomatic weight attached to European relations. They should not, however, be angled at the thrust of the FTA policy itself. It is true that the British were reacting to events rather than setting the pace after autumn 1955 and that the FTA was a conservative proposal. Yet it did represent an attempt to adjust Britain's commercial interests and concentrate on trade policy which was a priority in Europe. Ultimately, the Six presented a challenge to Britain to which there was no perfect solution; for all its faults, Plan G was an understandable response to the developments on the Continent and in the Commonwealth and marked an advance in British attitudes towards European integration.

Otto Clarke, the Treasury official who had been greatly involved in post-war economic policy and was responsible for Plan G's development in Whitehall, later described Britain's long-term course as having been 'to display remarkable ingenuity to retain the status quo'.[50] It is in this light that Britain's FTA proposal has to be seen. Through the formulation of Plan G, Whitehall had concluded that Britain had to develop a new relationship with Europe to defend its established policies and meet Europe's rise within the geometry of the three circles. Doubtful about the long-term potential of the Six, opposed to their form of European co-operation, and yet fully aware of the necessity of securing Britain's position in Europe, British policy-makers designed the FTA to meet these divergent criteria. This was a difficult balancing act by any standards, especially when complicated by wider policies. In the final analysis, the FTA was an ingenious plan when viewed from Britain's position. Its failure was that when viewed from European and especially French perspectives, by threatening the future of the EEC the FTA was 'too ingenious for its own good'.[51]

Notes

Introduction

1　M. Camps, *Britain and the European Community 1955–1963* (London, 1964).
2　The two most significant works on British policy from June to December 1955 remain S. Burgess and G. Edwards, 'The Six plus One: British Policy Making and the Question of European Economic Integration, 1955', *International Affairs*, Vol. 64, No. 3 (1988), pp. 393–413, and J.W. Young, '"The Parting of the Ways"? Britain, the Messina Conference and the Spaak Committee, June–December 1955', in M. Dockrill and J.W. Young (eds), *British Foreign Policy 1945–56* (London, 1989), pp. 197–224.
3　On the historiographical trend see A. Lane, 'Diplomatic History', in L.J. Butler and A. Gorst (eds), *Modern British History: a Guide to Study and Research* (London, 1997), pp. 168–82, esp. p. 178; and J.W. Young, 'Britain and "Europe": the Shape of the Historiographical Debate' in B. Brivati, J. Buxton and A. Seldon (eds), *The Contemporary History Handbook* (Manchester, 1996), pp. 207–14. For four notable surveys, see B. Brivati and H. Jones (eds), *From Reconstruction to Integration: Britain and Europe since 1945* (Leicester, 1993); S. George, *An Awkward Partner: Britain in the European Community* (Oxford, 1990); S. Greenwood, *Britain and European Cooperation Since 1945* (Oxford, 1992); and J.W. Young, *Britain and European Unity, 1945–1992* (London, 1993). A.S. Milward also dedicates specific attention to the issue in Chapter 7 of *The European Rescue of the Nation-State* (London, 1992), pp. 345–433. More generally, see J. Barnes, 'From Eden to Macmillan, 1955–1959' in P. Hennessy and A. Seldon (eds), *Ruling Performance* (Oxford, 1987), pp. 98–149; R. Bullen, 'Britain and "Europe" 1950–1957' in E. Serra (ed.), *Il rilancio dell'Europa e i trattati di Roma* (Bruxelles, 1989), pp. 315–38; M. Charlton, *The Price of Victory* (London, 1983); and R. Lamb, *The Failure of the Eden Government* (London, 1987), pp. 59–101.
4　R.T. Griffiths and S. Ward, '"The End of Thousand Years of History". The Origins of Britain's Decision to Join the European Community 1955–1961', in R.T. Griffiths and S. Ward (eds), *Courting the Common Market: the First Attempt to Enlarge the European Community 1961–1963* (London, 1996), pp. 7–37; and similarly R.T. Griffiths, 'A Slow One Hundred and Eighty Degree Turn: British Policy Towards the Common Market, 1955–60' in G. Wilkes (ed.), *Britain's Failure to Enter the European Community 1961–63* (London, 1997), pp. 35–50; W. Kaiser, *Using Europe, Abusing the Europeans: Britain and European Integration, 1945–1963* (London, 1996), pp. 28–60; A. Moravcsik, *The Choice for Europe. Social Purpose and State Power from Messina to Maastricht* (London, 1998), esp. pp. 86–158; and H. Young, *This Blessed Plot. Britain and Europe from Churchill to Blair* (London, 1998).

5 For this view, C.A. Wurm, 'Britain and European Integration, 1945–63', *Contemporary European History*, Vol. 7, Part 2 (1998), pp. 249–61, esp. p. 255.

6 R. Mayne, *The Recovery of Europe* (London, 1970), p. 252. For cautious support of this view, H.J. Küsters, 'West Germany's Foreign Policy in Western Europe, 1949–58: the Art of the Possible', in C. Wurm (ed.) *Western Europe and Germany* (Oxford, 1995), pp. 55–85, esp. p. 71; A. Deighton 'Missing the Boat. Britain and Europe 1945–61', *Contemporary Record*, Vol. 3, No. 3, Feb. 1990, pp. 15–17. For more definite assessments, Charlton, *Price*, p. 198; Greenwood, *Britain and European Co-operation*, p. 68; R. Lamb, *The Macmillan Years 1957–1963* (London, 1995), p. 111.

7 J.R.V. Ellison, 'Perfidious Albion? Britain, Plan G and European Integration, 1955–1956', *Contemporary British History*, Vol. 10, No. 4 (1996), pp. 1–34; Kaiser, *Using Europe*, pp. 28–87; E. Kane, *Tilting to Europe?: British Responses to Developments in European Integration 1955–1958* (Unpublished DPhil thesis, Oxford, 1996); M. Schaad, 'Plan G – a "Counterblast"? British Policy towards the Messina Countries, 1956', *Contemporary European History*, Vol. 7, Part 1 (1998), pp. 39–60; and Young, *Britain and European Unity*, p. 50.

8 While Kaiser covers aspects of the negotiations he does so only as part of his greater analysis of policy development from 1958 onwards, see *Using Europe*, pp. 88–107. Kane has also dealt with the negotiations but her analysis is written largely from the perspective of the Foreign Office, see *Tilting*, pp. 93–165.

9 On 1961–63 see N.P. Ludlow, *Dealing with Britain. The Six and the First UK Application to the EEC* (Cambridge, 1997); also see the contributions in Griffiths and Ward (eds), *Courting the Common Market*, and in Wilkes (ed.), *Britain's Failure*. The only study of the Six and the FTA negotiations is E. Bloemen, 'A Problem to Every Solution. The Six and the Free Trade Area' in T.B. Olesen (ed.), *Interdependence Versus Integration* (Odense, 1995), pp. 182–96. Other studies on the policies of members of the Six will be referred to throughout this book.

10 Milward, *Rescue*, p. 395. Roger Bullen passes a similar judgement, 'The fear voiced in 1950 that Great Britain would become merely an island off the west coast of Europe was rapidly becoming a reality', 'Britain and "Europe" 1950–1957', pp. 315–38.

11 Bullen, 'Britain and "Europe" 1950–1957'; Greenwood, *Britain and European Co-operation*; J.W. Young, *Britain, France and the Unity of Europe 1945–51* (Leicester, 1984) and J.W. Young, 'Towards a New View of British Policy and European Unity 1945–57' in R. Ahmann, A.M. Birke and M. Howard (eds), *The Quest for Stability: Problems of West European Security 1918–1957* (Oxford, 1993). Milward, *Rescue*; also A. S. Milward, *The Reconstruction of Western Europe 1945–51* (London, 1984) and A.S. Milward and G. Brennan, *Britain's Place in the World. A Historical Enquiry into Import Controls 1945–60* (London, 1996).

12 Bullen, 'Britain and "Europe" 1950–1957', p. 324; Greenwood, *Britain and European Co-operation*, pp. 42–60; Young, 'Towards a New View...' p. 436 and Chapter 2 of *Britain and European Unity* in general. Also, Deighton, 'Missing the Boat', pp. 15–17.

13 Bullen, 'Britain and "Europe" 1950–1957', p. 319. Also Young, 'Towards a New View', p. 450.

14 Bullen, 'Britain and "Europe" 1950–1957', pp. 330–31; Young 'Towards and New View' p. 450. Also see Young's chapters on the EDC and the Schuman Plan in J.W. Young (ed.), *The Foreign Policy of Churchill's Peacetime Administration 1951–1955* (Leicester, 1988) pp. 81–108 and pp. 109–35 respectively.

15 For a detailed diplomatic analysis of Britain's decision not to participate in the ECSC discussions see Young *Britain, France and the Unity of Europe* pp. 141–67. Also for a published collection of documents, R. Bullen and M.E. Pelly (eds), *Documents on British Policy Overseas*, Series II, Vol. I, *The Schuman Plan, The Council of Europe and Western European Integration, 1950–1952* (London, 1986), Chapter 1. For more recent critical studies, E. Dell, *The Schuman Plan and the British Abdication of Leadership in Europe* (Oxford, 1995) and C. Lord, *Absent at the Creation: Britain and the Formation of the European Community, 1950–2* (Aldershot, 1996).

16 On the ECSC see J.W. Young, 'The Schuman Plan and British Association' in Young (ed.), *Churchill's Peacetime Administration* pp. 109–34. For a more detailed discussion of 1951–52 see J.W. Young 'Churchill's "No" to Europe: the "rejection" of European Union by Churchill's post-war government, 1951–2', *Historical Journal*, Vol. 28 (1985), pp. 923–31. For an interesting discussion of Eden's policy see H.J. Yasamee, 'Anthony Eden and Europe', *FCO Historical Branch Occasional Papers*, No. 1 (Nov. 1987), pp. 39–50. On the EDC see E. Fursdon, *The European Defence Community: a History* (London, 1980); S. Dockrill, 'The Evolution of Britain's Policy Towards a European Army 1950–54', *Journal of Strategic Studies*, Vol. 12, No. 1 (March 1989), pp. 38–62; S. Dockrill, *Britain's Policy for West German Rearmament, 1950–55* (Cambridge 1991). For studies focusing on German rearmament through the perspective of the Cold War, see S. Mawby, *Containing Germany: Britain and the Arming of the Federal Republic* (London, 1999), and K. Ruane, *The Rise and Fall of the European Defence Community: Anglo-American Relations and the Crisis of European Defence 1950–1955* (London, 2000).

17 Greenwood, *Britain and European Co-operation*, p. 69.

18 See A. Deighton, 'The Last Piece of the Jigsaw: Britain and the Creation of the Western European Union, 1954', *Contemporary European History*, Vol. 7, Part 2 (1998), pp. 181–97, and Ruane, *Rise and Fall*.

19 Young, 'Towards a New View' pp. 456–57. Also, Bullen, 'Britain and "Europe" 1950–57', p. 331; Deighton, 'Last Piece of the Jigsaw', pp. 194–6; Ruane, *Rise and Fall*, pp. 175–99.

20 Milward, *Rescue*, p. 345 and p. 390.

21 Milward, *Rescue*, p. 390.

22 Milward, *Rescue*, pp. 349–56. For similar conclusions, A. Cairncross, *Years of Recovery. British Economic Policy 1945–51* (London, 1985), pp. 234–99 and A. Cairncross, *The British Economy Since 1945* (Oxford, 1992), pp. 10–11.

23 Milward, *Rescue*, p. 356.

24 Milward, *Rescue*, p. 358.

25 Milward, *Rescue*, p. 386.

26 Moravcsik, *Choice*, pp. 122–35.
27 See Milward, *Rescue*, p. 395.
28 R. Bullen and M.E. Pelly (eds), *Documents on British Policy Overseas*, Series II, Vol. II, The London Conference. Anglo-American Relations and Cold War Strategy January–June 1950 (London, 1987), Doc. 33, p. 115.
29 A. Eden, *Full Circle* (London 1960) p. 12.
30 These were Austria, Belgium, Denmark, France, the Federal Republic of Germany, Greece, Iceland, Ireland, Italy, Luxembourg, the Netherlands, Norway, Portugal, Sweden, Switzerland, Turkey and the United Kingdom.
31 C. Thorne, *Border Crossings. Studies in International History* (Oxford, 1988), p. 107.

1 Malicious Conception: the Counter-Initiative, June–December 1955

1 Hansard, *House of Commons Debates*, 5th series, vol. 542, cols. 593–610, 15 June 1955.
2 *Correspondence arising out of the Meeting of the Foreign Ministers of the Governments of Belgium, France, the Federal Republic of Germany, Italy, Luxembourg and the Netherlands held at Messina on June 1–2, 1955*, Macmillan to Bech, 15 June 1955, Cmd. 9525 (HMSO, 1955), p. 9.
3 Burgess and Edwards, 'Six plus One', pp. 393–413; Young, '"Parting of the Ways"?', pp. 203–11.
4 Compare Kaiser, *Using Europe*, pp. 28–60, Milward, *Rescue*, pp. 424–7 and H. Young, *Blessed Plot*, pp. 78–98.
5 Moravcsik, *Choice*, pp. 122–35.
6 Two recent doctoral theses covering the evolution of Plan G do not employ Board of Trade archives and underestimate the Board's role in policy development, see Kane, *Tilting* and M.P.C. Schaad, *Anglo-German Relations during the Formative Years of the European Community* 1955–61 (Unpublished DPhil Thesis, Oxford, 1995). While Kaiser has used Board of Trade files, *Using Europe* makes no substantial link between the counter-initiative studies and Plan G.
7 Public Record Office (PRO) CAB128/29, CC(55) 19th meeting, 30 June 1955; Cmd 9525, p. 10, Macmillan to Beyen, 1 July 1955. The Spaak Committee was named after its chairman, the Belgian Foreign Minister, Paul-Henri Spaak; see Spaak, *Battle*, pp. 227–52.
8 On Bretherton's role, Burgess and Edwards, 'Six plus One', pp. 399–400; Young '"Parting of the Ways"', pp. 203–4. Also, Charlton, *Price*, p. 179. Bretherton was accompanied by P. Nicholls of the Treasury, and E.B. Boothby and J.C. Peterson, both from the Brussels Embassy, PRO FO371/116044/134, MAE/CIG Doc. No. 54, 26 July 1955.
9 PRO CAB134/1029, MAC(55)147, 4 Aug. 1955. Burgess and Edwards, 'Six plus One', pp. 399–407; Young '"Parting of the Ways"?', pp. 203–11.
10 CAB134/1026, MAC(55) 45th meeting, 27 Oct. 1955.
11 CAB134/889, ES(55) 8th meeting, 1 Nov. 1955.
12 Most recently, H. Young, berates the Office for its 'sonorous vacuities', *Blessed Plot*, p. 96.

13 Ruane, *Rise and Fall*, p. 196. Also see Deighton, 'Last Piece of the Jigsaw', pp. 181–97.
14 Kaiser, *Using Europe*, pp. 36–42, esp. p. 37.
15 Kaiser, *Using Europe*, p. 41 and pp. 42–60.
16 The WOD papers for 1955–57 were released ten years after the thirty year rule in 1997. For background on the WOD, M. Beloff, *New Dimensions in Foreign Policy. A Study in British Administrative Experience 1947–59* (London, 1961), p. 124.
17 On the late 1940s, S. Greenwood, *The Alternative Alliance: Anglo-French Relations Before the Coming of NATO, 1944–48* (London, 1996), pp. 59–65, esp. p. 62; J.W. Young, *Britain, France and the Unity of Europe, 1945–51* (Leicester, 1984), pp. 118–28.
18 DBPO, Series II, Vol. II, Doc. No. 33, p. 115.
19 On early policy towards NATO, P. Foot, 'Britain, European Unity and NATO, 1947–50', in F.H. Heller and J.R. Gillingham (eds), *NATO: the Founding of the Atlantic Alliance and the Integration of Europe* (London, 1992), pp. 57–72, esp. pp. 68–9.
20 DBPO, Series II, Vol. I, Doc. No. 392, FO Brief for the Secretary of State, 31 Oct. 1951, pp. 742–4.
21 J.W. Young, 'British Officials and European Integration, 1944–1960', *Discussion Papers on Britain and Europe* (Leicester University, 1994), p. 11.
22 On association with the ECSC, C. Lord, '"With but not of": Britain and the Schuman Plan, a Reinterpretation', *Journal of European Integration History*, Vol. 4, No. 2 (1998), pp. 23–46; Young, 'The Schuman Plan and British Association', pp. 109–34. On the EDC and the WEU in general, Dockrill, *Britain's Policy for West German Rearmament, 1950–55*; Mawby, *Containing Germany*; Ruane, *Rise and Fall*; and J.W. Young, 'German Rearmament and the European Defence Community' in Young (ed.), *Peacetime Administration*, pp. 81–108.
23 DBPO, Series II, Vol. I, Doc. No. 413, PUSC(51)12(Final), 12 Dec. 1951, pp. 781–8, esp. p. 785.
24 DBPO, Series II, Vol. I, Doc. No. 413, PUSC(51)12(Final), 12 Dec. 1951, pp. 781–8, esp. p. 786.
25 FO371/118580/25, Weir to Hood, 16 March 1955; FO371/118580/31, Hood minute, 19 April 1955.
26 FO371/116038/1, Edden minute, 14 May 1955.
27 FO371/116038/1, Coulson minute, 20 May 1955.
28 Economic specialists were small in number within the Office; the MAD and the Economic Relations Department were thought to be out of place within the Office structure; comments made to author by John Moore Heath (First Secretary, MAD, FO, 1956–8), interview with author, Aug. 1994, and also by Sir Guy Millard (Private Secretary to Prime Minister 1955–56), interview with author, June 1996. On this point at an earlier stage, A. Adamthwaite, 'The Foreign Office and Policy-making' in Young (ed.), *Peacetime Administration*, pp. 18–19.
29 H. Macmillan, *Riding the Storm, 1956–1959* (London, 1971), p. 67.
30 FO371/116042/114, Stretton 'Record of Conversation', 29 June 1955.
31 FO371/116042/114, Stretton 'Record of Conversation', 29 June 1955.

32 Comment made by Alan Edden (Head of the MAD, FO, 1954–58), let-
    ter to Sir Denis Wright, 21 Dec. 1987, by kind permission of Sir Denis
    Wright (Assistant Under-Secretary of State, FO, 1955–59), interview with
    author, Sept. 1995.
33 Kaiser, *Using Europe*, pp. 42–60.
34 On these issues, H. Macmillan, *Tides of Fortune, 1945–1955* (London,
    1969).
35 FO371/116048/224b, Macmillan minute, 19 Sept. 1955.
36 PRO T232/432, Butler minute, 20 Sept. 1955. Macmillan sat in the
    Council of Europe Assembly at Strasbourg from 1949 to 1951, Alistair
    Horne, *Macmillan 1894–1956* (London, 1988), p. 322.
37 FO371/116040/52G, Edden minute, 29 June 1955; FO371/116041/74,
    Warner, Brussels to FO, 9 July 1955; FO371/116045/162, Boothby, Brussels
    to FO, 8 Aug. 1955.
38 FO371/116050/275, Ellis Rees to Macmillan, 1 Oct. 1955; FO371/116052/
    316, Jebb to FO, 8 Nov. 1955; also, FO371/116052/312G, Edden minute,
    9 Nov. 1955.
39 FO371/118586/7b, Harrison minute, 10 Aug. 1955. Also see J.W. Young,
    'The Geneva Conference of Foreign Ministers October–November 1955',
    Discussion Papers in Diplomacy No. 9 (University of Leicester: Centre
    for the Study of Diplomacy, 1995).
40 FO371/118557/136, Hood to Caccia, 10 Dec. 1955.
41 See also L. Kane, 'European or Atlantic Community? The Foreign Of-
    fice and "Europe" 1955–1957', *Journal of European Integration History*,
    Vol. 3, No. 2 (1997), pp. 83–98.
42 FO371/118559/57, Edden minute, 3 Dec. 1955.
43 FO371/116056/365, Wright to Labouchere, 6 Dec. 1955.
44 FO371/124783/1, Bushell minute, 17 Jan. 1956.
45 PRO T234/181, Trend minute, 26 Oct. 1955.
46 Comment made by Sir Guy Millard in interview with the author, June
    1996.
47 FO371/116052/312G, Edden minute, 9 Nov. 1955.
48 FO371/116054/347, Kirkpatrick to Jebb, 24 Nov. 1955.
49 T232/432, Bridges minute, 20 Sept. 1955; also, T234/700, Hubback brief,
    29 Sept. 1955.
50 On the Economic Section, CAB134/1029, MAC(55) 136, 14 July 1955;
    Burgess and Edwards, 'Six plus One', p. 403.
51 See Butler's comments in Charlton, *Price*, pp. 194–5; On OFD, T234/
    23, van Loo to Clarke, 29 Oct. 1955; Bank of England Archives (BOE)
    OV47/7, doc. 37b, Extract, Governor's Note, 12 Oct. 1955; Burgess
    and Edwards, 'Six plus One', p. 403. On the Bank, BOE OV47/7, doc.
    48, Parsons to Governor, 25 Oct. 1955.
52 T234/23, van Loo to Clarke, 29 Oct. 1955.
53 On policy from 1945 to 1950, Milward, *Reconstruction*, pp. 237–9; S.
    Newton, 'Britain, the Sterling Area, and European Integration, 1945–
    1950', *Journal of Imperial and Commonwealth History*, Vol. 13, No. 3
    (1985), pp. 163–82; Young, *Britain, France and the Unity of Europe*, pp.
    118–28. For the 1950s, Cairncross, *The British Economy Since 1945*, pp.
    90–133; Milward, *Rescue*, pp. 348–66; G.D.N. Worswick in G.D.N.

Worswick and P.H. Ady (eds), *The British Economy in the Nineteen-Fifties* (Oxford, 1962), pp. 1–75. In general, B.W.E. Alford, *Britain in the World Economy Since 1880* (London, 1996); J.C.R. Dow, *The Management of the British Economy 1945–60* (Cambridge, 1964); A. Shonfield, *British Economic Policy Since the War* (London, 1958); Strange, *Sterling and British Policy*.

54 Camps, *Britain*, p. 47.
55 T234/181, Trend minute, 26 Oct. 1955.
56 T234/181, Treasury meeting, 28 Oct. 1955.
57 K. Middlemas, *Power, Competition and the State,* Vol. I (London, 1986), pp. 250–3.
58 Charlton, *Price*, p. 168; Middlemas, *Power*, p. 252. On East-West trade, J.W. Young, 'Winston Churchill's Peacetime Administration and the Relaxation of East-West Trade Contols, 1953–54', *Diplomacy and Statecraft*, Vol. 7, No. 1 (March 1996), pp. 125–40.
59 PRO CAB129/59, C(53)70, 19 Feb. 1953.
60 CAB134/1029, MAC(55)135, 13 July 1955.
61 On the late 1940s, Milward, *Reconstruction*, p. 237.
62 PRO BT241/294, McIntosh on EP(55)38, 11 Oct. 1955.
63 PRO T236/4033, Dean minute, 9 Nov. 1954.
64 Central Statistical Office (CSO), *Annual Abstract of Statistics (AAS)*, Nos. 93 and 97, 1956 and 1960.
65 PRO BT11/5715, Lee minute, 20 Sept. 1955.
66 BT11/5715, Bretherton minute, 17 Nov. 1955. For criticism of Bretherton, Peter Jenkins, 'The Bretherton syndrome of "Britain knows best"', *The Independent*, 6 Nov. 1991; for a recent defence, H. Young, *Blessed Plot*, p. 70 and pp. 86–98.
67 BT11/5715, Swindlehurst POM609, 24 Oct. 1955.
68 'Walled garden' from *The Economist*, 'Critical Months for Free Trade', 22 March 1958.
69 CAB134/889, ES(55) 8th meeting, 1 Nov. 1955. On Lee, P. Hennessy, *Whitehall* (London, 1989), p. 160.
70 FO371/116052/306, FO to Paris, 2 Nov. 1955; FO371/116052/313, Labouchere, Brussels to FO, 7 Nov. 1955; FO371/116055/361, MAE/CIG No. 360, 14 Nov. 1955.
71 FO371/116052/313, Munro minute, 11 Nov. 1955.
72 *The Economist*, 'Britain and Europe's "Third Chance"', 19 Nov. 1955; FO371/116054/344, Meiklereid to Edden, 15 Nov. 1955. Also, Sir Roy Denman, *Missed Chances. Britain and Europe in the Twentieth Century* (London, 1996), p. 198, and H. Young, *Blessed Plot*, pp. 92–4.
73 CAB134/1226, EP(55) 11th meeting, 11 Nov. 1955.
74 T234/700, FO to Washington, 17 Nov. 1955.
75 FO371/116035B/122, Ellis Rees to FO, 7 Dec. 1955.
76 FO371/116054/341, Watson, Washington to Edden, 10 Nov. 1955.
77 T234/181, Wright to Bretherton, 18 Nov. 1955; FO371/116035A/108, Bretherton to Wright, 19 Nov. 1955.
78 T234/181, Cairncross, No. 10, to Petch, 19 Nov. 1955.
79 FO371/116054/347, Jebb to Kirkpatrick, 18 Nov. 1955.
80 FO371/116056/369, Millar to Kirkpatrick, 2 Dec. 1955.

81 FO371/116056/365, Labouchere to Harrison, 24 Nov. 1955; FO371/ 116035B/124, Mason to FO, 10 Dec. 1955.
82 T234/181, Note for the Record, 2 Nov. 1955.
83 FO371/116035B/123, Mason to FO, 10 Dec. 1955; FO371/116035B/138, Hope minute, 15 Dec. 1955.
84 FO371/116055/349, FO brief, 18 Nov. 1955; FO371/116054/345, Strath minute, 18 Nov. 1955; T234/181, Bridges minute, 21 Nov. 1955.
85 National Records and Archives Adminstration, Washington, DC, USA (NARA) RG59/840.00/11–2155, Brussels to State, 21 Nov. 1955.
86 FO371/116057/384, Macmillan to FO, 15 Dec. 1955; Macmillan Papers, Bodleian Library, Oxford, MS Macmillan dep.d.24*, diary, 14 Dec. 1955; Macmillan, *Riding*, p. 72 and Spaak, *Battle*, pp. 232–5.
87 FO371/116035/35, C.E. Brief(55)120, 11 Dec. 1955.
88 FO371/116056/378, Jebb to FO, 13 Dec. 1955; FO371/116035B/130, Jebb to FO, 14 Dec. 1955; FO371/116057/388, Jebb to FO, 23 Dec. 1955.
89 FO371/116057/398, Clarke, Rome to FO, 23 Dec. 1955.
90 FO371/116035A/110, Millar to FO, 19 Nov. 1955.
91 *Foreign Relations of the United States (FRUS)*, 1955–57, Vol. IV, doc. 141, Dulles, Paris to State, 17 Dec. 1955.
92 FO371/115999/12, Munro minute, 7 Dec. 1955.
93 FO371/116035A/112, Makins to FO, 22 Nov. 1955; FO371/115999/14, Makins to Caccia, 23 Dec. 1955; FO371/116056/382b, Dulles to Macmillan, 13 Dec. 1955. Also, J.E. Helmreich, 'The United States and the Formation of EURATOM', *Diplomatic History*, Vol. 15, No. 3 (Summer 1991), pp. 387–410.
94 *FRUS*, 1955–57, Vol. IV, doc. 129, National Security Council meeting, 21 Nov. 1955; FO371/116057/385, Hancock minute, 15 Dec. 1955.
95 For a clear exposition of US policy, *FRUS*, 1955–57, Vol. IV, doc. 143, Memo. of Conversation, 21 Dec. 1955.
96 *FRUS*, 1955–57, Vol. IV, doc. 139, Dulles to Eisenhower, 17 Dec. 1955.
97 *FRUS*, 1955–57, Vol. IV, doc. 144, The Hague to State, 21 Dec. 1955.
98 On this, Burgess and Edwards, 'Six plus One', pp. 412–13; Charlton, *Price*, p. 194; Greenwood, *Britain and European Cooperation*, p. 67; Lamb, *Eden Government*, p. 79; Young, '"Parting of the Ways"?', p. 217.
99 FO371/116047/386, Edden minute, 14 Dec. 1955. Avon Papers, University of Birmingham (by kind permission of the Avon Trustees), AP23/ 48/83, Eden to Macmillan, 22 Sept. 1967.
100 CAB134/1226, EP(55)11th meeting, 11 Nov. 1955.
101 BOE OV47/7, doc. 48, Parsons to Cobbold, 25 Oct. 1955. Also, BOE OV47/7, doc. 42a, Cobbold note, 19 Oct. 1955; BOE OV47/7, doc. 52, Bank minute, 2 Nov. 1955.
102 BT11/5715, Bretherton note, 22 Oct. 1955.
103 Camps, *Britain*, p. 34 and pp. 38–9.
104 BT11/5715, Bretherton note, 22 Oct. 1955.
105 CAB134/889, ES(55)8th meeting, 1 Nov. 1955.
106 CAB134/1030, MAC(55)211, 11 Nov. 1955. Also, T234/181, Note of an informal meeting, 9 Nov. 1955.
107 CAB134/1026, MAC(55)48th meeting, 16 Nov. 1955.
108 T234/700, Edden to Trend, 19 Oct. 1955.

109   See for example C.J. Bartlett, *British Foreign Policy in the Twentieth Century* (London, 1989), p. 117; Milward, *Rescue*, p. 433; Young, 'Towards a New View', p. 460.
110   Macmillan, *Riding*, p. 69; N. Henderson, *Channels and Tunnels. Reflections on Britain and Abroad* (London, 1987), pp. 153–4; comments made by various retired civil servants to the author. Also, A. Nutting, *Europe Will Not Wait. A Warning and a Way Out* (London, 1960), pp. 83–4.
111   Examples of this school are, A. Cairncross, *British Economy*, pp. 129–30; Deighton, 'Missing the Boat', pp. 15–17; Lamb, *Eden Government*, pp. 59–101; Milward, *Rescue*, pp. 424–33. For brief mention of this, Dell, *The Schuman Plan*, p. 303.
112   Camps, 'Missing the boat at Messina and other times?' in B. Brivati and H. Jones, *From Reconstruction to Integration* (Leicester, 1993), pp. 134–43; Greenwood, *Britain and European Cooperation*, pp. 73–6; Griffiths and Ward, ' "Thousand Years" ', pp. 31–2; Kane, *Tilting*, pp. 38–9; Young, ' "Parting of the Ways" ', pp. 217–18.
113   Wurm, 'Britain and European Integration, 1945–63', pp. 249–61, esp. p. 255.
114   Kaiser, *Using Europe*, pp. 54–6.
115   Moravcsik, *Choice*, pp. 131–5.
116   T234/700, cited by Clarke to Edden, 29 Oct. 1955.
117   CAB134/1228, EP(55)53, 7 Nov. 1955.
118   CAB134/1228, EP(55)54, 7 Nov. 1955.
119   CAB134/1228, EP(55)55, 7 Nov. 1955.
120   Milward, *Reconstruction*, pp. 248–50.
121   BT11/5715, Swindlehurst POM609, 24 Oct. 1955.
122   T232/433, Watts to Hall, 14 Oct. 1955.

2   Fresh Impetus: Formulating Plan G, January–May 1956

1   A. Eden, *Full Circle* (London, 1960), pp. 317–19.
2   Macmillan to his official biographer, Horne, *Macmillan Vol. 1*, pp. 379–80. Also, Macmillan, *Riding*, pp. 686–97.
3   Horne, *Macmillan Vol. 1*, p. 385; Macmillan, *Riding*, pp. 692–3.
4   D. Carlton, *Anthony Eden* (London, 1981), pp. 388–9.
5   Camps, *Britain*, pp. 51–2.
6   On the importance of Mollet's government to the Six's development, F. Duchêne, *Jean Monnet. The First Statesman of Interdependence* (New York, 1994), p. 288; H.J. Küsters, 'The Origins of the EEC Treaty', in E. Serra (ed.), *Il rilancio dell'Europa e i trattati di Roma* (Brussels, 1989), pp. 211–38, esp. p. 233; Milward, *Rescue*, p. 207. Also, Macmillan, *Riding*, p. 74 and Nutting, *Europe*, pp. 88–9. In general, M. Larkin, *France Since the Popular Front* (Oxford, 1988), pp. 251–6.
7   FO371/124421/22, Jebb to FO, 13 Jan. 1956; FO371/124712/2, Hood minute, 23 Jan. 1956; PRO PREM11/1848, Jebb to FO, 30 Jan. 1956.
8   T234/182, Clarke minute, 16 Jan. 1956.
9   CAB134/1282, MAC(56) 2nd meeting, 10 Jan. 1956; CAB134/1283, MAC(56)6 (Final), 13 Jan. 1956.

10 FO371/122022/1, Hood and Edden minutes, Jan. 1956.
11 FO371/122022/8, Harrison minute, 16 Jan. 1956.
12 FO371/122023/20, Nutting to Lloyd, 10 Jan. 1956; FO371/124727/1, Nutting minute, 20 March 1956.
13 FO371/122024/46, Wright to Labouchere, 3 March 1956.
14 On Eden's view, Carlton, *Eden*, p. 300; J. Charmley, *Churchill's Grand Alliance. The Anglo-American Special Relationship 1940–57* (London, 1995), pp. 360–1; D. Dimbleby and D. Reynolds, *An Ocean Apart* (London, 1988), p. 227; D. Dutton, *Anthony Eden: a Life and Reputation* (London, 1997), pp. 253–4; R. Rhodes James, *Anthony Eden* (London, 1986), pp. 352–3.
15 FO371/122022/11, Thorneycroft to Eden, 20 Jan. 1956.
16 FO371/122022/11, Rodgers minute, 26 Jan. 1956, Munro minute, 25 Jan. 1956, Edden minute, 26 Jan. 1956.
17 FO371/124543/4(2), Caccia minute, 4 Jan. 1956.
18 For minutes of the meetings, Avon Papers (University of Birmingham, by kind permission of the Avon Trustees), AP20/29/2A, Visit of the Prime Minister and the Secretary of State to Washington, January 30th–February 3rd 1956, Document No. 1, 'Record of a meeting at the White House on Monday, January 30th, 1956, at 2.30 pm'.
19 CAB128/30, CM10(56)1, 9 Feb. 1956. Also, Eden, *Full Circle*, pp. 336–7.
20 Hansard, *House of Commons Debates*, 5th series, vol. 548, cols. 2082–3, 13 Feb. 1956.
21 *FRUS*, 1955–57, Vol. IV, doc. 150, Dulles to Embassy, Belgium, 26 Jan. 1956; NARA RG59/840.00/2-356, Memo. of Conversation: Rothschild and Sprouse, 31 Jan. 1956; *FRUS*, 1955–57, Vol. IV, doc. 156, Dillon, Paris to State, 7 Feb. 1956 and doc. 162, Memo. of Conversation: Dulles and Martino, 1 March 1956.
22 CAB129/60, C(53)108, 19 March 1953. Macmillan was Minister of Housing and Local Government from 1951–54.
23 Macmillan, *Riding*, p. 72.
24 T234/183, Macmillan to Rowan, 23 Jan. 1956.
25 Macmillan Papers, Bodleian Library, Oxford, MS Macmillan dep. d.25*, diary, 28 Jan. 1956.
26 T234/100, Macmillan to Bridges, 1 Feb. 1956.
27 Papers of the 1st Viscount Norwich, Churchill College, Cambridge, DUFC 4/7, Duff Cooper despatch, 30 May 1944.
28 T234/100, Macmillan to Bridges, 1 Feb. 1956.
29 T234/183, Macmillan minute, 6 Feb. 1956.
30 T234/100, Clarke minute, 10 Feb. 1956. On the relationship between these two mandarins see A. Cairncross (ed.), *The Robert Hall Diaries, Vol. II 1954–1961* (London, 1991), pp. 167–8.
31 On HOPS, Beloff, *New Dimensions*, p. 154, and S. Brittan, *The Treasury under the Tories 1951–1964* (Harmondsworth, 1964), p. 172.
32 On *de facto* convertibility, Cairncross, *British Economy*, pp. 124–5; Milward, *Rescue*, p. 387.
33 T234/100, Rowan minute, 22 Feb. 1956; T234/101, Rowan minute, 28 May 1956.

34 Quoted in Brittan, *Treasury under the Tories*, p. 200. The Radcliffe Committee was a public enquiry into the workings of the monetary system, Cairncross, *British Economy*, pp. 97–9.
35 T234/100, Macmillan minute, 24 Feb. 1956.
36 T234/701, Clarke minute, 11 Feb. 1956.
37 For a critical analysis of the Collective Approach, Milward, *Rescue*, pp. 358ff.
38 T234/701, Clarke minute, 11 Feb. 1956.
39 In general, see A. Cairncross and N. Watts (eds), *The Economic Section 1939–1961* (London, 1989).
40 Hall's diary entry, 30 July 1958, in Cairncross (ed.), *Robert Hall Diaries Vol. II*, p. 167.
41 Hall's diary entries, 1 Oct. 1954 and 30 Aug. 1956, in Cairncross (ed.), *Robert Hall Diaries Vol. II*, p. 17 and pp. 73–4 respectively.
42 T234/196, Watts to Figgures, 3 Aug. 1956; PRO T230/395, Note by Economic Section, 17 Aug. 1956.
43 For a contemporary critical analysis of economic policy see Shonfield, *British Economic Policy*.
44 CAB129/59, C(53)70, 19 Feb. 1953.
45 BT11/5402, Kipping to Lee, 20 Feb. 1956.
46 For interesting analysis of business attitudes, A. McKinlay, N. Rollings and J. Smyth, 'British Business and European Integration, 1945–1964' in M. Davids, F. de Goey and D. de Wit (eds), *Proceedings of the Conference on Business History, Oct. 1994, The Netherlands* (Rotterdam, 1995), pp. 330–41. For the classic study of parties, élites and pressure groups, R.J. Lieber, *British Politics and European Unity* (London, 1970), esp. pp. 54–8; also, Charlton, *Price*, pp. 193–4.
47 PRO BT205/238, Swindlehurst POM231, 10 March 1956.
48 BT241/296, McIntosh minute, 18 April 1956; BT205/238, Lee minute, 19 April 1956.
49 Middlemas suggests the Salisbury Group never forgave Thorneycroft for his criticism of the Sterling Area, *Power*, p. 253.
50 BT241/295, Swindlehurst POM63, 16 Jan. 1956.
51 BT205/242, Thorneycroft to Eden, 9 Nov. 1956.
52 BT205/238, Gibbs minute, 23 April 1956.
53 T234/182, Clarke minute, 16 Jan. 1956.
54 T234/701, Bretherton to Figgures, 27 Jan. 1956.
55 T234/701, Bretherton, 'Possible Forms of Association by the United Kingdom with the European Common Market', Jan. 1956.
56 See, for example, BT205/220, Currall minutes, 6 Sept. 1955 and 24 Sept. 1955.
57 Camps, *Britain*, pp. 38–40. Also, Kaiser, *Using Europe*, pp. 67–8.
58 A.G. Harryvan and A.E. Kersten, 'The Netherlands, Benelux and the Relance Européenne 1954–1955', in Serra (ed.), *Il rilancio*, pp. 125–57, esp. pp. 137–8. Also, W. Asbeek Brusse, *West European Tariff Plans, 1947–1957. From Study Group to Common Market* (Unpublished PhD thesis, European University Institute, Florence, 1991), pp. 230–51.
59 Milward, *Rescue*, p. 195.
60 FO371/122050/1, Munro minute, 9 Jan. 1956.

61 FO371/122023/23 and /25, Labouchere to FO, 13 Feb. 1956 and 14 Feb. 1956 respectively.
62 T234/103, Spaak to Eden, 7 Feb. 1956; Charlton, *Price*, pp. 200–1.
63 Charlton, *Price*, pp. 200–1.
64 T234/103, Hood to Clarke, 18 Feb. 1956; T234/103, Macmillan minute, 21 Feb. 1956; T234/103, Figgures to Clarke, 24 Feb. 1956.
65 Spaak, *Battle*, pp. 233–4.
66 Macmillan, *Riding*, p. 75.
67 FO371/122022/17, Rodgers minute, 1 Feb. 1956. Also, see Helmreich, 'The United States and the Formation of EURATOM', pp. 387–410; P. Winand, *Eisenhower, Kennedy and the United States of Europe* (London, 1992), pp. 83–108.
68 FO371/121950/42, Millar to FO, 16 Feb. 1956; FO371/121951/76, Jebb to Kirkpatrick, 21 Feb. 1956. Also, see Marjolin, *Architect*, p. 299.
69 FO371/122048/30, Millar to FO, 2 Feb. 1956.
70 FO371/121950/45, Millar to FO, 18 Feb. 1956.
71 FO371/121975/3 and /4, Note of a discussion and Note of a meeting, 23 Feb. 1956 and 22 Feb. 1956 respectively.
72 For this view, Schaad, *Anglo-German Relations*, pp. 81–90.
73 FO371/121972/11, Record of Conversation, 16 Feb. 1956.
74 FO371/121922/74, Thorneycroft to Macmillan, 18 Feb. 1956.
75 FO371/121922/74, Hope to Lloyd, 21 Feb. 1956.
76 FO371/121922/74, Wright minute, 23 Feb. 1956; also, FO371/121922/74, Edden minute, 22 Feb. 1956.
77 FO371/121922/74, Record of Meeting, 23 Feb. 1956.
78 FO371/121918/2, Minutes of the 316th Meeting of the OEEC Council, 28/29 Feb. 1956. An OEEC Special Committee on Nuclear Energy was established at this meeting to examine measures to be taken within the OEEC and also the relationship between any new OEEC machinery and Euratom. Also see Camps, *Britain*, p. 93.
79 FO371/122044/18, Ellis Rees to FO, 3 March 1956.
80 Hansard, *House of Commons Debates*, 5th series, vol.549, col. 869, 27 Feb. 1956; Lord Gladwyn, *The Memoirs of Lord Gladwyn* (London, 1972), p. 289.
81 Camps, *Britain*, p. 93; NARA RG59/840.00/5–956, London to State, 9 May 1956.
82 *FRUS*, 1955–57, Vol. IV, doc. 173, Dulles to Embassy, Belgium, 24 May 1956.
83 FO371/121919/17, Reports on conversation between Macmillan and Ramadier, 27 Feb. 1956. Also, Macmillan, *Riding*, p. 75.
84 PREM11/1337, Macmillan to Eden, 28 Feb. 1956. Also, Macmillan Papers, Bodleian Library, Oxford, MS Macmillan dep. d.25*, diary, 28 Feb. 1956, and Macmillan, *Riding*, pp. 75–6.
85 PREM11/1337, Eden to Macmillan, 3 March 1956.
86 FO371/122024/44, Wright minute, 6 March 1956.
87 FO371/122024/50, Report of the first meeting of the Working Group, 6 March 1956.
88 T234/100, Clarke minute, 7 March 1956.
89 CAB134/1373, AOC(56)2nd meeting, 5 March 1956. AOC was chaired

by the Cabinet Secretary, Sir Norman Brook, and staffed by senior officials from the Foreign Office, the Ministry of Defence, and the Treasury.

90   T234/100, Macmillan to Clarke, 12 March 1956; T234/701, Macmillan to Clarke, 16 March 1956; T234/100, RWBC/I.E./7, 20 March 1956. On Harrod's wider communications with Macmillan, PREM11/2973.

91   *Manchester Guardian*, 'Outside Europe's Market: I – The British Dilemma' and 'II – A Free Trade Area?', 14/15 March 1956. On Meade, Cairncross and Watts, *Economic Section*, pp. 113–31.

92   T234/701, Meade, LSE, to Figgures, 24 Jan. 1956; T234/701, Figgures to Bretherton, 25 Jan. 1956.

93   T234/701, Bretherton to Figgures, 27 Jan. 1956; T234/701, Figgures to Bretherton, 31 Jan. 1956.

94   FO371/122044/21, RWBC/I.E./4, undated, received 15 March 1956.

95   T236/6018, Symons to France, 19 March 1956.

96   FO371/122024/63, France minute, undated, received 27 March 1956.

97   FO371/122025/79, RWBC/I.E./15 (Final), 20 April 1956.

98   On the original Council of Europe idea, see Young, *Britain and European Unity*, p. 24.

99   BT11/5715, Bretherton minute, 24 April 1956; also, T234/101, Cohen to France, 8 May 1956.

100   BT11/5715, Swindlehurst POM390, 11 May 1956.

101   FO371/122028/107, Thorneycroft, 'Initiative in Europe', 22 May 1956.

102   T234/101, Macmillan to Clarke, 28 May 1956.

103   T234/101, Minutes of a Meeting, 24 April 1956; T234/101, Meeting at the House, 8 May 1956; T234/101, Rowan minute, 28 May 1956.

104   T234/100, Macmillan minute, 24 Feb. 1956; J. Turner notes an earlier clash between Macmillan and the Treasury over this plan, *Macmillan* (London, 1994), p. 83. For HOPS and the Economic Section, T234/101, Clarke minute, 29 May 1956; T230/395, Day to Figgures, 11 May 1956.

105   T234/101, Clarke minute, 29 May 1956. For minutes of the key Working Group meetings, FO371/122024/64, RWBC/I.E./4th meeting, 26 March 1956; FO371/122025/72, RWBC/I.E./6th meeting, 11 April 1956.

106   T234/101, Clarke minute, 29 May 1956.

107   Kaiser argues to the contrary, *Using Europe*, pp. 71–2.

108   T234/100, Clarke minute, 21 Feb. 1956.

109   FO371/122024/21, RWBC/I.E./4, undated, received 15 March 1956.

110   BT11/5715, Sanders minute, 22 May 1956.

111   This is the view of Kaiser, *Using Europe*, pp. 62–3.

112   CAB134/1282, MAC(56)11th, 20 March 1956; FO371/122024/66, RWBC/I.E./5th meeting, 29 March 1956.

113   FO371/122044/21, Edden and Laskey minutes, both 12 March 1956. FO371/122025/79, Wright minute, 30 April 1956. Also see Schaad, 'Counterblast', p. 53.

114   Comment made by Sir Denis Wright, Assistant Under-Secretary of State, Foreign Office, 1955–59, interview with the author, Sept. 1995.

115 FO371/122028/108, Caccia minute, 30 May 1956.
116 Comment made by Alan Edden, Head of the Mutual Aid Department 1954–58, Edden to Sir Denis Wright, 21 Dec. 1987, by kind permission of Sir Denis Wright.
117 T234/103, Hood to Clarke, 18 Feb. 1956. Also see Kane, 'European or Atlantic Community?', pp. 88–90.
118 CAB134/1373, AOC(56) 2nd meeting, 5 March 1956; AOC(56) 3rd meeting, 12 April 1956; AOC(56)2, 17 Feb. 1956; AOC(56)3 Revised, 22 March 1956; AOC(56)4 (Final), 26 April 1956.
119 PREM11/1365, Millar to Lloyd, 16 March 1956.
120 CAB129/81, CP(56)112, 2 May 1956; also CAB128/30, CM(56)35, 10 May 1956 and CAB129/81, CP(56)142, 15 June 1956.
121 FO371/122025/65, Brief on European Integration, undated, received 8 May 1956.
122 For Treasury reservations, T234/103, Figgures and Clarke minutes, 20 and 21 Feb. 1956 respectively.
123 T234/101, Minutes of Meeting, 31 May 1956.
124 For wider perspective on these internal Conservative Party positions, S. Onslow, *Backbench Debate Within the Conservative Party and its Influence on British Foreign Policy, 1948–57* (London, 1997), pp. 78–106.
125 Plan E was actually designated Plan K in the first draft of Clarke's directive to officials, T234/195, Clarke 'Initiative in Europe – Plan G', 5 June 1956.
126 Minister of Housing and Local Government, Duncan Sandys, was an example of this group, see Papers of Baron Duncan Sandys, Churchill College, Cambridge, DSND 15/4, Sandys to Thorneycroft, 23 July 1956.
127 Charlton, *Price*, p. 210.
128 PREM11/1366, Record of a Meeting between Brentano and Thorneycroft, 2 May 1956.
129 B. Bouwman, *The British Dimension of Dutch European Policy (1950–1963)* (Unpublished DPhil thesis, Oxford, 1993), in general and pp. 175–221 in particular.
130 Spaak, *Battle*, p. 239.
131 NARA RG59/840.00/3–756, Bonn to State, 7 March 1956.
132 Asbeek Brusse, *West European Tariff Plans*, p. 252.
133 Charlton, *Price*, p. 202.
134 Camps, *Britain*, p. 169.

3 Deliberation, Delay, Decision, June–December 1956

1 Hansard, *House of Commons Debates*, 5th series, vol. 561, cols. 53–54, 26 Nov. 1956.
2 Clarke's phrase, T234/195, Clarke minute, 5 June 1956.
3 Snoy's comment, Charlton, *Price*, p. 203.
4 'Communiqué on the talks between the Foreign Ministers of members of the European Coal and Steel Community, Venice, 30 May 1956', Royal Institute of International Affairs, *Documents on International Affairs 1956* (Oxford, 1959), pp. 695–6. On the Venice meeting, Küsters,

'Origins of the EEC Treaty' in Serra (ed.), *Il rilancio*, pp. 227–8 and Milward, *Rescue*, pp. 211–13.

5 Camps, *Britain*, p. 96.

6 FO371/121957/302, Jebb to FO, 1 June 1956; FO371/122027/95, Clarke to FO, 1 June 1956; FO371/122028/109, Tahourdin to Edden, 6 June 1956.

7 FO371/122028/109, Edden to Caccia, 13 June 1956.

8 FO371/122044/30, Edden minute, 13 June 1956.

9 FO371/122028/110, Lloyd to Jebb, 19 June 1956.

10 FO371/121959/337, Record of Conversation: Nutting and Faure, 15 June 1956; also, Nutting, *Europe*, p. 86; FO371/122029/125, Johnston minute, 4 July 1956, and Edden minute, 29 June 1956.

11 On the Saar agreement, F. Roy Willis, *France, Germany and the New Europe 1945–1967* (Oxford, 1968), pp. 208–9.

12 FO371/124491/25, Millar to FO, 7 June 1956.

13 For an excellent analysis of European tariff policies, Asbeek Brusse, *West European Tariff Plans*, esp. pp. 183–278. Much of the following summary is indebted to this source.

14 Abandonment of quantitative import restrictions was vital for convertibility as a method of freeing monetary reserves.

15 For explanation of the various standpoints of these countries, Asbeek Brusse, *West European Tariff Plans*, pp. 196–206.

16 Milward, *Rescue*, p. 385.

17 FO371/122025/74, RWBC/I.E./8th meeting, 13/16 April 1956.

18 CAB129/82, CP(56)172, 9 July 1956.

19 CAB129/82, CP(56)171 and CP(56)172, both 9 July 1956. Also, CAB134/1282, MAC(56) 18th and 19th meetings, 5 and 12 June 1956 respectively.

20 CAB128/30, CM(56) 49th meeting, 12 July 1956.

21 Lamb, *Eden Government*, p. 95.

22 Macmillan, *Riding*, pp. 78–9.

23 FO371/122051/33, Bretherton minute, 23 July 1956.

24 Asbeek Brusse, *West European Tariff Plans*, p. 265.

25 CAB134/1282, MAC(56) 23rd meeting, 11 July 1956; CAB134/1286, MAC(56)96 (Final), 13 July 1956.

26 FO371/121920/46, Ellis Rees to FO, 13 July 1956.

27 See F.M.B. Lynch, 'Restoring France: the Road to Integration', in A.S. Milward *et al.*, *The Frontier of National Sovereignty. History and Theory 1945–1992* (London, 1993), pp. 59–87, esp. pp. 83–4.

28 FO371/122020/41, Swindlehurst minute, 24 April 1956; Hansard, *House of Commons Debates*, 5th series, vol. 555, cols. 1674–80, 5 July 1956. Also, Camps, *Britain*, pp. 95–6.

29 FO371/122051/33, Bretherton minute, 23 July 1956.

30 Papers of Duncan Sandys, Churchill College, Cambridge: DSND 9/3/22, Macmillan 'European Integration', 16 Jan. 1952. For Cabinet differences, J.W. Young, 'Churchill's 'No' to Europe: The 'Rejection' of European Union by Churchill's Post-War Government, 1951–52', *Historical Journal*, Vol. 28, No. 4, (Dec. 1985), pp. 933–5.

31 T234/195, Gilbert minute, 8 June 1956.

32 PREM11/2136, Thorneycroft to Eden, 8 June 1956.

33 PREM11/2136, GEN.535/1st meeting, 22 June 1956.

34 T234/195, Thorneycroft to Macmillan, 25 June 1956.
35 BT205/240, UK/Australian Trade Discussions, 5 July 1956.
36 BT205/240, UK/Australian Trade Discussions: meeting held at No. 10 Downing Street, 13 July 1956.
37 BT205/238, Glaves Smith POM416, 28 May 1956.
38 BT205/240, UK/Australian Trade Discussions, 16 July 1956; BT205/240, UK/Australian Trade Discussions: meeting held at No. 10 Downing Street, 20 July 1956.
39 BT11/5716, Thorneycroft to Amory, 3 July 1956.
40 BT11/5715, Macmillan to Eden, 18 June 1956.
41 BT11/5715, Macmillan to Thorneycorft, 21 June 1956. On the Commonwealth meeting, see Carlton, *Eden*, p. 402; Macmillan, *Riding*, pp. 77–8; Rhodes James, *Eden*, p. 441.
42 T234/195, 'The Probable Development of the Commonwealth over the Next Ten or Fifteen Years', June 1956; T234/195, Armstrong minute, 28 June 1956.
43 BT11/5716, Amory to Thorneycroft, 29 June 1956; also, T234/195, Amory to Macmillan, 29 June 1956.
44 FO371/122031/144, EI(56) 13, 4 July 1956.
45 FO371/122029/129, EI(56) 2nd meeting, 27 June 1956; FO371/122029/125, Wright minute, 9 July 1956; FO371/122032/156, Wright and Edden minutes, 24 and 27 July 1956 respectively.
46 T234/195, Gilbert note, 26 July 1956; T234/195, Gilbert to Petch, 25 July 1956; T234/195, Figgures to Cohen, 10 July 1956.
47 T234/195, Maude to Macmillan, 26 July 1956; T234/195, Macmillan minute, 26 July 1956.
48 CAB129/82, CP(56) 191, 27 July 1956.
49 CAB128/30, CM(56) 52nd meeting, 24 July 1956.
50 T234/195, Figgures to Gilbert, 9 July 1956.
51 CAB129/82, CP(56) 192, 28 July 1956.
52 CAB134/1229, EP(56) 15th meeting, 1 Aug. 1956; CAB134/1231, EP(56)67, 1 Aug. 1956; CAB128/30, CM(56) 57th meeting, 2 Aug. 1956.
53 T234/196, Cobbold to Macmillan, 7 Aug. 1956.
54 FO371/122033/174, Butler memorandum, 9 Aug. 1956.
55 PREM11/2136, Amory to Butler, 3 Sept. 1956.
56 CAB129/83, CP(56)207, 7 Sept. 1956. Also, FO371/122034/229, Home to Macmillan, 3 Sept. 1956.
57 CAB134/1231, EP(56) 72, 31 Aug. 1956.
58 T234/104, Boyle to Macmillan, 13 Sept. 1956.
59 PREM11/2136, Stuart to Eden, 14 Sept. 1956.
60 T230/395, Watts to Allen, 11 July 1956.
61 T234/196, Watts to Figgures, 3 Aug. 1956; T230/395, 'Rates of Growth Abroad', 17 Aug. 1956.
62 T234/197, Clarke to Petch, 13 Sept. 1956.
63 CAB134/1231, EP(56) 70, 31 Aug. 1956.
64 Macmillan, *Riding*, p. 82. Also see Macmillan Papers, Macmillan Papers, Bodleian Library, Oxford, MS Macmillan dep. d.27, diary, 5 Sept. 1956.
65 T234/196, Macmillan to Eccles, 12 Aug. 1956.

66 CAB128/30, CM(56) 65th meeting, 14 Sept. 1956. Also, CAB129/82, CP(56)208, 11 Sept. 1956.
67 CAB134/1231, EP(56)68 ('Plan G and the Moment in British History'), 23 Aug. 1956.
68 CAB128/30, CM(56) 65th meeting, 14 Sept. 1956. Also, FO371/122034/222G, Thorneycroft to Butler, 23 Aug. 1956.
69 CAB128/30, CM(56) 66th meeting, 18 Sept. 1956.
70 Kilmuir (David Maxwell Fyfe) had been a supporter of closer Anglo-European relations for sometime, see Kilmuir, *Political Adventure: the Memoirs of the Earl of Kilmuir* (London, 1964), pp. 185–9.
71 See, for example, Charmley, *Churchill's Grand Alliance*, pp. 298–9.
72 Avon Papers, University of Birmingham (by kind permission of the Avon Trustees), AP20/1/29–32, 14 Sept. 1956.
73 Macmillan Papers, Bodleian Library, Oxford, MS Macmillan dep. d.27, diary, 2 Oct. 1956.
74 Papers of R.A. Butler, Trinity College, Cambridge, G31/88, Butler 'Reminiscences Ending with Suez', 18 April 1957.
75 PREM11/2136, Meeting at the Hotel Matignon, 27 Sept. 1956. See Kane, *Tilting*, pp. 71–80. Also, P.M.H. Bell, *France and Britain 1940–1994. The Long Separation* (London, 1997), pp. 155–8, and G. Warner, 'Aspects of the Suez Crisis' in E. di Nolfo (ed.), *Power in Europe? II: Great Britain, France, Germany and Italy, and the Origins of the EEC, 1952–1957* (Berlin, 1992), pp. 43–66.
76 PREM11/1352, GEN.551/ 2nd meeting, 1 Oct. 1956; CAB130/120, GEN.553/ 1st meeting, 4 Oct. 1956; CAB130/120, GEN.553/1, 9 Oct. 1956.
77 PREM11/1352, GEN.551/1, 22 Sept. 1956.
78 CAB130/120, GEN.553/1st meeting, 4 Oct. 1956; PREM11/1352, GEN.551/2, 22 Sept. 1956.
79 CAB128/30, CM(56) 67th meeting, 26 Sept. 1956.
80 CAB130/120, GEN.553/1st meeting, 4 Oct. 1956.
81 T234/196, FO to Macmillan, 16 Aug. 1956.
82 T234/101, Hood to Odgers, 23 Oct. 1956.
83 CAB130/120, GEN.553/2nd meeting, 11 Oct. 1956; CAB130/120, GEN.553/1, 9 Oct. 1956.
84 H.J. Küsters, 'The Federal Republic of Germany and the EEC Treaty', in Serra (ed.), *Il rilancio*, pp. 495–506, esp. pp. 500–1; G. Schmidt, '"Tying" (West) Germany into the West – But to What? NATO? WEU? The European Community?' in Wurm (ed.), *Western Europe*, pp. 137–74, esp. p. 154.
85 FO371/124559/5, Hancock minute, 21 Nov. 1956.
86 CAB134/1315, PR(56)3, 1 June 1956. On the support payments issue see S. Dockrill, 'Retreat from the Continent? Britain's Motives for Troop Reductions in West Germany, 1955–1958', *Journal of Strategic Studies*, Vol. 20, No. 3 (1997), pp. 45–70.
87 CAB134/1373, AOC(56) 3rd meeting, 12 April 1956; CAB134/1373, AOC(56) 4th meeting, 9 May 1956; CAB134/1373, AOC(56) 5th meeting, 9 Aug. 1956.
88 FO371/122033/200, Hugh Jones minute, 17 Aug. 1956.

89 *FRUS* 1955–57, Vol. IV, doc. 32, Memo of Conversation: Dulles and Makins, 29 June 1956; doc. 33 Memo of Conversation: Dulles and Makins, 13 July 1956; and doc. 34, Eden to Eisenhower, 18 July 1956.
90 Macmillan, *Riding*, pp. 82–4.
91 CAB128/30, CM(56) 68th meeting, 3 Oct. 1956.
92 T234/363, Statements by the Chancellor and the President, 3 Oct. 1956.
93 Macmillan, *Riding*, p. 85.
94 BOE OV47/7, Bolton, Washington to Bank, Oct. 1956.
95 FO371/122035/249, Macmillan to Spaak, 3 Oct. 1956.
96 FO371/122035/270, Macmillan to Spaak, 16 Oct. 1956.
97 FO371/122035/276, Labouchere to FO, 17 Oct. 1956; BT11/5716, Glaves-Smith POM773, 24 Oct. 1956.
98 Lamb, *Eden Government*, p. 97.
99 T234/213, Jebb to Nutting, 2 Oct. 1956.
100 *Manchester Guardian*, 16 Oct. 1956.
101 FO371/122036/295, Isaacson to FO, 23 Oct. 1956.
102 Schaad, *Anglo-German Relations*, pp. 110–11.
103 Schaad, *Anglo-German Relations*, pp. 112–16. Also, Küsters, 'The Federal Republic of Germany and the EEC Treaty' in Serra (ed.), *Il rilancio*, pp. 495–506, esp. p. 501.
104 Cf. Küsters, 'The Origins of the EEC Treaty', pp. 225–6 with Lynch, 'Restoring France', pp. 77–87, Milward, *Rescue*, p. 215, A.S. Milward, 'Conclusions: the Value of History' in Milward *et al.* (eds), *Frontiers*, pp. 182–201, esp. p. 188, and Moravcsik, *Choice*, p. 119.
105 F.M.B. Lynch, 'De Gaulle's First Veto: France, the Rueff Plan and the Free Trade Area', *European University Institute Working Papers in History HEC No. 98/8* (Department of History and Civilization, EUI, Florence, 1998), p. 5.
106 FO371/122035/279, Berne to FO, 17 Oct. 1956.
107 T234/702, Clarke to Maude, 19 Oct. 1956. Also, T234/200, Clarke to Makins, 2 Nov. 1956.
108 CAB129/84, CP(56)256, 6 Nov. 1956; on the Suez crisis, D. Carlton, *Britain and the Suez Crisis* (Oxford, 1988), p. 162.
109 BT11/5716, Swindlehurst, POM740 and 741, 4 Oct. 1956; BT11/5716, Swindlehurst POM762, 10 Oct. 1956; FO371/122037/333, Kipping to FBI members, 13 Oct. 1956; BT11/5717, Robinson minute, 26 Oct. 1956.
110 'West Germany's Increased Openings for British Exporters', *The Board of Trade Journal*, Vol. 170, No. 3088, 7 Apr. 1956, pp. 308–10; 'Minister of State Underlines the Case for Mutual Free Trade Area in Europe', *The Board of Trade Journal*, Vol. 171, No. 3119, 10 Nov. 1956, p. 969.
111 FO371/122035/267, Millar to Johnston, 9 Oct. 1956; FO371/122035/269, Jebb to FO, 16 Oct. 1956; FO371/122036/280, Tahourdin to FO, 18 Oct. 1956; FO371/122037/310, Bretherton minute, 18 Oct. 1956; FO371/122046/116, Isaacson to Wright, 23 Oct. 1956; FO371/122036/301, Isaacson to FO, 24 Oct. 1956.
112 FO371/122035/279, Berne to FO, 17 Oct. 1956; FO371/122036/280, Tahourdin to FO, 18 Oct. 1956; FO371/122036/283, Henderson to FO, 18 Oct. 1956; FO371/122036/282, Stirling to FO, 19 Oct. 1956; FO371/

122036/284, Wallinger to FO, 19 Oct. 1956; FO371/122036/285, Copenhagen to FO, 19 Oct. 1956; FO371/122036/289, Clarke to FO, 19 Oct. 1956; FO371/122036/296, Barclay to FO, 22 Oct. 1956.

113   FO371/122038/345, FO weekly telegram, 30 Oct. 1956.

114   T234/200, Clarke to Makins, 12 Nov. 1956; CAB129/84, CP(56)261, 12 Nov. 1956.

115   *FRUS* 1955–57, Vol. IV, doc. 200, CFEP 539/3, 15 Nov. 1956.

116   CAB128/30, CM(56) 85th meeting, 20 Nov. 1956. See V. Rothwell, *Anthony Eden* (Manchester, 1992), p. 222 and p. 243.

117   CAB128/30, CM(56) 83rd meeting, 13 Nov. 1956.

118   CAB134/1238, ES(EI)(56) 13th meeting, 25 Oct. 1956. For examples of the mixed reports of this meeting, FO371/122036/295, Isaacson to FO, 23 Oct. 1956; FO371/122036/297, Millar to FO, 23 Oct. 1956; FO371/122036/299, Labouchere to FO, 24 Oct. 1956.

119   FO371/122038/361, Millar to FO, 8 Nov. 1956; FO371/122038/362, Isaacson to FO, 9 Nov. 1956.

120   See T234/196, Gilbert minute, 7 Aug. 1956. The Committee included officials from the main Whitehall departments, but also from the Ministry of Labour, Ministry of Fuel and Power, Customs and Excise, and the Bank of England. See, in general, CAB134/1238.

121   CAB134/1238, ES(EI)(56) 16th meeting, 8 Nov. 1956.

122   FO371/122054/112G, Rodgers minute, 19 Nov. 1956.

123   CAB134/1238, ES(EI)(56) 17th and 18th meetings, 15 Nov. 1956 and 22 Nov. 1956 respectively.

124   CAB134/1240, ES(EI)(56)79 (Final), 22 Nov. 1956.

125   T234/199, Clarke minute, 31 Oct. 1956.

126   Hansard, *House of Commons Debates*, 5th series, vol. 561, col. 108, 26 Nov. 1956.

127   Camps, *Britain*, pp. 105–10; Macmillan, *Riding*, pp. 87–8.

128   Hansard, *House of Commons Debates*, 5th series, vol. 561, cols. 163–4, 26 Nov. 1956.

129   FO371/122056/170, Bretherton note, 8 Dec. 1956.

130   FO371/122041/459, Brussels to MAD, FO, 7 Dec. 1956.

131   FO371/122056/170, Bretherton note, 8 Dec. 1956; T234/200, Figgures to Clarke, 10 Dec. 1956.

132   FO371/122056/171, Ellis-Rees to FO, 14 Dec. 1956 & FO to Brussels, 20 Dec. 1956.

133   FO371/122039/405, Rodgers minute, 27 Nov. 1956.

134   FO371/122056/158, FO to UKDEL Paris, 9 Dec. 1956.

135   FO371/122051/46, OEEC C/WP17/W(56)1, 6 Sept. 1956.

136   FO371/122057/174, Report by the UK representative on the Sixth Meeting of WP17, 12 Dec. 1956; FO371/122057/182, Ellis-Rees to FO, 22 Dec. 1956; FO371/120815/22, Gore-Booth minute, 6 Dec. 1956; FO371/122042/467, Jebb to FO, 12 Dec. 1956.

137   BT11/5717, Glaves-Smith POM887, 18 Dec. 1956; CAB134/1238, ES(EI)(56) 22nd meeting, 20 Dec. 1956; FO371/122042/494, Rodgers minute, 5 Jan. 1957.

138   For example, FO371/122054/114, Ellis-Rees to FO, 7 Nov. 1956.

139   FO371/122055/135, Ellis-Rees to FO, 21 Nov. 1956; T234/231, Cahan

to Bretherton, 16 Nov. 1956; T234/231, Figgures minute, 14 Dec. 1956; CAB134/1238, ES(EI)(56) 22nd meeting, 20 Dec. 1956.

140 FO371/122057/172(C), C/WP17/W(56)58(Final), 26 Dec. 1956.

141 FO371/122057/172(C), Heath minute, 2 Jan. 1957.

142 Also see Barnes, 'Eden to Macmillan', p. 131. In general, C.J. Bartlett, *British Foreign Policy in the Twentieth Century* (London, 1989), pp. 116–17. Mollet's directeur adjoint de cabinet (Chief of Staff), Emile Noël, claimed retrospectively that during the four months of meetings leading up to the Suez Crisis Mollet 'tried to convince his [British] counterparts to make a move into the European Community, and said that France would make it easier for them'; see H. Young, *Blessed Plot*, p. 109.

143 Nutting in Charlton, *Price*, p. 220; Lord Gladwyn, interview with author, Dec. 1993. Also, P. Guillen, 'Europe as a Cure for French Impotence? The Guy Mollet Government the Negotiation of the Treaties of Rome', in E. di Nolfo (ed.) *Power in Europe? II. Great Britain, France, Germany, Italy and the Origins of the EEC, 1952–1957* (Berlin, 1992), pp. 505–16; Warner, 'Aspects of the Suez Crisis', *Power*, pp. 43–65.

144 FO371/122431/64, Jebb to FO, 26 Nov. 1956.

145 FO371/124491/51, Millar to FO, 29 Nov. 1956.

146 PREM11/1138, Eden minute, undated, distributed on 28 Dec. 1956.

147 For evaluation of this with particular reference to the end of Empire, P.J. Cain and A.G. Hopkins, *British Imperialism: Crisis and Deconstruction 1914–1990* (London, 1993), pp. 281–91; also, G. Krozewski, 'Sterling, the 'minor' territories, and the end of formal empire, 1939–1958', *Economic History Review*, Vol. 46, No. 2 (1993), pp. 239–65.

148 FO371/124193/14, Clarke to Lloyd, 7 Dec. 1956.

4 Perfidious Albion? January–May 1957

1 See, for example, C.J. Bartlett, *'The Special Relationship': a Political History of Anglo-American Relations since 1945* (London, 1992), pp. 77–106, and Carlton, *Britain and the Suez Crisis*, pp. 103–5.

2 On nuclear policy, I. Clarke, *Nuclear Diplomacy and the Special Relationship* (Oxford, 1994), esp. pp. 1–106, and J. Melissen, *The Struggle for Nuclear Partnership* (Groningen, 1993), esp. pp. 35–62.

3 On this, Cain and Hopkins, *British Imperialism*, pp. 289–91; R.F. Holland, 'The Imperial Factor in British Strategies from Attlee to Macmillan, 1945–63', *Journal of Imperial and Commonwealth History*, Vol. 12, No. 2 (Jan. 1984), pp. 165–86; and G. Krozewski, 'Finance and Empire: the Dilemma Facing Great Britain in the 1950s', *International History Review*, Vol. 18, No. 1 (Feb. 1996), pp. 48–69.

4 For such a view, Bartlett, *British Foreign Policy in the Twentieth Century*, p. 115, and Warner, 'Aspects of the Suez Crisis', pp. 63–5.

5 Macmillan, *Riding*, pp. 198–200.

6 On France, Guillen, 'Europe as a Cure', pp. 504–16.

7 For a similar view, Dimbleby and Reynolds, *Ocean Apart*, p. 221; Schmidt, '"Tying"', pp. 157–8.

8 CAB129/84, CP(57)6, 5 Jan. 1957.

9 See the brief coverage in Greenwood, *Britain and European Co-operation*, p. 71; H. Young, *Blessed Plot*, p. 116; and Young, *Britain and European Unity*, pp. 59–60. Beloff, *New Dimensions*, pp. 112–16 and Camps, *Britain*, pp. 119–21, concentrate on the Grand Design's insitutional proposals, both writing before the release of Lloyd's Cabinet paper under the thirty-year rule.

10 Kaiser, *Using Europe*, pp. 98–100.

11 For another study which attempts to explain Foreign Office policy and the Grand Design in a broader perspective, Kane, 'European or Atlantic Community?', pp. 92–8. Also, Kane, *Tilting*, pp. 80–92.

12 *FRUS*, 1955–57, Vol. IV, doc. 47, US Del. NAC to State, 13 Dec. 1956.

13 FO371/124559/5, Hancock and Starkey minutes, 21 and 28 Nov. 1956 respectively. Also, Schmidt, '"Tying"', p. 154.

14 CAB129/84, CP(57)6, 5 Jan. 1957.

15 FO371/130966/2/G, Hancock minute, 7 Jan. 1957.

16 FO371/130966/2/G, Hugh-Jones minute, 7 Jan. 1957.

17 FO371/130966/2/G, Gore-Booth to Kirkpatrick, 8 Jan. 1957.

18 T225/714, Makins to Macmillan, 5 Jan. 1957.

19 T225/714, Makins to Macmillan, 8 Jan. 1957.

20 T225/714, Clarke minute, 7 Jan. 1957.

21 DO35/7127, Laithwaite to Home, 7 Jan. 1957.

22 FO371/130969/103/G, Dean to Lloyd, 7 Jan. 1957.

23 PREM11/2998, Lloyd to Macmillan, 15 Feb. 1960.

24 Lloyd's biographer makes only a passing reference to the Grand Design, see D.R. Thorpe, *Selwyn Lloyd* (London, 1989), p. 258. Lloyd's reputation is still not high; he has recently been described as 'an incorrigible second rater', H. Young, *Blessed Plot*, p. 113.

25 CAB130/122, GEN.564/1st meeting, 18 Dec. 1956.

26 On Amery and Suez, see D. Carlton, *Britain and the Suez Crisis* (Oxford: Blackwell, 1988), pp. 57–8; also, PREM11/1333, Amery to Macmillan, 12 June 1957, and documents quoted from 1962 in S. Greenwood, *Britain and European Integration since the Second World War* (Manchester, 1996), pp. 138–41.

27 Anthony Nutting, *Europe Will Not Wait. A Warning and a Way Out* (London, 1960), pp. 119–22.

28 P. Fischer, 'West German Rearmament and the Nuclear Challenge' in Heller and Gillingham (eds), *NATO*, pp. 381–401, esp. pp. 395–6; Guillen, 'Europe as a Cure', pp. 514–15; M. O'Driscoll, '"Les Anglo-Saxons", F-I-G and the Rival Conceptions of "Advanced" Armaments Research & Development Co-operation in Western Europe, 1956–58', *Journal of European Integration History*, Vol. 4, No. 1 (1998), pp. 105–30; P. Pitman, 'French Sectoral Strategies and the Diplomacy of European Integration during the 1950s', *1995 ECSA Conference Papers* (Maastricht, 1995), pp. 13–20; Schmidt, '"Tying"', pp. 156–9.

29 FO371/130966/26/G, Steel to Powell, 24 Jan. 1957.

30 Melissen, *Nuclear Partnership*, p. 39.

31 Schmidt, '"Tying"', pp. 156–7.

32 CAB128/30, CM(57) 3rd meeting, 8 Jan. 1957.

33 FO371/130967/63, Hood to Coulson, 11 March 1957.

34 FO371/130967/40, Warner to Hancock, 8 Feb. 1957.
35 CAB134/1857, ES(EI)(57)39, 8 Feb. 1957; CAB134/1855, ES(EI)(57) 10th meeting, 28 Feb. 1957.
36 FO371/128317/34, Rodgers minute, 4 Feb. 1957.
37 CAB134/1240, ES(EI)(56)79(Final), 22 Nov. 1956.
38 PREM11/2136, Thorneycroft to Macmillan, 21 Jan. 1957.
39 Cmnd. 72, *A European Free Trade Area. United Kingdom Memorandum to the Organisation for European Economic Co-operation* (HMSO, 7 Feb. 1957). For Cabinet authorisation, CAB128/31, CC(57) 8th meeting, 7 Feb. 1957.
40 T234/200, Amory to Eccles, 11 Feb. 1957.
41 CSO, *AAS*, No. 96, 1959.
42 PREM11/2136, Bishop minute, 21 Jan. 1957; T234/105, Figgures minute, 1 Feb. 1957.
43 T234/104, Note of a meeting, 15 Jan. 1957.
44 For example, FO371/128333/97, Isaacson to Wright, 25 Jan. 1957; FO371/128333/85, The Hague to FO, 26 Jan. 1957; FO371/128334/126, Scarlett to FO, 30 Jan. 1957; FO371/128334/141, Barclay to FO, 6 Feb. 1957.
45 FO371/128332/46, Hood and Edden minutes, 21 and 22 Jan. 1957 respectively.
46 BT11/5552, Swindlehurst POM28, 11 Jan. 1957; T234/231, France minute, 3 Jan. 1957.
47 T234/231, Clarke minute, 4 Jan. 1957.
48 FO371/128317/40, Ellis Rees to FO, 13 Feb. 1957.
49 FO371/128317/45, Ellis Rees to FO, 14 Feb. 1957.
50 T234/200, Figgures minute, 7 Feb. 1957.
51 T234/200, Note of a meeting, 19 Feb. 1957.
52 FO371/128333/97, Isaacson to Wright, 25 Jan. 1957; T234/200, Warner minute, 31 Jan. 1957.
53 *Resolution of the Council of 13th February 1957*, C(57)30, 14 Feb. 1957 in Cmnd.641. *Negotiations for a European Free Trade Area. Documents Relating to the Negotiations from July, 1956, to December, 1958* (HMSO, 1959), pp. 7–8. For the Working Parties, *Resolution of the Council of 8th March 1957*, C(57)42, 9 March 1956, Cmnd.641, pp. 8–9.
54 T234/200, ES(EI)(57)26(Final), 6 Feb. 1957; T234/200, ES(EI)(57)46, 26 Feb. 1957.
55 Nutting, *Europe*, p. 93.
56 FO371/128333/97, Isaacson to Wright, 25 Jan. 1957; FO371/128333/86, Henderson to Lloyd, 24 Jan. 1957.
57 T234/200, Figgures minute, 7 Feb. 1957.
58 PREM11/2133, Macmillan to Thorneycroft, 11 Feb. 1957.
59 PREM11/2136, Ramsden to Prime Minister, 31 Jan. 1957; PREM11/2133, Eccles to Macmillan, 10 Feb. 1957.
60 BT213/86, President's Informal Advisory Group on Exports. Minutes of the 23rd Meeting, 6 March 1957.
61 See also, Camps, *Britain*, p. 111.
62 BT11/5552, Bretherton minute, 25 Feb. 1957. This view was also held in the Treasury, T234/200, Figgures minute, 7 Feb. 1957.
63 T234/104, Note of a meeting, 15 Jan. 1957.

64 FO371/128333/97, Isaacson to Wright, 25 Jan. 1957.
65 FO371/128333/111, Mason to Lloyd, 1 Feb. 1957; FO371/128334/147, Cohen to Wright, 1 Feb. 1957. In general, see B. Bouwman, '"Longing for London": The Netherlands and the Political Cooperation Initiative, 1959–62' in A. Deighton (ed.), *Building Postwar Europe* (London, 1995), pp. 141–58, esp. pp. 141–4.
66 Bouwman, *British Dimension*, pp. 204–5; see pp. 175–222 for a full discussion.
67 FO371/128333/111, Heath minute, 7 Feb. 1957.
68 FO371/128317/37, Ellis Rees to FO, 12 Feb. 1957; FO371/128336/209, Ellis Rees to Wright, 14 Feb. 1957.
69 On Erhard, Bloemen, 'Problem', esp. pp. 188–9; and S. Huth, *British–German Relations between 1955 and 1961* (Unpublished PhD thesis, Cambridge, 1993), pp. 138–40. Also, S. Lee, 'German Decision-Making Elites and European Integration: German 'Europolitik' during the Years of the EEC and Free Trade Area Negotiations' in Deighton (ed.), *Building Postwar Europe*, pp. 38–54.
70 T234/35, Rowan to Makins, 27 March 1957.
71 T234/35, Makins minute, 27 March 1957; FO371/128337/256, Steel to Gore-Booth, 27 Feb. 1957.
72 FO371/128334/146, Hayter to Wright, 4 Feb. 1957; T234/35, Spicer minute, 26 March 1957. Also, Huth, *British–German Relations*, pp. 138–9.
73 BT11/5552, Swindlehurst POM28, 11 Jan. 1957.
74 FO371/128317/38, Ellis-Rees to FO, 13 Feb. 1957.
75 T234/204, Hayles minute, undated.
76 FO371/128376/52, Jebb to FO, 1 Feb. 1957; FO371/128376/52, Heath minute, 4 Feb. 1957.
77 CAB134/1238, ES(EI)(56) 19th meeting, 6 Dec. 1956; FO371/122056/171, Ellis Rees to FO, 14 Dec. 1956; T234/104, Note of a meeting, 15 Jan. 1957. Also, BT11/5552, Cohen minute, 4 Jan. 1957.
78 FO371/128336/219, Jebb to FO, 20 Feb. 1957.
79 FO371/128336/232, Jebb to FO, 22 Feb. 1957; FO371/128336/238, Wright minute, 22 Feb. 1957.
80 See Guillen, 'Europe as a Cure', pp. 508–9.
81 FO371/128338/268, Edden minute, 1 March 1957.
82 See C. Schenk, 'Decolonization and European Economic Integration: The Free Trade Area Negotiations, 1956–58', *Journal of Imperial and Commonwealth History*, Vol. 24, No. 3 (Sept. 1996), pp. 444–63.
83 T234/200, Note of an *ad hoc* meeting, 8 March 1957.
84 Hall's diary entry, 7 March 1957, in Cairncross (ed.), *Robert Hall Diaries Vol. II*, p. 103.
85 PREM11/2133, Macmillan to Thorneycroft, 5 March 1957.
86 PREM11/2133, Thorneycroft to Macmillan, 11 March 1957.
87 T234/200, Note of an *ad hoc* meeting, 8 March 1957.
88 CAB130/123, GEN.580/1st meeting, 8 March 1957.
89 FO371/128337/257, Wright to Clarke, 5 March 1957. For the American record, *FRUS*, 1955–57, Vol. IV, doc. 225, Memo of Conversation, 26 Feb. 1957.
90 CAB134/1674, EA(57) 7th meeting, 27 March 1957.

91 FO371/128338/283, Gore-Booth to Stirling, 15 March 1957.
92 CAB129/86, C(57)81, 30 March 1957.
93 T234/105, Clarke to Makins, 22 March 1957.
94 CAB128/31, C(57) 29th meeting, 3 Apr. 1957; CAB129/87, C(57)107, 30 Apr. 1957; CAB128/31, C(57) 38th meeting, 6 May 1957.
95 FO371/128343/511, '... meeting with M. Maurice Faure', 7 May 1957; cf. NARA RG59/440.002/5-1057, Paris-State, 2133, 10 May 1957.
96 Bloemen, 'Problem', pp. 184–5; Schenk, 'Decolonization', p. 455.
97 FO371/128378/119, Ellis Rees to FO, 19 March 1957; FO371/128378/ 128, Ellis Rees to FO, 20 March 1957.
98 FO371/128378/128, Gore-Booth and Hugh Jones minutes, 23 and 25 March 1957 respectively.
99 FO371/128338/278, 'Record of the meeting...', 9 March 1957.
100 FO371/128338/280, Figgures to Wright, 6 March 1957.
101 FO371/128339/315, Thorneycroft minute, undated; FO371/128341/400, Heath minute, 5 Apr. 1957. This is confirmed by Macmillan's diary, see Macmillan Papers, Bodleian Library, Oxford, MS Macmillan, dep. d.28*, diary, 9 March 1957.
102 PREM11/2133, Macmillan minute, 8 March 1957.
103 CAB128/31, CC(57) 21st meeting, 18 March 1957; Cmnd. 124 *Defence, Outline of Future Policy* (HMSO, 4 Apr. 1957). W. Rees, 'The Sandys White Paper: New Priorities in British Defence Policy', *Journal of Strategic Studies*, Vol. 12, No. 2 (June 1989), pp. 215–29; Reynolds, *Britannia*, p. 211.
104 Clarke, *Nuclear Diplomacy*, pp. 38–45.
105 CAB128/31, CC(57) 13th meeting, 22 Feb. 1957.
106 PREM11/2136, Ramsden to Prime Minister, 31 Jan. 1957. Also see O'Driscoll, '"Les Anglo-Saxons"', pp. 113–14.
107 PREM11/1831A, 10 Downing St. Communiqué, 9 March 1957.
108 CAB128/31, CC(57) 17th meeting, 12 March 1957.
109 *FRUS*, 1955–57, Vol. XXVII, doc. 277, Memo. of a Conversation, 22 March 1957; *FRUS*, 1955–57, Vol. XXVII, doc. 288, Macmillan to Eisenhower, 23 March 1957. Also, NARA RG59/740.00/3-1457, London to State, 14 March 1957. On Bermuda, CAB129/86, C(57)88, 2 Apr. 1957. Also, Bartlett, *Special Relationship*, pp. 88–9, and M. Dockrill, 'Restoring the "special relationship". The Bermuda and Washington conferences, 1957' in D. Richardson and G. Stone (eds), *Decisions and Diplomacy. Essays in Twentieth-Century International History* (London, 1995), pp. 205–23.
110 *FRUS*, 1955–57, Vol. XXVII, doc. 292, Agreed Note on Military Nuclear Programmes of Fourth Countries, 23 March 1957. As to the motivation for this document, cf. Melissen, *Nuclear Partnership*, p. 39, and, G. Warner, 'Eisenhower, Dulles and the unity of Western Europe, 1955–1957', *International Affairs*, Vol. 69, No. 2 (1993), pp. 319–29, esp. pp. 323–4.
111 FO371/128342/447, FO to Paris and Gore-Booth minute, both 17 Apr. 1957.
112 FO371/128339/300, Jebb to FO, and Heath minute, 14 and 15 March 1957 respectively.

113 NARA RG59/440.002/5–257, London to State, 5969, 2 May 1957.
114 Cf. Young, *Britain and European Unity*, p. 60.
115 Lamb, *Macmillan Years*, p. 111.
116 FO371/128341/400, Figgures to Sanders, 3 Apr. 1957.
117 BT11/5553, 'Record of a meeting held at 10 Downing Street', 18 Apr. 1957.
118 T234/201, Figgures to Clarke, 23 Apr. 1957; PREM11/2133, Trend to Prime Minister, 1 May 1957.
119 BT11/5553, Lee to Eccles, 26 Apr. 1957.
120 PREM11/1844, Jebb to Lloyd, 27 Apr. 1957; T234/201, Makins minute, 2 May 1957.
121 PREM11/1844, Jebb to Lloyd, 27 Apr. 1957.
122 See FO371/128337/241(a), Jebb to Lloyd, 23 Feb. 1957; FO371/128338/268, Hood minute and Hood to Jebb, 28 Feb. and 1 March 1957 respectively; FO371/128337/241(a), Lloyd to Jebb, 4 March 1957. Also, see FO371/128337/241(a), Edden and Hoyer Millar minutes, 26 and 28 Feb. 1957 respectively.
123 FO371/128341/400, Wright minute, 8 Apr. 1957.
124 CAB134/1240, ES(EI)(56)79(Final), 22 Nov. 1956.
125 FO371/128337/241(a), Lloyd to Jebb, 4 March 1957.
126 BT11/5553, Lee to Eccles, 26 Apr. 1957.
127 NARA RG59/440.002/4-2057, Dulles circular, 1481, 20 Apr. 1957.
128 FO371/128317/39, Ellis Rees to FO, 13 Feb. 1957; also Nutting, *Europe*, p. 92.
129 Schaad, *Anglo-German Relations*, pp. 128–9.
130 FO371/128377/75, Ellis Rees to FO, 16 Feb. 1957.
131 The Foreign Office was concerned about misunderstanding on this issue, FO371/128338/264, Hood minute, 27 Feb. 1957.
132 Bouwman, *British Dimension*, p. 199.
133 Macmillan, *Riding*, p. 246.
134 CAB128/31, CC(57) 14th meeting, 28 Feb. 1957; CAB128/31, CC(57)15th meeting, 4 March 1957. In general, Camps, *Britain*, pp. 121–2.
135 Huth, *British–German Relations*, pp. 85–7.
136 CAB128/31, CC(57) 13th meeting, 22 Feb. 1957.
137 See Camps, *Britain*, pp. 119–21. Also, PEP (Political and Economic Planning), 'European Unity – a Review', *Planning*, Vol. 25, No. 436 (28 Sept. 1959), pp. 163–84, esp. pp. 177–80.
138 *FRUS*, 1955–57, Vol. IV, doc. 227, State to Certain Diplomatic Missions, 735, 6 March 1957.
139 FO371/128341/433, Tennant (Federation of British Industry) to Wright, 12 Apr. 1957.
140 FO371/128341/433, Wright minute, 15 Apr. 1957.
141 PREM11/1841, FO to Bonn, 17 Apr. 1957.
142 NARA RG59/740.00/3-1457, London to State, 4867, 14 March 1957.
143 BT11/5553, Lee to Eccles, 26 Apr. 1957.
144 T234/201, Clarke minute, 8 May 1957. On Jebb's conversion, Gladwyn, *Memoirs*, pp. 288ff. Lord Gladwyn maintained that these accusations were untrue, interview with author, Dec. 1993.
145 G. Bossuat, 'The Choice of "La Petite Europe" by France (1957–1963).

An Ambition for France and for Europe' in Griffiths and Ward (eds), *Courting*, pp. 59–82, esp. pp. 60–1.

146 Bossuat, 'The Choice', pp. 60–1; Lynch, 'De Gaulle's First Veto', p. 5.

147 FO371/121920/46, Ellis Rees to FO, 13 July 1956.

148 In general, Marjolin, *Architect*.

149 NARA RG59/440.002/4–1257, Paris to State, 1944, 12 Apr. 1957. Also, see Robert Hall's diary entry, 5 May 1957, in Cairncross (ed.), *Robert Hall Diaries Vol. II*, p. 112.

150 NARA RG59/440.002/5–2757, Memo. of Conversation, 27 May 1957.

151 FO371/128378/128, Hugh Jones minute, 25 March 1957.

152 CAB129/87, C(57)106, Note by the Chancellor of the Exchequer, 30 Apr. 1957.

153 CAB129/87, C(57)106, 'Next Steps', Report by Officials, 30 Apr. 1957.

154 CAB128/31, CC(57) 37th meeting, 2 May 1957.

155 PREM11/2133, Macmillan to Poole, 18 Apr. 1957.

156 FO371/128327/26, Meade to FO, 2 May 1957; also, Camps, *Britain*, p. 120.

157 FO371/128343/495, FO to Brussels, 6 May 1957; FO371/128343/496, FO to Paris, 6 May 1957; T234/105, 'Summary Record of Discussion', 6 May 1957.

158 FO371/128343/511, '. . . Meeting with M. Maurice Faure', 7 May 1957.

159 CAB134/1674, EA(57) 10th meeting, 8 May 1957.

160 Macmillan, *Riding*, p. 435.

161 Macmillan, *Riding*, p. 291; PREM11/1829A, de Zulueta to Macmillan, 6 May 1957.

162 Schaad, *Anglo-German Relations*, pp. 138–42.

163 Macmillan, *Riding*, p. 295; FO371/130972/194, 'Record of a meeting held in Palais Schaumberg, Bonn at 4:30pm on May 8, 1957', undated.

164 T234/706, Figgures minute, 9 May 1957.

165 Macmillan Papers, Bodleian Library, Oxford, MS Macmillan, dep. d.28*, diary, 8 May 1957.

166 T234/201, 'Ad hoc meeting . . .', 23 May 1957; FO371/128347/596, FO to Ankara, 6 June 1957.

167 NARA RG59/740.00/5-1557, London to State, 6240, 15 May 1957.

168 On the GATT suspension, BT205/261, TN(FT)(57)20, 25 Apr. 1957.

169 NARA RG59/440.002/5-2257, Brussels to State, 1381, 22 May 1957; *FRUS, 1955–57*, Vol. IV, doc. 237, Memo. of Conversation, 26 May 1957; NARA RG59/440.002/5-2757, Memo. of Conversation, 27 May 1957.

170 The speech was reported in NARA RG59/440.002/5-2957, London to State, 3044, 29 May 1957.

171 *The Times*, 28 and 30 May 1957; NARA RG59/440.002/5-3157, London to State, 6606, 31 May 1957.

172 FO371/128347/611, Thorneycroft to Eccles, 4 June 1957.

173 NARA RG59/440.002/5-2957, London to State, 3044, 29 May 1957.

174 Comment made by Sir Denis Wright, interview with author, 6 Sept. 1995. On Office intervention, FO371/128347/611, various minutes, 29 May–8 June 1957.

175 FO371/128377/98, Eccles to Thorneycroft, 4 March 1957; FO371/128337/254, Eccles to Lloyd, 4 March 1957.

176 NARA RG59/440.002/5-3157, London to State, 6606, 31 May 1957.
177 See Camps, *Britain*, p. 124, and Griffiths and Ward, '"Thousand Years"', p. 13.
178 Nutting, *Europe*, p. 87.
179 G. Warner, 'The Anglo-American Special Relationship', *Diplomatic History*, Vol. 13, No. 4 (Fall 1989), pp. 479–99, esp. p. 487.
180 C. Wurm, 'Two Paths to Europe: Great Britain and France from a Comparative Perspective' in C. Wurm (ed.), *Western Europe and Germany*, pp. 175–200, esp. pp. 179–80.
181 Carlton, *Britain and the Suez Crisis*, pp. 102–5.
182 Nutting, *Europe*, p. 92. Also, Camps, *Britain*, pp. 113–15.
183 NARA RG59/740.00/5-1557, London to State, 6240, 15 May 1957.
184 *Economist*, 'Albion in the Dock', 11 May 1957.
185 See R.T. Griffiths, 'The United Kingdom and the Free Trade Area: a Post Mortem', in Olesen (ed.), *Interdependence*, pp. 167–81, esp. p. 170.
186 PREM11/2133, Macmillan to Lloyd, 26 May 1957.
187 PREM11/1841, Lloyd to Macmillan, 28 May 1957.
188 PREM11/2133, Thorneycroft to Macmillan, 28 May 1957.

5 Philosophies Apart, June–October 1957

1 *FRUS*, 1955–57, Vol. XXVII, doc. 299, Macmillan to Eisenhower, 12 June 1957.
2 On the French governmental crisis, Larkin, *France*, p. 260.
3 Macmillan, *Riding*, pp. 435–6.
4 Macmillan, *Riding*, p. 377.
5 T234/117, UK High Commissioner, Canada, (UKHCC) to CRO, 8 July 1957.
6 PREM11/2133, Macmillan to Home, 30 June 1957; PREM11/2133, UKHCC to CRO, 12 July 1957.
7 The Economist Intelligence Unit, *The Commonwealth and Europe* (London, 1960), p. 7, Table 2.
8 B.W. Muirhead, 'Britain, Canada, and the Collective Approach to Freer Trade and Payments, 1952–1957', *Journal of Imperial and Commonwealth History*, Vol. 20, No. 1 (Jan. 1992), pp. 108–26.
9 PREM11/2133, UKHCC to CRO, 12 July 1957.
10 On Commonwealth policy, CAB128/31, CC(57) 44th meeting, 4 June 1957.
11 PREM11/2133, Eccles to Prime Minister, 27 June 1957; PREM11/2133, Home to Prime Minister, 28 June 1957.
12 PREM11/2133, Thorneycroft to Macmillan, 27 June 1957; PREM11/2133, Lloyd to Macmillan, 4 July 1957.
13 PREM11/2133, Eccles to Prime Minister, 27 June 1957; PREM11/2133, Home to Prime Minister, 28 June 1957.
14 PREM11/2133, unauthored minute, 11 July 1957.
15 Kane, *Tilting*, pp. 104–6.
16 PREM11/2133, Macmillan to Home, 30 June 1957.
17 Figures from *FRUS*, 1955–1957, Vol. XXVII, doc. 379, London to State, 9 Sept. 1957.

18 CAB128/31, CC(57) 50th meeting, 9 July 1957.
19 T234/202, Clarke to Makins, 11 July 1957.
20 BT11/5553, Lee minute, 2 July 1957.
21 PREM11/2133, UKHCC to CRO, 12 July 1957; also see Rowan's comments in NARA RG59/440.00/7-1257, London to State, 346, 12 July 1957.
22 CAB129/88, C(57) 164, 17 July 1957.
23 CAB128/31, CC(57) 56th meeting, 23 July 1957.
24 T234/201, Thorneycroft to Macmillan, 28 May 1957.
25 BT205/262, TN(FT)(57) 31, 27 June 1957.
26 This was confirmed in the Commons, Hansard, *House of Commons Debates*, 5th series, vol. 572, col. 1301, 2 July 1957; also, written answer, col. 87, 2 July 1957.
27 T234/217, CO(FTA)(57) 1st meeting, 8 July 1957.
28 T234/217, CO(FTA)(57) 2nd meeting, 8 July 1957.
29 T234/217, FO to Paris and all European posts, 11 July 1957.
30 NARA RG59/440.00/7-1257, London to State, 346, 12 July 1957.
31 T234/217, CO(FTA)(57) 3, 4 July 1957; T234/217, CO(FTA)(57) 4th meeting, 9 July 1957.
32 T234/218, CRO to Treasury, 12 Sept. 1957.
33 FO371/128353/792, Sykes to Wright, 26 July 1957.
34 FO371/128353/792, Wright to Boothby, 31 July 1957.
35 Principles based on Articles 3 and 4 of the *Treaty Establishing The European Economic Community*, in Sweet and Maxwell's Legal Editorial Staff, *European Community Treaties* (London, 1977), pp. 61–138.
36 *Report by the Chairman of Working Party No. 21 to the Chairman of the Council*, FTA(57) 51, 11 July 1957, Cmnd. 641, p. 11. On the WP reports, also see Camps, *Britain*, pp. 125–7.
37 On national standpoints and the origin issue, FO371/128387/390, Ellis Rees to FO, 26 July 1957.
38 *Report by the Chairman of Working Party No. 22 to the Chairman of the Council*, FTB(57) 7, 20 July 1957, Cmnd. 641, p. 26. Also, BT11/5553, Bretherton to Cohen, 3 July 1957; FO371/128386/362, Ellis Rees to FO, and Edden minute, 13 and 15 July 1957 respectively.
39 *Report by the Chairman of Working Party No. 23 to the Chairman of the Council*, FTC(57) 1, 19 July 1957, Cmnd. 641, p. 30. Also, FO371/128383/244, FO to Paris, 27 May 1957.
40 *Free Trade Area Negotiations. Report by the Chancellor of the Exchequer*, C(57) 168, 19 July 1957, Cmnd. 641, pp. 42–4.
41 Macmillan, *Riding*, pp. 436–7.
42 Macmillan Papers, Bodleian Library, Oxford, MS Macmillan dep.d.29*, diary, 11 July 1957.
43 PREM11/2133, Macmillan minute M.333/57, 15 July 1957. Also, Macmillan, *Riding*, p. 436–7.
44 T234/201, Clarke to Figgures, 6 June 1957.
45 PREM11/2133, Macmillan minute M.333/57, 15 July 1957. Also, see comments in CAB130/123, GEN.580/2nd meeting, 12 July 1957; CAB130/123, GEN.580/3rd meeting, 30 July 1957.
46 PREM11/1844, Jebb to Lloyd, 28 April 1957.
47 FO371/130972/224, Macmillan to Lloyd M235/57, 3 June 1957.

48 For early plans, CAB134/1240, ES(EI)(56) 87, 20 Nov. 1956.
49 CAB130/123, GEN.580/3rd meeting, 30 July 1957.
50 FO371/128350/670, Figgures 'Note for the Record', 21 June 1957.
51 FO371/130972/224, Hood minute, 6 June 1957.
52 NARA RG59/440.002/7-1557, The Hague to State, 39, 15 July 1957.
53 CAB130/123, GEN.580/2, 25 July 1957; CAB130/123, GEN.580/3rd meeting, 30 July 1957.
54 PREM11/2133, Macmillan minute M.333/57, 15 July 1957; CAB130/123, GEN.580/2nd meeting, 12 July 1957.
55 FO371/128351/732, Paris to MAD, and Edden minute, 11 and 22 July respectively.
56 FO371/128348/647, FO Minute, 17 June 1957; Hansard, *House of Commons Debates*, 5th series, 1956–57, vol. 573, cols. 944–5, 16 July 1957.
57 PREM11/2133, Ramsden to Prime Minister, 11 July 1957; PREM11/2132, 'Record of Conversation', 19 July 1957; FO371/128354/801, Jebb to Gore-Booth, 30 July 1957.
58 FO371/128354/819, Jebb to Gore-Booth, 24 July 1957.
59 T234/202, 'EFTA: Meeting with Sir Gladwyn Jebb on 15th July 1957', 17 July 1957.
60 FO371/128349/669, Figgures minute, 12 July 1957.
61 FO371/128351/726, Bonn to FO, 13 July 1957; FO371/128353/778, Steel, Bonn to FO, 26 July 1957.
62 FO371/128388/405, Hancock minute, 30 July 1957.
63 R. Maudling, *Memoirs* (London, 1978), p. 65 and p. 67.
64 *The Times*, 'Preparing for Free Trade Area Negotiations', 8 Aug. 1957.
65 On Maudling, N. Beloff, *The General Says No* (Harmondsworth, 1963), p. 79; Lieber, *British Politics*, p. 140; Lamb, *Macmillan Years*, p. 110; Young, *Britain and European Unity*, p. 60.
66 PREM11/2132, Macmillan to Thorneycroft, 22 July 1957; Macmillan, *Riding*, pp. 437–8.
67 Lieber, *British Politics*, p. 140. Macmillan would repeat this tactic in preparing the first application for EEC membership, N.P. Ludlow, 'A Mismanaged Application: Britain and EEC Membership 1961–1963', A. Deighton and A.S. Milward (eds), *Widening, Deepening and Acceleration: the European Economic Community, 1957–63* (Brussels, 1999).
68 PREM11/2132, Macmillan to Thorneycroft, 22 July 1957.
69 CAB128/31, CC(57) 61st meeting, 2 Aug. 1957. *The Times*, 'Preparing for Free Trade Area Negotiations', 8 Aug. 1957.
70 PREM11/2132, Macmillan to Thorneycroft, 22 July 1957.
71 T234/373, Macmillan to Thorneycroft, 26 July 1957.
72 Maudling, *Memoirs*, p. 67.
73 PREM11/2132, Macmillan to Maudling, 5 Aug. 1957; Maudling, *Memoirs*, p. 67.
74 PREM11/2132, Macmillan to Thorneycroft, 22 July 1957; PREM11/2132, Norman Brook to Prime Minister, 1 Aug. 1957.
75 PREM11/2132, Norman Brook to Macmillan, 1 Aug. 1957. Mr Liverman confirmed that Coulson's appointment was an attempt to give the Foreign Office a greater role in the FTA negotiations, letter to author, 21 Dec. 1996.

76 CAB134/1835, ES(57) 4th meeting, 11 July 1957.

77 CAB134/1835, ES(57) 4th meeting, 11 July 1957; CAB134/1676, EA(57) 85, 12 July 1957.

78 CAB134/1835, ES(57) 4th meeting, 11 July 1957; CAB134/1676, EA(57) 83, 12 July 1957; CAB134/1674, EA(57) 22 meeting, 24 July 1957.

79 FO371/128354/798, Ormsby-Gore and Edden minutes, both 29 July 1957. In general see B. Wells, *Discordant Allies: Security Policy Objectives as a Factor in British-German Relations 1955–61* (PhD thesis, London School of Economics and Political Science, in preparation. The author is grateful to Ms Wells for draft sections from her thesis).

80 FO371/128358/929, Steel to Millar, 12 Sept. 1957.

81 T234/202, Clarke minute, 21 Aug. 1957.

82 FO371/128356/863, 'Possible Inducements in the Free Trade Area Negotiations', 21 Aug. 1957; T234/202, Figgures minute, 16 Aug. 1957.

83 PREM11/2133, Jebb to Prime Minister and Bishop to Jebb, 17 and 19 June 1957 respectively. Also, Gladwyn, *Memoirs*, p. 298. On the secret agreement, see Chapter 4. For the wider context of this issue, M. O'Driscoll, 'Missing the Nuclear Boat? British Policy Towards French Military Nuclear Ambitions during the EURATOM Foundation Negotiations, 1955–56', *Diplomacy and Statecraft*, Vol. 9, No. 1 (1998), pp. 135–62.

84 FO371/128388/410, FO to Ankara, etc., 6 Aug. 1957.

85 FO371/128388/412, FO to Ambassadors, 6 Aug. 1957.

86 FO371/128356/885, Paris to FO, enclosing Records of Conversation, 22 Aug. 1957.

87 On Gaillard, Marjolin, *Memoirs*, p. 283.

88 FO371/128362/1022, Labouchere to FO, 4 Oct. 1957; FO371/128363/ 1039, Record of Talks between Mr R. Maudling and Italian Ministers, 5 Oct. 1957.

89 FO371/128362/1038, Bonn to FO, enclosing Records of Conversation, 5 Oct. 1957.

90 FO371/128360/958, Heath minute, 25 Sept. 1957.

91 FO371/128361/1006, Ellis Rees to Coulson, 30 Sept. 1957.

92 FO371/128362/1038, Conversation with German Ministers, 5 Oct. 1957; FO371/128362/1021, Bonn to FO, 4 Oct. 1957.

93 Schaad, *Anglo-German relations*, pp. 143–5.

94 Bloemen, 'Problem', pp. 186–9.

95 Cabinet Office, Free Trade Area Office Papers (hereafter FTAO Papers) Box 18, 'Record of Conversation with Professor Erhard', 4 Oct. 1957.

96 Bloemen, 'Problem', pp. 186–9.

97 PREM11/2531, Macmillan to Maudling, 13 Aug. 1957.

98 PREM11/2531, Maudling to Macmillan, 14 Aug. 1957.

99 FO371/128362/1038, Conversation with German Ministers, 5 Oct. 1957.

100 Figgures in Charlton, *Price*, p. 222. On rumours, NARA RG59/440.002/ 9-1257, London to State, 631, 12 Sept. 1957; FO371/128361/987, Bonn to FO, 27 Sept. 1957.

101 Macmillan, *Riding*, p. 438.

102 CAB129/88, C(57) 188, 24 Aug 1957.

103 Articles 38–47 of the *Treaty Establishing The European Economic Com-*

munity, in Sweet and Maxwell's Legal Editorial Staff, *European Community Treaties*, pp. 73–7.

104   T234/200, Amory to Eccles, 11 Feb. 1957.
105   PREM11/2531, Butler to Macmillan, 24 Aug. 1957.
106   CAB128/31, CC(57) 62nd meeting, 27 Aug. 1957.
107   CAB128/31, CC(57) 72nd meeting, 8 Oct. 1957.
108   Macmillan, *Riding*, p. 439; CAB129/89, C(57) 218–222, 4 Oct. 1957.
109   See PREM11/2531, Makins to Macmillan, 23 Sept. 1957; CAB134/1835, ES(57) 6th meeting, 24 Sept. 1957; CAB129/89, C(57) 222, 4 Oct. 1957.
110   CAB129/89, C(57) 219, 4 Oct. 1957.
111   PREM11/2531, Trend to Prime Minister, 5 Oct. 1957.
112   CAB128/31, CC(57) 72nd meeting, 8 Oct. 1957.
113   CAB129/89, C(57) 222, 4 Oct. 1957.
114   FO371/128361/1003, Gore-Booth minute, 26 Sept. 1957.
115   FO371/128362/1035, Bretherton minute, 2 Oct. 1957.
116   CAB129/89, C(57) 218, 4 Oct. 1957. Also, T234/202, Clarke to Liverman, 20 Aug. 1957.
117   FO371/128351/724, Gore-Booth minute, 18 July 1957.
118   CAB129/89, C(57) 222, 4 Oct. 1957.
119   For early explanation of this strategy, see comments made to American officials, NARA RG59/440.002/9-1957, London to State, 1953, 19 Sept. 1957.
120   FO371/128362/1033, Edden minute, 9 Oct. 1957.
121   FO371/128362/1035, Bretherton minute, 2 Oct. 1957.

6   The Negotiations Begin, October–December 1957

1   CAB129/89, C(57) 222, 4 Oct. 1957.
2   Macmillan, *Riding*, p. 438.
3   CAB129/88, C(57) 194, 1 Sept. 1957.
4   CAB129/88, C(57) 200, 9 Sept. 1957. Also, CAB129/88, C(57) 187, 23 Aug. 1957.
5   CAB128/31, CC(57) 62nd meeting, 27 Aug. 1957.
6   CAB129/89, C(57) 213, 17 Sept. 1957.
7   Lee minute, 10 Sept. 1957, attached to CAB129/89, C(57) 213, 17 Sept. 1957.
8   CAB128/31, CC(57) 69th meeting, 19 Sept. 1957.
9   Also see Camps, *Britain*, pp. 127–9.
10   FO371/128361/998, Isaacson, Paris to Gore-Booth, 26 Sept. 1957.
11   T234/218, France 'Note for the Record', 9 Oct. 1957.
12   FO371/128369/1217, Figgures minute, 14 Nov. 1957.
13   CAB130/132, GEN.613/2nd meeting, 14 Oct. 1957.
14   FO371/128364/1080, Coulson minute, 21 Oct. 1957.
15   PREM11/2531, Eccles to Lloyd, 2 Dec. 1957.
16   For example, PREM11/2533, Amory to Macmillan, 11 Sept. 1957 and PREM11/2533, UKHCC to CRO, 3 Oct. 1957.
17   T234/202, Thorneycroft minute, 4 Oct. 1957; T234/202, M(57) 58, 8 Oct. 1957; CAB130/132, GEN.613/2nd meeting, 11 Oct. 1957.

18 FO371/128393/573, FO to Bonn, enc. Thorneycroft to Erhard, 14 Oct. 1957; T234/202, 'Record of a Meeting between the Chancellor of the Exchequer and the Secretary General of NATO', 16 Oct. 1957.
19 FO371/128393/575, Ellis Rees to FO, 16 Oct. 1957.
20 Camps, *Britain*, p. 135.
21 *Note of the Interim Committee for the Common Market and Euratom*, CES/7.117, 15 Oct. 1957, Cmnd. 641, pp. 44–48.
22 FO371/128393/576 and /577, both Ellis Rees to FO, 16 Oct. 1957; FO371/128393/580, Ellis Rees to FO, 17 Oct. 1957.
23 *Resolutions of the Council*, C(57) 221 and 222, 17 Oct. 1957, Cmnd. 641, pp. 48–50.
24 FO371/128394/584, Ellis Rees to FO, 19 Oct. 1957.
25 Camps, *Britain*, p. 135.
26 On the Action Committee in general, Monnet, *Memoirs*, pp. 405–30 and p. 450. Marjolin, *Memoirs*, pp. 317–22.
27 FO371/128362/1018, De Peyer 'Conversation with M. Max Kohnstamm', 9 Oct. 1957.
28 Duchêne, *Jean Monnet*, p. 321.
29 PREM11/2531, Eccles to Maudling, 21 Oct. 1957.
30 PREM11/2531, Macmillan minute, 21 Oct. 1957.
31 FO371/128360/955, Anderson minute, 17 Sept. 1957.
32 Camps makes this point, *Britain*, p. 130.
33 FO371/128327/53, Edden to Liverman, 14 Oct. 1957.
34 FO371/128327/57, Meade to FO, 23 Oct. 1957.
35 FO371/128327/64, Council of Europe Recommendation 152, 30 Oct. 1957.
36 FO371/128327/59, Meade to FO, 25 Oct. 1957.
37 FO371/128369/1221, FO circular telegram, 28 Nov. 1957.
38 CAB128/31, C(57) 72nd meeting, 8 Oct 1957; CAB129/89, C(57) 221, 4 Oct. 1957.
39 FO371/128364/1068, Ormsby-Gore minute, 16 Oct. 1957.
40 FO371/128394/601, Labouchere to FO, 25 Oct. 1957.
41 FO371/128394/601, Heath minute, 28 Oct. 1957.
42 BT205/262, TN(FT)(57) 60, 18 Nov. 1957.
43 BT205/262, TN(FT)(57) 60, 18 Nov. 1957.
44 BT11/5595, Garran minute, 26 Sept. 1957; *FRUS*, 1955–57, Vol. IV, doc. 242, Memo. of Conversation: Dillon and Eccles, 26 Sept. 1957.
45 *FRUS*, 1955–57, Vol. XXVII, doc. 310, Dulles to Eisenhower, 21 Oct. 1957.
46 *FRUS*, 1955–57, Vol. XXVII, doc. 330, Memo. of Conversation: Dillon and Lloyd, 25 Oct. 1957.
47 CAB130/132, GEN.613/3rd Meeting, 22 Oct. 1957; CAB130/134, GEN.613/1, 23 Oct. 1957; CAB130/132, GEN.613/4th Meeting, 25 Oct. 1957.
48 *Annotated Agenda Prepared by the Chairman*, CIG(57) 1, 31 Oct. 1957, Cmnd. 641, pp. 50–9.
49 See Camps, *Britain*, pp. 137–8.
50 FO371/128369/1217, Figgures minute, 14 Nov. 1957.
51 Camps, *Britain*, p. 137; Kaiser, *Using Europe*, pp. 70–1.

52 See Milward, *Rescue*, pp. 213–5.
53 CAB130/132, GEN.613/9th meeting, 19 Nov. 1957.
54 CAB130/132, GEN.613/10th meeting, 2 Dec. 1957; BT11/5616, CCI/ 51st meeting, 9 Dec. 1957.
55 CAB130/132, GEN.613/8th meeting, 11 Nov. 1957.
56 PREM11/2341, Symons to de Zulueta, 29 Aug. 1957.
57 PREM11/2341, Macmillan to Adenauer, 16 Sept. 1957; PREM11/2341, Macmillan minute, undated.
58 PREM11/2341, Macmillan to Adenauer, 10 Oct. 1957.
59 PREM11/2341, Lloyd, Bonn to Macmillan, 11 Oct. 1957.
60 FO371/128358/927, Bonn to FO, 11 Sept. 1957.
61 FO371/128392/547, Ellis Rees to FO, 3 Oct. 1957. Also, NARA RG59/ 440.002/9-3057, Bonn to State, 574, 30 Sept. 1957.
62 FO371/128366/1108, Lee minute, 31 Oct. 1957. Also, FO371/128356/ 871, BBC Monitoring Report, 14 Aug. 1957; FO371/128359/939, Bonn to Board of Trade, 12 Sept. 1957.
63 FO371/128367/1165, Marjoribanks to Edden, 11 Nov. 1957.
64 See Bouwman, '"Longing for London"', pp. 143–4.
65 FO371/128389/440, Mason to Lloyd, 15 Aug. 1957; FO371/128363/ 1049, Mason to FO, and FO minute, 14 and 18 Oct. 1957 respectively; FO371/128365/1089, Mason to Gore-Booth, 24 Oct. 1957; FO371/ 128371/1262, The Hague to FO, 6 Dec. 1957.
66 FO371/128394/601, Labouchere to FO, 25 Oct. 1957; FO371/128367/ 1168, Labouchere to Lloyd, 15 Nov. 1957.
67 FO371/128367/1161, Scarlett to Gore-Booth, 13 Nov. 1957, and Edden minute, 22 Nov. 1957.
68 FO371/128366/1134, Barclay to FO, 12 Nov. 1957; FO371/128372/1268, Barclay to FO, 10 Dec. 1957, and Heath minute, 12 Dec. 1957.
69 T234/202, 'EFTA. Note of a Meeting', 2 Dec. 1957.
70 On the response to Sputnik see Eisenhower's memoirs, *The White House Years, Waging Peace, 1956–1961* (London, 1966), pp. 205–6 and p. 226. In general, see J.L. Gaddis, *Strategies of Containment* (Oxford, 1982), pp. 183–5. On collaboration with Britain, Bartlett, *Special Relationship*, p. 93; Clarke, *Nuclear Diplomacy*, pp. 77–107; Dimbleby and Reynolds, *Ocean Apart*, pp. 223–4; Eisenhower, *Waging Peace*, p. 219; Melissen, *Nuclear Partnership*, pp. 42–6.
71 Macmillan, *Riding*, p. 321. On the Washington Conference, Dockrill, 'Restoring the "Special Relationship"', pp. 215–20.
72 CAB128/21, CC(57) 74th meeting, 21 Oct. 1957.
73 The papers of R.A. Butler, Trinity College, Cambridge, G31/118, 22 Oct. 1957.
74 For the Declaration, Macmillan, *Riding*, pp. 756–9; also, *FRUS*, 1955–57, Vol. XXVII, doc. 334, Memo. of Conversation: Eisenhower and Macmillan, 25 Oct. 1957.
75 Macmillan Papers, Bodleian Library, Oxford, MS Macmillan dep.d.30', diary, 24 Oct. 1957; also, Macmillan, *Riding*, p. 323.
76 CAB128/31,CC(57) 76th meeting, 28 Oct. 1957; Also see CAB129/90, C(57) 271, 15 Nov. 1957. For officials' views see CAB134/1835, ES(57) 7th meeting, 11 Nov. 1957.

77 CAB128/31, CC(57) 76th meeting, 28 Oct. 1957; Macmillan, *Riding*, pp. 319–25.
78 See Warner, 'Eisenhower', p. 327.
79 The French had been dissatisfied with American attitudes towards the Algerian War for some time, see Warner, 'Eisenhower', p. 328.
80 Macmillan, *Riding*, p. 331. Also see Horne, *Macmillan*, Vol. II. p. 35.
81 Melissen, *Nuclear Partnership*, p. 39, and Warner, 'Eisenhower', p. 324. Also, S. Ambrose, *Eisenhower the President* (London, 1984), p. 478, and Bartlett, *Special Relationship*, p. 93.
82 PREM11/1830A, Jebb to FO, 21 Nov. 1957.
83 FO371/128370/1238, Lamb to Gore-Booth, 2 Dec. 1957.
84 PREM11/1830A, Lloyd to Dulles, 21 Nov. 1957.
85 PREM11/1830A, Lloyd to Dulles, 26 Nov. 1957; PREM11/2531, Communiqué of the Macmillan–Gaillard meetings, 26 Nov. 1957.
86 PREM11/1830A, Macmillan to Diefenbaker, 27 Nov. 1957.
87 Papers of Selwyn Lloyd, Churchill College, Cambridge, SELO 4/22, Lloyd minute, 'Reflections written Aug. 1960'. For confirmation of ill favour, NARA RG59/641.51/11-2657, Paris to State, 2707, 26 Nov. 1957.
88 Quote taken from Eisenhower, *Waging Peace*, p. 231. For the NATO meetings, *FRUS*, 1955–57, Vol. IV, docs. 75–82, 17–19 Dec. 1957.
89 For Eisenhower's view, *Waging Peace*, pp. 231–2.
90 CAB128/31, CC(57) 84th meeting, 12 Dec. 1957; CAB128/31, CC(57) 85th meeting, 20 Dec. 1957. Macmillan, *Riding*, pp. 334–41.
91 Macmillan, *Riding*, p. 338.
92 *FRUS*, 1955–57, Vol. IV, doc. 75, US Delegate, NATO meetings to State, 17 Dec. 1957.
93 See O'Driscoll, '"Les Anglo-Saxons"', pp. 114–15.
94 PREM11/2531, Maudling to Macmillan, 6 Dec. 1957.
95 On Italy's intervention, F. Fauri, 'Italy and the Free Trade Area Negotiations, 1956–58', *Journal of European Integration History*, Vol. 4, No. 2 (1998), pp. 47–66, esp. pp. 50–4.
96 PREM11/2531, Macmillan to Maudling, 7 Dec. 1957.
97 FO371/128370/1248, Maudling to Eccles, 3 Dec. 1957.
98 FO371/128370/1249, Hoyer Millar minute, 25 Nov. 1957; FO371/128369/1220, Figgures minute, 27 Nov. 1957; PREM11/2351, Eccles to Selwyn Lloyd, 2 Dec. 1957.
99 FO371/128370/1248, Maudling to Eccles, 3 Dec. 1957. Also, Bloemen, 'Problem', pp. 188–9.
100 FO371/128396/642, Ellis Rees minute, 5 Dec. 1957. Also, FO371/128371/1262, The Hague to FO, 6 Dec. 1957.
101 FO371/128370/1235, Coulson 'Record of Conversation with Baron Snoy', 28 Nov. 1957.
102 FO371/128367/1156, Paris to FO, 13 and 14 Nov. 1957.
103 T234/373, Figgures to Clarke, 5 Dec. 1957.
104 FO371/128366/114, Jebb to FO, 13 Nov. 1957. Also NARA RG59/440.002/11-2157, Paris to State, 2620, 21 Nov. 1957.
105 T234/373, Makins minute, 5 Dec. 1957.
106 FO371/128371/1257, Rodgers minute, 20 Dec. 1957.
107 FO371/128365/1086, Bretherton minute, 21 Oct. 1957, and Edden

minute, 2 Nov. 1957. Also, T234/373, Clarke minute, 12 Oct. 1957.
108 NARA RG59/440.002/10-1457, London to State, 2434, 14 Oct. 1957.
109 FO371/128368/1196, Warner to Edden enclosing 'Rec. of Conversation', 28 Nov. 1957.
110 FO371/128372/1284, FO Minute, undated, received 16 Dec. 1957.
111 FO371/128370/1236, Eccles to Lloyd, 2 Dec. 1957.
112 See M. Schulte, 'Challenging the Common Market Project. German Industry, Britain and Europe 1956–1963', unpublished paper presented to a conference at St Antony's College, Oxford, March 1996. Also, for a more detailed analysis, M. Schulte, 'Industrial Interest in West Germany's Decision against the Enlargement of the EEC. The Quantitative Evidence up to 1964', *Journal of European Integration History*, Vol. 3, No. 1 (1997), pp. 35–61.
113 FO371/128370/1248, Maudling to Eccles, 3 Dec. 1957.
114 NARA RG59/440.002/11-1557, Memo. of Conversation, 15 Nov. 1957.
115 Comment made by Sir Michael Palliser (Paris Embassy, 1956–60), interview with the author, Sept. 1995.
116 Schaad, *Anglo-German Relations*, pp. 153–8. Also see Bloemen, 'Problem', pp. 188–90.
117 See Macmillan's recollections of the NATO meeting, *Riding*, p. 330 and pp. 334–5. Also see Turner, *Macmillan*, pp. 137–8.
118 Warner, 'Eisenhower', pp. 327–8; also, O'Driscoll, '"Les Anglo-Saxons"', pp. 114–15.
119 FO371/128360/966, 'Note of a meeting between the President and Sir Christopher Steel', 6 Sept. 1957.
120 For evidence of strained relations, see Charlton, *Price*, p. 207; Dimbleby and Reynolds, *Ocean Apart*, p. 241; Horne, *Macmillan*, Vol. II, pp. 32–4; Turner, *Macmillan*, p. 214.
121 By the close of 1957, ratification was complete in the parliaments of all Six powers, FO371/128369/1221, FO circular telegram, 28 Nov. 1957.
122 T234/373, Figgures minute, 5 Dec. 1957.

7 Impending Crisis, January–May 1958

1 Milward, *Rescue*, p. 223. See also Marjolin, *Architect*, pp. 308ff.
2 FO371/134486/23, Jebb to FO, 9 Jan. 1958.
3 FO371/134486/24, Edden minute, 14 Jan. 1958. Also, T234/374, Figgures to Coulson, 10 Jan. 1958.
4 CAB130/139, GEN.624/1st meeting, 6 Dec. 1957, and GEN.624/1, 16 Dec. 1957. For Eden's Policy Review, see Chapter 3.
5 The Foreign Office document containing these objectives, GEN.624/5, remains closed although its contents are revealed in CAB130/139, GEN.624/2nd meeting, 4 Feb. 1958.
6 CAB130/139, GEN.624/2, 2 Jan. 1958.
7 CAB130/139, GEN.624/3, 21 Jan. 1958.
8 CAB130/139, GEN.624/3, 21 Jan. 1958.
9 CAB134/1679, EA(58) 5, 24 Jan. 1958 and EA(58) 15, 5 March 1958; CAB134/1678, EA(58) 1st meeting, 29 Jan. 1958.
10 CAB130/139, GEN.624/3rd meeting, 18 Feb. 1958.

11 CAB130/139, GEN.624/10, 9 June 1958; CAB130/153, GEN.659/1st meeting, 14 July 1958.
12 Macmillan, *Riding*, p. 411. On the Commonwealth tour, see pp. 375–414.
13 PREM11/2531, Brook to Macmillan, 20 Feb. 1958.
14 Macmillan Papers, Bodleian Library, Oxford, MS Macmillan dep.d.31', diary, 21 Feb. 1958; also Macmillan, *Riding*, p. 441.
15 Maudling's comments in *The Times*, 'Progress over free trade', 17 Jan. 1958; BT11/5554, Bretherton minutes, 17 Jan. and 20 Feb. 1958.
16 *Draft Outline of an Agreement on Agriculture and Fisheries*, CIG(58) 4, 6 Jan. 1958, Cmnd. 641, pp. 190–6.
17 See also Camps, *Britain*, pp. 138–9.
18 PREM11/2531, 'Extract from talks between P.M. and P.M. of Australia', 11 Feb. 1958.
19 *Swiss Memorandum on the Continuation of Studies on the Draft Agreement on Agriculture and Fisheries*, CIG(58) 25, 7 March 1958, Cmnd. 641, pp. 197–8.
20 See Milward, *Rescue*, p. 220 and Chapter 5 in general.
21 Schaad, *Anglo-German Relations*, pp. 160–2.
22 See N.P. Ludlow, 'British agriculture and the Brussels negotiations: a problem of trust', in Wilkes (ed.), *Britain's Failure*, pp. 108–19.
23 CAB129/91, C(58) 27, 30 Jan. 1958; CAB128/32, CC(48) 14th meeting, 4 Feb. 1958.
24 BT11/5648, Lee to Cohen, 28 Jan. 1958; on alternative projects, BT11/5648, Bretherton to Lee, 17 Jan. 1958; CAB130/132, GEN.613/13th meeting, 22 Jan. 1958; T234/374, Clarke to Makins, 24 Jan. 1958.
25 *The Times*, 'M. Gaillard's view on the free trade zone', 28 Jan. 1958 and the *Economist*, 'Free Trade Area. Double Entendre', Jan. 1958.
26 FO371/134488/80, Jebb to FO, 27 Jan. 1958.
27 CAB128/32, CC(58) 7th meeting, 20 Jan. 1958; Also, NARA RG59/440.002/1-2358, London to State, 23 Jan. 1958.
28 Melissen, *Nuclear Partnership*, pp. 106–9; O'Driscoll, '"Les Anglo-Saxons"', pp. 116–30.
29 T234/374, Makins minute, 28 Jan. 1958. Also, *The Times*, 'Three Power Agreement on Arms', 22 Jan. 1958.
30 Lynch, 'De Gaulle's First Veto', p. 7.
31 Bossuat, 'The Choice', pp. 61–2.
32 FO371/134489/135, Wright minute, 17 Feb. 1958. Also, T234/202, 14/48/2 meeting, 18 Feb. 1958.
33 FO371/134492/238, Clarke to FO, 6 March 1958; FO371/134492/237G, Ellis Rees to FO, 6 March 1958. The counter-plan was not officially received until 20 March, FO371/134496/323, Warner to Figgures, 20 March 1958.
34 FO371/134492/234, Coulson to Maudling, 27 Feb. 1958.
35 BT11/5555, Bretherton minute, 12 March 1958.
36 T234/204, Hayles minute, undated. See Chapter 4.
37 The *Economist*, 'Free Trade Area: The French View', 1 March 1958.
38 T234/375, Figgures to Clarke, 7 March 1958.
39 'Walled garden' from The *Economist*, 'Critical Months for Free Trade', 22 March 1958.

40 FO371/134493/265, Steel to FO, 4 March 1958; FO371/134492/231, Ellis Rees to FO, 5 March 1958; FO371/134493/250, Wright minute, 5 March 1958.

41 FO371/134493/267, Coulson minute, 5 March 1958; BT11/5555, Bretherton minute, 6 March 1958; FO371/134493/263, Clarke to FO, 11 March 1958.

42 FO371/134493/267, Coulson minute, 5 March 1958.

43 FO371/134493/245, Kirk to Edden, 6 March 1958.

44 BOE OV47/19, doc. 10A, Rootham to Stevens, 11 March 1958.

45 BT11/5555, Bretherton minute, 12 March 1958; FO371/134495/307, Edden minute, 2 Apr. 1958. According to the Dutch, 'both parties threw their lobsters at one another', FO371/134495/307, Kirk to Edden, 20 March 1958.

46 BT11/5555, Bretherton minute, 12 March 1958.

47 FO371/134494/284, Kirk to Edden, 13 March 1958. Also see Bloemen, 'Problem', p. 191; Camps, *Britain*, p. 147; Lynch, 'De Gaulle's First Veto', p. 8.

48 BT11/5555, Bretherton minute, 17 March 1958.

49 *The Times*, 'Free Trade Area Talks in Paris Held Up', 1 Apr. 1958. Also, BOE OV47/20, doc. 46B, Stobbs minute, 3 Apr. 1958.

50 FO371/134495/318, Hugh Jones minute, 3 Apr. 1958.

51 FO371/134495/318, 'Note by the Prime Minister', 17 March 1958.

52 PREM11/2531, Eccles to Lloyd, 2 Dec. 1957. Maudling had also recommended this to Macmillan, PREM11/2531, Maudling to Macmillan, 6 Dec. 1957; see Chapter 6.

53 FO371/134492/235, Hayter minute, 13 March 1958; BT11/5555, Bretherton minute, 17 March 1958.

54 FO371/134495/307, Kirk to Edden, 20 March 1958; T234/708, Heath to Figgures, 23 Apr. 1958. Also, *The Times*, 'Six-Power View on Proposed Free Trade Area. Clarification by Prof. Hallstein', 21 March 1958.

55 CAB129/92, C(58) 65, 21 March 1958; BOE OV47/20, doc. 44, Stobbs minute, 2 Apr. 1958.

56 T234/203, Clarke to Lee, 21 March 1958; PREM11/2531, Trend to Macmillan, 26 March 1958; FO371/134495/308G, Edden minute, 26 March 1958; BT11/5555, Bretherton minute, 26 March 1958; CAB129/92, C(58) 67, 26 March 1958; CAB128/32, CC(58) 27th meeting, 27 March 1958.

57 CAB129/92, C(58) 67, 26 March 1958.

58 T234/375, Clarke minute, 26 March 1958.

59 *Report by the Group of Trade Experts on the Definition of Origin of Goods in the Free Trade Area*, CIG(58) 12, 31 Jan. 1958, Cmnd. 641, pp. 104–47.

60 'Percentage content' referred to the percentage value of the product derived from non-FTA origin; 'processing criterion' referred to specified processes carried out in a FTA member country which conferred FTA origin on the resulting product. *Summary Report on the Negotiations Concerning the Establishment of a Free Trade Area*, C(58) 287, 31 Dec. 1958, Cmnd. 641, pp. 59–96, esp. para. 14.

61 The *Economist*, 'Free Trade Area: Italian Bridge', 15 March 1958. See Fauri, 'Italy', pp. 54–5; also, Maudling, *Memoirs*, p. 71.

62 *Proposals by Mr. Carli Relating to the Definition of Origin*, CIG(58) 27, 11 March 1958, Cmnd. 641, pp. 147–9.
63 BOE OV47/19, doc. 34, Page to Stobbs, 27 March 1958.
64 BT11/5555, Bretherton minute, 17 March 1958.
65 BT11/5555, Swindlehurst minute, 19 March 1958; FO371/134495/322, Gore-Booth to Unwin, 1 Apr. 1958; Also, *The Times*, 'Balancing Tariffs in Europe. Italian Plan Sent To Experts', 13 March 1958.
66 Macmillan Papers, Bodleian Library, Oxford, MS Macmillan dep.d.31˙, diary, 17 March 1958; also, Macmillan, *Riding*, p. 442; CAB128/32, CC(58) 28th meeting, 1 Apr. 1958.
67 CAB134/1836, ES(58) 5th meeting, 4 March 1958.
68 FO371/134495/317, Dillon to Caccia, 27 March 1958; *FRUS*, 1955–57, Vol. VII, doc. 16, State Dept. circular 911, 28 March 1958. Also, Winand, *United States of Europe*, p. 118.
69 FO371/134496/344, Edden minute, 10 Apr. 1958; FO371/134495/317, Gore-Booth minute, 27 March 1958. Also, FO371/134495/317, Gore-Booth to Caccia, 27 March 1958.
70 NARA RG59/440.002/3-2058, State Dept. circular CA-8152, 20 March 1958. On sharing preferences, NARA RG59/440.002/2-1058, Tuthill, Paris to State, 10 Feb. 1958.
71 On this advance in US policy, cf. instructions in *FRUS*, 1955–57, Vol. IV, doc. 243, Herter to Embassy, Paris, Topol 1019, 10 Oct. 1957 with updated instructions in *FRUS*, 1958–60, Vol. VII, doc. 8, State Dept. circular CA-7021, 13 Feb. 1958 and doc. 12, State Dept. circular CA-8151, 20 March 1958. Also, NARA RG59/440.002/3-2058, State Dept. circulars CA-8152 and CA-8153, both of 20 March 1958.
72 On American economic aims, see A.P. Dobson, *The Politics of the Anglo-American Economic Special Relationship 1940–1987* (Brighton, 1988), pp. 173–83, and F. Romero, 'Interdependence and integration in American eyes: from the Marshall Plan to currency convertibility' in Milward *et al.*, *Frontiers*, pp. 155–181.
73 *FRUS*, 1958–60, Vol. VII, doc. 12, State Dept. circular CA-8151, 20 March 1958.
74 FO371/134495/318, 'Note by the Prime Minister', 17 March 1958; CAB129/92, C(58) 65, 21 March 1958; T234/375, Clarke to Makins, 1 Apr. 1958; Cabinet Office, FTAO Papers, Box 84, 'Dr Adenauer's Visit to London. Brief on Item 2(a). Free Trade Area', undated.
75 FO371/134501/501, 'Draft Record of Meeting', 18 Apr. 1958; PREM11/2341, FO News Dept. Communiqué, 18 Apr. 1958.
76 CAB130/132, GEN.613/26th meeting, 18 Apr. 1958. FO371/134498/400(a), Mason to FO, 17 Apr. 1958; PREM11/2341, Hoyer Millar to Lloyd, 14 Apr. 1958. Also, Camps, *Britain*, p. 152.
77 PREM11/2341, Steel to Lloyd, 10 Apr. 1958 and Maudling to Macmillan, 11 Apr. 1958; Macmillan Papers, Bodleian Library, Oxford, MS Macmillan dep.d.31˙, diary, 19 Apr. 1958. For further evidence of growing German suspicion of Britain, Huth, *British–German Relations*, pp. 147–50.
78 *The Times*, 'Dr Adenauer in London To-day' and 'M. Gaillard Resigns', both 16 Apr. 1958.

79 See Küsters, 'Germany's Foreign Policy', in Wurm (ed.), *Western Europe*, p. 74.
80 Schaad, *Anglo-German Relations*, pp. 168–70.
81 Cabinet Office, FTAO Papers, Box 84, 'Record of a meeting held with German officials at 11am on April 17th at Gwydyr House', 17 Apr. 1958; FO371/134498/400(a), Mason to FO, 17 Apr. 1958.
82 T234/203, Coulson minute, 22 Apr. 1958.
83 Schaad, *Anglo-German Relations*, pp. 172–3.
84 *Report on the Proposals by Mr. Carli*, CIG(58) 33, 25 March 1958, Cmnd. 641, pp. 153–163; *Proposals by Mr Carli*, CIG(58) 35, 29 March 1958, Cmnd. 641, pp. 163–4.
85 BOE OV47/20, doc. 70, Stobbs minute, 16 Apr. 1958; T234/203, Millard minute, undated (around 29 Apr. 1958).
86 *Report by the Group of Trade Experts . . .*, CIG(58) 12, 31 Jan. 1958, Cmnd. 641, p. 112, para. 5.
87 See report attached to CAB129/93, C(58) 110, 16 May 1958.
88 For the original position, see paragaphs 2 and 23 of the FTA White Paper, Cmnd. 72. For a more recent explanation of the limits of British policy, CAB129/89, C(57) 218 (Annex B, paragraph 7), 4 Oct. 1957.
89 CAB134/1836, ES(58) 10th meeting, 8 May 1958.
90 CAB134/1836, ES(58) 8th, 9th and 10th meetings, 2, 7 and 8 May 1958 respectively.
91 CAB130/123, GEN.580/4th meeting, 16 May 1958; Macmillan, *Riding*, p. 443.
92 CAB130/123, GEN.580/3, 12 May 1958.
93 CAB129/82, CP(56) 208, 11 Sept. 1956.
94 CAB134/1679, EA(58) 14, 19 May 1958.
95 BT11/5555, Lee minute, 14 May 1958. Also see BT11/5555, Cohen minute, 14 May 1958.
96 Comment made by Sir Denis Wright, interview with author, Sept. 1995.
97 CAB134/1678, EA(58) 12th meeting, 20 May 1958. Also see CAB134/1679, EA(58) 40, 16 May 1958.
98 See Camps, *Britain*, pp. 150–1.
99 Larkin, *France*, pp. 263–9.
100 FO371/134501/516, Steel to FO enclosing Record of Conversation between Coulson and Müller-Armack, 22 May 1958.
101 CAB128/31, CC(58) 45th meeting, 22 May 1958.
102 FO371/134500/470, Maudling to Erhard, 5 May 1958.
103 T234/720, Figgures minute, 1 Oct. 1959. Also see P. Gore-Booth, *With Great Truth and Respect* (London, 1974), p. 249. For historical views, cf. Camps, *Britain*, p. 144 and Young, *Britain and European Unity*, p. 63.
104 BT11/5555, Bretherton minute, 5 May 1958.
105 BT11/5648, Bretherton to Lee, 15 Jan. 1958; BT11/5648, Golt minute, 7 March 1958; BT11/5648, Bretherton to Cohen, 28 March 1958. Also see R. Maurhofer, 'The Quest for the Lesser Evil: Britain, Switzerland and the Decision to Create EFTA', paper presented to the Annual Congress of the Swiss Political Science Association, Balsthal, 5 Nov. 1999.
106 Consider the tone in BT11/5555, Bretherton minutes, 17 and 26 March 1958.

107 T234/375, Figgures minute, 27 Feb. 1958; FO371/134493/266, Makins minute, 5 March 1958; BT11/5555, Bretherton minute, 17 March 1958.
108 See M. af Malmborg and J. Laursen, 'The Creation of EFTA' in Olesen (ed.), *Interdependence*, pp. 197–212 and W. Kaiser, 'Challenge to the Community: the Creation, Crisis and Consolidation of the European Free Trade Association, 1958–1972', *Journal of European Integration History*, Vol. 3, No. 1 (1997), pp. 7–33. On links between industrial organisations, Lieber, *British Politics*, p. 65.
109 FO371/134488/91G, Edden and Ormsby-Gore minutes, 31 Jan. and 3 Feb. 1958 respectively.
110 FO371/134491/180, Wright minute, 17 Feb. 1958; FO371/134492/235, Hoyer Millar and Edden minutes, 14 and 28 March respectively.
111 BT11/5648, Clarke to Cohen, 23 Jan. 1958; T234/374, Clarke to Makins, 24 Jan. 1958.
112 T234/375, Clarke minute, 10 March 1958; T234/375, Rowan to Makins, 13 March 1958; T234/203, Clarke minute, 1 Apr. 1958.
113 T234/376, Figgures to Clarke, 8 May 1958.
114 T234/376, Clarke to Makins, 13 May 1958.
115 On 1943, Horne, *Macmillan*, Vol. I, pp. 153–90, and Turner, *Macmillan*, pp. 49–53.
116 Young, *Britain and European Unity*, p. 63.
117 Griffiths and Ward, '"Thousand Years"', p. 13.
118 See Bloemen, 'Problem', pp. 194–5, and Lamb, *Macmillan Years*, p. 116.
119 Maudling, *Memoirs*, p. 72.

8 The Demise of the Free Trade Area, June–December 1958

1 For a recent example of the General's attitude, PREM11/2338, Jebb to Lloyd, 24 March 1958. Also, Willis, *New Europe*, p. 273.
2 *FRUS*, 1958–60, Vol. VII Part 2, doc. 12, Elbrick to Herter, 27 May 1958.
3 PREM11/2345, 'Record of Conversation', 7 June 1958.
4 On de Gaulle's return to power in general, Jean Lacouture, *De Gaulle: the Ruler 1945–1970* (translation by A. Sheridan, London, 1991), pp. 185–229. On de Gaulle's attitude towards the EEC see Bossuat, 'The Choice', p. 63; Lynch, 'De Gaulle's First Veto', pp. 10ff; G.-H. Soutou, 'French Policy Towards European Integration, 1950–1966' in M. Dockrill (ed.), *Europe within the Global System 1938–1960* (Bochum, 1995), pp. 118–131, esp. pp. 126–8.
5 *FRUS*, 1958–60, Vol. VII Part 2, doc. 14, Paris to State, 31 May 1958.
6 See, for example, CAB130/134, GEN.613/12(Revise), 2 June 1958.
7 CAB130/132, GEN.613/35th meeting, 17 June 1958; CAB130/134, GEN.613/15(Revise), 17 June 1958.
8 T234/376, Clarke to Makins, 12 June 1958; FO371/134504/591, Bretherton to Wright, 16 June 1958.
9 CAB130/123, GEN.580/5th meeting, 23 June 1958.
10 Papers of R.A. Butler, Trinity College, Cambridge, G32/100, Butler minute, 6 June 1958.

11 CAB130/123, GEN.580/5, 13 June 1958 and GEN.580/6, 20 June 1958.
12 See in general, H. Macmillan, *The Blast of War 1939–45* (London, 1967). Also, Horne, *Macmillan*, Vol. I, pp. 153–90, and Turner, *Macmillan*, pp. 49–53.
13 Macmillan, *Riding*, pp. 444–5.
14 CAB130/123, GEN.580/5th meeting, 23 June 1958.
15 Macmillan Papers, Bodleian Library, Oxford, MS Macmillan dep.d.32˙, diary, 23 June 1958.
16 PREM11/2315, Macmillan to Lloyd and Amory, 24 June 1958.
17 T234/203, Makins to Amory, 26 June 1958.
18 T234/203, Amory minute, undated.
19 T234/203, 'Note of a Meeting', 27 June 1958.
20 For Macmillan's briefs, FO371/134505/608, Edden minute, 26 June 1958; PREM11/2531, Maudling to Macmillan and to Lloyd, both 27 June 1958. Also, PREM11/2531, Figgures minute, 28 June 1958.
21 Macmillan Papers, Bodleian Library, Oxford, MS Macmillan dep.d.32˙, diary, 30 June 1958; Macmillan, *Riding*, p. 448. For the meetings, PREM11/2326, 'Record of Converstation', 29 June 1958.
22 Macmillan, *Riding*, p. 448.
23 See the various records of conversations in PREM11/2326.
24 PREM11/2531, 'Extract from Record of Conversation', 30 June 1958 and Macmillan to de Gaulle, undated.
25 Macmillan Papers, Bodleian Library, Oxford, MS Macmillan dep.d.32˙, diary, 4 July 1958.
26 CAB128/32, CC(58) 51st meeting, 1 July 1958.
27 BT11/5556, Currall minute, 1 July 1958.
28 PREM11/2531, de Gaulle to Macmillan, 5 July 1958.
29 PREM11/2573, Dulles to Lloyd, 7 July 1958; for the American record, *FRUS*, 1958–60, Vol. VII Part 2, doc. 35, Memorandum by Sec. of State Dulles, 5 July 1958.
30 FO371/134505/624, Ellis Rees to FO, 8 July 1958; FO371/134505/638, Ellis Rees to FO, 11 July 1958.
31 PREM11/2531, Macmillan to de Gaulle, 19 July 1958.
32 CAB134/1837, ES(58) 32, 16 July 1958; CAB134/1836, ES(58) 13th meeting, 18 July 1958; T234/377, Clarke minute, 21 July 1958.
33 FO371/134506/648, Commercial Dept., Paris to FO, 19 July 1958.
34 FO371/134506/652, Ellis Rees to FO, 22 July 1958.
35 CAB128/32, CC(58) 63rd meeting, 22 July 1958.
36 BT11/5649, Bretherton 'Note of Meeting', 23 July 1958.
37 PREM11/2531, Maudling to Macmillan, 28 July 1958. Also see Maudling's statement to the Commons, Hansard, *House of Commons Debates*, 5th series, 1958–59, vol. 592, cols. 1369–1372, 30 July 1958.
38 CAB130/132, GEN.613/43rd meeting, 28 July 1958.
39 BT11/5556, Lee minute, 1 July 1958; BT205/371, Currall minute, undated.
40 PREM11/2531, Macmillan to Maudling, 3 Aug. 1958.
41 PREM11/2531, Eccles to Macmillan, 14 July 1958.
42 T234/377, Makins to Amory, 16 July 1958.
43 PREM11/2531, Maudling to Macmillan, 5 Aug. 1958.
44 PREM11/2531, Macmillan minute, 6 Aug. 1958.

45 T234/377, Clarke minute, 21 July 1958.
46 T234/377, Clarke minute, 6 Aug. 1958.
47 PREM11/2671, de Zulueta to Maude, 30 Aug. 1958; PREM11/2671, Amory memo., 8 Sept. 1958.
48 On German scepticism, K.-J. Müller, 'Adenauer and De Gaulle – De Gaulle and Germany: a Special Relationship', The Konrad Adenauer Memorial Lecture 1992 (St. Antony's College, Oxford, 1992), pp. 4–5.
49 For the *Die Welt* quote see Willis, *New Europe*, p. 279. In general, C. de Gaulle, *Memoirs of Hope* (trans. by T. Kilmartin, London, 1971), pp. 174–79. Also, S. Lee, 'Anglo-German Relations 1958–59: the Post-war Turning Point?', *Diplomacy and Statecraft*, Vol. 6, No. 3 (Nov. 1995), pp. 787–808, esp. pp. 794–5.
50 See also, Camps, *Britain*, p. 156 and Griffiths and Ward, '"Thousand Years"', p. 14. Also, The *Economist*, 'Deceptive Sunshine in Venice', 27 Sept. 1958.
51 BT11/5557, Warner to Coulson, 7 Oct. 1958.
52 On the Dutch, Bouwman, *British Dimension*, pp. 217–9.
53 Lynch, 'De Gaulle's First Veto', p. 15.
54 Schaad, *Anglo-German Relations*, pp. 185–6. Also see Bloemen, 'Problem', pp. 192–3.
55 FO371/134509/751, Ellis Rees to FO, 29 Sept. 1958. Also, FO371/134508/742, Holliday to Isaacson, 17 Sept. 1958 and FO371/134509/775, Mackenzie to Ellis Rees, 3 Oct. 1958.
56 PREM11/2531, Maudling to Macmillan, 28 July 1958.
57 See also, Camps, *Britain*, p. 154 and The *Economist*, 'Mr Maudling in The Castle', 2 Aug. 1958.
58 T234/204, Figgures to Clarke, 26 Sept. 1958.
59 T234/378, Richards minute, 2 Oct. 1958.
60 BT205/371, Currall minute, undated. For the state of play by October, *Interim Report by the Steering Board for Trade on the Work Done in Pursuance of Mandate CIG(58) 49(Final)*, CIG(58) 57, 14 Oct. 1958, Cmnd. 641, pp. 178–88.
61 PREM11/2532, Maudling to Macmillan, 30 Sept. 1958.
62 See the comments of M. Vavasseur, Ministry of Industry official, in BT11/5556, Currall minute, 1 July 1958.
63 T234/378, Richards minute, 2 Oct. 1958.
64 PREM11/2532, Maudling to Macmillan, 20 Sept. 1958.
65 Lynch, 'De Gaulle's First Veto', pp. 12–15 and p. 28.
66 CAB130/123, GEN.580/9, 19 July 1958; CAB129/94, CAB(58) 181–4, all 9 Sept. 1958; CAB128/32, CC(58) 71st meeting, 11 Sept. 1958. Also, BT11/2532, Trend to Macmillan, 10 Sept. 1958.
67 On the results of the Commonwealth Conference, *Commonwealth Trade and Economic Conference. Report of the Conference*, Cmnd. 539 (HMSO, 1958), esp. paras. 6 and 40. Also, FO371/134509/771, Foreign Office circular telegram, 9 Oct. 1958.
68 PREM11/2532, Maudling to Macmillan, 30 Sept. 1958.
69 PREM11/2328, 'Record of Meeting', 8 Oct. 1958. For the brief, FO371/134510/791, Holliday to Gore-Booth, 2 Oct. 1958.
70 Macmillan, *Riding*, pp. 454–5. Also see Macmillan Papers, Bodleian

Library, Oxford, MS Macmillan dep.d.33˙, diary, 9 Oct. 1958.

71 For de Gaulle's proposals, *FRUS*, 1958–60, Vol. VII Part 2, doc. 45, de Gaulle to Eisenhower, 17 Sept. 1958.

72 On Adenauer's reaction, Schaad, *Anglo-German Relations*, p. 187–8; on French isolation, Lynch, 'De Gaulle's First Veto', pp. 16–21.

73 Griffiths and Ward, '"Thousand Years"', pp. 14–15; Huth, *British–German Relations*, p. 68; and Turner, *Macmillan*, p. 216.

74 Huth, *British–German Relations*, p. 68.

75 PREM11/2352, Macmillan to Lloyd, 15 Oct. 1958.

76 PREM11/2352, Macmillan to Lloyd, 26 Oct. 1958.

77 T234/378, Clarke minute, 16 Oct. 1958.

78 T234/378, Rowan minute, 16 Oct. 1958.

79 FO371/134545/3, Rumbold minute, 16 Oct. 1958.

80 FO371/134545/3, Gore-Booth minute, 17 Oct. 1958.

81 PREM11/2532, Lloyd to Macmillan, 31 Oct. 1958.

82 *FRUS*, 1958–60, Vol. VII Part 1, doc. 36, Telegram from the Embassy in the United Kingdom to the Department of State, 23 Oct. 1958.

83 Macmillan Papers, Bodleian Library, Oxford, MS Macmillan dep.d.33˙, diary, 26 Oct. 1958; also Macmillan, *Riding*, p. 455.

84 CAB130/132, GEN.613/48th meeting, 2 Oct. 1958.

85 CAB130/132, GEN.613/49th meeting, 6 Oct. 1958.

86 T234/378, 'Record of a Meeting', 14 Oct. 1958. On Wormser, Camps, *Britain*, p. 163.

87 FO371/134510/803, Figgures to Clarke, 15 Oct. 1958.

88 *Memorandum from the European Economic Community*, CIG(58) 60, 20 Oct. 1958, Cmnd. 641, pp. 96–104. Also see Camps, *Britain*, pp. 156–63.

89 CAB130/132, GEN.613/52nd meeting, 15 Oct. 1958.

90 BT11/5557, Bretherton minute, 2 Nov. 1958.

91 CAB128/32, CC(58) 79th meeting, 30 Oct. 1958.

92 Macmillan Papers, Bodleian Library, Oxford, MS Macmillan dep.d.33˙, diary, 31 Oct. 1958; CAB130/123, GEN.580/6th meeting, 31 Oct. 1958.

93 PREM11/2532, Macmillan to Amory, 31 Oct. 1958.

94 PREM11/2532, Adenauer to Macmillan, 3 Nov. 1958.

95 FO371/134512/894, Gore-Booth to Hoyer Millar, 10 Nov. 1958. Also, FO371/134512/894, Holliday to Marjoribanks, 19 Nov. 1958.

96 T234/204, Clarke minute, 4 Nov. 1958.

97 CAB129/95, C(58) 229, 4 Nov. 1958.

98 FO371/134513/924, 'Record of Talks with M. Couve de Murville', 6 Nov. 1958.

99 FO371/134513/924, 'Record of a Meeting held at 10 Downing Street', 6 Nov. 1958.

100 FO371/134513/924, 'Record of a Meeting held at 10 Downing Street', 6 Nov. 1958; Macmillan Papers, Bodleian Library, Oxford, MS Macmillan dep.d.33˙, diary, 6 Nov. 1958.

101 BT205/264, TN(FT)(58) 26 Supplement, 21 Nov. 1958.

102 Translation taken from Camps, *Britain*, pp. 164–5.

103 PREM11/2352, de Gaulle to Macmillan, 15 Nov. 1958.

104 PREM11/2352, Macmillan to de Gaulle, 7 and 17 Nov. 1958.

105 Hansard, *House of Commons Debates*, 5th series, vol. 595, cols. 845–52, 17 Nov. 1958; FO371/134514/944, FO to Oslo and other non-Six capitals, 17 Nov. 1958. See *The Times*, 'France the Wrecker', 18 Nov. 1958 and The *Economist*, 'Free Trade Area. The Negotiation Game', 13 Dec. 1958.
106 Macmillan, *Riding*, p. 457.
107 T234/205, Makins to Amory, 17 Nov. 1958. Also see FO371/134514/928, Gore-Booth to Caccia, 18 Nov. 1958.
108 CAB130/123, GEN.580/11, 25 Nov. 1958.
109 Macmillan papers, Bodleian Library, Oxford, MS Macmillan dep.d.33*, diary, 28 Nov. 1958; PREM11/2532, Macmillan to Lloyd, 28 Nov. 1958.
110 FO371/134518/1086, Marjoribanks to Hancock, 3 Dec. 1958. Also, FO371/134517/1036, Ellis Rees to FO, 28 Nov. 1958. For numerous reports on the Bad Kreuznach meeting, see FO371/134517 and FO371/134518. Also, Horne, *Macmillan*, Vol. 2, pp. 111–12.
111 PREM11/2532, Maudling to Macmillan, 2 Dec. 1958.
112 De Gaulle, *Memoirs of Hope*, pp. 179–80. Also see Schaad, *Anglo-German Relations*, pp. 196–8.
113 FO371/134517/1036, Etherington-Smith to FO, 28 Nov. 1958.
114 FO371/134519/1110, Millard 'Record of a Meeting', 4 Dec. 1958.
115 On the Berlin Crisis, S. Lee, 'Perception and Reality: Anglo-German Relations during the Berlin Crisis 1958–1959', *German History*, Vol. 13, No. 1, 1995, pp. 47–69.
116 Lee, 'Anglo-German Relations', p. 796.
117 This is the thesis of Huth, *British–German Relations*, p. 248. See de Gaulle's allusion, *Memoirs of Hope*, p. 180. Also, Camps, *Britain*, p. 175 and Kaiser, *Using Europe*, p. 97.
118 PREM11/2826, Adenauer to Macmillan, 12 Dec. 1958.
119 PREM11/2532, Macmillan to Lloyd, 28 Nov. 1958; FO371/134518/1069, Hancock minute, 28 Nov. 1958.
120 CAB130/135, GEN.613/31, 5 Nov. 1958; CAB134/1836, ES(58) 14th meeting, 20 Nov. 1958; CAB130/123, GEN.580/8th meeting, 27 Nov. 1958.
121 CAB134/1678, EA(58) 27th meeting, 26 Nov. 1958.
122 CAB130/135, GEN.613/33, 7 Nov. 1958.
123 T234/378, Clarke to Bell, 10 Nov. 1958; T234/379, Clarke to Makins, 26 Nov. 1958.
124 CAB128/32, CC(58) 80th meeting, 11 Nov. 1958; CAB130/123, GEN.580/11, 25 Nov. 1958; CAB130/123, GEN.580/8th meeting, 27 Nov. 1958. For the Foreign Office, FO371/134514/928, Gore-Booth to Caccia, 18 Nov. 1958.
125 FO371/134517/1036, Etherington-Smith to FO, 28 Nov. 1958.
126 CAB130/123, GEN.580/12, 2 Dec. 1958.
127 BT11/5558, Bretherton minutes, 25 Nov. and 3 Dec. 1958.
128 The *Economist*, 'Europe. A French Success', 29 Nov. 1958.
129 See The *Economist*, 'Free Trade Fundamentals', 22 Nov. 1958.
130 BT11/5558, Bretherton minute, 11 Dec. 1958. On Ministerial agreement to the Board's proposals, CAB130/154, GEN.670/2nd meeting, 11 Dec. 1958; CAB130/123, GEN.580/10th meeting, 12 Dec. 1958.
131 *The Times*, 'Paris "No" to Free Trade Area', 15 Dec. 1958. Also, *Sum-*

mary Report on the Negotiations Concerning the Establishment of a Free Trade Area, CIG(58) 287, 31 Dec. 1958, Cmnd. 641, pp. 59–96.

132 Gore-Booth, *With Great Truth*, pp. 250–1. Also see Lord Gladwyn, *Memoirs*, p. 307. *The Times*, 'Anglo-French Clash on Trade Discrimination', 16 Dec. 1958.

133 For the chancellor of the exchequer's report to the prime minister on the meeting, PREM11/2826, Ellis Rees to FO, 16 Dec. 1958. For Cabinet discussion, CAB128/32, CC(58) 86th meeting, 18 Dec. 1958.

134 Lord Gladwyn, *Memoirs*, p. 316.

135 See Bloemen, 'Problem', p. 193. On the eventual solution to this issue, Camps, *Britain*, pp. 180–1 and *FRUS, 1958–60*, Vol. VII Part 1, doc. 52, Editorial Note.

136 T234/204, Millard minute, 29 Sept. 1958; CAB130/132, GEN.613/53rd meeting, 17 Oct. 1958; FO371/134515/964, Ellis Rees to FO, 19 Nov. 1958.

137 T234/205, McKean minute, 12 Dec. 1958.

138 BT11/5650, Bretherton 'Note for the Record', 3 Dec. 1958.

139 BT11/5557, Sallis minute, 3 Nov. 1958; BT11/5557, Sallis 'Note of a Meeting', 5 Nov. 1958; T234/378, Lee 'Note for the Record', 5 Nov. 1958. See also Chapter 7.

140 CAB130/132, GEN.613/57th meeting, 18 Nov. 1958; CAB130/123, GEN.580/10, 21 Nov. 1958; CAB130/123, GEN.580/13, 2 Dec. 1958.

141 See PREM11/2532, Trend to Macmillan, 3 Dec. 1958.

142 FO371/134520/1149G, Holliday, Wright, Gore-Booth and Hoyer Millar minutes, all 4 Dec. 1958. See also in general, FO371/134545.

143 PREM11/2531, Eccles to Macmillan, 14 July 1958; PREM11/2532, Eccles to Macmillan, 8 Dec. 1958.

144 CAB130/123, GEN.580/10th meeting, 12 Dec. 1958; CAB130/154, GEN.670/3rd meeting, 22 Dec. 1958. The Swedish and British industrial federations had formulated their proposals by this stage, FO371/134519/1137, Hankey to FO, 18 Dec. 1958.

145 See in general, Camps, *Britain*, pp. 210–32; Malmborg and Laursen, 'The Creation of EFTA', pp. 197–212, Kaiser, 'Challenge to the Community', pp. 7–33 and Maurhofer, 'Quest for the Lesser Evil', pp. 12–32.

146 In general, Cairncross, 'Economic Policy and Performance', Floud and McCloskey (eds), *Economic History*, p. 64. Alford, *Britain in the World Economy*, p. 237.

147 CAB130/139, GEN.624/10, 9 June 1958.

148 On this, J. Fforde, *The Bank of England and Public Policy 1941–1958* (Cambridge, 1992), pp. 585–6.

149 For the Treasury's analysis, Fforde, *Bank*, p. 592; for the approach to the prime minister, PREM11/2671, de Zulueta to Maude, and Amory memo., 30 Aug. and 8 Sept. 1958 respectively.

150 T234/377, Clarke minute, 6 Aug. 1958; T234/378, Rowan minute, 16 Oct. 1958. For an interesting analysis of the motives for convertibility in 1958, see S.M. Schwaag, 'Currency Convertibility and European Integration', unpublished paper presented to a conference at St. Antony's College, Oxford, March 1996, p. 9.

151 This was according to agreements reached by the OEEC in the sum-

mer of 1955, see M. Dickhaus, 'The Functioning of the European Payments Union (EPU) 1950–1958', in Olesen (ed.), *Interdependence*, pp. 82–95, esp. p. 87, and J.J. Kaplan and G. Schleiminger, *The European Payments Union: Financial Diplomacy in the 1950s* (Oxford, 1989), pp. 205–8.

152 See also, BOE OV44/22, Stevens to Rickett, 4 Nov. 1958.

153 PREM11/2671, 'Exchange Rate Policy. Note of a Meeting held at 10 Downing Street', 5 Nov. 1958.

154 PREM11/2671, 'Exchange Rate Policy. Note of a Meeting held at 10 Downing Street', 27 Nov. 1958.

155 PREM11/2671, Amory to Macmillan, 10 Dec. 1958 and 'Exchange Rate Policy. Note of a Meeting held at 10 Downing Street', 12 Dec. 1958. Also, BOE OV44/23, Stevens to Deputy Governor, 12 Dec. 1958. Also, Robert Hall's diary entry for 30 Dec. 1958, in Cairncross (ed.), *Robert Hall Diaries, Vol. II*, p. 180.

156 PREM11/2671, Amory 'Record of Conversation: Unicorn', 17 Dec. 1958.

157 See Camps, *Britain*, pp. 181–2. Also, P.M. Pitman, 'Le programme de réforme financière français et le rétablissement de la convertibilité en éurope occidentale', *Du franc Poincaré à l'écu*, colloque tenue 3 et 4 dec. 1992, (Paris, 1993), pp. 451–70, esp. p. 469, (the author is grateful to Dr Pitman for a translation of this article).

158 See comments in PREM11/2671, 'Exchange Rate Policy. Note of a Meeting', 5 Nov. 1958.

159 P.M. Pitman, 'Le programme', pp. 451–70; Schwaag, 'Currency Convertibility', pp. 15–23.

160 Lynch, 'De Gaulle's First Veto', esp. pp. 15–28.

161 Lynch, 'De Gaulle's First Veto', pp. 27–8.

162 De Gaulle, *Memoirs of Hope*, pp. 179–80.

163 Lacouture, *De Gaulle*, p. 213.

164 Bossuat, 'The Choice', pp. 63–6 and pp. 74–5; Lynch, 'De Gaulle's First Veto', pp. 10ff. Also, Soutou, pp. 126–8.

165 See, for example, G. Warner, 'The United States and the Western Alliance, 1958–63', *International Affairs*, Vol. 71, No. 4 (Oct. 1995), pp. 801–18. Also, de Gaulle, *Memoirs of Hope*, pp. 202–3.

166 NARA RG59/440.002/11-358, Dept. of State circular, CG-227, 3 Nov. 1958; NARA RG59/440.002/11-2058, Memo. of Conversation: Herter and Joxe, 20 Nov. 1958. Also, see Griffiths and Ward, '"Thousand Years"', p. 15.

167 FO371/134518/1064, MacLehose to Robinson, 3 Dec. 1958.

168 FO371/134509/762B, Bonn to FO, 8 Oct. 1958.

169 FO371/134518/1064, MacLehose to Robinson, 3 Dec. 1958.

170 FO371/134519/1147, Makins to Rumbold, 16 Dec. 1958.

171 For Whitehall frustration, FO371/134520/1151, Gore-Booth minute, 16 Dec. 1958, and various other minutes in this file. Also, Papers of Sir Paul Gore-Booth, Bodleian Library, Oxford: MS Gore-Booth c.4555/folios 172–3, Cohen minute, 17 Nov. 1958, and folio 174, Lee minute, 17 Nov. 1958. For the Dulles meeting, PREM11/2826, Jebb to FO, 16 Dec. 1958.

172 For a discussion of policy development in 1959/60, see, for example,

J. Ellison, 'Accepting the Inevitable: Britain and European Integration' in W. Kaiser and G. Staerck (eds), *British Foreign Policy, 1955–64: Contracting Options* (London, 2000) pp. 171–89; Kaiser, *Using Europe*, pp. 88–151; K. Steinnes, 'The European Challenge: Britain's EEC Application in 1961', *Contemporary European History*, Vol. 7, No. 1 (1998), pp. 61–81; J. Tratt, *The Macmillan Government and Europe. A Study in the Process of Policy Development* (London, 1996), pp. 30ff.

173 PREM11/2826, de Zulueta to Macmillan and Macmillan minute, both 30 Dec. 1958.

174 T234/359, Ellis Rees 'Note for the Record' and Clarke minute, 23 Jan. and 27 Jan. 1959 respectively.

Conclusion: Threatening Europe

1   Camps, *Britain*, pp. 509–10 and p. 517. Similar judgements have been sustained by Hugo Young's recent study, see *Blessed Plot* in general.

2   Young, 'Towards a New View', p. 460. Also see Young, *Britain and European Unity*, p. 171.

3   Milward, *Rescue*, p. 433.

4   Kaiser, *Using Europe*, Ch. 1 'What Bus? The Messina Conference, 1955', pp. 28–60.

5   Also see Wurm, 'Britain and European Integration', p. 255.

6   Kaiser, *Using Europe*, pp. 72–87, for example.

7   Moravcsik, *Choice*, p. 123.

8   See Ellison, 'Perfidious Albion?', pp. 1–34; Kaiser, *Using Europe*, pp. 61–87; Kane, *Tilting*, pp. 40–70; Schaad, *Anglo-German Relations*, pp. 90–134; Schaad, 'Counterblast', pp. 39–61.

9   Cf. Camps, *Britain*, p. 510.

10 BT11/5715, Bretherton note, 22 Oct. 1955.

11 BOE OV47/7, doc. 48, Parsons to Cobbold, 25 Oct. 1955.

12 CAB134/1373, AOC(56) 2nd meeting, 5 March 1956.

13 Camps, *Britain*, p. 510.

14 CAB134/1238, ES(EI)(56) 17th and 18th meetings, 15 Nov. and 22 Nov. 1956 respectively.

15 CAB134/1240, ES(EI)(56) 79(Final), 22 Nov. 1956.

16 T234/201, Clarke to Figgures, 6 June 1957.

17 These documents can be found in T234/720 dated from July 1959 to Feb. 1960. Officials involved included Bretherton, Clarke, Coulson, Figgures, France, Gore-Booth and Wright. For a commentary see R.T. Griffiths, 'The United Kingdom and the Free Trade Area: a Post Mortem' in Olesen (ed.), *Interdependence*, pp. 167–81.

18 T234/720, Clarke 'Thoughts in Retrospect on the Free Trade Area Negotiations: 1956–1959', 18 Jan. 1960.

19 Camps, *Britain*, p. 509.

20 Kane, *Tilting*, p. 173.

21 Cf. Moravcsik, *Choice*, p. 123.

22 Turner, *Macmillan*, p. 272.

23 Kaiser, *Using Europe*, p. 74.

24 FO371/122028/107, Thorneycroft, 'Initiative in Europe', 22 May 1956.
25 FO371/122025/65, Brief on European Integration, undated, received 8 May 1956.
26 FO371/128317/34, Rodgers minute, 4 Feb. 1957.
27 PREM11/2985, SC(59) 40, 27 Oct. 1959.
28 On the Foreign Office conversion to Europe, H. Young, *Blessed Plot*, pp. 176–81.
29 Cf. Moravcsik, *Choice*, pp. 122–35.
30 Kaiser, *Using Europe*, p. 87.
31 Duchêne, *Jean Monnet*, p. 359.
32 On the Six during 1961–63 see Ludlow, *Dealing with Britain*, esp. pp. 241–4.
33 FO371/130970/156, Jebb to Lloyd, 28 April 1957.
34 FO371/130973/228, Bushell minute, 26 July 1957.
35 See Milward and Brennan, *Britain's Place in the World*, Ch. 6, esp. pp. 198–208.
36 T234/720, Figgures 'Free Trade Area Negotiations: Post Mortem', 1 Oct. 1959. Also see Camps, *Britain*, p. 111.
37 See Camps, *Britain*, pp. 168–9.
38 Schaad, *Anglo-German Relations*, p. 211.
39 Bouwman, *British Dimension*, pp. 218–19.
40 On French tactics in the Brussels negotiations, Ludlow, *Dealing with Britain*, pp. 239–40.
41 T234/218, France 'Note for the Record', 9 Oct. 1957.
42 T234/720, Bretherton to Clarke, 3 Feb. 1960.
43 Camps, *Britain*, p. 169. For a revised opinion, Young, *Britain and European Unity*, p. 63.
44 T234/374, Makins minute, 28 Jan. 1958.
45 T234/720, France to Clarke, 21 July 1959; T234/720, Coulson to Clarke, 4 Sept. 1959; T234/720, Figgures 'Free Trade Area: Post Mortem', 1 Oct. 1959.
46 PREM11/2532, Macmillan to Lloyd, 28 Nov. 1958.
47 Young, *Britain and European Unity*, p. 180.
48 Kaiser, *Using Europe*, p. 211 and pp. 212–27.
49 On this see A.S. Milward, 'Allegiance. The Past and the Future', *Journal of European Integration History*, Vol. 1, No. 1 (1995), pp. 7–21. Also see Young, 'Britain and "Europe": the shape of the historiographical debate', pp. 207–14.
50 Sir R. Clarke, *Anglo-American Economic Collaboration in War and Peace, 1942–1949* (Oxford, 1982), p. 70.
51 Marjolin, *Architect*, p. 319.

Bibliography

1. Unpublished sources

Public Record Office, Kew

BT11   Board of Trade Commercial Relations and Exports Department: Departmental and General
BT205   Board of Trade Tariff Division
BT213   Board of Trade Commodity and General Division
BT241   Board of Trade Commercial Relations and Export Division: Policy, General and Record
CAB128 Cabinet minutes
CAB129 Cabinet memoranda
CAB130 *Ad hoc* Cabinet Committees: General and Miscellaneous Series
CAB134 Cabinet Committees: General Series from 1945
DO35   Dominions Office and Commonwealth Relations Office: Original Correspondence
FO371   Foreign Office General Correspondence
PREM11 Prime Minister's Office
T225   Treasury Defence and Material Division
T230   Treasury Economic Advisory Section
T232   Treasury European Economic Co-operation Committee
T234   Treasury Home and Overseas Planning Staff Division
T236   Treasury Overseas Finance Division

Cabinet Office Historical Section, Hepburn House, London

Various Boxes Free Trade Area Office Files

Bank of England Archives, Threadneedle Street, London

OV44   Convertibility Measures
OV47   European Integration General

National Archives and Records Administration, College Park, MD, USA

Record Group 59, State Department Central Decimal Files, 1955–58

Private papers

Avon, Lord (Anthony Eden), Birmingham University Library
Butler, R.A., Trinity College, Cambridge
Duff Cooper, A., Churchill College, Cambridge
Duncan Sandys, D.E., Churchill College, Cambridge
Gore-Booth, P.H., Bodleian Library, Oxford
Lloyd, J. Selwyn B., Churchill College, Cambridge
Macmillan, Harold, Bodleian Library, Oxford

Interviews and correspondence

Gladwyn, Lord (interview, 8 Dec. 1993)
Heath, John Moore (interview, 24 Aug. 1994)
Liverman, John G. (letter, 21 Dec. 1996)
Mayne, Richard (interview, 6 July 1994)
Millard, Sir Guy (letter, 2 May 1996; interview, 13 June 1996)
Palliser, Sir Michael (interview, 20 Sept. 1995)
Wright, Sir Denis (interview, 6 Sept. 1995)

2. Published sources

Command papers (HMSO), various numbers, 1955–1959
Bullen, R. and Pelly, M.E. (eds), *Documents on British Policy Overseas*, Series II, Vol. I (HMSO, 1986) and Vol. II (HMSO, 1987).
Central Statistical Office, *Annual Abstract of Statistics* (HMSO, 1956 and 1960).
Foreign Relations of the United States (FRUS):
    Vol. IV, 1955–1957, Western European Security and Integration (Washington, 1986)
    Vol. XXVII, 1955–1957, Western Europe and Canada (Washington, 1992)
    Vol. VII, Part 1, 1958–1960, Western European Integration and Security; Canada (Washington, 1993)
    Vol. VII, Part 2, 1958–1960, Western Europe (Washington, 1993)
Hansard, *House of Commons Debates*, 5th series, various volumes, 1955–1958.
Royal Institute of International Affairs, *Documents on International Affairs*, various years.
Sweet and Maxwell's Legal Editorial Staff, *European Community Treaties* (1977).

3. Memoirs and diaries

Note: unless otherwise stated, the place of publication is London.

Cairncross, A. (ed.) *The Robert Hall Diaries, Vol. II 1954–1961* (1991).
De Gaulle, C. *Memoirs of Hope* (trans. by T. Kilmartin, 1971).
Eden, A. *Full Circle* (1960).
Gladwyn, Lord *The Memoirs of Lord Gladwyn* (1972).
Gore-Booth, Sir P. *With Great Truth and Respect* (1974).
Eisenhower, D.D. *The White House Years, Waging Peace, 1956–1961* (1966).
Henderson, N. *Channels and Tunnels. Reflections on Britain and Abroad* (1987).
Kilmuir, Lord *Political Adventure: the Memoirs of the Earl of Kilmuir* (1964).
Macmillan, H. *The Blast of War, 1939–45* (1967).
Macmillan, H. *Tides of Fortune, 1945–1955* (1969).
Macmillan, H. *Riding the Storm, 1956–1959* (1971).
Marjolin, R. *The Architect of European Unity* (1989).
Maudling, R. *Memoirs* (1978).
Monnet, J. *Memoirs* (1978).
Roll, E. *Crowded Hours* (1985).
Spaak, P.-H. *The Continuing Battle* (1971).

4. Secondary works

Note: unless otherwise stated, the place of publication is London.

Ahmann, R. et al. (eds) *The Quest for Stability: Problems of West European Security 1918–1957* (Oxford, 1993).

Alford, B.W.E. *British Economic Performance, 1945–1975* (Cambridge, 1995).

Alford, B.W.E. *Britain in the World Economy Since 1880* (1996).

Ambrose, S. *Eisenhower the President* (1984).

Bartlett, C.J. *British Foreign Policy in the Twentieth Century* (1989).

Bartlett, C.J. *'The Special Relationship': a Political History of Anglo-American Relations since 1945* (1992).

Bell, P. M. H. *France and Britain 1940–1994. The Long Separation* (1997).

Beloff, M. *New Dimensions in Foreign Policy. A Study in British Administrative Experience 1947–59* (1961).

Beloff, N. *The General Says No* (Harmondsworth, 1963).

Beloff, N. *The Transit in Britain* (1973).

Bloemen, E. 'A Problem to Every Solution. The Six and the Free Trade Area', in Olesen (ed.), *Interdependence*, pp. 182–96.

Brittain, S. *The Treasury under the Tories 1951–1964* (Harmondsworth, 1964).

Brivati, B. and Jones, H. (eds) *From Reconstruction to Integration. Britain and Europe Since 1945* (Leicester, 1993).

Brivati, B., Buxton, J. and Seldon A. (eds) *The Contemporary History Handbook* (1996).

Bullen, R. 'Britain and 'Europe' 1950–1957', in Serra (ed.) *Il rilancio*, pp. 315–38.

Butler, L.J. and Gorst, A. (eds) *Modern British History: a Guide to Study and Research* (1997).

Cain P.J. and Hopkins, A.G. *British Imperialism: Crisis and Deconstruction 1914–1990* (1993).

Cairncross, A. *Years of Recovery. British Economic Policy 1945–51* (1985).

Cairncross, A. and Watts, N. *The Economic Section 1939–1961* (1989).

Cairncross, A. *The British Economy Since 1945* (1992).

Carlton, D. *Anthony Eden* (1981).

Carlton, D. *Britain and the Suez Crisis* (Oxford, 1988).

Camps, M. *Britain and the European Community 1955–1963* (1964).

Charlton, M. *The Price of Victory* (1983).

Charmley, J. *Churchill's Grand Alliance. The Anglo-American Special Relationship 1940–57* (1995).

Clarke, I. *Nuclear Diplomacy and the Special Relationship* (Oxford, 1994).

Clarke, Sir R. *Anglo-American Economic Collaboration in War and Peace, 1942–1949* (Oxford, 1982).

Deighton, A. (ed.) *Building Postwar Europe. National Decision-Makers and European Institutions, 1948–63* (1995).

Deighton, A. and Milward, A.S. (eds) *Widening, Deepening and Acceleration: the European Economic Community, 1957–63* (Brussels, 1999).

Dell, E. *The Schuman Plan and the British Abdication of Leadership in Europe* (Oxford, 1995).

Denman, Sir R. *Missed Chances. Britain and Europe in the Twentieth Century* (1996).

Dickhaus, M. 'The Functioning of the European Payments Union (EPU) 1950–1958', in Olesen (ed.), *Interdependence*, pp. 82–95.

Dobson, A.P. *The Politics of the Anglo-American Economic Special Relationship 1940–1987* (Brighton, 1988).

Dockrill, M. and Young, J.W. (eds), *British Foreign Policy 1945–56* (1989).

Dockrill, M. (ed.), *Europe within the Global System 1938–1960* (Bochum, 1995).

Dockrill, S. *Britain's Policy for West German Rearmament, 1950–55* (Cambridge, 1991).

Dow, J.C.R. *The Management of the British Economy 1945–60* (Cambridge, 1964).

Duchêne, F. *Jean Monnet. The First Statesman of Interdependence* (1994).

Dutton, D. *Anthony Eden: a Life and Reputation* (1997).

Economist Intelligence Unit *The Commonwealth and Europe* (1960).

Fforde, J. *The Bank of England and Public Policy 1941–1958* (Cambridge, 1992).

Floud, R. and McCloskey, D. (eds) *The Economic History of Britain Since 1700, Vol. 3, 1939–1992* (Cambridge, 1994).

Gaddis, J.L. *Strategies of Containment* (Oxford, 1982).

George, S. *An Awkward Partner* (Oxford, 1990).

Greenwood, S. *Britain and European Cooperation since 1945* (Oxford, 1992).

Greenwood, S. *Britain and European Integration since the Second World War* (Manchester, 1996).

Greenwood, S. *The Alternative Alliance: Anglo-French Relations Before the Coming of NATO, 1944–48* (1996).

Griffiths, R.T. and Ward, S. (eds) *Courting the Common Market: the First Attempt to Enlarge the European Community 1961–1963* (1996).

Griffiths, R.T. and Ward, S. '"The End of a Thousand Years of History". The Origins of Britain's Decision to Join the European Community, 1955–1961', in Griffiths and Ward (eds), *Courting*, pp. 7–37.

Hampsher-Monk, I. and Stanyer, J. (eds) *Contemporary Political Studies* (Exeter, 1996).

Heller, F.H. and Gillingham, J.R. *NATO: the Founding of the Atlantic Alliance and the Integration of Europe* (1992).

Hennessy, P. *Whitehall* (1989).

Hennessy, P. and Seldon, A. (eds) *Ruling Performance* (Oxford, 1987).

Horne, A. *Macmillan 1894–1956* (1988).

Horne, A. *Macmillan 1957–1986* (1989).

Kaiser, W. *Using Europe, Abusing the Europeans. Britain and European Integration, 1945–63* (1996).

Kaiser, W. and Staerck, G. *British Foreign Policy, 1955–64: Contracting Options* (2000)

Kaplan, J.J. and Schleiminger, G. *The European Payments Union: Financial Diplomacy in the 1950s* (Oxford, 1989).

Küsters, H.J. 'The Federal Republic of Germany and the EEC-Treaty', in Serra (ed.) *Il rilancio*, pp. 495–506.

Küsters, H.J. 'The Origins of the EEC Treaty', in Serra (ed.) *Il rilancio*, pp. 211–38.

Küsters, H.J. 'West Germany's Foreign Policy in Western Europe, 1949–1958: the Art of the Possible', in Wurm (ed.) *Western Europe*, pp. 55–85.

Lacouture, J. *De Gaulle: the Ruler 1945–1970* (trans. by A. Sheridan, 1991).

Lamb, R. *The Failure of the Eden Government* (1987).

Lamb, R. *The Macmillan Years 1957–1963* (1995).

Larkin, M. *France Since the Popular Front* (Oxford, 1988).

Lieber, R.J. *British Politics and European Unity* (1970).

Lord, C. *Absent at the Creation: Britain and the Formation of the European Community, 1950–2* (Aldershot, 1996).

Ludlow, N.P. *Dealing with Britain. The Six and the First UK Application to the EEC* (Cambridge, 1997).

Mayne, R. *The Recovery of Europe* (1970).

Melissen, J. *The Struggle for Nuclear Partnership* (Groningen, 1993).

McKinlay, A., Rollings, N., and Smyth, J. 'British Business and European Integration, 1945–1964', in Davids, M., de Goey, F. and de Wit, D. (eds) *Proceedings of the Conference on Business History, Oct. 1994, The Netherlands* (Rotterdam, 1995), pp. 330–41.

Middlemas, K. *Power, Competition and the State*, Vol. I (1986).

Milward, A.S. *The Reconstruction of Western Europe, 1945–51* (1984).

Milward, A.S. *The European Rescue of the Nation State* (1992).

Milward, A.S. *et al.* (eds) *The Frontier of National Sovereignty. History and Theory 1945–1992* (1993).

Milward, A.S. and Brennan, G. *Britain's Place in the World. A Historical Enquiry into Import Controls 1945–60* (1995).

Moravcsik, A. *The Choice for Europe. Social Purpose and State Power from Messina to Maastricht* (1998).

Nolfo, E. di (ed.) *Power in Europe? II. Great Britain, France, Germany, Italy and the Origins of the EEC, 1952–1957* (Berlin, 1992).

Nutting, A. *Europe Will Not Wait. A Warning and a Way Out* (1960).

Olesen, T.B. (ed.) *Interdependence Versus Integration. Denmark, Scandinavia and Western Europe, 1945–1960* (Odense, 1995).

Onslow, S. *Backbench Debate within the Conservative Party and its Influence on British Foreign Policy, 1948–57* (1997)

Reynolds, D. *Britannia Overruled* (1991).

Rhodes James, R. *Anthony Eden* (1986).

Richardson, D. and Stone, G. (eds) *Decisions and Diplomacy. Essays in Twentieth-Century International History* (1995).

Rothwell, V. *Anthony Eden* (Manchester, 1992).

Roy Willis, F. *France, Germany and the New Europe 1945–1967* (Oxford, 1968).

Ruane, K. *The Rise and Fall of the European Defence Community. Anglo-American Relations and the Crisis of European Defence 1950–1955* (2000).

Schmidt, G. '"Tying" (West) Germany into the West – But to What? NATO? WEU? The European Community?', in Wurm (ed.), *Western Europe*, pp. 137–74.

Serra, E. (ed.) *Il rilancio dell'Europa e i trattati di Roma* (Bruxelles, 1989).

Shonfield, A. *British Economic Policy Since the War* (1958).

Strange, S. *Sterling and British Policy* (Oxford, 1971).

Taylor, A.J.P. *The Origins of the Second World War* (1963 edition).

Thorne, C. *Border Crossings. Studies in International History* (Oxford, 1988).

Tratt, J. *The Macmillan Government and Europe. A Study in the Process of Policy Development* (1996).

Turner, J. *Macmillan* (1994).
Urwin, D. *The Community of Europe* (1991).
Winand, P. *Eisenhower, Kennedy and the United States of Europe* (1992).
Worswick, G.D.N. and Ady, P.H. (eds) *The British Economy in the Nineteen-Fifties* (Oxford, 1962).
Wurm, C. (ed.) *Western Europe and Germany* (Oxford, 1995).
Young, H. *This Blessed Plot. Britain and Europe from Churchill to Blair* (1998).
Young, J.W. *Britain, France and the Unity of Europe, 1945–51* (Leicester, 1984).
Young, J.W. (ed.) *The Foreign Policy of Churchill's Peacetime Administration, 1951–55* (Leicester, 1988).
Young, J.W. *Britain and European Unity, 1945–1992* (1993).

5. Articles and working papers

Burgess, S. and Edwards, G. 'The Six plus One: British Policy Making and the Question of European Economic Integration, 1955', *International Affairs*, Vol. 64, No. 3 (1988), pp. 393–413.
Deighton, A. 'Missing the Boat. Britain and Europe 1945–61', *Contemporary Record*, Vol. 3, No. 3 (Feb. 1990), pp. 15–17.
Deighton, A. 'The Last Piece of the Jigsaw: Britain and the Creation of the Western European Union, 1954', *Contemporary European History*, Vol. 7, Part 2 (1998), pp. 181–96.
Dockrill, S. 'The Evolution of Britain's Policy Towards a European Army 1950–54', *Journal of Strategic Studies*, Vol. 12, No. 1 (1989), pp. 38–62.
Dockrill, S. 'Retreat from the Continent? Britain's Motives for Troop Reductions in West Germany, 1955–1958', *Journal of Strategic Studies*, Vol. 20, No. 3 (1997), pp. 45–70.
Ellison, J.R.V. 'Perfidious Albion? Britain, Plan G and European Integration, 1955–1956', *Contemporary British History*, Vol. 10, No. 4 (1996), pp. 1–34.
Fauri, F. 'Italy and the Free Trade Area Negotiations 1956–59', *Journal of European Integration History*, Vol. 4, No. 2 (1998), pp. 47–66.
Helmreich, J.E. 'The United States and the Formation of EURATOM', *Diplomatic History*, Vol. 15, No. 3 (Summer 1991), pp. 387–410.
Holland, R.F. 'The Imperial Factor in British Strategies from Attlee to Macmillan, 1945–63', *Journal of Imperial and Commonwealth History*, Vol. 12, No. 2 (Jan. 1984), pp. 165–86.
Jenkins, P. 'The Bretherton syndrome of "Britain knows best"', *The Independent*, 6 Nov. 1991.
Kaiser, W. 'Challenge to the Community: The Creation, Crisis and Consolidation of the Free Trade Association, 1958–1972', *Journal of European Integration History*, Vol. 3, No. 1 (1997), pp. 7–33.
Kane, L. 'European or Atlantic Community? The Foreign Office and "Europe"': 1955–1957', *Journal of European Integration History*, Vol. 3, No. 2 (1997), pp. 83–98.
Krozewski, G. 'Sterling, the "minor" territories, and the end of formal empire, 1939–1958', *Economic History Review*, Vol. XLVI, No. 2 (1993), pp. 239–65.
Krozewski, G. 'Finance and Empire: The Dilemma Facing Great Britain in the 1950s', *International History Review*, Vol. 18, No. 1 (Feb. 1996), pp. 48–69.

Lee, S. 'Perception and Reality: Anglo-German Relations during the Berlin Crisis 1958–1959', *German History*, Vol. 13, No. 1, 1995, pp. 47–69.

Lee, S. 'Anglo-German Relations 1958–59: The Postwar Turning Point?', *Diplomacy and Statecraft*, Vol. 6, No. 3 (Nov. 1995), pp. 787–808.

Lord, C. ' "With but not of": Britain and the Schuman Plan, a Reinterpretation', *Journal of European Integration History*, Vol. 4, No. 2 (1998), pp. 23–46.

Lynch, F.M.B. 'De Gaulle's First Veto. France, the Rueff Plan and the Free Trade Area', Working Papers in History HEC No. 98/8 (Department of History and Civilization, European University Institute, Florence, 1998).

Milward, A.S. 'Allegiance. The Past and the Future', *Journal of European Integration History*, Vol. 1, No. 1 (1995), pp. 7–19.

Muirhead, B.W. 'Britain, Canada, and the Collective Approach to Freer Trade and Payments, 1952–1957', *Journal of Imperial and Commonwealth History*, Vol. 20, No. 1 (Jan. 1992), pp. 108–26.

Müller, K.-J. '*Adenauer and De Gaulle – De Gaulle and Germany: a Special Relationship*', *The Konrad Adenauer Memorial Lecture 1992* (St. Anthony's College, Oxford, 1992).

Newton, S. 'Britain, the Sterling Area, and European Integration, 1945–1950', *Journal of Imperial and Commonwealth History*, Vol. 13, No. 3 (1985), pp. 163–82.

O'Driscoll, M. 'Missing the Nuclear Boat? British Policy Towards French Military Nuclear Ambitions during the EURATOM Foundation Negotiations, 1955–56', *Diplomacy and Statecraft*, Vol. 9, No. 1 (1998), pp. 135–62.

O'Driscoll, M. ' "Les Anglo-Saxons", F-I-G and the rival Conceptions of "advanced" Armaments Research and Development Co-operation in Western Europe, 1956–1958', *Journal of European Integration History*, Vol. 4, No. 1 (1998), pp. 105–30.

PEP (Political and Economic Planning), 'European Unity – a Review', *Planning*, Vol. 25, No. 436 (28 Sept. 1959), pp. 163–84.

Pitman, P. M. 'Le programme de réforme financière français et le rétablissement de la convertibilité en éurope occidentale', in *Du franc Poincaré à l'écu*, colloque tenue 3 et 4 dec. 1992 (Paris, 1993), pp. 451–70.

Rees, W. 'The Sandys White Paper: New Priorities in British Defence Policy', *Journal of Strategic Studies*, Vol. 12, No. 2 (June 1989), pp. 215–29.

Schaad, M. 'Plan G – a "Counterblast"? British Policy towards the Messina Countries, 1956', *Contemporary European History*, Vol. 7, Part 1 (1998), pp. 39–60.

Schenk, C. 'Decolonization and European Economic Integration: The Free Trade Area Negotiations, 1956–58', *Journal of Imperial and Commonwealth History*, Vol. 24, No. 3 (Sept. 1996), pp. 444–63.

Schulte, M. 'Industrial Interest in West Germany's Decision against the Enlargement of the EEC. The Quantitative Evidence up to 1964', *Journal of European Integration History*, Vol. 3, No. 1 (1997), pp. 35–61.

Steinnes, K. 'The European Challenge: Britain's EEC Application in 1961', *Contemporary European History*, Vol. 7, Part 1 (1998), pp. 61–79.

Warner, G. 'The Anglo-American Special Relationship', *Diplomatic History*, Vol. 13, No. 4 (Fall 1989), pp. 479–99.

Warner, G. 'Eisenhower, Dulles and the Unity of Western Europe, 1955–1957', *International Affairs*, Vol. 69, No. 2 (1993), pp. 319–29.

Warner, G. 'The United States and the Western Alliance, 1958–1963', *International Affairs*, Vol. 71, No. 4 (Oct. 1995), pp. 801–18.

Wurm, C.A. 'Britain and European Integration, 1945– 63', *Contemporary European History*, Vol. 7, Part 2 (1998), pp. 249–61.

Young, J.W. 'Churchill's 'No' to Europe: The 'Rejection' of European Union by Churchill's Post-War Government, 1951–52', *Historical Journal*, Vol. 28, No. 4 (Dec. 1985), pp. 923–37.

Young, J.W. 'Winston Churchill's Peacetime Administration and the Relaxation of East-West Trade Controls, 1953–54', *Diplomacy and Statecraft*, Vol. 7, No. 1 (March 1996), pp. 125–40.

Young, J.W. *'The Geneva Conference of Foreign Ministers October–November 1955', Discussion Papers in Diplomacy No. 9* (University of Leicester: Centre for the Study of Diplomacy, 1995).

6. Unpublished theses and papers

Asbeek Brusse, W. *West European Tariff Plans, 1947–1957. From Study Group to Common Market* (Unpublished PhD thesis, European University Institute, Florence, 1991).

Bouwman, B. *The British Dimension of Dutch European Policy (1950–1963)* (Unpublished DPhil thesis, Oxford, 1993).

Huth, S. *British–German Relations between 1955 and 1961* (Unpublished PhD thesis, Cambridge, 1993).

Kane, E. *Tilting to Europe?: British Responses to Developments in European Integration 1955–1958* (Unpublished DPhil thesis, Oxford, 1996).

Maurhofer, R. 'The Quest for the Lesser Evil: Britain, Switzerland and the Decision to Create EFTA', unpublished paper presented to the Annual Congress of the Swiss Political Science Association, Balsthal, 5 November 1999.

Pitman, P. 'French Sectoral Strategies and the Diplomacy of European Integration during the 1950s', *1995 ECSA Conference Papers* (Maastricht, 1995).

Schaad, M.P.C. *Anglo-German Relations during the Formative Years of the European Community 1955–61* (Unpublished DPhil thesis, Oxford, 1995).

Schulte, M. 'Challenging the Common Market Project. German Industry, Britain and Europe 1956–1963', unpubished paper presented to a conference at St Antony's College, Oxford, 21–24 March 1996.

Schwaag, S.M. 'Currency Convertibility and European Integration', unpublished paper presented to a conference at St Antony's College, Oxford, 21–24 March 1996.

Wells, B. *Discordant Allies: Security Policy Objectives as a Factor in British–German Relations 1955–61* (PhD thesis, London School of Economics and Political Science, in preparation).

7. Newspapers and periodicals

The Board of Trade Journal
The Economist
The Independent
The Times

Index